NEWER ISLAMIC MOVEMENTS IN WESTERN EUROPE

DAMES
Dansk Center for Migration
og Etniske Studier

**EUROPEAN RESEARCH CENTRE
ON MIGRATION & ETHNIC RELATIONS**

Newer Islamic Movements in Western Europe

LARS PEDERSEN Ph.D
Department of Ethnography and Social Anthropology
Aarhus University, Denmark

LONDON AND NEW YORK

First published 1999 by Ashgate Publishing

Reissued 2018 by Routledge
2 Park Square, Milton Park, Abingdon, Oxon, OX14 4RN
711 Third Avenue, New York, NY I 0017, USA

Routledge is an imprint of the Taylor & Francis Group, an informa business

Copyright © Lars Pedersen 1999

All rights reserved. No part of this book may be reprinted or reproduced or utilised in any form or by any electronic, mechanical, or other means, now known or hereafter invented, including photocopying and recording, or in any information storage or retrieval system, without permission in writing from the publishers.

Notice:
Product or corporate names may be trademarks or registered trademarks, and are used only for identification and explanation without intent to infringe.

Publisher's Note
The publisher has gone to great lengths to ensure the quality of this reprint but points out that some imperfections in the original copies may be apparent.

Disclaimer
The publisher has made every effort to trace copyright holders and welcomes correspondence from those they have been unable to contact.

ISBN 13: 978-1-138-32374-2 (hbk)
ISBN 13: 978-1-138-32375-9 (pbk)
ISBN 13: 978-0-429-45124-9 (ebk)

Contents

Preface viii

1 Introduction 1
  1.1 Islam in Western Discourse 5
    1.1.1 The Nomenclature Problematic - Explanatory Notes 12
  1.2 Islamism 14
  1.3 The Background to this Thesis 16
  1.4 An Outline of this Thesis 20

2 Islamic Organisations in Western Europe 23
  2.1 Germany 26
    2.1.1 Turkey as Administrator of Islam in West Berlin 27
    2.1.2 Non-governmental Islamic Organisations 31
  2.2 France 32
    2.2.1 Turkey as Administrator of Islam in France 32
    2.2.2 Non-state Islamic Organisations 34
    2.2.3 The Structuring of Islam by the French State 36
    2.2.4 Algeria as Administrator of Islam in France 39
  2.3 Denmark 42
  2.4 The Institutionalisation of Islam in Holland, Belgium and Britain 46
    2.4.1 Holland 46
    2.4.2 Belgium 49
    2.4.3 Britain 51
  2.5 Summary 53

3 Avrupa Millî Görüş Teşkilâtleri (AMGT):
The Union of the New World Vision in Europe 56
  3.A The Structure of the Organisation 59
  3.A.1 Denmark 59
    3.A.1.1 A Millî Görüş Cemaat in Aarhus 65
  3.A.2 France 69
  3.A.3 Berlin 74
    3.A.3.1 The Relationship between AMGT-BB and
    Islamische Föderation Berlin 78
    3.A.3.1.1 The Case of the Islamic Primary School:
      Islam Kolleg 80

	3.A.4 AMGT Hac Organizasyonu'ndan	88
	3.A.5 Ramadan	89
	3.B 'The Islamic Outlook'	90
	3.B.1 Millî Görüş and the Rushdie Affair	91
	3.B.2 Millî Görüş and Anti-Semitism	92
	3.B.3 Millî Görüş and Political Events in Eastern Europe (1989/90)	94
	3.B.4 The Islamic Outlook and the Community	98
	3.B.4.1 Faith and the Need for Solidarity	100
	3.B.4.2 Islam as the Guiding Thread	103
	3.C Summary	105
4	Islam in Daily Life	108
	4.1 The Structure of Religious Life in Aarhus	113
	4.1.1 Koran-i-kerim kürsü - Koranic Courses for Children	119
	4.1.2 The Growth in the Number of Mosques, 1979-1992	122
	4.2 Islamism as the Manager of Islamic Identity	123
	4.3 Changes	136
5	On the Periphery of Islamism: Jama'at al-Tabligh	139
	5.1 Denmark	142
	5.2 France	145
	5.2.1 An Interview and its Context - Meeting Sheikh Mohammed Hammami	147
	5.3 On the Periphery of Islamism	149
6	Migration, Marginalisation and Social Identity – Islam and 'Cultural Release'	153
	6.1 Muslim Minorities, Labour Market Affiliation and Social Identity	154
	6.2 Reflections on 'Systemworld' and 'Lifeworld'	160
	6.3 Social and Cultural Interests among Muslim Minorities in Western Europe	163
	6.4 Public Institutions and Multicultural Society	172
	6.5 Cultural Release, Marginalisation and Social Identity	182
7	Islamism in a Multicultural Western Europe	187
	7.1 The Conspiracy and the Islamic Community	187
	7.2 With Islam at the Helm	188
	7.3 Muslim Immigrant Milieux and the Dialectic of Marginalisation Processes	191
	7.4 Multicultural Society and Equal Rights	195
	7.5 Islamism in Multicultural Society	197
	7.6 The Concept of Minority Rights in Multicultural Society	202

Postscript	208
Bibliography	222
Appendix A Interview with Mehmet	232
Appendix B Interview with Yahya Schülzke	237
Appendix C Yahya Schülzke's Defense Statement	241
Appendix D AMGT Hac.	245
Appendix E What is Millî Görüş?	247
Appendix F 'Muslims of all the World, Unite'	252
Appendix G Islamische Föderation Statement on the Rushdie Case	256
Appendix H Islamische Kulturzentren Statement on the Conflict in Azerbaijan, 1989	257
Appendix I 'The Islamic Alternative'	259
Appendix J Letter from Senator für Schulwesen	267
Appendix K Flyer for the Alternative (Islamic) Theatre in Berlin	270
Appendix L Interview with Mustafa Doğan	271
Appendix M Letter from the Danish Directorate for Aliens	276
Appendix N Letter from the Danish Directorate for Aliens	278
Summary	279

Preface

This Ph.D thesis is the outcome of a lengthy process. It is primarily based on fieldwork carried out among Islamists in the years from 1989-1993, and on later observations of the response from within Danish public institutions to themes related to immigration generally, and to Islamic forms of expression in particular.

The research project of which this thesis is a result has, over the years, been supported financially by the Danish Research Council for the Humanities, and the Danish Social Science Research Council, while I was attached to the Dept. of Ethnography and Social Anthropology, Aarhus University, Denmark.

First and foremost, I should naturally like to thank the many people, ordinary members as well as leaders, of the various Islamic groups in Europe who had sufficient confidence in me to invite me in - no names mentioned, and none forgotten.

I have received a great deal of encouragement and advice from my two tutors: Dr. Klaus Ferdinand, former head of department, now professor emeritus, Dept. of Ethnography and Social Anthropology, Aarhus University, has been an engaged and supportive tutor over the years. On the whole, Klaus Ferdinand is the person who has contributed above all, both prior to and during the project, to enabling me to focus my interest in Islam and Islamism in relation to Muslim immigrant societies in Western Europe. His contribution cannot be overestimated.

Dr. Carl-Ulrik Schierup, Dept. of Sociology, Umeå University has been a great source of inspiration in the attempt to pair traditional ethnographic theory with other relevant social science outlooks. One could say that in this way the theoretic eclecticism here corresponds to the eclecticism of multicultural society. Carl-Ulrik Schierup has been an outstanding critical reader of the thesis and came up with numerous suggestions, not all of which were met with enthusiasm on my part, but which nevertheless have been valuable to the final result. While I have good reason to thank these two tutors, I am, however, the only one who can and should be held accountable for whatever shortcomings this thesis might contain.

One other person who deserves thanks is Dr Kirsten Haugaard Bach who specialises in Egypt. Kirsten has been a thorough and very critical reader of this work. She has come up with suggestions for improvements and has pointed out inconsistencies - despite which, we remain good friends!

I should like to thank the Danish Research Council for the Humanities for making an English version of the thesis possible with their economic support. Finally, Jamal Mahjoub deserves thanks for having delivered a firm and accurate translation of the thesis from the Danish original. Jamal is also responsible for providing the final camera-ready-copy.

August 1998
Lars Pedersen

1 Introduction

The significance of the influence of Islamic movements in the Middle East as well as among immigrants in Europe is a theme that crops up time and again, not least of all in the media. These movements constitute one of the greatest political challenges facing nation states in the Middle East, alongside the unresolved question of national identity.

In Europe *Islamism* is often regarded as a statement of demarcation made by immigrant Muslims who consciously seek to avoid 'integration' and whose way of life subscribes to certain norms and values that are at odds with those of the majority of society. Islamism in Europe stresses *Islam* as a relevant medium in the formulation of cultural heritage and identity among immigrant Muslims.

There are historic precedents for Islam being used as a part of political argumentation in the Middle East. King Hassan II of Morocco, for example, claims that he is a *Sharif,* in other words that he is a descendent of the prophet's clan; the Saudi royal family trace their ancestors to the religious reformists who were involved in the local power struggle towards the end of the last century, moreover, they call themselves the Protectors of Islam's two holy sites; President Sadat sought increasingly to be filmed in a mosque whenever he was to appear on Egyptian television.

The Arab nationalism which the Ba'thist party in Iraq has stood for since 1968 is founded on secularism. But despite the basis of the state being secular this has not outruled the use of language carrying religious connotations being utilised to gain legitimacy. President Saddam Hussein, for example, made the following statement in Najaf, a town sacred to the Shi'ites, in 1979:

> Iraq will fight and triumph against injustice everywhere with the swords of Imam Ali, Husayn, Khalid al Walid, Salah al-Din, all Arab strugglers and Islamic leaders of the land of Arabism and of the message of Islam (Broadcast on Baghdad radio, 17th October 1979; in; Dam 1983, p.131).

According to the secularism being developed in Iraq, *Shia* and *Sunni* Islam share a common cultural heritage. The heroes of Shi'ite history are on an equal par with those in *Sunni* Muslim history.[1]

In that same year (1979) Saddam Hussein accused Syria of being behind an attempted coup staged against him. He structured his accusations so as to draw a parallel between the conflict between the two Ba'th parties in Iraq and Syria respectively, and the story of the rivalry in the 7th century between the fourth, and last, so-called Rightly Guided caliph, Ali, who controlled most of Iraq, and Mu'awiyah, who was the governor of Syria but who himself wanted to be caliph and therefore did not recognise Ali (ibid.)

Nor did Islam manage to avoid being invoked in the run up to the Gulf conflict of 1991-92. Saddam Hussein called for a *Jihad* (holy war) against the infidels. This man, who had formerly stood for a secular form of Arab nationalism, appealed for full mobilisation, using a term that in the West denotes the essence of religious fanaticism. A few days later a sigh of relief was heard when it was announced that Saudi Arabia had engaged 290 theologians from 60 countries who had unanimously rejected the threat. Saddam Hussein could not, according to these experts, call for a *Jihad* under the circumstances.

What we are seeing, then, is the search for legitimacy at state level via the use of religiously-charged language. Political argumentation in the Middle East has, over the last 15-20 years, become increasingly Islamicised. Social revolutionaries also have argued their case from an Islamic standpoint. Islam has, as such, discovered a role as a frame of reference for socio-political groups in opposition: In Egypt there is the illegal Muslim Brotherhood, as well as mass Islamic organisations, such as student groups, and there are also violent underground groups. In Algeria there is The Islamic Front (FIS). In Tunesia, The Islamic Tendency. Pakistan has its own equivalent and so does Turkey. The Soviet occupation of Afghanistan was met by armed opposition from a group that defined itself as Islamic. In the Phillipines and in Thailand it takes the form of a struggle for minority rights. In Iran opposition to the Shah found a means of self expression in Islamism, and following the revolution an Islamic opposition movement continued the struggle against the Islamic regime

---

[1] The Imam Ali and his son Hussein are the earliest and most significant figures in the history and mythology unique to Shia Islam; Khalid al-Walid was a general under the first caliph - the successor to the Prophet Muhammed - he was one of the key figures in the early Arab-Islamic conquests; Saladin was the very famous Kurdish Muslim leader of the army that recaptured Jerusalem from the crusaders.

installed by Khomeni. The Iranian Islamic revolution marked the arrival of this politicisation, not least of all in the Western media.

This however also marked the emergence of a new means of dealing with politics which replaced the social models of former years which had suffered defeat. The Islamic wave won support when it became obvious that Arab socialism could not deliver its promises and that, in the case of Iran, capitalism did not lead to welfare for all, as had been previously claimed.

The Islamic wave which I shall analyse in this treatise lies parallel to that which has been in existence in political opposition in the Muslim world. It is a variation which takes Islamic theology as its starting point in its criticisim of the existing system. Following on from this the Islamic wave takes a rejection of state history associated with Islam as its point of departure. The new movements also take as their central landmarks the well known works of state criticism by Islamic philosophers and politicians such as Ibn Taymiya, Hassan al-Banna, Sayed Qutb, Maulana Maududi and Khomeini, who attacked political tyranny as well as the part played in this by the Islamic scholars, the *Ulema*.

The Islamic movements seek to confront injustices in the state apparatus, social need, and economic exploitation. In their view Islam, as a model for society, offers an alternative to suffering.

In the form it takes in the Middle East, it can be said that this kind of *Islamism* seeks to confirm Islamic identity through stressing the need for radical social change. Society is regarded as being characterised by social injustice, economic arbitrariness and political irresponsibility, along with cultural and religious alienation. In other words, Islam contains the motivation, but also the model for future society, a third way. As such, Islamism stresses the socio-political dimension in a religious context.

Using Islam as their chosen means, Muslim minorities in Western Europe are developing a region of consciousness and culture in which the social norms of the majority society do not count. The development which this expresses exists not only at an individual level, but also at a collective one, in that new organisational parameters are being established. These new organisations not only break with established political unions among ethnic minorities, but also with forms of religious-political expression such as are represented by national cultural associations which often refer back to official religiosity and politics of their country of origin.[2]

In this treatise I describe and evaluate the development of the new cultural discontinuity which Islamism represents among Muslim minorities in Western Europe. My interest is aimed at a clarification of Islamism's

---

[2] Attention has been drawn to this situation previously in Pedersen (1991c).

ability to contribute to strengthening the pillar upon which Muslim minorities base their identity, formulated as it is on a specifically Islamic foundation. Furthermore, I shall evaluate Islamism's alternative and potential to formulate an opposition strategy - one that could be transformed into a political movement.

My analysis of the European dimension of Islamism draws on experience that is primarily based on empirical material relating to the dominant Turkish Islamist movement, Millî Görüş, in three countries, namely; Denmark, West Germany, and France. Two conflicting tendencies emerge in the development of Islamic movements in Western Europe. *In part* the same movements are to be found in several countries at the same time which hints at an international organisation with the emphasis on one's country of origin. There is also, *in part*, a break with this tendency as noted in more recent movements, not least of all among the young, where there is an increasing orientation towards the sense of being part of a minority.

Existing studies of Islamism in Europe are all quite recent. There have been no attempts to analyse the tendency in a broader synthesis that seeks to gather experiences from around Europe. In this sense the present work is a pioneering study, both in the international context as much as in the Danish.

In any analysis of Islamism there are valid reasons why the nomenclature used to describe this world should be queried from the very outset. What exactly do we mean when we use the word *Muslim* as an adjective?

Here we have an apparent paradox: *Muslim* is used quite broadly. We have accustomed ourselves to encountering *Islam* and *Muslim* in the written form as well as in the mass media and the politiological, sociological, historic and anthropological literature.

These terms are to a large degree an integral part of our tools of expression, and comprise elements in our understanding of the world; they order and explain existence to us, and they provide it with meaning. In short, these terms and all that they convey can be used by anyone. But it is precisely the ease with which we believe that we understand what terms like *Islam* and *Muslim* mean that creates problems. It is precisely the apparently obvious nature of these terms which should give cause for us to pause and reflect for a moment.

In the following I shall run through the ways in which Islam and Muslims are presented in Western discourse. In part I shall begin with the discourse of the press, and then introduce how the recent Islamic wave is interpreted in the mainstream of social science analyses. After that I shall define the term Islamism, which is a term that I - like others - apply as a collective term for the Islamic movements. To end this conclusion I shall look at the background to my conducting this work and outline its construction.

1.1 Islam in Western Discourse

What role does the journalist ascribe his subjects? The degree to which we speak of 'the others' is not insignificant. During my own field investigations I have on numerous occasions experienced Muslim immigrants expressing scepticism about my work. Likewise, while carrying out fieldwork previously in Egypt I encountered scepticism. Anthropological colleagues have also confirmed that they too had similar encounters during the course of their work.

The scepticism encountered among Muslim immigrants, and not least of all when I approached religious institutions, or when I wished to discuss Islam, was however, more reluctant. When I enquired about the reasons for this scepticism, leaders and ordinary members of Islamic organisations referred to negative experiences in previous encounters with the media. In the Muslim immigrant circles there exists a strong awareness of the meaning of these terms, and that non-Muslims should not produce representations of Islam.

When, after my first few encounters with representatives of the Islamic Cultural Centre (Islamisk Kulturcenter) in Aarhus, I asked why they were so reserved in response to my questions, they responded by referring to an article in a local paper (*Aarhus Onsdag:* 12.12.1984) in which the journalist's visit to the centre was illustrated with photographs of the Ayatollah Khomeini. Using very evocative language the journalist managed to construct a link which the 'victims' felt was intimidating. During a subsequent interview with a representative of the Islamic Cultural Centre in Copenhagen an article in the national daily, *Politiken* (14.11.1986), was put forward as evidence of the kind of distortion of the lives of Muslims and their religious organisations which can occur when the description is left to non-Muslims. The experience of representatives of Islamic congregations tells them that there is good reason to exercise caution. In the Aarhus case I was actually confronted with the article more than two years after it had been published!

On the basis of this I began to take an interest in the way the media portrayed Muslim immigrants. Previous investigations into this subject

(Hammer 1984, and Hedman 1985) describe the kind of themes that dominate coverage of immigrants in Danish and Swedish newspapers. Both investigations show that both the Danish and the Swedish papers, generally speaking, display a positive attitude towards immigrants. In both cases, however, it is noted that the crucial point is that immigrants are represented either in conflicts or in controversial contexts. This implies that, despite them taking a *positive* stance, the newspapers nevertheless manage to impart a *negative* message.

What themes do we find associated with *Islam* and *Muslims* if we are to go by what is written in the serious and more thorough newspapers, where the coverage of immigrants, for example, or events in the Middle East is in the hands of journalists who are experienced in dealing with such material?: The main themes are fanaticism, religious fanaticism in political life, and the suppression of women in daily life.

In another context I carried out an analysis of the coverage of Muslims in the Danish national daily newspaper *Information*, from 1986 through to September 1987 (Pedersen 1988). The material on Muslims and immigrants turned out to be based, on the whole, on themes of conflict: war, flight, racism - and cultural conflict, a new topic in the 1980s.

Information's attempt to deal with such an area suggests that we can presumably take their coverage to be representative of engaged, fair and responsible journalism. Indeed, specialist experts were often brought in to ensure this. Assuming, however, the integrity of this newspaper, allows us to touch upon what Edward Said describes as 'latent Orientalism'. (Said 1978, p.206). In other words, this example highlights the subconscious element, or substance, which to a large extent is taken as being self-explanatory, that is generally accepted and which promotes images and associations which are not questioned in any fundamental manner. This is something which constitutes Europe's shadow, something alien, the Other, a product of the 'geography of the fantasy' as he also refers to it.

Islam and *Muslims* were *never* mentioned during the period in question in any context other than conflict or war. As regards the Middle East, the message was clear and simple: one could read about Mubarek's crisis, the worst since Sadat was killed by *religious fanatics*, about *Islamic fundamentalists* or *militant Muslims* threatening stability in Tunisia, how in the Sudan the election was thankfully won by *moderate* Muslims. There was nothing about Iran in the way that there was, say, about Pakistan, Egypt, Iraq and Jordan, but only about the *Ayatollah Khomeini*'s Iran, the *Ayatollah's army*, the *war machine, authority*. There is mention of an

Ayatollah-factor, of the *Ayatollah*'s (or 'wizard') *apprentices* and of the forces which the *Ayatollah*'s seizure of power in Tehran had let loose everywhere. Moreover, one could read about Islam's suppression of women.

My investigation shows that Islam was always linked to fundamentalism, fanaticism, and militancy or terror. The term *Islam* was used as an explanation of why this or that action had been carried out. *Islam* was the key which explained everything, bringing order to our understanding of an otherwise chaotic world. Taken separately, in each individual case the explanatory terms could be regarded as being used innocently and naturally. Together, however, they build up an excessive opinion which forms a pattern of abnormality and threats which are posed against nothing less than mankind itself. The use of these terms allows the reader to understand what message the journalist is trying to get across. Our familiarity with these terms signals that 'we' have reason on our side, a reason that is up against 'their' (the Muslims') fanaticism and lack of reason. At the same time it is made clear that the dictators whom the 'extremists' are up against, have the desire and aptitude for democracy. They possess the very same reason that we do!

The newspaper *Information* tells us that there is no formal distinction between religion and politics in Islam. However, even the most orthodox Sunni-Muslims happily accept this distinction, they write. According to the authors, Sunni-Islam renounces the stipulations of Islam and is not, therefore, in accordance with holy scripture in the same way that Shia-Islam is. This implies also that the newspaper is suggesting that true, authentic Islam is Shia Islam, other forms are partly or completely heretical! How close does this conclusion come to providing a true picture of how Islam is seen in the West? At present Islam in the West is equated with Shia-Islam. It is difficult to use the word Islam today without summoning up certain fluctuating political phenomena - in this case, Khomeini-ism.

The case of Israel demonstrates how it is Islam in particular upon which these latent politics are imposed. Israel's Jericho rocket, whose range allows it to reach Arab capitals, has never been called 'Jewish', while Pakistan's equivalent has been called 'Muslim'. It is only the extreme right wing Tehiya party and the ultra racist rightist Kach party which are called Jewish, despite Israel, as a Zionist state, being founded precisely on an interweaving of religion and state. All Zionist parties are built upon a religious doctrine, and almost all Israeli parties are Zionist. My point is not, of course, that the predicate 'Jewish' should be added to everything as an all-embracing explanatory term, in the same way as the predicate 'Muslim' is, but, on the contrary, that Muslims can be presented as being something other than just 'Muslims', in the way that Jews are usually presented as something other than 'Jews'.

Immigrants with a Muslim background have in recent years become 'hot property'. Everyone has an opinion about them, and this despite the fact that very few Danes actually come into contact with any of them on a daily basis, and that factual information about them is quite incomplete (Körmendi 1986).

The material dealing with immigrant related issues that appeared in *Information*, during the period that I conducted my investigation, fell roughly into three categories, 1) the arrival of refugees and the regulation of legislation dealing with this area, 2) racism and anti-foreign sentiments, and 3) cultural conflict. The order in which they appear here conforms to the proportion in which they appeared. 'The flow of refugees' mostly appeared as immediate news or daily reportage, while the perspective of racism and anti-foreign feeling came under debate primarily when preceded by the release of a book, and secondly when prompted by clashes between immigrants and Danes. The theme of cultural conflict was mainly linked to seminars and conferences. Only very few articles have taken the form of investigative journalism within immigrant circles.

The suppression of women is a prominent aspect of the debate surrounding immigrant culture. We read now about Muslim culture and what we hear is that it is patriarchal, suppressive and that the individual is subordinate to the collective.

The immigrants depicted in *Information* are also to be found in the traditional pathological role of immigrants as being a victim of their own culture. I am in no doubt that many immigrants never had the opportunity to gain extensive school education, and I am in no doubt that arranged marriages exist. What, however, is presented to us in the articles referred to here, is what 'we' 'know' about 'them' already - inescapable truths, no new angles, no surprises. Those immigrants interviewed live up to their roles as immigrants and tell the journalists what they want to hear.

Information also examined conditions within immigrant families. Their lives, according to the newspaper, were particularly characterised by conflict. During the period in which I conducted my investigation there were at least half a dozen articles on immigrant families and the conflicts within them - only one single one was based on actual news. The articles were instead based on 1) a ministerial report on 'immigrant children and the environment they grow up in', and 2) a conference on social work with under-privileged, alienated and oppressed groups.

What answer are we given then, on why there are conflicts in Turkish families, for example? These conflicts are about generation problems, a conflict between parents and children. Conflicts of this kind would not appear particularly sensational when in the context of a Danish family. But, whereas the conflicting relationship between young Danes and their parents is often interpreted as a stage in personal development, the process of liberation, and the inter-generation conflicts among Turks are seen as tragic, and an expression of cultural conflict in which the children are torn between two cultures and the parents attempt to force the children to conform to Turkish cultural norms.

Young immigrants become, then, the victims of culture. As the cultural-sociologist, Jonathan Schwartz, writing in *Information* - about the paper's coverage of a number of cases in which children were forcibly removed from Turkish families, noted that it is rare to hear the problems within Danish families being described as cultural - they are social problems. In other words, immigrants have (too much) culture - whereas Danes have society!

Only a few of the, in total 105 articles and commentaries, which do not deal with cultural conflict, racism/anti-foreign sentiment, or laws on refugees: 1) six articles and commentaries touched on conditions in the labour market, 2) seven articles dealt with criminal material in a series on 'The Suit Mystery'; in which the newspaper covered, at great length, the case of a Turkish immigrant accused of murder, 3) one article dealt with immigrant radio, and 4) a brief notice explained how immigrant women were now giving birth to fewer children than previously - the birth rate was now only double that of Danish women.

To be a Muslim is, at one and the same time, both a simple and a very difficult matter, according to the analysis outlined above. Simple in so far as Islam is taken as a religion of laws. If one learns certain simple laws and obeys certain conditions then one can become a Muslim and have a firm anchor point in the world. This implies the embracing of a *stationary, conservative cultural form*. Transplanted to the West, as an immigrant, the Muslim immediately acquires a problem: It is *not possible to be a guided Muslim in a modern democratic welfare state*. If one wishes to be modern, one has to discard one's Muslim identity, with the subsequent loss of culture. If one wishes to remain Muslim, one is at odds with development and must renounce its fruits. This gives rise to an inevitable cultural clash.

The themes and the perspectives in which 'Islam' and 'Muslims' are treated reappear throughout the Western world's media coverage (see also Dindler and Olesen (eds.) 1988 and Said 1981). And not only in the media, but also in the discourse of power regarding 'them'. That is to say that these comprise the form of the manner in which foreigners/immigrants are talked about in public institutions in the same way as it does that of academics. It is a case of a reputation which represents certain truths, which to a great extent is taken for granted.

If we examined an overview of existing research on Middle Eastern societies it would show that references to Islam's mythology have shot up on a regular basis - since 1979, the Islamic revolution in Iran being the immediate reason. Today, *Islam* appears in every single book on the Middle Eastern region - this was far from being the case in the first half of the 1970s.

Social science is also now subject to the kind of treatment reserved for fiction, in the same way as journalism is - each description and analysis is pared down, thus losing some of its sense, and thereby being reduced.

There is nothing new about ideologies, religion and politics providing mutual support for one another. This applies both when it comes to Islam as well as in other matters. There is, however, a quite specific hybrid form which exists on Muslim territory between religion and politics which is known as *Islamism*, and this I shall explain here.

The emergence of Islamism is often seen as a return to the past, an archaism, a rejection of modernisation and technology. A point of view that Gibb (1947); Halpern (1963); Rahman (1970); Berger (1970); Israeli (1979) and Curtis (1981) all express. Halpern, furthermore, is of the view that Islamic movements are a desperate attempt to attain upward mobility within traditional society rather than in progressive modern society (op.cit., p.138 ff). In other words the Islamic movements are an outcome of the tensions and dislocations of the modernisation process, though condemned to be forgotten in the fullness of time, overcome by modernisation (op.cit., p.153). In the long term, as we have seen, this view has been contradicted by history. Those Islamic movements which were at their height in the Muslim world during the 1930s certainly lost their popular appeal in the 50s and 60s, but resurfaced towards the end of the 1970s.

The writers mentioned above do not only agree on the point that there is a contrast between the religiously formulated movements and modernisation, they are also united on the matter of Islam and modernisation being incompatible; a choice has to be made.

Many more recent analyses are an extension of these viewpoints, but at the same time attempt to define the emergence of Islamism as a perspective created out of the permanent structural crisis of integration in Middle Eastern society as a whole. In other words they regard Islamism as being a result of the restricted development opportunities produced by the priorities made in the international division of labour.

This situation has been analysed in various ways: Thus this kind of political Islam is seen as an expression of *traditionalist* critique, a defensive standpoint (Arjomand 1984). Johansen (1981) describes the critique as *pre-bourgeois* - political culture defined as a product of the conflict between the *pre-bourgeois* forms of religion and secular political cultural forms. Baber Johansen begins with the term 'structural heterogeneity' which comprises the coexistence of both traditional and modern societies. This, then, is to preserve forms of religion which have not been transformed into secular political culture.

Bassam Tibi, who starts from the same basic point as Johansen, with the term structural heterogeneity, defines Islamic political expression as *pre-industrial* culture (Tibi 1981 & 1985). This cultural form can not transform traditional society into functional differentiation. The industrialisation necessary to overcome the structures of underdevelopment rests on what is, in the final instance, a hegemonic 'technical-scientific' culture. This means that the answer to modernity cannot lie in forms based on religion, but in *secularisation*. Although Tibi (and others) at first hand appear to show some sympathy for the Islamic project, in that it expresses 'cultural awareness', it is, in the final instance seen as being both irrelevant and reactionary in the face of a superior 'technical-scientific cultural system'.

Despite the differences, the two analyses shown above work within the same modernisation theoretical framework: *Islam* can be considered as a cultural system which not only has to stand up to 'change' but which in addition provides an inadequate response to 'modernisation'. Secularisation on the other hand is regarded as a necessity for 'modernisation', and it is presumed that these two phenomena progress together in a process that is both linear and irreversible. It is assumed that secularisation takes place both at the institutional *and* the cultural ideological level.

One of the points I would make in relation to the literature and views outlined above, is that Islam cannot be taken as a homogeneous object which can be ascribed to one independent cause that acts ontologically, or can be taken as a reaction to other (similarly reified) forces and which therefore cannot a priori be defined as anti-modern. Islam is treated in this thesis not as a societal agent, but as a language - and therefore as an opportunity for legitimisation. The perspective is shifted towards the level of the societal players.

1.1.1 The Nomenclature Problematic - Explanatory Notes

It could perhaps be said that it makes little difference how we regard Muslims, except for the fact that political decisions are being taken based on this matter. *Islam* and *Muslims* have been politicised, not least of all in European society. One could say that this is where political Islam really begins, precisely here where we make assumptions about 'the Others' and produce actions that will have consequences for them.

There is a tendency for us to put down *Islam* as the cause of everything, the radicalism and the suppression. Even here we already have something of a problem in explaining this as it is Islam's latent significance which provides the reference point. We all think we know what *Islam* and being a *Muslim* are - and it is precisely this which is our first problem.

Sivanandan (1983) claims that whereas formerly the relationship of power regarding foreign cultures was based on the conviction of the superiority of 'our' culture, it is now based on our superior understanding of other cultures. What he means by this is that the term culture takes material form, so to speak, when it is a part of a larger control apparatus. Taking culture as the cause of sociality there is a tendency to separate talk of 'them' from time and place, 'they' lose their history and identity, reduced as they are to cultural caricatures.

This conclusion requires, however, that in general we clearly define the matter, in a manner that also satisfies the actual historical content: are *Islam* and *Muslim*, in other words, terms that can, with complete authority, contain and explain the countless cultural variations which they have to cover? Can it honestly be true that a uniform culture is to be found in all the geographic regions where Islam exists? Islam is found in the Philippines to the east and in Morocco to the west, in Central Asia and in Bosnia Herzegovina in the north and in Sudan and Nigeria to the south. There is a huge cultural gap between the 'orthodox' Islam of a high scholar in Cairo and the 'popular Islam' of a peasant in Turkey. Within Islam there are a large number of sects with quite different ritual practices and large differences in their approach to Islamic religious thought. Khomeini's radical political views are not necessarily shared by Chinese Muslims, Turkish Alevite-Muslims or by Nigeria's Ibadi-Muslims.

How can it then be claimed that *Islam* and *Muslim* are meaningful terms which, quite literally, cover every eventuality in terms of class, social, political, ethnic and national difference? Is it sufficient to subdivide Islam according to its sectarian, regional, ethnic and social forms of expression, or should we continue *ad infinitum* until we get down to the individual Muslim and attempt to define his or her particular type of Islam?

To provide a relevant answer to these questions we could, for example, consider how the relationship between *Islamic* and *Muslim* is articulated in two widespread and fundamentally different forms, both of them problematic in their own way, namely, the case where *Islam* is everything, and the case in which nothing is *Islam*.

In the first case *Islam* is seen as *source* of identity. Here, *Muslim* is taken as the starting point of a comprehensive reductionism: Identity, society, war and history are all referred back to holy scripture and become, as such, both *Islamic* and *Muslim*. The chain linking them is as follows: The Koran (along with the other holy texts) provides an Islamic identity which gives rise to an Islamic society, Islamic wars and an Islamic history.[3]

In the second case a clear division is evident between Islam and society. One of the principles at stake in clarifying this basic assumption has been the distinction between the terms *Islamic* and *Muslim*. Implicit in any declaration that a certain condition is *Islamic* is the claim that this is an authentic core substance of which there can be no doubt of its being genuine Islam. The discussion would be of its extent. Muslim implies a broad cultural definition, referring to cultures which have Islam as their religion, but manifested in different ways. In this variation it is believed that it is possible to distinguish between what is Islam and what is not, and thereby what social significance can be ascribed to it.[4] The societies, history and politics can be evaluated thereafter on the basis of their adherence or deviation to or from Islam.

If, however, we turn to the Muslim debate, we are faced with the historic fact that Islamic scholars have persistently sought to elucidate the importance of Islam in the world. We, as non-Muslims, must indeed take into account the fact that there is now, and has been over the course of 1400 years, an ongoing and highly qualified discussion about Islam which has not resulted in a definition of a mode of practice about which all are in agreement.[5] In actual fact there was an 'agreement to disagree' in the 9th and 10th centuries. To respect this discussion implies, as far as I can tell, that we cannot provide a true definition of *Islam* and what is *Muslim*.

---

[3] The classic, and also very impressive work, The Cambridge History of Islam (1970) is editorially structured around this basic concept.

[4] An attempt to put apply such a distinction in a Danish context can be found in Olsen (1988).

[5] Which is why Turner's suggestion that Islam actually conforms more to an *orthopraxy*, which presumes a common practice and ritual community, than to an *orthodoxy* which presumes a common belief, is not satisfactory (Turner 1974).

I shall therefore refrain from doing so and shall instead take up a third position which views *Islam* as a character, as a circumstance which always carries meaning and which can be studied. Muslim culture is to be found in the discussion of what it means to be a Muslim. This interpretation cannot be evoked in a discussion of how far this or that phenomenon is in line with Islam. There are, in other words, no positions of privilege, only representations. When, therefore, I apply the terms Islamic or Muslim, it is not so as to direct the line of argument back towards the holy texts, nor is it to judge the degree of authenticity. On the contrary, it is the utilisation of terms which deal with and represent the players' actual understanding of themselves.

1.2 Islamism

One can be a *Muslim* without being an *Islamist*. While the first refers to a cultural heritage that dates back centuries, the second refers to a political-religious phenomenon which has an associated historical character. Francois Brugat (1988) and Bruno Etienne (1987) distinguish this term, as they do between the 'classical Muslim', and followers of certain mystical practices, such as the Sufis. They also stress that the term *Islamist* is the term most often used by the Islamists themselves. They use the term *Islamiyyine* to distinguish themselves from the rest of the *Muslimine* (the Muslims).

Here too, of course, there is another obvious nomenclature problem with some of the terms which are often used to refer to the same kind of political Islam: *traditionalism, fundamentalism,* and *Islamism*.

Clearly, some of the views held by the Islamists can be pointed out as being anti-modern. Although it ought to be possible to agree with people such as Sivan (1985) in there being a disparity between the dominant Islamic movements and pervasive popular culture, while, at the same time, studies of Islamism show that we are forced to deal with quite a different picture: The activists in the Islamic movements are linked to the form of modern existence. It is not the case that young people are excluded from modernity and therefore express their opposition to it, but that the young are a product of modernity and are included in it. The movement is based in big cities rather than in rural areas. In terms of education the movement emerged more from within the fields of technology rather than the centres and institutions of religious learning. This is not then a rebellion by the religious institutions. It is a movement with a popular base, more concerned with the character of the political project than with matters of a strictly religious nature. The widespread Islamic wave comprises modern aspects and includes a sharp critique of tradition. The Islamists are not opposed to the modern mass media, but seek rather to take control of them.

'The enemy is not modernity (...) but...tradition' explained Olivier Roy (1985). Olivier Roy writes that traditionalism's privileged approach to religion comes from:

> In the end it is about habits and customs: women's clothing, the upbringing of girls, the obedience of children and respect for hierarchy (op.cit. 1985, p.28).

In short, all the values which are closely bound to the normative sphere of religion. In contrast to Islamism, traditionalism does not lay the foundations for 'the political project' writes Roy, who points on the other hand towards 'tout ce qui est conservateur' (...); 'sa nostalgie du passé est par ailleurs, plus moralisante que mue par un desir de justice sociale', which is precisely the theme which the Islamists emphasise strongly.

Islamism's theoreticians are themselves very aware of their role as critics of tradition and of the fact that their message also has a claim in the struggle over the meaning of Islam. In this context Rached Ghannouchi, leader and theoretician of the Tunisian Harakat al-Itijah al Islami (Islamic Tendency Movement, better known by its French title Mouvement de la Tendence Islamique, MTI), states:

> (The Islamic message) has encountered internal hindrances as a consequence of the inherited traditionalist image of Islam (...), by this I mean from the spiritual education that comes from different cults, which is produced later and which has no connection with Islam: sufism, the dervish movement, visiting the graves of the ancestors, hadra, or 'sufi seances, saint cults, etc' (Burgat 1988, p.16).

While *Islamism* can be said to be formulated on the basis of being a critique of *traditionalism*, *fundamentalism* can be said to constitute the foundations of *Islamism*. *Islamism* separates itself from k in stressing the socio-political dimension of the religious framework, while *fundamentalism*'s project can more accurately be defined as being a reiteration of the authenticity of the holy scripture. As such the *Islamists* can be said to be *fundamentalists*, while the reverse does not necessarily follow.

Abdelsalam Yassine, one of the leading figures in the Moroccan Islamist movement, Mouvement de la Jeuness Islamique, explains here the limits of fundamentalism:

> What some of the ulema do is very interesting, but it is not sufficient. They are (undoubtedly) a part of the opposition, (but there is) an opposition in principles which is infinite. They do no more than point out what they believe to be immoral. It is not sufficient to do that, one must go a step further, to the next stage, which is to see a project (...) These ulema only preach about the immoral. Only in a few rare exceptions do they talk of economic problems, and only very rarely about political ones, but it is essential to be aware that there is a very close relationship between immorality and the economic and political system. (...) We want to assume power (...); it is permitted by democracy, that is what we want (Burgat 1988, p. 30).

The question of the authority of state and politics is central to the Islamists. The fundamentalists are criticised for limiting themselves to the moral sphere and for not raising a question mark above the political power at the centre, in the same way as they are criticised for not raising questions about the constitution of the financial sector. On the other side the Islamists argue for their involvement in the political sphere with a view to winning power.

The use of the term *Islamism* is (as outlined in Burgat 1988) an attempt to coin a term that covers: 1) quite a variety of institutional forms, be they local groups or international networks, 2) very different political forms, underground as well as tolerated, in opposition, or, as in Iran, agents of the state, and 3) very different methods of action, ranging from encouraging conversion from within the mosques to more radical social action and this, lest we forget, also includes violent action.

The Islamic wave can therefore quite well be bound to the same historic frame of explanation - despite it having quite different forms of expression.

1.3 The Background to this Thesis

I have, on previous occasions, conducted interviews and ethnographic fieldwork among Islamists in Egypt. In 1982-83 I carried out a survey among Islamists at Cairo University as part of my education. Later this led to a more general investigation into the Islamic position in Egypt (C.f. Pedersen 1984 & 1986).

My interest in conducting an investigation into Islamism in Western Europe arose, however, from the experience gained on a research project into cultural identity among young Muslim immigrants in Denmark (c.f. Pedersen & Selmer 1991). To my great surprise I discovered a strong Islamic tendency among young, so-called, 'second generation' immigrants. And not least of all among youths who had grown up in Denmark. While it came as little surprise that Islamic movements found some resonance within the Middle East it struck me as being less than obvious what role they might serve in a European context - I had, in any case, not seen any analyses of the phenomenon.

Islamism in Western Europe has particularly gained a foothold among the so-called, 'second generation' immigrants, who are not entirely comfortable adopting norms that apply in a Turkish rural village, for example, or in the Turkish state, and who also find difficulty in recognising themselves in the Western representations which I have described above.

Although here we are not dealing with a culture which represents any kind of majority among young immigrant Muslims, this is, nevertheless, a group which is central in the reformulating of the collective identity. This is a new cultural phenomenon within the European context which articulates its own values centred around Islam. A new region of consciousness is therefore being defined, one which demands space within a multi-cultural Europe. I discovered a group of youths along these lines, able to identify positively with Islam, and who at the same time used this to relate both theoretically and in practice, to Western society, and who insisted on the right to exist as fully fledged citizens i.e., as *Danish Muslims* in Denmark.

The subsequent investigation looks specifically at the Turkish Islamist movement in Europe, Millî Görüş, while at the general level it represents an analysis of Islamism in Western Europe. The analysis is largely built on material collected personally. Gathered in part in the form of structured interviews and in part in the form of a field investigation into an Islamist circle in Denmark.

I have conducted interviews with representatives of various Islamic organisations in Europe, both state run and non-state run organisations Among the non-state run organisations I have primarily interviewed people representing the Turkish Islamist movement in Europe, Millî Görüş. In the case of Denmark and France I interviewed the foremen of the organisations. In the case of Berlin a special spokesman was referred. In Berlin, I also, at the same time, had the opportunity to interview imams linked to the movement. Moreover, I interviewed the leaders of the Turkish state's own Islamic organisations in Denmark, West Berlin and France. And in the case of France, also the representative of the Algerian state.

Alongside the structured interviews which were aimed at the construction and aims of the organisations, I conducted fieldwork within an Islamist community in Aarhus. This community was structured along the lines of a Danish union, (or social club) with a number of general activities available. Among the basic activities of the members are sports and the use of information technology. Similarly, the union's premises resembled a place that functioned as an informal meeting place, a place to get away from the cold, a place for people linked to the union who were out of work.

In the wider sense the community is also a religious community in that religious activities, such as prayer and Koran courses, also take place on the premises. More accurately however, this community is a Millî Görüş *cemaat*, or community, and is thereby a part of the dominant brand of Turkish Islamism.

The field research took the form of occasional - brief or extended - stays on the community's premises, conducting conversations with whoever was present. The aim of this was to maintain broadly informal contact and ensure that I was known in the environment. Along with these conversations another key element of the research was to conduct a number of structured, open, in-depth interviews with selected people.[6]

The circumstances pertaining to my interviews with the leaders of organisations is a practical example of the problems facing Islamic organisations in gaining legitimacy with a non-Muslim public. Those groups with the greatest degree of public recognition proved to be those which were the easiest to gain access to regarding interviews.

My interest began with my encounter with the Turkish Islamist community in Aarhus. As far as I could tell this was a unique and dynamic environment. I held a couple of meetings with some of the groups leaders who knew me. I outlined my plans and at first experienced strong opposition to my project as they were worried about the exposure that this could give rise to. They would have preferred to define the time and the place for any public debate. The project was nevertheless accepted after further discussion.

I had expected that my contacts here would open further doors for me. This was not quite the case. Although I had established good relationships with the leading figures in the community, none of them was willing to provide me with access to the organisation's Danish leader. I had to resort to the telephone company's directory enquires before I could introduce myself to him. He was greatly surprised when I introduced

---

[6] I conducted interviews of this type with eleven young men in total. Each of these people was interviewed 3-4 times for about 2-3 hours each time, i.e. between 6 and 12 hours per person. None of the subjects wished to be interviewed using a tape recorder.

myself and outlined the aims of my project to him. He was not willing to give me an interview straight away, but demanded a copy of the project outline as well as copies of previous articles along with the names of members of the Aarhus group whom he was intending to contact for further verification about me. A few weeks later I was invited to interview him, although without a tape recorder. 'It is unnecessary', I was told. The chairman explained that his earlier reticence was due to the fact that public exposure could have a damaging effect on the organisation on account of the large amount of suspicion which surrounded Islam.

The reaction of the chairman of the organisation in France was almost the exact opposite. I telephoned the organisation's head mosque in Paris and an interview was immediately granted for that same day. The chairman of the organisation in France is a 'public' person and is, for example, a member of a newly established advisory body set up by the French Ministry of the Interior to deal with Islam.

In the case of Berlin the reaction was somewhere between the two extremes encountered in Denmark and France. The organisation is openly established with mosques and the leadership expresses itself publicly, albeit cautiously in the face of politicised public criticism. The spokesman did not wish his name to be mentioned out of fear that this might create obstacles for him in his application for naturalisation as a German citizen. In the case of both France and Berlin I was able to use a tape recorder.

Here we have perhaps touched upon one of the reasons why there is no existing research work based on interviews and conversations with people who are involved in the front line of the movement. Existing analyses refer, by and large, to material which is related to the (party) political landscape in Turkey during the first half of the 1970s.

How, in the light of this, can I then consider my material to be authentic - especially when taking into account my lack of knowledge of the Turkish language? I could, supposedly, be misled. I could have been provided with interpreters who supplied a more liberal version of events.

My lack of competence in Turkish does, of course, impose certain limitations on the degree to which any analysis can be taken. This condition is, I believe, taken into consideration in the concluding phase of my analysis of the movement. My confidence that no sleight of hand was at work feeding me cleverly crafted statements for the purposes of external propaganda is based in part on the fact that, taken as a whole, the arguments presented make sense logically. In part also, it is the fact that, by and large, there was a consensus of viewpoints, regardless of whether I was in Aarhus, Copenhagen, Berlin or Paris. Regardless also of which level of the organisation I was addressing.

1.4 An Outline of this Thesis

In the following work I shall present the new cultural trend which the more recent Islamic movements represent among Muslim minorities in the form of various analysis strategies and levels. I have attempted to integrate these in a progressive disputation.

In the course of this introduction I have criticised the use of *Islam* and *Islamism* in Western discourse. Western discourse on *Islam* and *Islamism* defines a problematic mental landscape for the establishment of a multi-cultural society. My criticism is based on an analysis of the representation in the media. Just as I criticised the Western social science representations of the Islamic movement, which has made substantial inroads in the Middle East over recent years. I went on to attempt a more accurate definition of the term *Islamism*, to which my analysis is related.

In *Chapter 2* I present a layout of the institutionalisation of Islam in Western Europe. The intention being to clarify the reasons for the continued growth of the Islamic organisations, and to show that the desire of the Islamic organisations to function as European organisations is to a large degree limited by political and legal conditions. The development of autonomous Islamic organisations is contested even at the levels of state politics and administration.

Millî Görüş which is recognised as the most important Turkish Islamic movement in Western Europe is presented in *Chapter 3*. The intention is to make clear what kind of perspectives a particular Islamist group offers to the (primarily Turkish) Muslim minorities in the European context. What type of community the members are offered. What kind of organisational framework is associated with involvement in the movement. I describe the organisations in Denmark, Berlin, and France and present the background material for the subsequent analysis of the movements positions.

In *Chapter 4* we move on to a description of the position occupied by Islam in the context of local organisations. The case of Turkish-Danish Islamism in its Aarhus setting is taken as an example of how the Islamic movements establish a local communal space for redefining their cultural heritage. Islamism is similarly sketched at the individual level so as to clarify what crucial life experiences and interpretations are at the heart of joining an Islamist community and what social roles the community plays in relation to the development of social contacts.

This takes us on to an explanation of Islamism's position as the provider of an explicit religious identity. There are, however, Islamic movements which occupy the periphery of my definition of Islamism, which refrain from forming the link between an Islamic way of life and political rights. I have, therefore, made *Chapter 5* into an excursion into Jama'at al-Tabligh, which here constitutes an example of an Islamic fundamentalist movement. Jama'at al-Tabligh represents the view from the fringe of Islamism. Instead of pointing towards political factors, the movement consistently and unequivocally underlines the necessity of religious belief and practise in everyday life. This condition is seized in this context as a means of delineating the scope of Islamism. The bulk of Jama'at al-Tabligh's support comes from Pakistan. But while the Islamist groups organise themselves solely according to specific nationalities, Millî Görüş, for example with Turks - the Jama'at al-Tabligh has managed to establish itself internationally on a trans-national platform. This comes through in my example of the movement's roots being anchored among the North African immigrant community in France, but is confirmed also by my observations in Denmark.

It was my intention to try and produce an analysis of Islamism in Western Europe in such a manner that it did not reduce Islamism to an irrational psycho-social regression. It was my idea to show that we are dealing with social players, who seek to establish themselves meaningfully within a (modern) society, which is ruled by a dynamic that forces them out to the periphery, both economically and socially. Islamism thus gives rise to a discourse which is undoubtedly a rational and realistic response to the logic of social marginalisation. I also wanted to show that although this special 'player's-view' is exclusive, it is not an answer to particular anomalies or individual case histories. In contrast one can say that Islamism is a collective answer to a marginalised position in Western Society. In *Chapter 6*, therefore, I lay out the concrete historical and social context for the establishment of the new ethnic minorities in Western Europe. On the basis of this I introduce in this chapter what is a qualitative new level of analysis for the treatise, in that the discussion of Islam is combined with an attempt to combine the structural conditions for the societal processes in Western European capitalist society in general with those processes which are characteristic of the integration of the new ethnic minorities in particular. This takes us through a discussion in which the terms coined by Jürgen Habermas, *system* and *lifeworld*, comprise the centre of a general theoretical framework for the understanding of the Islamic movements articulation of social and cultural interests.

The Islamic movements respond to the social marginalisation processes which characterise the establishment of the new ethnic minorities in Western Europe and criticise the assault on the *lifeworld*. On the basis on the insights thus gained this thesis then rounds off in *Chapter 7* with a discussion of the critical relevance of Islamism. The Islamic movements' ruminations on the systemworld's infringement of the lifeworld is organised more as a defence of Islamic values as an alternative to secularist morals rather than being an explicit criticism of the social processes of marginalisation. The injustices appear to be undermined by the very act of creating new communities. At the same time this form of coexistence is, however, linked to another ideological level. Local resistance is bound to Islam as a medium to the global situation. One could say that it thereby becomes possible to link social marginalisation in Western Europe to global conflicts and hereby strengthen the impression of a universal conflict between Islam and the West.

The worldview which dominates the Turkish-European Islamist movement is perhaps formulated in a somewhat problematic fashion - seen from the vantage point of common Western perceptions of democracy. The advantage however is that it allows the construction of social identity centred around Islam, thus providing an alternative to lack of any affiliation with the job market. I place Islamism in a perspective which relates it to the economic and social marginalisation of immigrant milieus, stressing that the movement contributes in a positive sense to establishing a communal initiative in local society. This in fact includes the potential to relativise the limitations imposed by this worldview. For his reason I round off the thesis with a discussion of the degree to which Western European social institutions actually allow for the reception of Muslim minorities into their social strategies.

2 Islamic Organisations in Western Europe

The presence of Islam in Western Europe is essentially a consequence of the labour migration which took place in the 1960s and 1970s. European industries developed a relatively large demand for a work force that could only be satisfied by a reservoir of workers who arrived to a large degree from the Middle East. This marked the start of a new phase in European migration history which - regardless of regional variations - introduced a new factor into the debate on national identity and self-perception in Europe.

Immediately after the Second World War migration towards the European centres of expansion came mostly from Southern Europe. Greeks, Italians, Spaniards and Portuguese arrived. The colonial powers then supplemented this wave with people from the colonies.

It was however only in the 1960s that migration from the Middle East really began to take place on a large scale. And it was only during the 1970s that this group surpassed in numbers those coming from Southern Europe. Denmark was one of those countries which began to receive migrant workers very late on. It was only towards the end of the 1960s that one can begin to talk of a significant number of arrivals.

The arrival of immigrants from the Middle East and other Muslim regions gave rise to the establishment of Islamic institutions. These institutions did, however, only really begin to emerge in the 1980s - I would venture that this was not so much due to the fact that the construction of institutions takes time by nature, but rather that these institutions grew in what was, qualitatively speaking, a new social situation. Up until the mid-1970s the migrants were primarily men, married and unmarried. A male labour force was required and these men had hopes of being able to return home with the financial means to establish a new existence for themselves. Things did not turn out this way and the families were eventually reunited in Europe. The foreign workers became immigrants, and it was only then that the work of building up organisations and institutions began seriously - during a time that was marked by comprehensive social change.

Although Islam's European history extends further back in time, the development of Islamic institutions is, on the whole, linked to this more recent migration.

The settling of families in Europe was a new phase for the immigrants, new questions were raised, often by the immigrants themselves, questions concerning family life, questions of a moral and ethical character, questions are clearly concerned with religious matters. The ritualising of the most important events related to the cycle of life each have their own demands: childbirth, the circumcision of male children, weddings, deaths and funerals. The observation of religious celebrations also demands a certain amount of organisation (c.f. Pedersen & Selmer 1991).

The mosque associations that are established today among European Muslims developed first and foremost due to the initiative of the immigrant populations themselves. The associations, which nowadays are usually registered as unions, grew from local demand; the need is articulated locally, and the solutions are local. The mosques were established in housing areas often in small (basement) premises which housing associations passed on to them, or else in old buildings which have seen better days. It was never a case of setting up prestigious architectural structures, or finding buildings in attractive locations.

The expansion of this social type of religious institution still goes on - while being subject to difficult conditions. Developments from the mid-1980s onwards can be defined as a *state-political phase*. Existing mosque associations have been formalised and subject to new conditions which are actively defined by the state apparatus in the European nations. It has, furthermore, been characteristic of the formal institutionalisation of Islam that it has favoured the management of this to be in the hands of the Muslim state authorities. It has also, however, been characteristic of the immigrants that they have sought to bring an end to this dominance and point to the need for the establishment of their own recognised religious institutions independent of state interests in the countries of 'emigration' or 'immigration'.

The required efforts related to the religious and political life among the migrants of the 1970s reflected the political and religious ideas in their country of origin. The lines of conflict which existed, political and religious, were reproduced in exile. Existing traditions of religious and political organisation were transferred to the immigrant existence, as communal forms for the mobilisation of latent resources of identity.

Although some of the Islamic organisations were represented in Europe from early on in the course of the migration, it was only at the end of the 1970s that they first appeared in significantly large numbers. Religious-political divisions in the countries of origin are still of some importance but the organisations nowadays show a greater degree of rationality concerning their existence as migrants.

Dassetto and Bastenier (1984, p. 146) make the distinction between *da'wa movements* and *Islamist movements,* where the first group is characterised by the religious message while the latter group is seen to be characterised by the emphasis placed on the socio-political application of the religious stress. In this sense the *da'wa organisations* emerge as being non-political and purely religious while Islamist organisations do not stand out as being distinctively guided by religious motives and interests, which are more of a cover for political manipulation.

In contrast to this I would suggest that we should distinguish between two types of *da'wa* organisations, namely: 1) the Middle East states, and 2) the Muslim immigrant groups themselves. This sociological distinction stresses the political and legal conditions which make up the background upon which *Da'wa* is organised. A review of the institutionalisation of Islam in selected European states will not only shed light on the Islamic organisations, but at the same time it will also show that their future anatomy is intimately linked to Islam's legal status.

It is, as such, this condition which is seen here as being the crucial variable in the pattern of organisation. While studies rooted in the social and cultural characteristics and method of organisation of the various minority immigrant groups can, to a certain extent, explain why certain groups are more organised that others (see Gerholm & Lithman 1988; Rex, Joly & Wilpert 1987 and Baek Simonson 1990), they do not explain why particular patterns of organisation emerge in particular countries which are experiencing immigration.

In the following section I shall focus attention on the institutionalisation of Islam in Germany, France and Denmark which is the area covered by my investigation of Islamism. I shall, though, supplement my analysis of the situation in these countries with material that will shed some light on developments in Holland, Belgium and Britain. Similar material that would have provided insight into the situation in other Western European countries might have been interesting to include here. I have, however, been unable to acquire sufficient data to be able to extend the analysis to do this.

2.1 Germany

The establishment of Islam in West Germany is essentially due to immigration from Turkey which took place, broadly speaking, in the 1960s.[1]

Islam's history in Germany, which actually stretches back over around 250 years, was to enter a new era with the immigration of the 1960s and 1970s. This comprised a dramatic expansion of organised religious life and involved contributions from every possible part of the spectrum of Islamic movements.

The Turkish state then decided to compete with the independent Islamic associations. In part this was achieved through the appointment by the Turkish state of imams, and in part via the integration of religious education with teaching of the mother tongue which was administrated by the Turkish state.

Although Turkey has been despatching imams to Europe since 1975 it was only during the 1980s that attempts to systematically organise the religious life of the migrant Turks began to take effect - with the foundation, among other bodies, of the DITIB (the Diyanet Işleri Türk-Islam Birligi, i.e.: 'The Religious Authority's Turkish-Islamic Associations'). DITIB is - if not officially, then in effect - the Turkish state's body for religious affairs abroad. The *Turkish Diyanet Işleri Başkanligi*,[2] or Directorate for Religious Affairs, which is part of the prime minister's office, is responsible for the delegation of state imams and for organising the DITIB. In the beginning the delegated state-imams were paid for by local mosque associations which aligned themselves with the official Turkish line on Islam. From the end of the 1970s Turkey realised

---

[1] There are no exact figures for the number of immigrants since immigrants are not registered by religion. However, to give some quantitative idea of the situation it should be noted that in 1980 it was estimated that the Muslim population stood at 1.8 mil., of which about 1.5 mil. were originally from Turkey. A minority of around 120,000 came from Yugoslavia, 80,000 from the Arab countries, about 20,000 from Iran and a similar number from Pakistan. In comparison, immigrants of Southern European, non-Muslim origin numbered about the same, namely about 1.6 mil.; of these 600,000 were from Italy, and there were 500,000 non-Muslim Yugoslavs (Cibedo-Dokumentation 9/1980). In (West) Berlin the Muslim immigrant polulation made up about 130,000, of which about 110,000 were Turks. The city's population stood at about 2 million.

[2] *Diyanet Işleri Başkanligi* is referred to in daily speech as the *Diyanet*. I shall make use of this abreviation throughout the rest of this treatise.

that it was in their interests to organise and finance the imams who were to be posted themselves.

2.1.1 Turkey as Administrator of Islam in West Berlin

Formally speaking the DITIB is an independent umbrella organisation comprising a number of registered cultural unions, or so-called 'eingetragene Vereine' (e.V.). The association's articles make it clear that in certain matters there is clearly a desire to co-operate with the Turkish state system:

> *# 2:The objectives of the union:*
> 1. The objective of the union is to safeguard the interests of the Islamic religion in all areas, to inform about and educate in Islam, to establish and run suitable premises for religious devotions and education, to educate lay preachers, and to conduct language courses as well as social and cultural activities.
> 2. The union also has as its objective to produce and conduct programs for Islamic religious teaching in the schools of Berlin in co-operation with the Turkish republic's ministry of education and the leader of the Directorate for Religious Affairs.
> 3. The union offers organisational and financial support in making the hajj pilgrimage.
> 4. Depending on the economic circumstances the union will dispense educational and doctorate bursaries as well as help in the purchase of educational materials for young people in need.

As it becomes clear from the above articles of intention the DITIB is involved not only in organising religious services and religious teaching (Koran school), but it also regards its duties as including, in part at least, offering language lessons along with other social and cultural activities. In this context it is also interesting to note that the DITIB, in co-operation with the Turkish authorities, is also seeking to organise Islamic teaching in Berlin schools. Islamic education is actually arranged by an agreement between the Turkish state and the Berlin Senate in association with mother tongue education organised for the school authorities by the Turkish consulate. This education in the mother tongue is, as is the case in Denmark, voluntary, but it is still estimated that it manages to draw in about 30% of Turkish school children (Interview with Veli Bilgic, chairman of DITIB-Berlin, November 1989).

Formally speaking, DITIB is not part of the Turkish state apparatus. A small pamphlet ('Die Türkisch-Islamische Union (DITIB) in Kürze') stresses the point that the organisation does not have any 'organic links to official or private organisations within or outside Berlin'. The union is, it goes on to say, a 'forum based on volunteers who serve the general well being'. Likewise, it is stressed that this applies not simply to Turks, but to all Muslims. DITIB seeks, in this sense, to be an active member of Berlin union life, with the specific intention of organising and co-ordinating Islamic initiatives in Berlin.

DITIB comprises (in the autumn of 1989) 15 unions, of which 11 are organised with mosques and 4 unions are run as youth clubs, Koran schools, women's unions, and funeral unions respectively.

DITIB governs over 12 Turkish state imams based in Berlin on 4-year residence permits. DITIB is satisfied with running 11 out of a good 30 mosques in Berlin. It is said that the chairman of DITIB-Berlin is selected by the Turkish state imams in Berlin. He does, however, hold the title of social attaché and is the effective as well as the official representative of the Diyanet in Berlin. He himself describes the relationship as follows:

> DITIB - along with the social attaché - is a representative of the Diyanet. DITIB supports Diyanet in its work and has a very close relationship to it. Although he does stress at the same time that they are independent of one another. The actual Diyanet representative is the social attaché (Interview with Veli Bilgic, chairman of DITIB-Berlin, November 1989).

DITIB can, as such, be said to be the social attaché's legal tool in implementing the aims of the Diyanet. The social attaché organises regular gatherings of all the DITIB imams in Berlin with regard to common initiatives in certain situations so as to outline what theme should be the subject of the sermon for the coming Friday prayers.

DITIB also agree that there has been a politicisation of Islam in recent years, a position they distance themselves from. They only wish to deal with religious matters. 'We cannot take a political stance. It would do great damage if we were to do so. We are united in our religion', says Veli Bilgiç. Not everyone respects this division between religion and politics:

> Millî Görüş stresses the political and often allows politicians to speak in its mosques. This is not permitted! Diyanet does not recognise Millî Görüş and we will not have anything to do with them. The Islamic Federation has members from Millî Görüş, it is actually a Millî Görüş organisation.

Therefore, this is why they have a different understanding then we do. They are against the state. (Interview with Veli Bilgic, chairman of DITIB-Berlin, November 1989).

That DITIB believe that Islam is in an inferior position, culturally speaking, in the West is made clear by the fact that in their own short résumé of themselves, as mentioned above, they find it necessary to use a relatively large amount of space to explain that they support integration, that they are tolerant, and that they oppose any attempts to hitch Islam to the political wagon:

> In its activities, DITIB keeps itself to the legal norms. They are in favour of the exchange of opinions and ideas with tolerant non-Muslims. They are in favour of integration and against fanaticism, separation and violence.
>
> DITIB wishes to provide religious services without imposing them, and within certain limits which are based on rules decided for this. DITIB opposes any attempt to abuse Islam and Muslims for political or private interests.
>
> DITIB provides its services on a basis of love of mankind, brotherhood, unity and the general well-being ('Die Tükisch-Islamische Union (DITIB) in Kürze').

The evasive answer given in response to my question about the degree to which the Diyanet offered religious services to Turkish Alevi-Muslims, a Shi'a Muslim sect (See p.116), was as follows:

> When someone comes to us, we help. It does not matter whether they are black or white. Many African people come to our mosques. We know people who are Alevites and who also come to our mosques, who also pray there, and we stand alongside one another. They can come whenever they want (Interview with Veli Bilgic, chairman of DITIB-Berlin, November 1989).

The social attaché did not wish to comment on the quite specific religious needs which the *Alevites* have.

Every imam who is stationed abroad is given general guidelines by the Diyanet to which he must adhere. For the most part, however, the imam will work out his own theme when it comes to a particular social day of celebration or, in a specific case, direction will be given by the Diyanet. All imams also receive a journal published by the Diyanet, the 'Diyanet Gazetsi', every month. There are weekly meetings, or monthly in some cases, to talk things over with the social attaché; for example, in talking about the repression of Turkish Muslims in Bulgaria, or of the Rushdie Affair. In the case of Bulgaria DITIB organised a demonstration along with the other Turkish organisations in the city and about 50,000 people took part.

In the case of the Rushdie affair the imams received the outcome of the Diyanet's investigation of *The Satanic Verses* which they then preached in the mosque.

> Diyanet has examined this book, and the imams have read the results of this investigation and announced them.
>
> It is an inhuman thing which he (Rushdie/LP) has done. He is very negative. There have always been people who have wronged Islam. But Diyanet has not contributed by encouraging people to murder him.
>
> There is a big electronic screen near here. It is the largest screen in the world for showing the news electronically. They wanted to advertise Rushdie's book there, but we intervened and managed to prevent this (Interview with Veli Bilgic, Chairman of DITIB-Berlin, November 1989).

In the mosques, Koran courses are run for the very young. The age group ranges from 8 to 14 years. They attend for three hours 4-5 days a week, often 5 days if they do not have anything else to do. For people in the age group of 12 to 17 years there is a Koran school available which goes even further. The social attaché would not call it an imam school but 'it is to make up the shortages created when there is a lack of imams. Also nur eine Religiöse Erziehung'.

In 1986 the DITIB was put in charge of the old Turkish graveyard in Berlin, 'Berlin Türk Sehitligi', 'Der Türkische Friedhof zu Berlin' or 'Friedhof Tempelhof'. The graveyard is the property of the Turkish state. DITIB runs pilgrim trips to the *hajj*; in 1989 over 100 Turks set off from Berlin, and over a thousand journeys were organised by DITIB for Turks from all over Germany. Similarly, collections are organised for *zakat* and *fitre*, money which is distributed in Turkey to people who want an education but do not have the economic resources to do so. *Zakat* is for the poor, and the DITIB funds go towards the education of the poor. In actual fact 30 people are supported, of which half attend high school and the other half university.

As this demonstrates, the Turkish state is active in the administration of Islam among Turks in Berlin. DITIB provides the organisational framework for these activities.

Although the Turkish state is privileged in terms of founding an institutional framework for the religious lives of Turkish Muslims, the (outlawed) Turkish Islamic movements have also managed to gain a foothold in Germany.

2.1.2 Non-governmental Islamic Organisations

The leading case of Islamic organisational activity among migrants in West Germany worthy of mention is that of the so-called *Süleymanlis,* an Islamic brotherhood, or *tariqa,* organised along fiercely centralist principles. The order, which is named after its founder, Süleyman Hilmi Tunahan (1888-1959), is a branch of the Naqshibandiyya order. The strategic aim of the group is to see *shari'a* introduced in Turkey - by entering into various, and not always declared, working agreements with mainstream political parties. This group, which in principle is quite a closely sealed one became known through their establishing of Islamic cultural centres, in West Germany among other places, for initiating the first Koran courses at the end of the 1960s. The order runs the Union of Culture Centres in Europe, which in Germany is of the same magnitude as Millî Görüş and Diyanet (Blaschke 1985).

The *Nurcu* movement also goes in for the introduction of Shari'a in Turkey, but prefers to work strategically through secret alliances: among which there is the idea of gaining slow, gradual control of state administration. The Nurcu movement (The Fellowship of Light) is founded on the writings of Said Nursi (1871-1960), a Kurdish scholar. The movement, which is known for being characteristically intellectual, is concerned above all with the writings of their founding father. The movement has some characteristics of a tariqa but is not linked to the classical tradition. This is the smallest of the movements mentioned here (ibid.).

The largest Islamist group as far as the Turks in Europe are concerned however is Millî Görüş whose domestic movement in Turkey gave rise to a political party, The National Salvation Party (Millî Selamet Partisi, MSP), which, due to its being banned, was later renamed the

Welfare Party (Refah Partisi, RP). Throughout its history the party has sought legality and a parliamentary route to achieve the introduction of shari'a. They reject both the heterodoxy which Süleymanli rests on, and also the Nurcu movement's emphasis of the example set by their founder, Sheikh Said Nursis (ibid.). A radical fraction, *Tebliğ*,[3] splintered away from this group in 1983, complaining that Millî Görüş had been forced to compromise due to the structure of the party and that it was thereby in concordance with the Turkish constitution: Their ideal was, in contrast, along the lines of the Iranian model, - a movement in which the mosque is the central pillar (Interview with Schiffauer, November 1988;[4] Blaschke 1985; Binswanger & Sipahioglu 1988).

Although all four Islamic groups, as Algar (1976 & 1985) so convincingly demonstrates, are based on the peripheral edge of the Naqshibandi brotherhood - banned after the Kemalist revolution of 1925 - it is possibly only the Süleymanlis who are substantially influenced by the religiosity of the former order. In the other cases the religious heritage is of a slightly different character, the emphasis being on a methodical and conscientious way of life (Mardin 1984).

German law distinguishes between recognised and non-recognised religious communities, by 1990 none of the Islamic organisations had managed to achieve recognition, not even in Berlin where an Islamic federation (Islamische Föderation) had been trying since 1980.

2.2 France

Although the number of Turkish migrants in France is considerably smaller than that of Algerians, namely about 170,000 as opposed to 750,000 (1990 figures), Turkey has just as many imams in France as Algeria does.

2.2.1 Turkey as Administrator of Islam in France

Turkey first began sending imams to France in 1980. Today there are between 50 and 55 imams appointed by the Turkish state in France. These

---

[3] *Tebliğ*, also known as Kaplanists after their charismatic leader and founder, Cemalettin Kaplan.

[4] The ethnographer Werner Schiffauer has also written on migration and religiosity among a group of Turkish immigrants in West Germany. See Schiffauer (1988).

imams are located within the larger Turkish minority communities, while a number of them also tour around the smaller Turkish religious communities. The imams are provided with residence permits of six years duration in the same way as teaching envoys.

The practice of posting imams in France (and the rest of Europe) first began 'in order to oppose political Islam which is against Turkey's interests', the secretary of DITIB in France explained. It was to check the political development vis-à-vis Turkey in the immigrant communities. The politicising Islamic groups constitute a potential political problem that needs to be taken very seriously, he says (Interview with the secretary of the DITIB, May 1990).

DITIB also organises excursions to the hajj; although not in 1990 itself since there were only five people who wanted to go and therefore their trip was arranged by DITIB-Belgium.

DITIB is a Vakif organisation and therewith has property at its disposal. That is to say that it is the local immigrant associations who purchase the property and then hand responsibility for them over to DITIB. DITIB does not organise the purchases, but as the secretary says: 'we encourage them to do it!!'. So it is the local immigrant associations who are the buyers (Interview with the secretary for DITIB, May 1990).

DITIB has no contact with other Turkish Islamic organisations, because, as they put it, 'those organisations are against us!'.

A large proportion of the Turkish immigrants in France are Alevi-Muslims who have special religious requirements. As in West Berlin, DITIB in France does not feel that this matter requires special attention: 'We help all Turks who come and ask for our assistance. We are all Muslims and we do not discriminate'. When I persevered by insisting on some of their religious practices the response was restrained; of course they were welcome but the consulate had not, up until that time, received any requests for help.

The discussion of the veil is of limited interest to the Turks, the secretary told me. Only very few Turkish girls wear a veil. There has therefore been no need for DITIB to enter into the debate. The question had not been raised with DITIB by the Turkish community. 'The Turks know very well that this is not Islam, - and they also know our opinion!', The debate is considered to be politicising, and in the same way, supporters of the veil - in as much as they use the veil - are politicising Islam. It is a question which has also been politicised in the universities in Turkey (Interview with the secretary for DITIB, May 1990).

2.2.2 Non-state Islamic Organisations

Islam in France however relates in particular to the Arab population, and above all to the Algerians.[5]

Despite the fact that the immigration of Muslims dates back to the start of the century, supplemented by a later influx in the 1950s, *Islam* only became noticeable as a cultural factor in French society from the end of the 1970s. From 1970 until 1985 the number of known mosques, places of prayer and other cultural sites rose from about 10 to over 1000. Similarly, the number of officially recognised associations which defined themselves as 'Islamic' now adds up to a total of more than 600, while the number was minutely small in the early 1970s (Kepel 1987, p.9).[6]

---

[5] In 1986 the official known figure for immigrants was about 4.5 mil.: The North Africans made up around 1.5 mill. of these, of which 712,000 were Algerians, likewise Southern Europeans made up around 1.5 mill., of which 845,000 were Portugese (Voisard J. & C. Ducastelle 1988, p. 23ff.). According to Leveau (1988, p.109ff.) there were about 2.8 mill. Muslims in France in 1985, of which 1.5 mill. came from North Africa. Of these in turn, the number of *harkis* - Algerian soldiers enrolled into the French colonial army's regular units, and their descendents - was estimated to be around 400,000. In addition there is an unknown number of younger people whose parents are Algerian, but who have French citizenship, along with about 3000 French converts. According to French law anyone born in France of parents who were also born in France is entitled to French citizenship. This implies that children of parents born in Algeria prior to independence in 1962 have the right to French citizenship (Gillette A. & A. Sayed 1984, p. 108ff.). In sociological terms then, Islam is the second largest religion in France, in that the Protestants are estimated to number about 1 million and the Jews about ¾ mill. The following should be noted with regard to these population figures: The declarations of nationality refer to persons with *foreign* citizenship. It is quite possible for people who, for example, have an Algerian background to appear as French citizens today. The declaration of religious denomination is based on and estimate since nobody is registered according to their religion.

[6] Bruno Etienne, Arabist and director of the Institut de reserches et d'Etudes sur le Monde Arabe et Musulman, Aix-en-Provence, believes that it is impossible to form a clear picture of how many different groups exist. In Marseilles alone, for example, 125 unions were once counted, the national total is estimated to be about 800. In Etienne's view, however, the number is closer to 4000. He highlights the fact that this is a time of change, also as regards the formation of Islamic organisations, that there exists a distinctly public market for groupings (Interview with Bruno Etienne, October 1988).

The first independent attempt to organise Islam was the result of an initiative by the Alawi brotherhood who established a Zawiya in Paris in 1924.[7]

The most important Arabic Islamist movement in France is Groupement Islamique en France, which stems from the Mouvement de la Tendence Islamique (MTI) in Tunisia, Mouvement Islamiste d'Algerien, which is closely tied to the Front Islamique et salut in Algeria, an umbrella organisation for a number of Algerian Islamist groupings. The first and foremost group in Morocco is the Mouvement de la Jeunesse Islamique. Among the Turks, as in Germany, there is the European-wide Millî Görüş. The Islamic movements are very rarely trans-national but instead form networks within their own nationalities. One of the most notable exceptions to this on the European stage is *Jama'at al-Tabligh* which has its roots in Muslim India.[8] The movement does, however, finds some resonance among North Africans and mainly among Algerians, Tunisians and Moroccan immigrants in France where the movement is called *Foi et Pratique*. The charismatic leader of the movement here is Tunisian, while at the highest level the leadership is of North African origin (c.f. Kepel 1987).

Uniquely in the case of France, it was only in 1981 that foreign citizens were given the right to form organisations. Up until then it was a requirement that the leadership of every organisation should consist of French citizens.

The increase in the number of immigrant associations is, in this sense, something that is not solely dependent on internal factors within the immigrant groups, but can quite obviously also be attributed to changes in French policy towards immigrants. The consequence of this change of status has been the growth of associations of both a religious and secular nature, of organisations which impinge on a variety of spheres, education, work, culture and religion.[9]

---

[7] The Alawi brotherhood is named after Sheikh Ahmad al-Alawi (1869-1934). The brotherhood is a splinter group of the Shadhliyya order and became independent in 1913 (Lings 1961; Gellner 1981, p.131-148). See also note 28.

[8] See Chapter 5. Jama'at al-Tabligh was started by Muhammed Ilyas in the 1920s, and has its Euopean base among Pakistanis and its main headquarters in central England.

[9] The social anthroplogist Sossie Andezian notes, however, that the official goodwill towards religious organisations seen in the 1980s has ceased. In contrast to previously support is now only granted to organisations and activities that are not of a religious character. In this sense it is French society rather than immigrants

Although, in principle, the French state does not administrate religion, which explains why there is no mention in legal terms of recognition/non-recognition, it has most definitely involved itself actively in the life of such organisations.

2.2.3 The Structuring of Islam by the French State

The French state established La Mosqueé de Paris after the First World War in the 1920s, to give official recognition to the sacrifice made by Muslim soldiers for France during the war - the French colonial power saw itself, as Kepel (1987, p. 65) puts it, as a 'puissance musulman'. It is worth noting that France maintained control of the mosque until *1982* when it was handed over to the Algerian state.

Islam's revitalisation among North African immigrants resulted in 'la Mosqueé de Paris' changing its status. This change in status can also be viewed as a marked change in the symbolic meaning of relations with Islam. Whereas France had formerly considered Islam as an area of French responsibility, the state now relinquished this responsibility. Islam became a foreign element, and there is some attempt to view the relationship with Islam as being akin to those between nations. Kepel (op.cit.) shows that, in its day, the founding of the mosque also gave rise to colonial-political considerations. This viewpoint is supported by the fact that up until 1962 the running of the mosque fell to the Ministry of Foreign Affairs and not the Ministry of the Interior - where it was moved after Algeria gained independence.

By the close of the 1980s Islam clearly fell once more within the range of French state authority, and could therefore not be handed over to a foreign state. A committee was selected to advise the government on Muslim affairs. This 'Conseil consultatif de la communauté musulmane' which consisted exclusively of leading Muslims,[10] was established in

---

who are politicising, to an ever increasing degree, themes linked to immigrants (Interview with Andezian, October 1989).

[10] To begin with six 'sages' (wisemen) were nominated who were later supplemented by a further nine. There were three criteria in picking the 'sages', 1) they should represent a broad range in terms of nationality: The group consists therefore of a Tunisian, two Algerians, a Senegalese, a Comoran, a Turk,...In the selection process stress was placed on the group containing a majority of Muslims with French citizenship, 2) They should represent a spectrum in social and vocational terms: a couple of doctors, a worker, a student, a baker, an office clerk,

February 1990 by the Interior Minister which is also the 'ministre des cultes' or minister of the clergy. The aim of the council was formulated with a view to helping the government, 'and with its advice and recommendations to encourage the best possible concrete conditions for practising Islam in France' (Durand et al. 1990, p.22ff.).

The objective is not simply to form a council, which is 'representatif', but a council which is 'significatif', the Interior Minister explains: 'I have not tried to assemble people who represent Islam, but significant people' (op.cit.).

This confirms then, that it is not the case that the French state is now seeking to establish a body that would directly administrate the basic structural conditions for shaping the development of Islam in France. But rather a body that in terms of *significance,* and on the strength of its standing would be able to function as a negotiating body, and which in part would provide the state administration with an immediate insight into the developments in religious practise but which might also provide the state with a platform through which it can act considerately in potential conflict situations. The considerations concerning the formation of the council relate in this sense to the controversy surrounding *The Satanic Verses,* and to the political storm raised by Muslim schoolgirls wearing the veil (ibid.).

The dean of 'la Mosqueé de Paris', M. Tedjini Haddam, is a member of the Interior Minister's council. He explains the setting up of the council as follows:

> You are aware that Islam is the 2nd largest religion in France, there are between 3-4 million Muslims here. It is quite normal that the Interior Minister who is responsible for 'les cultes'/religion, that is to say, for Muslims, Christians, and Jews, seeks to help the religious organisations. With regard to Christianity there are no problems, Napoleon solved that - with the exception of Alsace and Mosel which have special statutes - Judaism was likewise regulated by Napoleon, there is a church council. Islam has no clergy, there is direct...it his HIM who has done it, it is not a person like me, it is HIM, himself....I said to Mr Joxe (the Interior Minister at the time/LP), that he is the Napoleon of this century, and it is true! He has tried to tackle a difficult problem, since Islam has no clergy. But the idea of a 'conseil superiuer islamique' exists in all Muslim countries. It is like this - I think it was in November - that he asked 6

---

a former ambassador..., varied, but clearly with a majority of senior positions, 3) they were to represent the most important geographic regions of France as far as Islam was concerned: Paris, Lyon, Marseille and Lille (Durand et al 1990, p. 25).

> people, known as 'sages'. (....) But it is also the task of this committee to reflect over how far Islam should be organised in France with regard to the French authorities, - in an impartial manner, and in a manner that represents the Muslim community. This committee of wise men worked for several months and submitted some interesting work to the minister. Following this the Interior Minister asked that the committee be expanded, the six became 15. It has now become a council that is a reflection of Islam in France ('Conseil de reflection sur islam en France'). This is a consultative council.

But what themes do the council discuss?

> I cannot tell you that, that is up to the minister. But I can say that it covers everything concerning Islam, everything is studied and re-studied by this council. But it is up to the minister to give you precise details, I do not have the right to tell you (Interview with Tedjini Haddam, dean of 'la Mosque de Paris', May 1990).

In the dean's view the formation of the consultative council is only a beginning:

> It is an intermediary phase, at the moment there is a consultative council., later it will automatically become representative and be expanded. It will not remain simply 15 members, the door has to be opened. The hindrances must be swept out of the way (Interview with Tedjini Haddam, dean of 'la Mosque de Paris', May 1990).

At least in some parts of the organisation of Muslim life it is clear that the formation of the consultative council provides the development of Islam in France with a place to stand, an opportunity to develop from a legal space that does not refer the administration of Islam to Middle Eastern states.

Turkey's 'Conseiller de Religion' in France (that is to say, DITIB) was neither invited to participate in this council of 'sages' nor aware of its existence: 'we are just a small minority which gets overlooked, most (of the members) are from North Africa'. The secretary did not, however, feel that Diyanet was interested in participating in the foundation of a common Islamic umbrella organisation for France (Interview with the secretary of DITIB-France, May 1990). On the other hand the Turkish Islamist movement in France, Millî Görüş, was represented by the chairman of 'Tendance Nationale Union Islamique en France' (TNUIF), Mustafa Doğan. Mustafa Doğan explained his participation in the council this way:

> The minister's decision has oriented us towards representing Islam in France, there is a fine point. It is up to us to become accepted by the Muslim population, we are between the state and the immigrant Muslims. We are between the government and the Muslim population, we are, in my opinion, duty bound to finding concrete solutions for the state authority that will be accepted by the Muslim community. We are intermediaries, if we can come up with something for the Muslim community and gain recognition from below, and if we can find solutions that satisfy the state authority (Mustafa Doğan, Appendix L).

Not all the independent Islamic associations however, see any significance in this new body. The imam of the French branch of 'Jama'at al-Tabligh' was not invited to participate and furthermore has no wish to take part:

> If the council comes up with rulings that serve Islam's best interests, it can only be good, and if they draw bad conclusions, then we are indifferent. We will continue to follow Islam anyway! (Interview with Sheikh Muhammed Hammami, 'Association Foi et Pratique, May 1990).

Muslims in France have, like everyone else, the freedom of religious choice, but, as in other European countries, this formal freedom has not resulted in the state viewing the various Islamic organisations or umbrella organisations that have developed as real partners in dialogue and negotiation. 'Mosqueé de Paris' is an officially recognised administrator of the organisation of Islam in France. It is the Algerian state that regulates this administration. The Turkish state is, however, recognised as having independent interests concerning the Turkish minority population.

2.2.4 Algeria as Administrator of Islam in France

As mentioned, it is Algeria which in effect in responsible for managing, in both real and symbolic terms, the most important institution in the structure of Islam in France, 'La Mosqueé de Paris'.

> The mosque organises all matters that touch on religion, everything which concerns Muslim culture: Prayer, marriage, initiation into Islam, ...certification that so and so is a Muslim, funeral services..., there is teaching in the Arabic language, there are conferences and courses, which are open to everyone. We are a social activity for society, furthermore we provide a service in the four difficult winter months, where we serve free meals three times a day, breakfast, dinner and supper, to between 300 and

> 600 people. We also have a special clinic for ritual circumcision (Interview with Tedjini Haddam, dean of the 'Mosqueé de Paris'. May 1990).

The dean is the leader not only of a mosque but of the large institution of which the mosque is a part. Apart from the religious sections there is a cultural section, a social section and an administrative section. The full name of this institution is the 'Institut Musulman de la Mosqueé de Paris'.

The mosque acts as a centre for the organisation of Islam throughout France, according to an Algerian-French convention. This convention regulates the purpose and length of stay for all associated visitors. In total fifty imams from Algeria are employed, usually on four-year contracts. Of these, seven imams operate directly from the institute in Paris. At Ramadan more imams are despatched from Algeria. In 1989, 31 extra imams were sent. The institute also administrates the teaching staff who are deployed to take care of teaching in the Arabic language.

> It is very expensive. For some years this was supported by the French government, although this has not happened for a long time. Over a long period, indeed, over a very long period in some cases, certain Muslim countries have assisted. Now though, it is only the Algerian government which provides finance and it is very dear (Interview with Tedjini Haddam, dean of 'la Mosquée de Paris', May 1990).

The mosque no longer deals with organising pilgrimages to the hajj. It did previously but stopped in 1990, for which there were a number of reasons:

> First of all because there are many private travel agencies outside the mosque who wish to cooperate with the mosque in running pilgrimage-campaigns. Secondly because the statutes of the mosque do not allow us to run a business. Therefore we must consider the fact that it might be illegal for us to organise for the hajj. We cannot contravene French law. When we are here we must respect French legislation (Interview with Tedjini Haddam, dean of 'la mosqueée de Paris', May 1990).

The mosque organises the collection of *zakat,* which the mosque has the right to do as part of its constitution since this is a religious act. The money which is collected in this way as *zakat, sadaqat al-fitr* and *sadaqa,* is sent home to Algeria 'to help Muslim associations...It is set aside for them'. On the other hand the mosque has not succeeded in gaining a certificate to produce *halal* meat. Because this is a matter with many interests of a business nature attached to it the French state will not issue a monopoly:

> *Halal* meat is a big problem. In principle the mosque can issue a certificate. But unfortunately there is an economic war, there is a 'grey market'. This is a great shame as it is a sacred matter which concerns moral responsibility. This has been eroded, partly due to the establishment of certain phantom organisations, etc. (.......)
> It is difficult to regulate, we try to get the imams to do it but it is not easy because it is about 'business'! On top of this French legislation will not provide anyone with a monopoly. This is up to the Ministry of Agriculture and the Ministry of the Interior (Interview with Tedjini Haddam, dean of 'la Mosquée de Paris', May 1990).

It was Algeria's monopoly of the leadership of 'la Mosquée de Paris' which provoked a number of attempts to create a national Islamic structure free of any state involvement. But what was the dean's view of the attempts made to try and unite the independent Islamic organisations? What was his reaction to the idea of gathering all the Islamic associations into a common federation, in a 'federation des federations', as Bruno Étienne for one, described it?:

> (Previous attempts..../LP)...were influenced by religious ideologies, but a collection of every trend in a common organism, that is something quite different, and will one day happen. That is one of the aims of Monsieur Joxes' initiative!
> It is difficult because in the matter of religion one can not....just look at the development of Christianity, Catholicism, Protestantism, and the current situation regarding Christianity. Is that how the pope actually gathers all Catholics together? Impossible! Why then do you want us to do that, there are so many more of us...... Excuse me, but there is an obvious advantage! It is not simply a practical question, it is, rather, an ideological one! (Interview with Tedjini Haddam, dean of 'la Mosquée de Paris', May 1990).

As mentioned above, Algeria's privileged position - in part due to it's control of la Mosquée de Paris - gave rise to a number of attempts to create a nation-wide Islamic organisation, free of state interference. These attempts have not, however, led to control of the mosque being withdrawn from Algeria. The coup d'etat in Algeria in 1992 did, however, have immediate consequences which might spell the beginnings of a process by which the mosque will have a new leadership structure. The mosque's above mentioned dean, Tedjini Haddam, was recalled to Algeria and installed in the new five-man state council. This has fuelled speculation among those who would like to see control of the mosque being located inside France (Conversation with Moustapha Diop,[11] February 1992).

La Mosquée de Paris still remains as the officially recognised managing body for the organisation of Islam in France. Until January 1992 it was the Algerian state that regulated this management. A question mark has, though, been raised about what kind of leadership the mosque should have in the future. The interests of the Turkish state are still recognised though.

2.3 Denmark

Today (1992) there are around 70,000 ethnic Muslims in Denmark, of which the largest group of immigrants is Turkish (30,000). It is estimated that 60,000 of these Muslims hold foreign nationalities while 9,000 are Danish. Sociologically speaking this means that Muslims make up the second largest religious community in Denmark ahead of Catholics (40,000), Jehovah's Witnesses (26,000) and Jews (9,000).[12]

---

[11] Dr. Moustapha Diop is a social anthropologist who has spent several years studying Islamic organisations in France. He is employed by INALCO, the Institut National de Langues et Civilisations Orientales, Paris.

[12] Neither Danish nor foreign citizens are registered according to their religious affiliation. In my opinion, the number of Muslims is based on the available official statistics on immigrant nationality, such as are to be found in 'Statistik om indvandrere og flygtninge 1991' in Dokumentation om INDVANDRE, nr. 2/1991. According to the Roman Catholic Church (1992) in Denmark there are 30,000 registered members of The Roman Catholic Church (1991/92) and an estimated 10,000 immigrants and refugees, who are not formally registered members of the church. There are 16,000 baptised Jehovas Witnesses (i.e. adults). The total number including children is estimated by the community as being about 26,000. According to the Jewish community (1991/92) the number of registered members is 3,600, this figure, however, comprises only adults. The total number of Jews in Denmark is estimated by the community as being around 9,000, including children and 'assimilated' Jews who are not members.

The oldest mosque in Denmark, dating back to 1974, is that of the Islamic Cultural Centre in Copenhagen.[13] Since then there has been a parting of the ways due to linguistic, national and political differences. Today these premises are mostly used by Pakistanis. Since the end of the 1970s the number of mosques and places of prayer has risen considerably to reach the present figure of about 50.[14]

The Islamic Cultural Centre in Copenhagen and its division in Aarhus are controlled by a group of Middle Eastern states through their ambassadors.[15] The same Middle Eastern states are also responsible for the rather ambitious plan to build a new Islamic cultural centre in Copenhagen,[16] plans which for the time being appear to have been shelved (*Dagbladet Information*, 10th December 1992).

Wheras religious affairs up until the 1980s were to a large extent in the hands of self-trained amateurs, the tendency now is for these people to be replaced by professional imams, in other words, paid imams in full-time employment with an education from a theological university: Paid for and provided by Kuwait, Libya, The Muslim World League, and Turkey.

Developments within the Turkish Islamic scene stand out in particular, in that the Diyanet has, since 1985, regularly sent out full time

---

[13] This ignores the Ahmadiya movement which established its own mosque as early as 1967 in Hvidovre. This movement is marginal to the dominant orthodox Islamic community.

[14] For a historic account of the establishment of a range of Muslim institutions and organised activities in Denmark, see Bæk Simonson (1990).

[15] According to Bæk Simonson (1990) the Islamic Cultural Centre is led by a committee comprising representatives of the Muslim embassies in Copenhagen: Morocco, Saudi Arabia, Egypt and Pakistan. In practical terms however, leadership of the two centres takes place locally.

[16] Copenhagen's magistrate issued an approval finally in February 1992 of the plans to build a new Islamic cultural centre on the site, which was leased from the Ministry of Defense. The political disagreement between the states involved during the Gulf War has however brought into question the matter of when the plans will be carried out - and the leadership of the centre. The initiative and leadership behind this new Islamic cultural centre came from Egypt, Turkey, Pakistan, Morocco, Saudi Arabia, Yemen, Libya and the PLO. The politicisation of the leadership of the Islamic Cultural Centre in the wake of the Gulf War was the immediate cause for the Danish converts to set up their own mosque (interview with Abdul Wahid Pedersen, February 1992). The centre should have been completed in 1996, the year when Copenhagen was to host a large international cultural program as the EU Cultural capital of the year.

imams on a regular basis to cater to the demands of the Turkish community in Denmark. In January 1989 there were a total of 18 Diyanet congregations in Denmark. The number of imams can vary due to administrative problems. At that point in time there were only 10 Diyanet imams in the country whereas the number has reached as high as 17. At the same time it was the ambition of the Diyanet to be able to serve a total of 24 congregations (interview with the social attaché at the Turkish consulate, January 1989). Denmark and Turkey have since arrived at an agreement whereby imams who are engaged and paid by the Turkish state can reside in Denmark for up to four years.[17]

Since 1985 the Diyanet has similarly been engaged in purchasing property with a view to setting up mosques. Ordinarily local Turkish immigrants would be encouraged to collect money in local circles and from among good Muslims with regard to providing the financial basis for buying a building. Support from the Diyanet is given on the condition that they are given control of the established funds, known as Vakif. This method has at times created tension between the Diyanet and the local unions which are usually Diyanet mosque associations. Tension is usually centred around the matter of who dictates the activities of the mosque and who is responsible for the continuous supply of money which is collected by the mosques. This gives associations normally loyally affiliated to the Diyanet the impression that the purpose of the Diyanet is not just to support local initiatives, but in a broader sense to channel resources into the creation of new mosques (Interview with the chairman of the Association of Turkish Labour Unions - Sammenslutningen af Tyrkiske Arbejderforeninger i Danmark, January 1990).

The Turkish state has, as such, via the Diyanet, focused its efforts on establishing its own religious centres for Turkish Sunni-Muslims. Although represented on the committee of the Islamic Culture Centre they did not involve themselves in its running. This, however, was to change in 1989. So as to put a halt to the Turkish Islamists they opposed the appointment of an imam nominated by them for Aarhus - instating one of their own instead.

Alongside the Turkish state's organisation of Islam in Denmark there is also a section of the largest Turkish European Islamist movement, Millî Görüş, which has organised a number of local mosque communities.

---

[17] According to The Directorate for Aliens this practise was introduced in 1989, prior to this they could stay in the country for up to 2 years (Appendix N).

The other Turkish-Islamic groups do not have an organisation but ally themselves solely with individual people. Similar direct state involvement is not shown by the remaining Muslim nationalities. Of the independent Islamic movements, Jama'at al-Tabligh makes an appearance within the Pakistani community.

Apart from the Danish *Folkekirke*, the national church, religious communities can be said to be either *recognised* or *unrecognised*. There are nine recognised, religious communities alongside the national church of which the Jewish community is the only non-Christian one. Among the benefits enjoyed by the recognised religious communities is the legal right to have their priests recognised which allows them to, for example, conduct weddings which are legally valid as civil marriages. This recognition of religious communities is said to have been trivialised in that a clause has been added to the laws governing marriage (pgf.16, stk.1, nr.3), which means that priests from unrecognised religious communities are now empowered to carry out weddings which are legally valid. The precondition for priests to have this authority is however,

> That the group in question is a proper religious community in the true meaning of the term, being thereby not simply a religious 'movement' or a religious or philosophical union, but an association or assembly (a religious community) whose primary purpose is the worship of God (cult) according to closely defined teachings and rites (Ægteskabsloven - the marriage laws of 1984).

Stenbæk (1987) maintains that the recognition of new religious communities is not considered relevant by the authorities on the basis of providing an opportunity for individual imams to attain the right to conduct weddings which are recognised as having 'civil validity', and furthermore, that this provides a solution to the problem surrounding residence permits. It is assumed, in other words, that the right to conduct validated civil weddings was the only real deficiency incurred by those religious communities which are not recognised. Attaining this right would in turn also solve all their other problems. An imam who has attained this right can extend his residence permit from 2 to 4 years (see Appendix N). An interview with a church ministry official confirmed the fact that the matter of the recognition of Islam as a religious community is not considered as being a significant one.

While the Muslim community has not, as yet, come up with a model which can guarantee them recognition as a religious community in

Denmark, the Turkish state has *de facto* control of imams coming to Denmark and thereby of the da'wa among Turks in this country.

Leaders of various independent Islamic organisations in Denmark claim that the lack of recognition leads to problems in at all getting entry visas for imams. They regard this unsympathetic stance as an expression of anti-Islamic sentiment. Recognition is not only of great symbolic significance but also of enormous practical importance.

The problem is more complex than the authorities realise. The matter is of great symbolic importance and this also influences the opportunities available for developing independent Islamic institutions. The lack of recognition creates large problems for independent Islamic organisations when trying to bring the imams they want into the country.

Today, the development of Islamic organisations in Denmark is in effect under the hegemony of the Muslim countries. Muslims, whether immigrants with foreign nationality who have lived in Denmark for perhaps 20 years, or Muslims with Danish citizenship cannot, on this important matter, be considered as being on equal terms, in terms of their rights, with the majority of the Danish population. This paradox is not going to diminish with the rise in the number of Muslims holding Danish nationality.

This is not simply a theoretical paradox, it is actually being articulated within Muslim minority circles today. There is now a Muslim lobby which opposes the creation of the new Islamic cultural centre in Copenhagen. The demand is, above all else, for there to be a democratic body supporting the centre before construction begins. This point is formulated among Muslims, not least of all among the Islamists - and most typically it is younger Muslims who have spent most of their lives in Denmark. It is, however, Danish Muslims (converts) who publicly voice criticism of the new Islamic cultural centre.

2.4 The Institutionalisation of Islam in Holland, Belgium and Britain

2.4.1 Holland

While the earliest Muslim population groups in Holland originate from the former colonies and can largely be said to have arrived in association with decolonisation, it is notable that the large influx of immigrants in the 1960s and 70s did not come from these regions, but from Turkey and Morocco.[18]

The formation of Muslim organisations began as early as the 1970s. In Holland - as in other places - in the majority of cases, by far, the religious life of Muslim immigrants is divided along lines of national allegiance. The few exceptional cases of mixed nationality mosques, such as Turkish/Moroccan or Surinamese/Moroccan, for example, do not appear to be the result of differences in ideology, but rather relate to settlement patterns.

The Turks are represented both by the Diyanet mosques and the Islamic movements: Süleymanli has been represented in Holland since 1972, which makes it the oldest Islamic movement for the organisation of religious life among immigrants in Holland. In 1988 Süleymanli was represented by about 20 mosques and 36 imams. Millî Görüş was represented by 15 mosque communities. Tebliğ, which splintered off from Millî Görüş, first appeared in 1983 and now runs 7 mosque communities. In the meantime, Diyanet, with around 90 mosque communities of its own, is the most important spokesman for Turkish Muslims. The Diyanet, which has sought to organise the religious life of Turkish Muslims in Holland since the start of the 1980s has about 65 imams stationed in Holland. They are given residence contracts of four years duration. Most of the buildings that the immigrants bought originally to house mosques are now Diyanet mosques, and are thereby under the control of the Diyanet (Interview with Doomernik, December 1988).[19]

While the Moroccan government is - unlike the Turkish - not directly engaged in despatching state imams, there is an active Moroccan government policy aimed at migrants, and there are alternative organisations, although these are considered by most researchers into the matter as being weak.

The Moroccan state authority seeks to protect its political interests in various ways and means, including that of an established religious legitimacy. In the migrant context these interests are pursued by means of

---

[18] The Muslim population in 1988 numbered around 350,000, the major part of which come from Turkey (180,000) and Morocco (120,000). After these come Surinam with about 25,000, about 8,000 from Pakistan and 7,000 molùccans from Indonesia (Slomp 1988).

[19] Jeroen Doomernik is a cultural anthropologist employed by the Institut Voor Sociale Geografie, Universiteit van Amsterdam, whose Ph.D project was on 'Turkish-Islamic institutions and integration'.

the establishment of *Amicales*,[20] a support organisation for migrants in Europe. Many Moroccans regard Amicales as being a network of informers for the Moroccan secret police, an extension of the governments arm and as spies. 'Activities harmful to the state' were reported among the migrant leaders and those in question risked imprisonment in Morocco. This analysis of Amicales is not uncommon among researchers into this organisation, although not all are in agreement on the matter.[21] There appears to be no doubt however that the Moroccan state authority enjoys widespread influence within migrant circles.

There is no historical tradition in Morocco for political organisations such as there is in Turkey. The Moroccan organisations are on the whole mosque-based.

Although there does not appear to be a particularly widespread tendency among Moroccan youth to break with the religious mainstream in Moroccan-Dutch Islam, there does appear to be a series of 'free' mosques emerging. These are organised, among others, by left wing political immigrant organisations (interview with Sijtsma, December 1988).[22] The largest of the immigrant organisations among Moroccans in Holland, KMAN (Committee of Moroccan Workers in Holland), is active in this, although they have a tradition of opposing religion. There is less of an affinity towards the international Islamist organisations.[23]

---

[20] Amicales Marocaines was formed by Morocco in 1973 in order to counter the infuence of political opposition groups within the sphere of European migrants. The formation of this organisation itself contributed to the growth of a large opposition precisely because the organisation was regarded as being a means of imposing ideological control (Dassetto & Bastenier 1984).

[21] Although Dassetto and Bastenier (1984, p. 186 ff) maintain that Amicales was founded with the aim of resisting the advance of political opposition within Moroccan migrant communities in Europe, they believe that the organisation must essentially be seen as being autonomous in relation to the government's formal authority and that it exists as an instrument of cultural and social support for Moroccan migrants. This viewpoint does not, however, change the fact that in terms of its religious alignment Amicales follows the religio-political line of the Moroccan state, which includes asserting the religious authority of the Moroccan king - via the title of sharif the Morocaan monarchy claims direct descendency from the Prophet Mohammed.

[22] Jelle Sijtsma is a cultural anthropologist at the Vakgroep Culturele Antropologie, Vrije Universiteit, Amsterdam, who was researching into the transfer of traditional Moroccan cultural traits to Moroccan-Dutch Islam.

[23] Morocco is, to begin with, the Maghreb country in which the Islamist movements are least organised.

2.4.2 Belgium

The majority of Muslim immigrants in Belgium come from North Africa and Turkey.[24]

Islam occupies a quite unique position in Belgium unlike anywhere else in Europe. Islam has been given official recognition and thereby is eligible for certain religious privileges. This quite special status enjoyed by Islam in Belgium is effected in such a way as to give the state a decisive hand in deciding how the institutionalisation of Islam should take place.

In the light of this the Belgium state has stipulated that there should be one Islamic authority to which it addresses itself, one authority with which to achieve consensus and to negotiate with and delegate responsibility to. Since the immigrant Muslims were not gathered under one authority, one 'church', it was decided in 1978 that one particular institution would be awarded this status. This was the Centre Islamique et Culturel de Belgique, which was formed in 1968 and led by the Muslim World League.[25] The centre has since been used as a central base for the league's European activities.[26]

The special status of the centre has given it rights which affect the entire Muslim immigrant community. It is the centre, as such, which appoints people to deal with the teaching of Islam and the mother tongue in Belgian schools, just as the centre has to approve the Imams who are to operate in the country. This is naturally only of significance to those imams

---

[24] The number of immigrants in Belgium is (in 1985) around 900,000, of these there are 200,000 of Muslim origin which makes them the second largest immigrant group, less than the approximate 320,000 Italians, but more than the 58,000 Spaniards. Around 130,000 Muslim immigrants come from the Maghreb countries, while around 70,000 come from Turkey. This immigration took shape in the 1960s but only really took off in the 70s (Bastenier 1988).

[25] *Muslim World League* or Rabitat al-Alam al-Islami, is a cooperative organisation which in principle consists of representatives from all the Muslim states, with the intention of propagating Islam (da'wa). The organisation whose main seat is in Mecca and which was founded in 1962 is accredited to the UN as an NGO. The league, which is primarily funded by Saudi Arabia, was set up on the initiative of Saudi Arabia as a political alternative to Arab socialism which at the time was on the rise with Nasser's Egypt in the vanguard.

[26] Muslim World League founded the Upper World Council of Mosques in 1975, which in 1980 set up le Conseil continental des mosquées en Europe, based in Brussels. This organisation formed the Institut Islamique pour la formation des prédicteurs et imams en Europe in 1982 (Kepel 1987, p.213 ff.).

who arrive from abroad and require work permits. The centre has no authority over those (often self-taught) imams who have lived in Belgium since the 1970s as migrant workers.

While Morocco partly exercises its influence through the centre, of which it is part of the leadership, and partly through Amicales (c.f. notes 20 & 21) the Turkish government seeks to maintain its authority through the offices of the Diyanet in Belgium. Belgium partly recognises the particular status of Turkey. This means that the Islamic Cultural Centre does not have any influence on the religious life organised by the Turkish *state*: The Turkish state decides itself who is to teach Islam and the mother tongue, as well as which imams are to operate in Belgium. The centre functions in that respect alone as an office of the Belgian state.

This special form which the institutionalisation of Islam has acquired in Belgium has not gone unchallenged by the immigrants themselves.

The organisation Culture et Religion Islamique (CRI) was founded in 1977 by a trans-national group of Muslims, as an organisational counterpart to Centre Islamique et Culturel de Belgique, and they criticise the centre's dependency on the immigrants' countries of origin, just as they criticise its centralised leadership (Dassetto & Bastenier 1984). Alongside these organisations, whose emergence is a direct consequence of the centre's official hegemony over Muslim religious life, we do, of course, also find the Turkish Islamist organisations mentioned earlier: Süleymanli, Millî Görüş, Tebliğ and Nurcu.

Among the North African immigrants Jama'at al-Tabligh occupies a significant position, but so do other North African Islamist movements. The Sufi orders also play an increasing role, although this has not as yet been investigated (interview with Dassetto, December 1988).

Since the mid-1980s the state has come to realise that it has not managed to centralise authority over Islam. This led to the formation of a 'conseil de sage' in 1991 to create a new situation. In contrast to what was the case in France the members of this council were chosen from among Muslims already active on the Belgian political scene. For this reason it has, according to Dassetto, no legitimacy among the Muslim public (Dassetto, seminar presentation February 1992).

2.4.3 Britain

The history of immigration in Britain is dominated by immigrants coming from the Indian subcontinent, i.e. what is present day Pakistan and Bangladesh. In addition there are large groups from Nigeria, East Africa, the Arab countries and, finally, there is a Turkish-Cypriot group.[27]

The earliest Muslim institutions established in Britain correspond to the spread of immigrants and are found in the large British ports. Just as it was the case in France, it was a disciple of Sheikh Ahmad al-Alawi (c.f. note 7) who, by establishing the zawaya (pl. zawiya) - at the close of the 19th century, created a centre for the religious activities of Muslims.[28] In the 1890s the first mosque appeared. Nielsen (1981) estimates that there exist around 500 mosques and places of prayer in Britain, while Ally (1979) estimates the number as being about 1000. Of these, writes Ally, most of them are occupied by a full-time imam. During the 1970s over 25 *jawami* were built.[29] Half of these large mosques - which are built in traditional style - were financed by foreign (predominantly Saudi Arabian and Libyan) donations. The other half are located in former factory or warehouse buildings and are financed by the congregation itself in each case. In association with these mosques Koran schools and libraries have been established. Furthermore, youth and women's organisations are also linked to them.

The first Islamist organisation to cover the entire country was founded in Britain at the start of the 1960s. The UK Islamic Mission whose Pakistani roots are in the *Jamaat-i-Islami* was already established in 1962 and is probably the best established and organised of all the Islamic

---

[27] There is a great deal of uncertainty about the numbers of Muslim immigrants, estimates vary from between ¾ to 1½ million (Nielsen 1987). The reason why Britain is the country where there is the highest degree of uncertainty about the religious faith of the immigrant population is because most are actually United Kingdom citizens. The estimated figures mentioned above are based on dated census material with an adjustment made for population growth. Although in the rest of Europe - similarly to Britain - residents are also not registered according to their religious convictions the registration of people's country of origin makes it possible to draw a more precise estimate of the number of Muslims present.

[28] These places which functioned not only as places of prayer, since the sheikhs also carried out other social functions, such as banking and social work, operated up until the 1st World War.

[29] *Jawami* (plural of *jami*) are large mosques which, in contrast to smaller local mosques (*masjid*) are also suitable for Friday prayers.

organisations in Britain. Aside from organising prayers and the religious aspects of family life, distributing the books, publishing periodicals, running language courses, Koran courses, they organised *halal* food products, Islamic clothing, legal advice, social counselling, sports arrangements and holiday camps (op.cit.). An Islamic student organisation was, likewise, established in 1962.

In recent years there has been a change to the religious organisation as represented by deobandi and barelwi, both of which are rooted in 19th century India.[30] The prominence of these two sects is a reflection of the fact that the majority of the Pakistani immigrant community are Pathans from North Western Frontier (deobandi) and Kashmir (barelwi) (Joly 1988).

Where the brotherhood-like religious organisational structures of the 1960s and 1970s were informal, there is now a formal structuring. The cause of this shift is to be found in the fact that public support for ethnic organisations in Britain has been altered, according to Jørgen Nielsen.[31] Previously, support was given to 'linguistic and cultural organisations'. This meant that the ethnic organisations' regulations were in concordance with the required aims. Now, however, support is given to 'cultural projects' which explains why the Sufi-based background now appears more prominently: religiously defined organisations can now perfectly well appear as organisers of these 'cultural projects'. Whereas the above named Sufi organisations formerly were not only informal but also local, they are now not only increasingly formal but there is also a tendency towards inter-regional organisation (according to an interview with Jørgen Nielsen, November 1988).

Markazi Jamiat Ahl-i Hadith too, like barelwi and deobandi, originated in 19th century India. Like deobandi this is a salafiyya movement which departs from Sufi thought on a number of central aspects (Joly 1988). *Jama'at al-Tabligh* which, like Jama'at-i-Islami is a phenomenon of this century, has its European base in central England (c.f. Chapter 5).

---

[30] *Deobandi*, which also comprises a defiance of sufi-oriented Islam was responsible in 1919 for the foundation of Jamiat ul-Ulama-i Hind. With the foundation of Pakistan they were able to open a section there, Jamiat ul-Ulama-i Islam. *Barelwi*, which evolves from a basis in the Naqshbandi-brotherhood is also called the Ahl-i Sunnat wa Jama'at, and is politically organised within Jamiat ul-Ulama-i Pakistan.

[31] Jørgen Nielsen is an Arabist and director of the Islamic Centre at Selly Oak Colleges in Birmingham.

English law does not operate on the basis of the recognition/non-recognition of religious communities, and nor does it emphasise, as is the case in most European countries, the country of origin of immigrants. In contrast to this the British government does not provide direct support to large organisations such as the UK Islamic Mission, according to Jørgen Nielsen. Indeed, government demands regarding the education of immigrant imams has, since the 1980s, become increasingly stringent, in that a university level qualification is now required. This is a demand which the large organisations are quite content with since it is a standard which they are in a position to deliver.[32] This government policy does, however, contradict the wishes of many families to 'import' an imam from their own village.

2.5 Summary

The development of Islamic organisations describes, in itself, the changing phases of Muslim immigration. In the earliest phase of immigration, when the first Muslim contract workers arrived in Europe, there were only very few centres of Muslim religious practise. In the 1970s, which, in immigration terms, was a decade of family re-unification, religious life was to a large extent in the hands of fellow migrants, Islamic lay people who had not received official education in an institution of theological learning.

The process of family re-unification marked the transformation from foreign worker to immigrant, and provided the impetus for the institutionalisation of religious life with the founding of various types of organisations with different aims in mind.

Based on the development of the Islamic scene in Europe it is clearly apparent that it is the political and legal conditions of the establishment of Islam which decide which sociological group plays the dominant role: either 1) the Muslim state apparatus, or 2) the Muslim immigrants themselves.

The earliest places of prayer were of a temporary nature. In some countries development of the first kind was favoured: this applies to Germany, France, Belgium and Denmark.

---

[32] These religious functionaries are issued at first with residence permits for 1 year at a time for 3 years and thereafter permits for periods of 3 years.

Although it can be said that the management of Islam lies in the hands of these two main groups of players, it can also be said that the European countries - whether or not they realise it - ultimately have the decisive hand in administrating Islam.

In those countries (in particular France and Belgium) where the state authority recognises its responsibility for the institutionalisation of Islam, it was decided that particular institutions be equipped with extensive powers, thereby giving them a degree of authority for which there is no consensus within the Muslim communities themselves. It is precisely in these countries that efforts to create alternative institutions have been greatest. In France and Belgium there is a strong tendency towards the view that the administration of Islam in the future should not be allocated to other states, but should be overseen by local forces. The new interventions remain unchanged in their overriding vision of the creation of a centralised Islamic authority. Nor is it the case in the other examples which I have covered that it is left up to the Muslim congregations to choose their own forms of organisational structure, here too, development to a great extent favours the initiative of the Middle Eastern states. A widespread and related problem encountered by Islamic organisations - in Denmark and Germany - is how to gain some kind of formal recognition as a religious community.

(ad 1) The da'wa of the Muslim states in Europe is usually regulated at the state level, as an agreement between individual states or groups of states, such as, for example, The Muslim World League and individual European states, or Turkey and individual European states.

(ad 2) The non-state da'wa in Europe has a lot of problems. The opportunities for bringing imams into the country in question are slim and this appears to be growing even more difficult, possibly as a result of rising anti-foreign feeling and a increasing involvement at the state level in Europe on the part of the Muslim countries.

In any case there is a clear tendency within European countries to favour the initiatives taken by Muslim states concerning the Islamic scene: This is the case in Germany, France, Belgium and in Denmark. Islam's social situation in Europe has to be regarded as constituting a democratic problem.

Even when looking at the same type of social networks and organisational traditions, the collective organisations of the new ethnic minorities assume different forms. The different models of institutions and traditions of organisation in the various European states become the determining factors.

In this sense the host immigration country actively shapes, and each does this in their own fashion, the collective organisation forms of the new ethnic minorities through the distribution of resources and privileges given to particular organisation structures. The new Islamic organisations must also define their function in relation to these models in order to attain credibility.

If we consider these organisations in relation to an identity problematic we must conclude therefore that the shaping of the collective identity is definitively influenced by the manner in which the state integrates these organisations.

It is apparent that the newer Islamic movements are of very different characters. In the following attempt to characterise significant aspects of Islamism's perception of the world I will limit myself to turning my attention to the Turkish Islamist movement Millî Görüş and the part of the Islamist movement associated with this.

3 Avrupa Millî Görüş Teşkilâtleri (AMGT): The Union of the New World Vision in Europe

Avrupa Millî Görüş Teşkilâtleri (AMGT) or, as it is more generally known, simply Millî Görüş, is an Islamist organisation of Turkish immigrants in Europe. The headquarters of the organisation are in Köln in Germany, but it consists of regional *bölgesi*, sub-divisions in European countries which have sufficient numbers of Turkish immigrants.

Most of the literature available on AMGT describes the organisation as being a sub-division of Millî Selamet Partisi (MSP) - what is now the Refah Partisi (RP) or Welfare Party. Although there is no doubt that AMGT and RP have common roots (politically speaking AMGT is part of RP's fundament, thus making it an existing, contributing element in Turkish politics), it would be misleading to reduce the role of the organisation to simply representing RP's Turkish-European supporters. AMGT exists in its own right within Turkish migrant communities who themselves define and set the agenda for the organisation. This is the premise that forms the perspective of the current investigation.

The term *Millî Görüş* is often translated as 'The National Standpoint' (e.g. Saribay 1985). The movement itself however is not content with this translation. A spokesman in Berlin claims that the term *millî* has a meaning which in Turkish differs from the term 'national'. Millî refers to the religious content which would mean that a more accurate translation of Millî Görüş would be 'The Religious Standpoint'. *Millî* is also a more general term than *Ummah*, which is the usual Islamic term used for the *Islamic* community. The term *millî* can be used as reference to groups of Abraham's people. One can, therefore, talk of Jewish *millet*, and Christian *millet*.

The organisation's Danish chairman interpreted the name as follows: It is, in so much as one adheres to the strictly literal sense of the words, correct to translate *Millî Görüş* into Danish as: 'The National Standpoint'. That the movement at all utilises the term *Millî Görüş* is historically rooted in the suppression of Islam in Turkey. The movement is forced to use a particular vocabulary in order to meet the requirements of Turkish law. The term *millî* satisfies the secular norm because it does also mean 'nation' in the secular sense. It is, however, also correct from an Islamic point of view to talk of *millî* because it has two meanings, 'nation' and *ümmet* (ummah). In the Koranic sense there is actually sociological parity between *millet* and *ummah*, according to the chairman. The Turkish population are Muslims and know very well that *millî* means *ümmet*. When Islam is once again free in Turkey it will no longer be necessary to live beneath the subjugation such impositions.

The Berlin spokesman for the organisation claims that the secular Turkish word for 'national' is *ulusal*. To translate *Millî* as 'national' would limit the movement to a Turkish nationalist standpoint, a standpoint which the organisation very clearly distances itself from. Indeed, on the contrary, it is asserted time and again that Islam is consistently anti-nationalist and universal. The union's own official German interpretation of 'Avrupa Millî Görüş Teşkilâteri' is 'Vereingung der Neuen Weltsicht in Europe' - or, 'The Union of the New World View in Europe'.

Already, even in the matter of nomenclature, a degree of compromise can be discerned. This refers back to the organisation's Turkish -national background, and more specifically it is due to secular legislation, which expressly forbids religious references in politics. The name also informs us that the organisation, in its Turkish context, does not wish to be considered illegal, but would prefer to operate openly. This also indicates that the supporters in Turkey have, on a political level - effected through their affiliation with Refah Partisi, sought to implement a democratic *parliamentary* strategy in attaining the Islamisation of the country.

It is Turkish state legislation which prevents the free formation of organisations, and which prevents organisations from freely working towards their own aims.[1] This condition is relevant not only in Turkey but also in Europe since the Turkish state authority also claims that its jurisdiction extends beyond Turkish territory and therefore applies to the social and political activities of Turkish citizens abroad, in other words, migrants in Europe.

Since Islam is generally regarded with great scepticism, and AMGT in particular is considered to be a potential haven for terrorist activities, the organisation has been quite reluctant to appear publicly.

---

[1] Turkish Penal Code, Article 163 explicitly forbids 'undermining secular order'. Flexibility in the formulation of the law invites a distinctly political interpretation. The law has from time to time been invoked for use against the Islamist movement.

Individuals have sought to protect themselves by remaining at least partially anonymous.

The person who was indicated as acting in the capacity of spokesman for AMGT Berlin Bölgesi (AMGT-BB: AMGT's Berlin section), refused to participate under his own name when I expressed a wish to interview a leading figure from the organisation. His concern was that by appearing publicly as a member of AMGT-BB he would damage his chances of attaining German citizenship, which he was in the process of applying for. The same argument was cited by the section leader, when he too refused to allow his name to be used in an interview.

Mehmet, as I shall call him, added that Turkey had quite a unique interpretation of the term 'secular', which is otherwise taken to mean the separation of state and religion. AMGT is of the view that Turkey, with its particular understanding of secularity (*laiklik*) *de facto* places religion under state authority. Diyanet, the Turkish directorate for religious affairs, is under the immediate control of the Prime Minister's Department. The intention is, in other words, to place religious life in Turkey in the hands of a state body. This state of affairs hinders the formation of any political organisation which openly seeks to call itself 'The Islamic Standpoint'.

The beginnings of Millî Görüş can be traced back to the end of the 1960s (more specifically to 1969) when Neçmetting Erbakan, the founder of the movement and its ideological inspiration formed the MSP (Millî Selamet Partisi). A year later the party ideology was already to be found represented among migrant workers in Berlin. At that time it was in the form of a union named 'Türk Kültür ve Yadimlasma Dernegi' ('Turkish Culture and Solidarity Union'). Later it assumed, as Binswanger (1988) also notes, the name 'Avrupa Türk Birligi' (The Turkish Union in Europe').

In 1973 the movement's ideology was outlined in a collection of texts by its charismatic founder. The book is entitled 'Millî Görüş' although this was not the name of the organisation right from the start, but that of an ideological current which first materialised in Turkey as a political party and later also spread through the circles of Turkish minorities in Europe.

It was only in 1981 that the organisation appeared publicly in West Germany under the name Millî Görüş. In 1985 the name was changed to the current one so as to make clear that it was now an umbrella organisation for a number of regional organisations in Europe: AMGT. AMGT now constitutes the organisational superstructure of an Islamic movement among the Turkish minority communities in Western Europe.

In the following section I shall outline how this, the most important Islamic movement in Europe, is organised. This chapter is based on material I have gathered through interviews with representatives of three of the movement's regions, i.e. Denmark, France and Berlin.

The first section (A) deals with the organisation's structure in these three regions and the considerable activities that are initiated on a regional basis - I shall briefly outline the planning that surrounds the *hajj*, and the particular conditions related to observing the month of fasting, Ramadan, which, within the Turkish context is also a measure of the religious orientation of the participants. Following on from this I present material in the second main section (B) which sheds light on Millî Görüş's position *vis-à-vis* Islam. Lacking sufficient material to provide a comprehensive outline of the movement's vision in an accessible, European, language, I have chosen to present material that illustrates briefly the general position of the movement. As this originally existed only in Turkish I have had to have this translated into Danish (Appendix E & F). In addition I have, in my interviews with the leaders, sought to supplement this with material which illustrates their position with regard to individual cases, and which also provides an insight into more general points of principle. In place of an appendix, I present an excerpt from one interview which I conducted with one of the movement's imams who attempts to outline the Islamic alternative.

In the first instance I have avoided going into an in-depth analysis of Millî Görüş's representation of the Islamic viewpoint in the context of the societal development process and have, on the whole, restricted myself to presenting material under specific, tangible headlines. In the concluding chapter however I shall return to this for the sake of formulating a perspective on the relevance of the movement's position.

3.A The Structure of the Organisation

In 1990, the organisation consisted of a total of 24 *bölgesi*. In West Germany each one of these corresponded to one of the Bunde *länder*. Berlin, likewise, constitutes a separate *bölgesi*. In France there are three. Countries other than these are covered as one *bölgesi* each. Denmark, for example, comprises one *bölgesi*. There is a sub-division in Australia which is also attached to AMGT (Interview with the spokesman for the organisation in Berlin, March 1990).

3.A.1 Denmark

According to the chairman of Millî Görüş in Denmark, the Islamic outlook, millî görüş, has always been in his heart, ever since he arrived in this country as a fifteen year-old in 1972. Danimarka Millî Görüş Teşkilâteri (DGMT) was first established as an *organisation* in Denmark in 1985, and was from the outset an independent division of AMGT. From this, it would not appear that the Islamic movement was previously organised in Denmark, nor does it appear under any of the names by which it was otherwise known in Germany. DMGT functions as a regional section and has no further local sub-divisions, as such. DMGT consists, rather, of a network of members in different towns. This network is though, organically bound to the Millî Görüş communities in Denmark - which have their own prayer houses (*cami* or *mescit*). In 1990 there were four Millî Görüş cemaat in Denmark (Helsingør, Kokkedal, Vejle, and Aarhus). In 1993 I counted at least 20. Only the mosque in Aarhus had its own imam, who had been trained in theology. The others were served by self-taught imams. By 1993 the movement had more trained imams in Denmark.

The chairman explains the reasons for forming a Danish Millî Görüş section as being:

> Now we are part of the Danish population. We want to stay here, we can't go back. Five years ago I told myself that I was all right here, that I would stay here. The second generation will be settled. They will be completely integrated, they should not just become manual workers, they should also receive the highest education. There will be Turks in all walks of life. They will preserve their Muslim roots, but they will be Muslim Danes!!
> Millî Görüş has no motive beyond Islam. Millî Görüş works for Islam. Millî Görüş is Islam. This does not mean that it distinguishes itself from others. There is nothing special about Millî Görüş: All Muslims are brothers, all people come from Adam and Eve, therefore we are brothers with all people. And with some we also share a common faith which makes out brotherhood even stronger.

The chairman pointed out that Islam's legal position in Denmark is deeply dissatisfactory: It is quite a problem for the various Millî Görüş cemaat that Islam is not an officially recognised religious faith in Denmark. The immediate consequence of this is that it is not particularly easy for them to bring the Imams they need into the country, and they can also be subjected to the processing of their cases being drawn out even longer.

The foreign imams have the right to be in Denmark for up to four years, but The Danish Directorate For Aliens has always laid obstacles in their path, including describing them as 'missionaries', which is why they have only been allowed to stay for 2 years, according to the chairman. But they are *not* missionaries, he says, an imam is a teacher and a guide to whom one can go in one's search of *ilm*, religious learning. The Danish Directorate for Aliens has, since 1989, given the Diyanet's hocas both work and residence permits lasting for up to four years, a right which DMGT imams have not been given.

It is quite a problem to bring independent Turkish imams into the country. The Directorate demands that the request go through the embassy each time, and due to the nature of their case the embassy will not endorse applications by Millî Görüş imams. The easiest option is to bring in imams who have a so-called 'green passport'. These imams are pensioned off in Turkey after having served for at least 25 years. They are allowed permission to stay in Denmark for up to two years. A former imam in Aarhus had just such a 'green passport'. These independent imams cannot, however, take advantage of the opportunity to attain a more permanent state of residence by gaining the right to perform marriages with the status of civil authority. In short, they can only enter the country with great difficulty. The old imams can be used in cases of emergency, but it is necessary to get hold of younger imams who have a better understanding and grasp of the situation of young people, explained the chairman.

There is no doubt, he claimed, that in the long term, Islam has to be recognised as a fully valid religious community with rights equal to those of the various Christian denominations and the Jewish faith. This is what Millî Görüş in any case hopes to achieve, he said, 'Islam is not a small religion, it is a world religion'.

Millî Görüş remains in permanent conflict with Diyanet. Diyanet is a part of the Turkish state apparatus which means that it is not exclusively concerned with Islam, but is driven rather by political considerations and interests of power. One example of how the Turkish state exploits Turkish immigrants is through the business of property via so-called *Vakif*,[2] the spokesman for the movement in Aarhus explained to me. He went on to say that the Diyanet's *Vakif* in Denmark was a bluff: The Turkish immigrants are given the false impression that *Vakif* is an officially registered foundation and that its properties cannot be touched by the Danish authorities. If it was not officially registered as a foundation then it would be regarded as being privately owned and could be conceivably be taken over privately, and people would not have much faith in it. Therefore, it is crucial to Turkey that the *Vakif* appears to be an official foundation. The structure of the leadership of these *Vakif*, which are run by the DTF (Danish Turkish Foundation) is quite obscure, and the foundation is not registered in any relevant Danish registry, as such. It is not possible to find out who is on the committee, nor what is stated in the regulations. In actual fact it is the Turkish Cultural attaché in Denmark who runs the foundation.

---

[2] An Islamic foundation.

There are, meanwhile, two types of *vakıf* in Denmark: *Genaza Vakf*, which is set up as an insurance concern, and can pay for transport in cases of returning the remains of people home to Turkey when they die; and the *Diyanet Vakf*, whose purpose is the acquisition of religious property.

People pay 100 Kroner (approx. 10 pounds Sterling) to join the *Genaza Vakf*. The money is paid to a funeral insurance but the resources are put into a common pool with those of the *Diyanet Vakf*. It is these resources, among others, which are used to acquire property for the Diyanet, the chairman explained.

When the Diyanet wishes to acquire a new property to establish a mosque, it usually happens as follows: The Diyanet encourages people to collect money for the purpose and promises that in return for their contribution they (the Diyanet) will put what amounts to perhaps forty percent of the value of the property into the scheme. The purchase will be administrated by a foundation to which there is no public access. When the property is paid for people are encouraged to continue to collect money, over and above the sixty percent needed, and the Diyanet absorbs the surplus.

Financial matters are one thing, but how does Millî Görüş differ from the Diyanet in matters relating to Islam? The organisation's Danish Chairman explains:

> There is no difference between us and the imams of the Diyanet, we are in agreement on Islam. They are also faithful people, who work to establish more hocas for the Turks and we are not hostile to them. But the Diyanet is still controlled by the Turkish government, and therefore they cannot always say what is right. Deep down in their hearts they know very well what is right.
>
> Millî Görüş is, on the other hand, independent, it comes from the grass roots and therefore we can disseminate Islam directly. The Diyanet only brings Islam to the Turks. They are forced to comply with state interests. Millî Görüş is completely free, we can open our hearts not only to Turks, but also to Danes, to Pakistanis and Africans. Islam is for the entire world. Islam is not only about this world, but also about life after death.

It is no longer possible to create a jointly accepted Islamic authority for the Islamic *ummah*, according to the foreman of Millî Görüş in Denmark. 'Islam is today spread across 48 Muslim countries and 20 states. Not even the Diyanet can plead for such authority. People must be allowed the freedom to live with their faith.[3] AMGT is working for the Islamic standpoint and has set up its own fatwa-commission to advise itself.[4]

> 'We must accept that we do not always completely understand what the holy texts are trying to tell us', the chairman explained. 'It was not possible in the day of the Prophet to know, for example, that television would one day be invented. Nevertheless this was anticipated in the Koran: The Prophet Muhammed told a story which today we can see contains a prediction about television. He foresaw, for example, that people would be able to move from one place to another faster than the eye can blink'.

Although the chairman explained that it was no longer possible nowadays to conceive of a commonly recognised religious authority, this does not mean that he was advocating an arbitrary or pluralist interpretation of Islam. While Mujtahid fatwa's can no longer be issued, imam-fatwa's can. Islam is founded on scholarship, he claimed. In order to evaluate what was right the Islamic ulama had to study the *kitab*, *sunnah*, *qiyas*, and *ijma* very thoroughly.

Despite Islam's legal status being weak in Denmark it is still possible to live in accordance with Islam, according to the chairman. All have a duty to follow Islam, only the mentally ill and the dying are exempt. In certain particular situations it can, however, provide problems: Not all employers, for example, like their employees to pray, even though some flexibility is allowed regarding the time of prayer. Millî Görüş takes the view that a Muslim should press his employer into accepting that he prays. It is, so to speak, an Islamic obligation to seek to gain that right. Millî Görüş however admits that even this can be difficult for the individual. If prayer is not possible then it must be compensated for on arriving home - as *kaza* (Arabic: kadha).

---

[3] Millî Görüş also has a different approach to the various *tarikat*, or Sufi brotherhoods. They are accepted in so far as they remain within Islam, e.g. *Nakshibendi*, while the *Haci Bektashi order* falls outside Islam, in his view. There is nothing, as such, wrong with Haci Bektash Veli - it is his heirs who have gone wrong (interview with the chairman of DMGT). The Haci Bektashi order is today run by the Alevites.

[4] The commission is under the leadership of the highly regarded imam, Mustafa Efe, who has translated the *Fetevayi Hindiyye* (i.e. Indian *Fatawa*) written by Indian *ulama* in the Hanafi tradition.

Today there are no *mujtahid* to be found. The great mujtahid are Abu Hanifa, Malik, Al-Shafi'i and Ibn Hanbal as founders of the four madhabib. The theologist Al-Ghazzali (11th -12 Th. century) is considered to be a *mujtahid*, the last *mujtahid* dates back to the 14th century.

Young people growing up now will represent Islam better than we can, said the chairman. Islam demands 'ilm' and the young have a better education than we do. Therefore, it is important that the young learn something, that they learn Danish well, but also that they gain a good knowledge of Islam.

There is a great social need for Islam, the chairman of DMGT explained:

> Denmark is a democratic society. It is a rich society, economically, in any case, and despite there being only 5 million inhabitants, there are around 60 suicide attempts a day, and 2 of these succeed. Every 40 minutes a suicide takes place somewhere in Germany. This is a result of the fact that we live in a materialist system, therefore there is a need for an Islamic organisation which can guide the way towards Islam.

Nowadays Islam exists under difficult conditions, and it is hard to get Danes to see what real Islam is. When a Turk or an immigrant makes a mistake it is immediately to the detriment of Islam, said the chairman, who went on to say that,

> The Danes knew nothing of Islam before we arrived here as immigrant workers. In Sweden there was contact with Islam all the way back to when King Karl XII[5] was at war with Russia and he turned to Turkey for help. In Denmark only very little is known of Islam, even with a high education. People have heard that the Ottoman Empire managed to reach the gates of Vienna in 1683. The first Turkish Immigrant workers arrived in Roskilde in 1967 and they can confirm how much people stared at them. Turks and other Muslims are still regarded with a great deal of suspicion.

For this reason DMGT is still not prepared to appear publicly in Denmark. For the same reason it was only after considerable deliberation that the union chairman consented to being interviewed by me. It was only after he had received some of my previous articles, and had enquired about me among Millî Görüş supporters in Aarhus.[6] The chairman of Millî Görüş did not wish for his interview to be recorded on tape, and his name was not to appear in the text. We also agreed that he should have a copy of my notes of the interviews, so that he might have the opportunity to respond to any misunderstandings or omissions.

---

[5] The 'warrior king' Karl XII (reigned 1697-1718) led the defeat of Peter the Great of Russia in the Battle of Poltava (1709). Karl XII escaped from Turkey where he attempted to persuade the Sultan to help him - in vain.

[6] The interview took place on the premises of the Helsingør Youth and Culture Union, whose local chairman was the brother of the union chairman.

DMGT also acts as a *hajj* organisation which runs the *hajj* through AMGT. The first time they sent people to the *hajj* was in 1987, they have sent people every year since then.

They also organise other activities within the parameters of AMGT. For instance, they organised a European competition for children, a competition about knowledge of the world, as much about Islam as about social conditions. This led to 18 people going to camp school in Malmø in Sweden during the period of the 22nd-24th December 1989. The winner later went on to take part in a European final in which only the very best participated.

What demands does the Millî Görüş leadership make regarding activities organised by the various cemaat? What restrictions are there? The only thing stipulated about the activities is that they be conducted under Islamic conditions. It is, for example, forbidden for money to be involved. Card playing is forbidden and professional football is also incompatible with Islam. There are four forms of sport and games which Islam regards as immediately being halal: Swimming, shooting and riding (in modern times this also means that driving a car is halal). Finally, it is halal to play with one's wife and children.

With regard to listening to music, this again must be evaluated according to whether or not it meets Islamic conditions. Music must not, for instance, be provocative. Rock music often seeks to stimulate feelings which are non-Islamic, and this applies to both aggressive or sexual feelings. It is quite all right to listen to rock music with the intention of studying it in order to understand Islam, but normally it would be a hindrance to Islam. In order to evaluate what is *halal/haram* in Islam, one has to progress in an informed manner and Millî Görüş can utilise its *fatwa-commision* in this.

The movement's most important activities are still those which are organised in the youth and cultural unions which form the local grass roots of DMGT - Millî Görüş cemaat.

3.A.1.1 A Millî Görüş Cemaat in Aarhus

The Aarhus Youth and Cultural Association (Aarhus Ungdoms og Kulturforening) was started in mid-1986. The union was based in the centre of town in Aarhus. The purpose of the union was, according to my interviews with the association leadership, to create a place specially for young people, a place that could 'fill the daily vacuum' with constructive activities. The place would be used as a starting point for:
-Improving the awareness of members about conditions in Denmark, in particular with regard to finding alternatives to

unemployment, by improving knowledge of vocations, education and training opportunities. Similarly, the association is working with an information federation, on the initiative of its members, to provide educational courses under the Fritidsloven (legislation governing leisure time education); These include a specially designed course in Danish, and a course on solar energy units. Members refer to the place as their 'school'.

-Cross cultural information work about Danish conditions and about what trade unions are available in Denmark. This includes inviting union representatives to speak.

-Discussing and learning more about Turkish culture.

-Making sports activities available.

These sports activities are decentralised and have their own boards. Strictly speaking, the association is only obliged to provide premises when there is a demand for meetings of the board and members, but is not responsible for the sports activities themselves. In order to organise the sport a sports club has been set up, ASIA, which has swimming and table tennis on its programme, as well as football. The Taekwon-do club which was affiliated when the association started has now fully joined.

The leadership is of the opinion that the association occupies a space within the spectrum of Turkish associations which would otherwise be empty. Several of the other clubs are effectively restricted to local housing zones, which The Aarhus Youth and Cultural Association is not, as it seeks to cover the entire Aarhus area. Many of the other associations are, they believe, aimed at somewhat older people and, similarly, the interpretation of Islam in these associations is linked to a political line which supports the particular interests of Turkey. In other words, what they are saying is that the Turkish government is exploiting Islam politically. They cite Islam's internationalism as their objection to this. Some Turkish immigrant unions in Aarhus completely reject Islam, which this union does not. Furthermore, they distance themselves completely from Turkish party politics, something which they are not certain that other unions can claim. They are also of the opinion that these other unions place too much emphasis on 'folklore'. It was characteristic up until 1990/91 that members of the association preferred to use the cross-national Islamic Cultural Centre as their religious gathering place, rather than the Turkish Diyanet-mosque in the western part of the city.

Up until that time the association had several good locations at its disposal, with a small kitchen, an office, board rooms, library and rooms with table tennis facilities. A single room was set aside to be used, apart from meetings and teaching, for prayer (the room is, however, in no way intended to replace the mosque, but is used only if one happens to be there at the time of prayer). The association's library contains for the most part religious literature in Turkish, cassette recordings of religious music, including *ilahiler* (religious hymns), also videos, often of a religious nature (film as sermons). The union also subscribes to a number of immigrant publications, as well as to newspapers and magazines from Turkey, often of a religious orientation. Various groups receive, from time to time, teaching in Koran reading, *ilahi* songs and the immediacy of Islam (*sohbet*)

Since 1991 the association has been well placed in a property in downtown Aarhus, which aside from a couple of other Islamic unions also houses the newly inaugurated Sultan Eyyub Cami mosque.

The aims of the association are to strengthen the young. It is the view that young people often have problems in relation to their parents. The parents were not sufficiently interested at an earlier stage in ensuring that their children received an education. Many of these parents, first generation immigrants, were concerned only that their children were able to earn money. Many of them were taken out of school, therefore, as early as possible. This is why it is vital to inform parents about the opportunities provided by education and about the benefits one can receive while gaining one, which would mean that the children could support themselves. This generation of parents has to be made to understand that in the long run this is a better investment, and one which will give rise to better job opportunities and better pay. They need to be reminded of the Turkish saying that: 'Education is a golden bracelet'.

The young Turkish girls experience greater problems than the boys, according to the association leaders. Not only do their parents want them to go out and earn money, but even earlier than the boys, at an age as young as 12 in some cases. The usual reasons cited for taking the girls out of school so early are to do with not wanting them to encounter information about sex, or having to take part in swimming/gymnastics, problems with camp school, etc. The local Millî Görüş leaders' view was that it would not make a great deal of difference as far as the girls were concerned, even if these subjects were made voluntary. The parents would simply find other excuses for removing their girls from school. For instance, they might refer to end of term parties or the mixed gender classes. The leaders remarked that it was interesting to note that in the Danish classes in the state schools (folkeskole) recent experiments were being made with all girl classes, with only women teachers!

The association has women members. In the beginning it was a case of a few individuals, with only sporadic activities arranged for them. The association is working on creating a special section for the women, but for the moment regards this as being a complicated task. Nothing would be achieved by declaring that the association was mixed, on the contrary it would scare people away. One of the problems is in finding the women leaders who would be needed for the project to succeed.

During my first encounter with members of the Aarhus Youth and Culture Association the idea that they were a part of Millî Görüş, as claimed by other Turkish immigrants, was persistently denied. One leader said:

> We share the same orientation as they do, (....) but we have nothing to do with them. We are Muslims, (....) and Islam is an integral part of Turkish culture and it occupies, therefore, a natural place among its members (Pedersen, 1991c, p. 126).

This interpretation is correct, but is far from being the whole story. Millî Görüş activists are responsible for setting up The Aarhus Youth and Culture Association, just as they are behind Helsingør Youth and Culture Association and the other Youth and Culture clubs or associations.

These associations have regulations which stipulate that anyone prepared to support their aims is allowed to join, and in the same way anyone can stand for election to the leadership. The associations are not, as such, exclusive in any way, or restricted to Millî Görüş members. In practice it is of course natural that only followers of the movement take part in the activities of these associations. On the other hand it can be said that the central leadership of Millî Görüş is not in a position to dictate the activities at the local level, if the association's members are not in agreement. The leaders of the associations can, for instance, only be elected and removed by members of the association.

This form of organisation is, like that of other immigrant organisations, tailored to suit the requirements that have to be met in order to qualify for public support. This form of organisation can be found in the structure of Millî Görüş throughout Europe, just as it applies to the structure of other immigrant groups.

In the early years of immigrant organisations there existed some degree of competition and powerplay between the various (political) groups trying to gain control of existing organisations. Today it seems that these groups have crystallised into independent unions, each with their own aims, all of which together make up the ordinary public supermarket of such associations, and where the choice is regulated by demand.

In terms of the running of Millî Görüş in Denmark, we can summarise the situation as being that there are communities which on the one hand are run along local, general, formal lines, registered as associations with publicly approved rules and regulations. On the other hand, Millî Görüş activists make up the bulk of the main tribe of these unions which are associated with DMGT and thereby to AMGT.

Since my interviews were conducted with the leaders of DMGT, the movement has not only expanded its activities quantitatively, but also qualitatively:

a) The movement has, since 1994, been the most active force among Turkish Muslims in the establishment of Islamic private schools.

b) In 1994 the movement managed to get two of its leading members elected into the Immigrant Council (Indvandrerrådet - what is now the Council for Ethnic Minorities - Rådet for Etnisk Minoriteter), which is an advisory body to the Minister of the Interior on questions of immigrant policy.

c) Since December 1994, the movement has been engaged in dialogue with other Danish, Islamic unions. To this end the movement took part in a conference, in December 1994, with other associations on the particular problems of Muslims in Denmark. The conference was an historic event in that it was the first of its kind in Denmark.[7] The dialogue has since been continued with a view to establishing a nation-wide umbrella organisation for the Islamic organisations in the country. One of the tasks which the planning group is working on is the question of the recognition of Islam as a religious faith (Interview with DMGT's representative at the meetings, December 1995).

3. A. 2 France

In France Millî Görüş is known as the Union Islamique en France (UIF). The UIF was formed in 1977 and , with its 21 sections in France, it makes up the French division of AMGT, according to its chairman Mustafa Doğan.[8]

The UIF's sections are most often, although not always, structured as unions around a mosque. The organisation has 16-17 imams who have graduated from a theological university. This number does not, however, meet the demand.

---

[7] During the conference, which took place in Aarhus, Arab, Turkish, Pakistani and Somali unions took part (the Dawah group, Millî Görüş, Braband Ungdomsforening, Muslim Youth League and the Somali Familieforening) as well as some cross-national unions, The Union of Muslim Students (FASM) Islamic Relief Organisation (ISRA), and the Union of Muslims In Denmark (MID 1995, p.3).

[8] Interview with Mustafa Doğan in May 1990 at the movement's French centre, Paris Fatîh Camisi (see Appendix M).

The movement has two women trained in Islam who can take care of the education of women. These two women are, like the imams, university trained: They received their education in Islam partly at university and partly at specialist schools and they also have teaching experience.

The organisation also has affiliated teachers - often students - who, on a voluntary basis, provide the Turkish school pupils with help in doing their homework and other supplementary teaching in relation to normal schooling, just as they also give lessons in the mother tongue, in Turkish culture, geography and history, but naturally, of course, also in Islam.

The organisation would like to make its advisory services more professional, for instance in dealing with solutions to individual social problems.

Millî Görüş in France seeks to organise Islamic life upon a number of planes. There is for example, a *hajj* organisation, which in 1990 sent around 200 pilgrims to Mecca, and the collection of zekât is also organised, primarily to be distributed as stipends to young people lacking the necessary finances, with a view towards education.

The UIF has a completely newly formed sports department. There have always been sports clubs available for followers of the movement, but they have been badly run. A parallel organisation has now been set up for sport in France: football, taekwon-do, and volleyball. As yet, no efforts have been made to organise sports for women.

The organisation does not run any departments specifically for young people. Instead, in each union there is a person responsible for youth. On the other hand there is a women's section which discusses social and cultural problems as well as family problems. The women also do handiwork as a part of the local section's activities.

> We are, as such, not a religious association in the strictest sense. We are an association which encompasses everything: the day to day life of people, life in the streets, the humanitarian, the spiritual life, the cultural, the social, the educational, financial, sports, etc (Mustafa Doğan, Appendix L).

Millî Görüş in France does not regard itself as a strictly religious association, but as an association which should seek to meet the needs of its members on all aspects of life.

Just as is the case in Denmark, the movement in France is founded on a double structure. On the one hand they are a part of an international organisation network (AMGT) and on the other they are rooted locally - and in this case tailored to the traditions of such unions in France. The UIF is run as an ASBL (Association But Non-Lucratif) according to French law of 1901, in other words as an officially registered association which serves general human aims.

In the case of France this has also given rise to a central French association which is not linked to AMGT. This association of French Millî Görüş unions is called Tendance National Union Islamique en France (TNUIF).

The TNUIF was formed in 1987 but from the start was created around the 'integration problem'. It can be said that the set-up of an organisation with such a profile was the result of a mental aberration. It was when perceptions about the temporary nature of labour migration were replaced by the realisation that one would actually be living in a state of permanent exile, as a minority, that the need for such an organisation, which concerned itself explicitly with integration into French society became clear:

> We demand that freedom, equality and fraternity shall be applied to all (....) We are prepared to be integrated into French society, which is why we have added the Tendence National to the Union islamique en France (op. cit.).

Co-operation with secular organisations which are working towards a solution to the problems associated with marginalisation and racism, such as SOS-Racism, are in no way dismissed, despite the UIF/TNUIF remaining firmly anchored in their Islamic identity. They see themselves as being part of the anti-racist movement, 'seeking to calm the spirit of phantasms which racism invokes among those who refuse to face facts' (op.cit.). The TNUIF occupies a niche here where it is possible for Islam to exist alongside other religions, thereby illuminating and increasing the opportunities for Islam's special and cultural integration into French society:

> Of course we can live in France and in Europe and remain Muslims, become Western and at the same time practise our religion. (...) We are working to integrate Islam into French society. There are around 4 million who are not recognised by the state authority, who have no form of representative organisation, and there are many problems (op.cit.).

The UIF and TNUIF exist side by side today. The UIF is a part of Millî Görüş (AMGT) but they are, broadly speaking, identical. They consist of the same associations. The activities within the two organisations are, on the whole, the same, that is to say that these organisations attempt to achieve concrete solutions for the children of immigrants who live in

France and, at the European level, through AMGT in Germany, says Doğan.

As mentioned, a council for Islam has been established in France, under the leadership of the Minister of the Interior (Pierre Joxe, at the time/ LP). UIF is represented on this council by Mustafa Doğan, precisely because he wishes to stress the problems facing Islam and the need for its integration in France, in the same way that he wishes to point out that the uncertainty surrounding Islam's rights also have to be seen in relation to the social unrest in immigrant environments - an unrest that in relation to French society is linked to the progress of French right wing tendencies, including Le Pen:

> The problems of Muslims have yet to be resolved. More than anything the problems of young people, the criminalisation, and marginalisation within society. These youth contribute to a radicalisation of French society (op.cit.).

The solution to these problems is, according to Millî Görüş, closely bound to Islam, in that 'insecurity regarding certain rights connected to Islam are indisputable, and also in relation to the young people who have need of a purpose' (op.cit.).

The French public politicise Islam, according to Mustafa Doğan. Not least of all the media, which contribute to presenting an image of Islam as a monster of fanaticism and terrorism. As an example of this he refers to the case of the Muslim schoolgirls use of the hijab. The use of the hijab is interpreted by the media and by certain politicians as being a political provocation, which is not the case. The hijab is a religious obligation made by God. 'It is God's order, passed down via the Koran. If one is a Muslim, you have to practise all of your faith' (op.cit.).

The opportunity to increase the teaching of Islam is one of the aims towards which Millî Görüş is working and planning. While it is not realistic to consider introducing the teaching of Islam in public French schools, it is possible to imagine that general non-proselytising education could be developed so as not to be in conflict with the religion. But Millî Görüş in France would also like to introduce Islamic private schools which can function at the same level as Jewish or Catholic schools.

Another example of the unresolved problems which Mustafa Doğan stresses that Muslims face in France, is the lack of control concerning *halal* butchers, and he points out that there is a need for the means to ensure the regulation of these butchers and certify their Islamic validity.

The Muslim organisations in France have, over the last 15 years, attempted on a number of occasions to form an umbrella organisation to promote their common efforts. As such the UIF is a member and co-founder of the Federation National de Musulmane de France, and along with others, lead by la Mosquée de la Paris have attempted to form a Rassemblement Islamique.

Up until now these attempts to form a common federation, a 'federation des federations' have not succeeded. This implies, according to Mustafa Doğan, that there is a need to rectifiy this. This is one of his motives for entering the consultative council of the Interior Minister, that it has the potential to act as a body which to a certain degree could act as a kind of umbrella for common Islamic interests.

Although the council only has a consultative status, does the organisation really feel that a non-Islamic, secular state ought to develop a council that has representative status for Islam? Mustafa Doğan sees the point as being, that it is the council which has to prove that it deserves to represent the Muslim population in France. The legitimacy of the council will depend on the decision it takes, and not on how it has been set up. It does not have, and cannot, *a priori*, purport to represent the popular opinion of the people. If the council manages to come up with proposals for solutions that in part, so to speak, manage to reach the Muslim population and gain their approval, and also in part manage to satisfy the needs of the state authority above them, then in effect they will have fulfilled the role of occupying an intermediate position, between the state and the Muslim population.

The most immediate question for Islam in France is the problem concerning the establishment of Muslim graveyards, halal butchers, the marginalisation of the young, and their education. These are very thorny problems, but problems which ought to be solved as soon as possible (op.cit.).

The relationship with Diyanet (which does not participate in the consultative council set up by the minister), on the basis of Mustafa Doğan's account, is one in which no love has been lost, although founded on peaceful co-existence. But he is in no doubt that it is Millî Görüş, with its freedom from state obligation, and its engaged and motivated members, which is best suited to providing an Islamic identity for the young. At the same time, however, he claims that the organisation lacks the financial resources to fully exploit this potential. It is still Diyanet which, as far as the Turkish Muslim minority is concerned, has the greatest economic resources.

At other levels too, Millî Görüş in France can be seen to be trying to contribute to the development of an Islamic platform along with the other Muslim minorities. In 1990 a consensus was reached among the Muslim communities concerning the start and end of the month of fasting, Ramadan. The UIF, like followers of the movement in other parts of Europe, does not adhere to the recommendations which the Turkish government issues in connection with this. Nor do they follow AMGT's suggestions to the letter.

3. A. 3 Berlin

In Berlin, AMGT has around 2000 members spread between nine mosque associations, all of which are known as so-called 'Eingetragende Vereine' (e.V.). They are all legally regulated associations, registered with the Berlin registry of unions. In each mosque a leadership is voted in, with a chairman. Between them the leaders of the individual mosques vote for a common leadership, with a regional chairman - a *bölge başkan* - at the top, who has to be approved by AMGT's main office. Together these *bölge başkan* make up the AMGT leadership.

It is difficult to estimate the quantitative strength of AMGT-BB with any accuracy. The number of members is around 2000 and these are people who have *membership cards* for the mosque associations which are associated with AMGT in Berlin. These people are very active, according to the spokesman, Mehmet, but the number of sympathisers is much greater. When, for example, the movement's ideological leader, Neçmettin Erbakan, visited Berlin in 1988 at least 5,000 people turned up. At the AMGT-BB's Afghanistan demonstrations around 3,000 turned up. Mehmet estimated that the movement has at least 10,000 sympathisers in Berlin, and seemed flattered but dismissive when I told him that Blaschke (1985) estimated them to come to around 15,000.

The regional leadership only has an advisory function regarding which activities the individual mosque associations should initiate. There are no means of forcing the individual mosques, which do not have to be in agreement. But, Mehmet says, normally there is agreement, they are after all working for the same common purpose and idea. The relationship of the mosques to Millî Görüş is not legally regulated. That is to say that although the mosques are 'e.V', this does not imply that they are bound together and under any obligation to the organisation AMGT. It is with this in mind, Mehmet explained, that: 'We share the same thoughts - we are all Millî Görüş supporters - (...) and that is why we gather together'. Millî Görüş is, as such, an organisation, but also a social movement and an ideological current.

In this way there is a formal difference between the mosques' connection to Millî Görüş and their official membership, at the same time, of the umbrella organisation, The Islamische Föderation. When an initiative has been decided by the Islamische Föderation, the member organisations have statutory responsibility for ensuring that the decision is actually implemented. The leadership of the mosque associations which make up the Millî Görüş network gather 3-4 times a year, while the regional leadership meet on a more regular basis and whenever otherwise required.

The task of the mosque leaders is of an organisational nature. Ideological and political discussions are not primarily conducted here. Mehmet explained that, for instance, in the run up to Ramadan, many imams wish to go to Turkey on holiday, but if 3-4 imams leave at the same time, there are too few left behind. It is up to the leaders to co-ordinate their departure times, so that the whole thing can continue to run smoothly. If one mosque, for example, experiences financial troubles then it is the leadership's task to find the resources between them, and if, for example, a demonstration of the distribution of flyers has to be organised, then it is also the mosque leaders who have to solve the practical problems associated with this. Questions of policy are on the other hand discussed in the mosque gatherings, such as, in connection with carrying out *vaaz* on weekends.

AMGT then, is an Islamic organisation which partly rests on democratic principles of representation, which ensure that the development of the organisation is based on its body of members, but at the same time it is bound together by a centralist principle which guarantees that the ideological foundation of the movement is maintained.

The nine Millî Görüş mosques in Berlin are each manned by an imam. There are a further three imams who are associated with the school of Islamic learning. These imams are paid by the individual mosques, since the organisation has no other way of doing this. They are paid mainly through the contributions of members to the mosque associations. These contributions are to cover salaries, rent for the mosques and other running costs. Since the contributions of the members are usually not sufficient to cover all of the costs, many mosques have a canteen, or a book sale in the mosque. Previously, for example, Helâl Gida, a Turkish foodstuff manufacturing chain in Berlin, made a substantial contribution, but since the company went out of business a few years ago this source has also been cut off.

The largest and most important part of the activities conducted by AMGT Berlin Bölgesi are centred around the mosque associations. The mosque unions each have a general secretary who oversees the daily administrative work. Each mosque organises:

-Tabligh, i.e. the actual preaching of Islam.
-Education, i.e. 'inner education' via Koran courses and other forms of Islamic learning (din dersi).
-Written material, e.g. such as the production of flyers and other kinds of printed matter.
-Sports activities.
-Youth work.

The women are not formally organised in any direct sense by the mosque associations, and therefore are not subject to their control. The mosque leaders cannot interfere with the work of the women's group, just as the women's groups cannot interfere in the mosques leaders. The women's associations, Cemiyet al Nisa, are actually independent unions - which can utilise the premises of the mosques. There are in fact only very few mosques which have associated unions of women, namely the Ahmet Sultan Mosque in Schöneberg along with Vakif and the Fatih Mosque in Kreuzberg.

The women are allowed to perform their prayers in the mosques, but not always. In contrast they do not come to the mosque for Friday prayers, when only men are present. The Prophet himself, Mehmet pointed out, did not wish for women to be allowed to enter a mosque for prayer. Women should only be allowed into the mosque exceptionally, when it is necessary for them. Women can attend, for example, the *terawith* (night prayers) during Ramadan. They also come to *vaaz* on Sundays where a hatip speaks to them: 'die Frauen kommen zu die vaaz um auch über den Islam zu lernen'. Women are to have special teaching in and about Islam, but this takes place in specially planned weekly sessions, only for them.

Millî Görüş in Berlin has two female *hatips* of its own. They are not hocas but they have a comprehensive grasp of Islamic learning which they pass on to other women. Every week they arrive to talk to the women's association in Millî Görüş's main mosque in Berlin, the Mevlana Mosque in Kreuzberg.

Furthermore, there is a series of associations and institutions which are not directly integrated into AMGT but which are counted as sympathisers, such a the student union, ASES at the Teknisches Universität and TFD (Türkischen Fernsehen Deutschland) which is a local Turkish language television channel which broadcasts for one hour a day.

The mosques' organisation of *tabligh*, 'education', 'PR', 'Sport' and 'Youth Work' is also co-ordinated at the *bölge* level: The youth work of the mosques is also linked to 'Berlin Islamci Gençlik Teşkilâti', 'The organisation for Berlin's Islamic Youth'. The youth association also arranges seminars and cultural activities, such as a theatre production arranged in March 1990, which criticised the Turkish state's suppression of Islam (Appendix K).

During the summer the youth associations arrange outings to recreational areas around Berlin, such as Grünewald, Tegel and Welter. They also organise 3-4 day summer trips for young people to other parts of West Germany where they can meet young people from some of the movement's other sub-divisions. The important things about this kind of common outing is that they strengthen fraternity and solidarity in the common spirit. The outings are intended to increase awareness and to stress that Muslims must understand one another as brothers, and that the suffering of one is also another's. Mehmet illustrated this with a reference to a *hadith*:

> God's messenger Muhammed, once said that if a *Mu'min*, a believer, cannot feel his brother's pain on the other side of the world, then he is not a true believer! (Mehmet, Appendix A,1).

Mehmet says that according to a particular *hadith*, the Prophet outlined certain forms of sport that were eminently suitable: swimming, riding and throwing a spear (i.e. shooting). Generally, however, it is not in these three disciplines that one tends to find young Turkish Muslims participating. First and foremost it is football and self-defence (karate and taekwon-do) which are the favoured sports activities, while swimming and body-building are also popular. The football club, 'Hilal-Spor' takes part in tournaments within the German youth league and is one of the leading clubs. This ethnographer's opinion that body building was a pastime inspired more by the participant's vanity than religious engagement was immediately rejected. New activities might be started up if some of the young people came forwards with a suggestion about this or that. The leadership would then consider whether or not to initiate it. The criteria for how far an activity should be pursued was based on whether it could be carried out in an Islamic manner: For instance, it was not permitted to wear tight clothing, men were to be covered from their navel to their knees, and when bathing they also had to be aware of not overstepping the rules about *hudud*. If these conditions were met, then the sport would be allowed, and this also applied to body-building.

There is also a women's sports union associated with the movement in Berlin. Here women are allowed to practise sports, mainly swimming, so long as the rules about Islamic clothing are observed, explains Mehmet. There is also the added condition that men must not be present, that is to say that the swimming coach must also be a woman.

Since Mehmet did not know of any women who participated in these sports himself, he was not in a position to say much more about this matter. He did though, dismiss the idea outright that it was furthermore required that the coach be a Muslim - a claim that I had been confronted with during a visit to the Berlin Senates Ausländerbeauftragte.

AMGT-Berlin Bölgesis also has a *zekât* committee. Mehmet explained that the committee was formed for those who could afford to give *zakât* but who could not of their own accord find a suitable recipient, which is in many ways the ideal situation. Via the *zekât* committee one can support students from Turkey who are not eligible for public stipends. In this manner AMGT helps young people to conduct their studies under reasonable conditions. But there is also a further advantage for Islam in that it aids the process of regaining the leading position in science which Islam once had. Islam wanted to serve mankind with its science, Mehmet explained. He pointed out the difference here between Millî Görüş and DITIB. Millî Görüş should be seen as a rejection of, and alternative to the, passive, ritually-orientated tradition. Instead it promotes the idea of Islam as a comprehensive lifestyle which argues, among other things, for raising the level of education:

> DITIB teaches people to pray five times a day, for example, to fast, pay zakat, and go on hajj to Mecca, but that is all that they teach. But in Islam that is not all. We seek, therefore, to go beyond that, to teach all of Islam (Mehmet, Appendix A,2).

3.A.3.1 The Relationship between AMGT-BB and Islamische Föderation Berlin

As noted AMGT-BB is run as a number of mosque associations, all of which are 'e.V.', or 'eingetragende Vereine'. AMGT-BB is not, as such, a registered union. That is to say the relationship between the individual 'e.V.' and AMGT-BB is not regulated by law. In contrast to this there is a legally regulated relationship between the same unions and another Berlin organisation, The Islamische Föderation Berlin.

Millî Görüş was the driving force behind the establishment of the Islamische Föderation in 1981 and this meant that it was involved in setting out the federation's aims. While the Islamische Föderation consisted at the outset of 10 groupings, of which 9 were a part of Millî Görüş and the last of which, namely Teblig, had broken away from them, today it comprises far more organisations. Although Millî Görüş is still the largest single grouping within the Islamische Föderation, the composition is now more varied. Alongside Tebliğ, the Nurcu movement has joined, as have the

Islamic-Iranian Student Union, the Islamic Afghani Student Fellowship, The Islamic-Iraqi Student Union, along with a couple of Turkish student unions. Women are represented by two unions. In 1986 the number of associated unions was 26.

From the beginning, the aim of the Islamische Föderation was to establish a structure that could gain official recognition and thereby stand as the official representative of Islam as far as the German state (Berlin) was concerned. It was hoped that by its formation the Islamische Föderation would gain recognition as 'Körperschaft des Öffentlichen Recht'. Such recognition if attained would mean, among other things, that the federation would be eligible to become responsible for Islamic religious education in German schools throughout the state school system.

The Islamische Föderation's organisational structure can be outlined as follows:

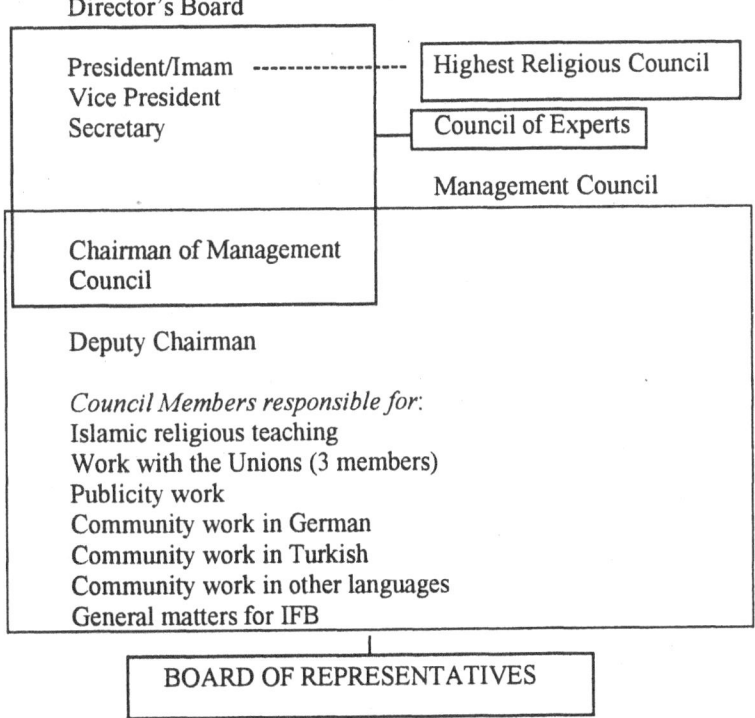

The Islamische Föderation is led by a board of representatives. Each union that is associated has at least one representative, depending on the size of the union. The board of representatives meets once a year to elect the day to day leadership and to make decisions about the union's working program.

The leadership consists of 4 persons: The Föderation's president (imam), a vice president, a secretary and a chairman for the so-called management council. The management council is, like the daily leadership elected by the board of representatives for a 3 year period, and conducts the federation's work in teaching Islam, working with the member organisations, PR work, and community work.

The federation's imam single-handedly picks out the members of The Highest Religious Council, which, according to the 1988 regulations comprises the federation's Fatwa commission. The vice-chairman of the Islamische Föderation, Yahya Schülzke, rejects the idea of calling it a fatwa commission as it is impossible today to issue fatwas. In contrast, the commission gives religiously founded advice, he explained. Furthermore, he stressed that in the Islamische Föderation ordinary rules about decisions applied, which in this case meant a majority in a referendum. The Islamische Föderation rejected, for instance Khomeini's so-called fatwa against Salman Rushdie (see appendix G). The High Religious Council consists only of persons who have been through an Islamic Theological university education. The federation's imam, likewise, selects a leader responsible for the Council of Experts, which in addition is set up *ad hoc* according to the nature of the task at hand.

The Islamische Föderation's ambition to be recognised as 'Körperschaft des Öffentlichen Recht', has been put aside for the moment since their application was turned down - the German authorities did not feel that they fulfilled the necessary criteria. On the other hand the federation is now seeking to attain juridical status as a 'religious community' ('Religionsgemeinschaft'). After several years - since 1982 - of attempting to submit the case to the 'Verwaltungsgericht', the Berlin administrative court, they succeeded in having the school authority's former standpoint, that the federation did not constitute a religious community, withdrawn. It still remains to get an administrative court to pass judgement, actually recognising them as such a community. If this judgement were to fall in favour of The Islamische Föderation, they would have access to organising the teaching of Islam within the framework of the Berlin county school system.

3.A.3.1.1 The Case of the Islamic Primary School: Islam Kolleg The Islamische Föderation will undoubtedly encounter a good deal of scepticism on the road ahead, testimony to which is the resistance which they have encountered in their establishment of a privately funded primary school. The argument which in the final instance is used against the school has no qualified substance to it, but is founded solely on the fact that the federation is regarded as a cover organisation for Millî Görüş.

When The Islamische Föderation attempted for the first time in 1982 to gain recognition as a 'religious community', and thereby achieve the right to organise teaching (of Islam) in the Berlin public school system, they were immediately opposed by the Senates responsible for the area. This rejection was defended on the basis that:
- The Islamische Föderation does not constitute a 'religious community', because its member organisations were not individually recognised as religious communities.
-That these member organisations could not be recognised as 'religious communities' because their religious objectives were not comprehensive enough.
-That the religious objectives of the Islamische Föderation were on an even ranking with their other aims i.e., social, legal, and cultural objectives.
-That The Islamische Föderation's religious objectives are not comprehensive enough.

The conclusion is that the federation is not a 'religious community', but is simply a religiously-oriented union.

The Senate's school board guards against any possible revision of the Islamische Föderation's structure that might enable it to evade the criticism, by simultaneously casting aspersions on the idea that Islam can at all meet the requirements for being approved as a 'religious community'. This refers to the course of development of school legislation and points at the situation of Islam in Berlin today, which cannot be compared to how it was in 1948, when the decision was fixed by the legislation (Appendix J). In December 1988 the Senate changed its stance after the case was brought before the 'Verwaltungsgericht'. By March 1990 however, the case had not yet been concluded; it still remained to verify the degree to which the Islamische Föderation can be considered a 'religious community'.

The vice-chairman of the Islamische Föderation, Yahya Schülzke, puts down the problems, such as those encountered in gaining recognition, to the fact that the evangelical church is opposed to this. The opposition from the church has been a crucial factor to the politicians, since the members of this church constitute, in his opinion, half of the electorate (Appendix B,1).

Since the Evangelical Church has not commented publicly on this particular case, Yahya Schülzke's opinions are founded on conversations he has had with (Christian) theologists, who have participated in the synods of the church in which the case has been discussed. According to these conversations the church is not opposed, as it previously was, to Islamic religious teaching in the schools, but is against the idea that the privilege of organising this should pass solely to the Islamische Föderation. The real objection which the church has is that they are being challenged on their own territory and would thereby lose an equivalent amount of influence. (Appendix B,2).

Yahya Schülzke claims that the Islamische Föderation finds it much easier to establish a dialogue with the Catholic Church than with the Evangelical Church. Basically, this is due to theological problems in the understanding of God, he says. Since The Second Vatican Council, the Catholics find it easier than the Protestants to recognise Islam as a means of believing in God. The Evangelical Church does not apparently consider the Christian and Islamic God to be one and the same. Ironically, the question appears, according to Yahya Schülzke, to be one of whether there is one God or several gods: 'For the Catholic Church and for the Muslims this is not a problem. For both of them there is only one God!' (Yahya Schülzke, Appendix B,2).

The fact that things are like this and that this conflict has been brought up within the ranks of the Evangelist Church itself, is demonstrated by the changes in the choice of words used by the Evangelist bishop in his message congratulating the Islamische Föderation in 1988/1989 in connection with the end of the month of fasting. In 1988 the bishop's message went as follows: 'We stand together with you, so as to contribute in fellowship to God's name being honoured' (Appendix B,2) - while in 1989, after having been criticised for his choice of words, he formulated himself this way: 'You have in recent weeks abstained a good deal and have undergone many exertions because of your faith and celebrate now a festival to honour your God' (op.cit.).

Another problem which the Islamische Föderation sees itself as being confronted by are the accusations of being controlled *de facto* by Millî Görüş. The organisation is not banned in Germany as it is in Turkey, but is, for example, categorised in the annually published 'Verfassungs- schutzberichte' as an 'Islamische extremistischer Organisation', which is a touch milder than the predicate 'strong religious fanaticism', by which Teblig was described. (e.g. Verfassungsschutzbericht 1985).

Just as I was in the middle of conducting my interview with the vice-president of the Islamische Föderation, Yahya Schülzke, the leader of the Senate's 'Auslanderbeauftragte', Barbara John, appeared on the television screen commenting on the parliamentary disturbances caused at the time by the federation's newly opened Islamic primary school. She described The Islamische Föderation as an organisation which was actually controlled by Milli Goruş, which again was described as an Islamic extremist organisation. The organisation was described as an exponent of religious *fanaticism*, whose aim was to *indoctrinate* children and *oppose integration*. The organisation was accused of *anti-Semitism*, and they were also professed to hold views that were highly *repressive of women*.

The Islamic private school was given the Senate's permission to begin a trial year in 1989. In December of that year the school was awarded the seal of professional approval by the Senate school committee. The level of education was satisfactory. The case was not, however, closed. A political debate was raised in the Senate, in which those who supported the founding of the school were accused of having ulterior motives. This led to a hearing of the parliamentary school committee in which questions were raised about the constitutional loyalty of the school leadership.

The matter at the heart of this political enquiry was whether the Koran and the constitution were at all compatible. The question, in effect, was: Could the Föderation's school leadership be loyal both to the constitution and to Islam at one and the same time? Or was it a case of the school having two very different and quite incompatible legal foundations. And, if in the final instance the school leadership were to favour Islam, this would make it impossible to consider it as being loyal to the German constitution. The Islamische Föderation responded to this by stating that there was a tradition in Islam for accommodating others, of reaching agreement with others and that such an arrangement was binding for Muslims. This was the situation for Muslims in Germany:

> Since we are living here we have an obligation to recognise the constitution, and we are ready to live according to it. I have tried to explain this. They only accepted this after Professor Steppart (German Islam expert/LP) had talked to them (Yahya Schülzke, Appendix B,3).

Yahya Schülzke was, as well as being chairman of the Islamische Föderation, also the leader of the school, and he was one of those who came under attack. Alongside a document thanking the Senate for 40 years of faithful service as a post inspector in Berlin, he presented a statement in his defence, which includes a presentation of the considerations raised in the Islamische Föderation concerning Islam's position in Europe as a part of a multi-cultural democratic society.

It is argued in this defence statement that the Föderation is loyal to the constitution, democratically minded, opposed to the repression of women, and in favour of integration. It concludes that Berlin society now faces the option of allowing Islam and Muslims to be an equal part of society - or of forcing them to continue to live in the ghetto. The arguments can be summed up in the following six points (for a full account of the defence document see Appendix C):

1. It is unheard of, and quite unprecedented to compare the compatibility of centuries-old divine laws (The Koran) with a modern

constitution. This was not the case previously with the Old and New testaments of the Bible.

2. The idea for a planned primary school arose among Muslim women who are organised within the Islamic 'Women's Union'. This is, cited as being, among other things, a reaction to the growing hostility towards foreigners in society. The project is conducted as a co-operative effort between Muslim men and women. It is unique and quite new for Muslim men and women to work together in a relationship as equals. This is a direct consequence of their integration in Europe. This is a new development, which leads away from the dominant nationalistic, state-Islam tradition of hostility towards women.

3. The primary school will be run by an organisation (The Islamische Föderation), which is the first Islamic organisation to have introduced democratic structures. There is, as such, talk of a special kind of integration. Such democratic structures are not found in the traditionalist and nationalistic organisations of state Islam organisations.

4. It is understandable that the federation's attempt to create an independent, European, Islamic community which implies the actual integration of Islam into European society, is not recognised by the politicians.

5. The Islamische Föderation is seeking to develop a dialogue with other religious and social forces with a view to promoting mutual recognition within a multi-cultural society.

6. The suppression of women is not Islamic, but is linked to nationalistic state-Islam. On the contrary the federation's discussions show that Islam regards women more highly than men!

The question of the Islamic primary school has now become a question of the degree to which Millî Görüş are behind it. It is not just Millî Görüş, but all Muslims who are seen as terrorists, according to Yahya Schülzke: 'Wir sind alle Terroristen, sehen sie das! Deshalb wollen die uns politisch hier keine Rechte einräumen' (Appendix B,3).

According to Yahya Schülzke, when the question of possible incompatibility between the Koran and the German constitution had been resolved by the intervention of an Islam expert, another excuse had to be found to prevent the school from being opened. When one has presented one particular problem to the Senate and cleared up all misunderstandings, new problems are quickly found to lay obstacles in the path of the Muslims. Now (March 1990) the problem was that Millî Görüş had never really provided any public exposition of themselves. The Islamische Föderation sought, unsuccessfully, to persuade German scholars familiar with Millî Görüş to make some contribution.

Although it is never stated outright that all Muslims are terrorists, Yahya Schülzke emphasised, as a Muslim one feels very badly treated and therefore it is easy to get the impression that one is regarded as a terrorist. There are many who do not wish to see the school given permission, including leading figures in the Senate 'Ausländerbeauftragte', and in the Turkish consulate. Others too, who have political influence are busy pulling strings.

What is also involved here, and perhaps first and foremost, is that the policy towards foreigners is based on the idea of them returning home. To create independent Islamic institutions does of course clash with the desire to see immigrants travel back to their country of origin. It is logical, therefore, to connect the religious life of Turks to Turkish state institutions (Appendix B,4).

Some Muslims dream of an Islamic state that would solve all the problems, in the same way that some Jews dream of a Messiah, Yahya Schülzke claims:

> Some people wait for the Messiah and believe that he will solve all their problems, while others say that he has already come and others still believe that he will not come. This is not how I look at it. I am also in favour of an Islamic state, but that is not a realistic question, neither in the BRD nor for that matter in Turkey or Iran.

Perhaps it might happen in 50 years, who knows? What is really at stake for Muslims is more to do with 'mit anderen kulturen zu leben', says Yahya Schülzke. It is about religious freedom and equality between people. On this basic point there is a parity between Islam and the bourgeois revolution:

> That which, for example, the French Revolution brought to Europe. The Prophet Muhammed had actually implemented fourteen hundred years ago! The French Revolution then, was in essence an Islamic revolution! (Yahya Schülzke, Appendix B, 5).

For Yahya Schülzke what matters is that we all must adjust ourselves to a multi-cultural society, where each individual can live on equal terms. But there is still a long way to go as far as the Federal Republic is concerned, in his view. One example is religious education. Arranging religious teaching is decided upon by each of the Länder individually. So that according to the legislation in Bremen today, for example, it is still not possible to conduct any religious teaching other than Christian biblical history. There is nothing available for Muslims, Jews, or Hindus, for example. 'This is, however, no legislation for a multi-cultural society!' In Yahya Schülzke's view it is important that the religions are given equal rights and can exist side by side. The Islamic federation's problems in gaining public recognition, first as a 'Körperschaft des Öffentliche Recht', and then as a 'religious community', and finally as leaders of a primary school appear to be typical of Islam's (political and mental) location in Berlin:

- The Muslim community exists with no publicly recognised religious representation.
- The Islamische Föderation seeks to define an Islamic-German field of action which is free of any foreign, nation-state interests.
- Public opposition to the recognition if The Islamische Föderation is not regarded as being professionally founded, but as a link in a politically motivated infringement of equal civil liberties.
- Opposition to recognising The Islamische Föderation's primary school is not based on criticism of the school's professional standards, of the curriculum, or the quality of the teaching staff, or of the school's administration.
- Opposition to the Islamische Föderation's initiative is based on the claim that it is guided by Millî Görüş.

The problem for the Berlin school authorities is, in the final analysis, due to the nature of the relationship between The Islamische Föderation and AMGT-BB.

The link between The Islamische Föderation and AMGT-BB can be illustrated by the diagram below:

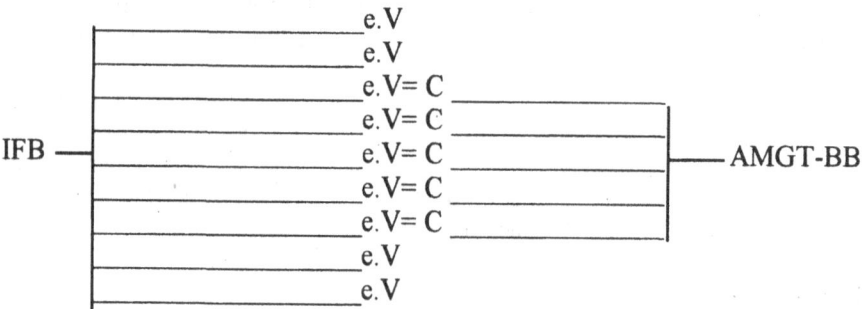

(e.V.: eingetragene Verein; Millî Görüş cemaat).

The problem for the school authorities is that on the one hand there are a number of 'e.V.', which, according to their union regulations are associated with the Islamische Föderation. A number of these 'e.V.' are simultaneously linked to AMGT-BB, although this is an informal relationship.

AMGT-BB is not concerned with the fact that these local mosque associations are 'e.v.', but that they are also Millî Görüş cemaat.

The worry of the public authorities, however, is that the 'e.v.' organised Millî Görüş cemaat are so heavily represented in the Islamische Föderation that power effectively resides with AMGT-BB and thereby potentially lies with the organisation's European headquarters in Köln, which, taken to its logical conclusion, could possibly mean the ideological founder of the movement, Necmettin Erbakan, whom, it should be recalled, is leader of the RP (The Welfare Party) in Turkey!

The question of the degree of influence which Millî Görüş has on The Islamische Föderation has been raised over a number of years by the Senate's 'Ausländerbeauftragte'. In April 1987 there appeared, in a supplement to a report entitled, 'Bericht über die räumliche Situation der islamischen Gemeinden in Berlin', the following:

> Within the Islamische Föderation, so far as we know, the fundamentalist Islam of a Turkish-national orientation (Millî Görüş - 'Nationale Sicht') is dominant. (...) For outsiders it is hard to evaluate accurately the influence and concrete intentions of the various currents on the work of the federation.. (Yahya Schülzke, Appendix B, 5).

One concludes as a result of this that attempts continue to be made: '...to involve Turkish national political aims into the associations work'.

There is no doubt that Millî Görüş is the largest Islamic organisation within The Islamische Föderation.. The mosque communities associated with AMGT-BB make up a majority, nine out of 12 mosque communities are linked to the Islamische Föderation. In addition to this there are a number of associations, including women's unions and student unions, which may represent Millî Görüş views in The Islamische Föderation. The vice-president of The Islamische Föderation claims that Millî Görüş does not have a dominant influence on the organisation's operations. We would appear to have to accept this if we stick to formal criteria. The student unions and women's unions are not official parts of Millî Görüş, they have no formal influence on Millî Görüş, just as Millî Görüş has no formal influence on them. Insofar as Millî Görüş should have *de facto* control over The Islamische Föderation is dependent on the state of Millî Görüş and the level of activities of its members.

But AMGT-BB itself rejects the idea that they have in any way control over The Islamische Föderation. They refer to the fact that although most of the associated unions are sympathisers of Millî Görüş the federation has many members who are not. If The Islamische Föderation really was simply a cover for Millî Görüş one would have to consider these other member unions as being stupid. AMGT-BB rejects the idea that they are a tightly disciplined and structured organisation, although they might well wish it were so: 'It is our wish and we would be happy if we had such a cemaat, and if everything simply worked!'.

To summarise then, it can be said that Millî Görüş, in the context of The Islamische Föderation's efforts to establish an Islamic primary school, is considered to be both an Islamic extremist movement which advocates the establishment of an Islamic state order, which would indicate a conflict with the German constitution, which is why the school leadership's loyalty to the constitution should be in question, and an Islamic organisation which professes to hold views that oppose integration in German society, are repressive of women and are anti-Semitic.

But as a German scholar explains in an interview: If one were to examine Catholic groups, for example, with a thorough eye, one would uncover similar 'loyalty problems', and the same view towards other social conditions, such as the view towards women.

This brings us back to the symbol of Islam in general and of Islamist groups in particular.

3.A.4 AMGT Hac Organizasyonu'ndan

AMGT also organises *hajj* and *umrah*. Turkish Muslims can choose between two hajj-organisations in that DITIB likewise offers similar assistance.

For 1990 the AMGT Hac Organizasyonu'ndna offered a one month stay in Saudi Arabia in June and July, culminating in the *Id* (*Kurban Bayram*), which that year was calculated to begin on the 3rd of July. If one chose to fly directly the trip cost 3350 DM, if one decided to travel by bus it cost 2300DM. The journey stretched out over 1 1/2 months and included 3-4 days in Turkey (Appendix D). The offers were more or less identical to those offered by DITIB.

In 1989 between 1000 and 1500 pilgrims joined AGMT's hajj program. 120 from Berlin alone, which was approximately the same number as DITIB recorded. The reason why AMGT organises *hajj* journeys at all and does not simply advise people to travel with DITIB is, according to the spokesman for the movement's Berlin section, Mehmet, that;

1) DITIB works with German banks and as such their operation involves the inclusion of interest and interest is forbidden according to Islam. The money which AMGT receives in payment for *hajj*, does not go into a bank account which provides interest 'because we in Millî Görüş, in Islam, are against interest' and,

2) that the hocas which DITIB sends out on the excursions do not know enough about the region, which results in the pilgrims 'seeing

nothing, hearing nothing, experiencing nothing!' (Mehmet, Appendix A 4&5). In contrast, the imams who belong to AMGT make a point of learning about the surroundings in Mecca so as to pass on that information to the pilgrims. They seek to tell the pilgrims about the life of the Prophet so that the pilgrims gain a more comprehensive experience.

3.A.5 Ramadan

AMGT insists that the beginning of Ramadan has to be decided by the appearance of the new moon, in contrast to Turkey and DITIB who work out the time and fix it in their annually distributed calendar.

A couple of years ago AMGT had the habit of sending a commission to Saudi Arabia where the conditions were good for observing the moon. This is no longer the case. In Berlin the Islamische Föderation is responsible for the fixing of the time. Die Islamische Föderation sends a commission to the city's observatory which begins to observe the moon a few days before the calculated time. When they see the moon the mosques are informed and the month of fasting can begin. It is not, however, the case that it always has to be done in Berlin, there is, for example, also an observatory in Hamburg.

During the time when a commission was sent to Saudi Arabia, it was so as to make one's own observations, but it did give rise to unhelpful criticism. Millî Görüş was accused of being dependent on Saudi Arabia and Iran, which is one of the reasons why they have stopped sending people to Saudi Arabia and now do all their observations in Europe instead.

The criticism does not stop there however. Conducting the fast on a time scale that in relation to the official Turkish one is a little off, provides a certain degree of visibility within the migrant environment and therewith also material for conflict. The spokesman, Mehmet, explains that Millî Görüş seeks to play down this potential conflict which can be manifested on individual families, but maintains that Millî Görüş cannot change a condition which they feel is a demand of the Prophet which they are following (Appendix A,6).

In other words, AMGT still insists that *Ramadan* should be observed on the basis of the Prophet's instructions and that the Diyanet's practise was in conflict with this. At the same time it is recognised that there is a socially conditioned problem in this different practise which legitimises the fact that being a single individual one can be obliged to give the appearance of following the general custom in Turkey.

This model of solution is, however, not always sufficient. If the conflict is in the home, for example, between generations, it is not possible to keep it covered up. Also this situation is solved differently today than it was before, which meanwhile sharpened differences in the home:

> So we suggested quite simply to our members that the sons did exactly as their fathers, because in Islam one should not offend the father and therefore we say to our friends, do as your father does and hope that God forgives you (Mehmet, Appendix A, 6).

As it is so often asserted in conversations with Millî Görüş supporters: 'Islam does not make life difficult for us, Islam is an easy religion'.

3.B 'The Islamic Outlook'

The task of developing an analysis of AMGT's ideological standpoint is one weighted with a considerable amount of difficulty. Existing attempts are based on old material, which is related in particular to the positions of the movement in Turkey during the first half of the 1970s. Although the movement today has to be regarded as being significant, no analyses of importance have now been conducted which examine the movement's actual base among immigrants in Western Europe. Existing analyses of the movement's ideology are sketchy and lack depth. There can be a number of reasons for this: 1) The movement expresses itself in Turkish and not in any of the main European languages. 2) The movement produces only very few programmatic publications in relation to the situation in Western Europe - the greater part of the written material produced is aimed at contributing to the national debate in Turkey, 3) those researchers who attempt to give some insight into the founding ideas of the movement are themselves sceptical or else hostile towards the movement, and do not give themselves enough time to conduct interviews, and 4) furthermore, the movement's members in Western Europe are not forthright in the matter of giving interviews - not least of all because of the political circumstances here. There are, therefore, fairly good conditions for growth when it comes to the formation of myth and suspicion surrounding the movement in Western Europe - a condition which, as mentioned above, is partly the fault of the movement itself.

In the following I will set out and comment on some of the movement's positions. I will briefly introduce the movement's stand on the Rushdie case, the position regarding the accusations of anti-Semitism, and the relationship to the collapse of communism in Eastern Europe in 1989/90. This I shall then attempt to relate to an analysis of two other Millî Görüş texts, one of which is intended to explain the movement's fundamental viewpoint. The second text is interesting to include here because it is more explicit but still seeks on a level of principle to provide an Islamic perspective on the social position of Muslims in Western Europe.

An attempt to conduct a proper analysis of the movement's universal aims in relation to the social processes will be presented only in the concluding chapter.

3.B.1 Millî Görüş and the Rushdie Affair

The Turkish-German Islamists in Millî Görüş have taken a stand on the Rushdie case. On the one hand they distance themselves from Khomeini's *fatwa* and on the other they have demanded that freedom of speech should not apply to blasphemy, which they consider Rushdie's book to be. Their point of view was made clear in a statement which they made along with the other organisations in Die Islamische Föderation Berlin, in March 1989 (Appendix G).

The Danish chairman of DMGT explains himself - expressing the same thoughts - as follows: Khomeini's *fatwa* concerning Salman Rushdie is wrong. Rushdie is not the first who has sought to take on Islam. The true Islamic answer to Rushdie's attack is not death threats, but to respond, to take his mistakes and distortions up.

The Rushdie case also though, reveals that freedom of speech is one-sided, he says. It is apparently all right to denigrate Islam, while Muslims are not allowed to criticise Thatcher, for example, or the Queen of Denmark. Christian values are not allowed to be criticised either, although it would, of course, also be against Islam to do such a thing, he claims. The view is that Islam, as such, is not harmed by Rushdie's critique, but that the feelings of Muslims were trampled being on. Millî Görüş does not feel that it should be allowed to belittle other people's faith, which is why they support the idea of limiting freedom of expression on this point.

Millî Görüş supporters, both in Denmark and Berlin, often express the view that *The Satanic Verses* is the result of a conspiracy. The work, they explain, is not that of Salman Rushdie alone, but is part of a shrewdly thought out slander campaign aimed at Muslims, arranged by the CIA and the British government.

3.B.2 Millî Görüş and Anti-Semitism

Abdulkadir Haas[9] believes that he has observed the development of a current of anti-Semitism within the Turkish minority environment in Berlin and West Germany since the mid-1980s, although he regards this trend as being a peripheral phenomenon. Unless Turkish religious culture is allowed better conditions for development within the Diaspora, he feels, that the conditions for the growth of anti-Semitism will improve. A significant factor in this is the existence of a Palestinian refugee community in Berlin, which, along with Israel's continued brutal conduct acts a catalyst in the development of such feelings which will not limit themselves to anti-Zionism.

This trend towards anti-Semitism stands out in contrast to the fact that Judaism in the Islamic world and not least of all in the Ottoman Empire over generations was met with far more tolerance than it was even in Christian Europe, just as Haas claims that the Jews in Turkey today are a recognised religious minority. He admits that in the Koran and in the handed down traditions there are instances which problematise the relationship between Jews and Muslims, but, he stresses, Turkish popular Islam has always formed an insurmountable barrier against anti-Semitic propaganda (Interview with Abdulkadir Haas, May 1990).

While Abdulkadir Haas is not of the view that the anti-Semitic undertones are linked to Millî Görüş, Binswanger and Sipahioglu's (1988) level a direct accusation at them. Their conclusion that Millî Görüş is to a certain degree anti-Semitic is based on a number of testimonies published in the daily paper Millî Gazete: Here there are examples of Adolf Hitler being described as 'the one who knew the Jews best' and 'The Jews were the cause of the Second World War'; 'The world is in the hands of the Jewish monopoly'; 'pornography is Jewish work, staged by Zionist world organisations to ruin the young and to incite people to revolt' (op.cit.,99).

The conclusion that the organisation AMGT is anti-Semitic, does not appear to be particularly well documented. The alleged anti-Semitic remarks appeared in Millî Gazete, but, in the light of the fact that the paper is not (In contrast to the authors' claims) an AMGT organ, and Binswanger and Sipahioglu (op.cit.) make no further attempt to prove their claim, just as they do not make any attempt to explain the context of these comments, they would not appear to be able to stand as factual testimony. What they

---

[9] As an expert attached to the Senate in Berlin, Abdulkadir Haas has produced an account of religious and religous-political developments among the Muslim population of Berlin. The report is not available publicly.

(op.cit.) do show, however, is that anti-Semitism must *also* be said to be a part of the Turkish Islamic movement's problemisation.

The movement's Berlin spokesman repudiates the claims of anti-Semitism in no uncertain terms. One was understandably anti-Zionist, but not anti-Semitic, he says. He explains that often in Millî Gazete people talked against the Jews when actually they meant to speak against the Israeli Jews, who are responsible for the Zionist state project (Appendix A, 7). We see here an awareness of a distinction between Jews and Zionists, which is analogous with Western European (left wing) anti-Zionism.

But why not then write 'Israeli' or 'Zionist' if that was what one wishes to say? Why write 'Jews' instead? The reason, according to the spokesman, is that Millî Gazete is a Turkish paper, which is published in Turkey. When one writes 'Jews', the reading public immediately understands that the context is *Israel*.

> When you use the word 'Jew' in Turkey one instantly understands 'Israel' (...) but, when you say 'Jew' *here* it is taken as referring first and foremost to the Jews in Germany (Mehmet, Appendix A, 7).

AMGT has attempted to draw the newspaper's attention to the problem, but without success, the spokesman explains, because of their lack of influence, '*Wir haben keine Weisungsbefugnisse*' (op.cit.).

The claim that Millî Görüş is anti-Semitic is repudiated, then, just as the spokesman claims, that also in other areas incorrect accusations are aimed at the organisations. He also explains that part of the problem is that there are so many people who speak out as Millî Görüş supporters in articles or flyers. Millî Görüş is actually not simply an organisation, there is also an ideological point of contact, he underlines. If these people express views that denigrate Germans or other Europeans and call them inhumane everyone thinks that Millî Görüş is like that. In the spokesman's view it was therefore, for this reason, high time that the organisation revealed itself publicly so that all could see what Millî Görüş actually stood for.

The statement from the movement's Danish chairman in connection with an analysis of the breakdown of communism confirms that anti-Semitism in Millî Görüş is a possibility. He actually says:

> Milli Görüş is of the opinion that the world's two ruling ideologies are on the verge of collapse. Communism is about to collapse and, as we see it now, capitalism is very sick. Social unrest is occurring everywhere, people are seeking freedom and equality, but cannot find any values. 'Allah al Haqq', God is truth. It is Judaism which, in the final instance, is the source of this decay. The ideology of capitalism came from the Jew Karl Marx.

> The ideologies of capitalism and communism come from the same (Jewish/LP) origins (Interview with the chairman of DMGT).

3.B.3 Millî Görüş and Political Events in Eastern Europe (1989/90)

AMGT does take a stand on international political events and has, for example, conducted demonstrations against the Soviet invasion of Afghanistan. The civil war in Afghanistan was not simply another war, but:

> ...a war between the Soviet Union and all the Muslims on earth (...) And all Muslims on earth have fought this war, and we have won this war, or shall we say almost won it (Mehmet, Appendix A,9).

While they have carried out their own demonstrations and collections of donations for the Afghani Mujahidin, they have also, in other contexts, worked together with other religiously minded organisations in Berlin, such as with DITIB and Die Islamische Kulturzentrum and Nurcular. This was the case in a demonstration aimed against the Soviet military intervention in Aserbaijan in 1990[10] and against Bulgaria's forced assimilation of the Turkish minority - in that demonstration the MHP supporters, *Ülküçlar*, the Idealist's League also participated.

My interviews with representatives for AMGT took place just as the breakdown of Eastern Europe's socialist order was gathering pace. They had not paid too much attention to the problems associated with the reunion of the two Germany's, but were more concerned with interpreting and disseminating knowledge about the new laws concerning foreigners, the consequences of which included a diminishment of the right to unlimited residence permits and the right to reunite families. They were, however, also clearly convinced that the foreign legislation was constructed with the idea in mind of getting rid of the Turkish minority population so as to make room for the other Germans and those who received German nationality by birth even though they might never have lived in the country - die Volksdeutschen.

While the potential problems created for Turkish Berliners by the disintegration of the DDR and the Eastern European social systems were not of immediate concern to them, the collapse of Eastern Europe gave some cause for optimism from an Islamic perspective. The line of reasoning was that the fall of communism was simply the first bastion, capitalism would then follow as the next bastion to fall, thus revealing

---

[10] Their response to the Soviet military intervention in Aserbajdsjan also appears on a flyer which they were co-signatories of (see Appendix H).

Islam's universal actuality. The reason why capitalism had a greater ability to survive than communism was that it had a greater flexibility and ability to adjust itself. This ability actually consisted of the fact that broadly speaking it could adopt partial elements from Islam. But the direction was obvious, the flow was towards an Islamic society.

> Communism has changed, its strength has broken down very quickly. The free market economy is changing, and we firmly believe that it will continue to turn in an Islamic direction. And we hope that at some point or another it will end up as Islam (Mehmet, Appendix A,10).

A Millî Görüş imam outlines the situation, and the Islamic perspective on the collapse of the East bloc, similarly:

> For years Muslims have lived in the various countries of the East bloc. After Perestrojka was set in motion in the Soviet Union the East Europeans began to search for a new form of society. It turned out that capitalism became the aim. However, not even capitalism can provide the solution for these people, since capitalism and communism are, to a certain degree, almost the same system. Muslims are oppressed under capitalism, just as they are under communism. That is to say that the Muslims cannot live freely. What is happening, for example, in the Soviet Union, in Azerbaijan, Tajikistan, and Kazakhstan clearly shows that this regime and *Perestrojka* have not brought any advantages for the Muslims. On the other hand Estonia, Latvia and Lithuania are now independent and are recognised as such by the Western world. The Western countries, that is to say the capitalist countries do not speak out against anything, even though so many people have been killed in Azerbaijan
>
> The great difference between the national movement in Lithuania and the movement in Azerbaijan is simply that while the first is Christian, the second is Muslim. That is why the Soviet regime has stepped in by using military power in Azerbaijan, but not in Lithuania, and for the same reasons the West has only supported the Lithuanian people and not the others!
>
> After Gorbachov and Bush met in Malta in 1989 they worked out some common rules.

The imam suggested that after this meeting Bush began his military oppression in Panama and Gorbachov did the same in Azerbaijan. Before they met Gorbachov had been in Italy with the pope in the Vatican - and who knows what suggestions and solutions were raised there? Although there are obviously differences within Christianity, it is, nevertheless, the same religion, which is why there is not the same violent suppression in Latvia and Lithuania.

The imam continued:

> After these events had taken place Gorbachov and Bush co-operated on reopening the former centre for Orthodox Christianity in Istanbul. There is a special aim in mind, in that Azerbaijan and the neighbouring regions inhabited by Muslims which, in passing, have beautiful natural surroundings, undoubtedly will reveal themselves as having many economic opportunities. That is why they seek to suppress these states. In time Islam will, however, regain its immediacy and reveal itself as an alternative to communism and capitalism and other systems. Therefore people like Gorbachov and Bush will mobilise any regime against Islam, to prevent Islam from appearing as a real alternative to the populations. The capitalist and communist systems will not accept the emergence of an Islamic state or power.
>
> As it appears in articles such as in Time Magazine, one can see that in the West there are two groups of Muslims. One group are the Muslims who pray and do their duty and the other group of Muslims are not so faithful and do not live up to their duties as Muslims. It is this last group which the West will support and not the others.

The Western capitalist system is no guarantee for man's freedom. Therefore the imam is of the firm conviction that that the capitalist system will prove not to be a viable alternative for the populations of Eastern Europe in general. From an Islamic perspective there is no great difference between capitalism and communism, the imam stresses: The greatest difference is that what is produced in the capitalist countries is offered to the population who therefore can live a little more freely. While on the cultural side the social conditions of the population are almost the same. In East Europe too, one can practise one's religion as a part of everyday life. One can virtually do what one likes - as in the West. On the other hand the people have no opportunity to develop their production and their economy freely. This is, however, just a small difference in capitalism's favour, which does not deserve to make it a real alternative. The population in the East bloc can perhaps in the current situation be amenable to the belief that the situation is as such because they now feel a new freedom. Later, however, they will come to see the reality of their situation, the imam believes.

The EU and the rest of Europe is Christian. There are religious, cultural and social differences between here and the Muslim regions and states, says the Imam. That is why the Vatican could win Europe over to its views. If, say, Turkey were allowed into the EU, the Turkish people would have to give up Islam, give up their culture and their history. Therefore Millî Görüş does not support the idea that Muslims should seek membership of EU.

The chairman of the Danish section of AMGT explains that they oppose Turkey's membership of the EU for several reasons:

> a) EU is dominated today, seen from the economic angle, by 50 monopolies. These monopolies would also come to rule over the Turkish economy.
> b) EU is a community of *Christian* countries. The incorporation of Turkey would come to mean a demand of assimilation. The Turks would lose their own culture, it could not remain a Muslim country.
> It was to stress Turkey's intentions regarding the EU's desire to suppress Islam that the current government banned women from wearing the headscarf, *basörtüsü*, and the Islamic head covering *tessettür* in Turkish educational institutions.
> c) In the case of national disorder occurring in a Turkey that lay within the framework of a strengthened and expanded EU, there would be no hesitation in sending the military in to put down the unrest, precisely because the Turks are *Muslims*. It is, as such, quite typical of the Soviet today that the place where national unrest is being put down militarily is in the Muslim regions, such as Azerbaijan and Tajikistan.

Millî Görüş is itself quite convinced that Turkey's application for membership of the EU will be turned down, simply because it is a Muslim country. One of the principles of the EU is that the majority of the population can have the final say in any decision taking, the above named Millî Görüş imam continued:

> If we, as Muslims, put forward our opinions they will not be accepted. We do not think that Muslims should enter into such an EU and ask for permission to have their rights met. We do not support the idea of Muslims who wish to practise their religion having to have special permission for this granted by the EU. The European community claims that it is a democratic community. This community ought to understand democracy as being that all people can live their lives according to their own values. It is not a democracy if we have to ask for permission to get what is obviously our right.

The conclusion of this point of view which is prevalent in AMGT, is that capitalism is not a real alternative to communism. To this Islamic movement Islam provides an alternative to both systems. It is also stressed that there are no true Islamic states in existence; there are only a number of speculations as to what form an Islamic alternative might take.[11]

---

[11] For one version of an Islamic alternative see my interview with a Millî Görüş imam from the Berlin section, Appendix I.

Let us, however, in the following section, attempt to link the actual political positions as we have seen with a more universal view which refers to the necessity of faith and solidarity.

3. B. 4 The Islamic Outlook and the Community

AMGT realised that they had a problem in that they had not attempted to explain themselves. Therefore, in 1989/90 they decided to re-issue a publication which in a brief manner sets out to explain some of their fundamental views - but only in Turkish.[12] The aim in re-printing this publication, as it is made clear at the beginning of the document, was that they did not want that,

> Those who say that they are religious and traditional should sully Millî Görüş and thereby come to stand side by side with the Zionists, communists, socialists and non-Muslims (Appendix E).

The publication stems from the early 1970s and was originally produced for use in Turkey. Despite this the organisation considers its authenticity to be intact and of general value to the Turkish-Muslim minority in Western Europe.

According to the text, joining Millî Görüş does not simply mean that one follows Islam at a personal level, but also in a political sense too:

> Even were the Meccans were to give me the sun in my right hand and the moon in my left, I would still preach the true faith, Islam, said the Prophet Muhammed to Abu Talib (op.cit.).

It would, then, not be acceptable for society to be led on the basis of materialistic values, which have a built in tendency to guide one astray from the true path.

A state whose population choose to base themselves on such an Islamic moral fundament is responsible for all of its subjects. The Islamic state must reciprocate the loyalty of its members and assure them a decent life. In the document there is a reference to the caliph Omar, the second caliph after the prophet Muhammed:

> 'If a wolf eats a sheep in Dicle, God will hold Omar responsible for it', said Omar. He also wrote to his Wali (Governor/LP) in Damascus, 'I have

---

[12] For the original text in Turkish, along with a translation of same, see Appendix E.

heard that you are building a palace. If you are paying for it from your own pocket then it is extravagance, but if it is from the state coffers then it is treachery,' he said, as he carried a sack of flour on his own back to the wife and children of a martyr (op.cit.).

Maintaining Islam as the fundament for all sociality means, according to the document's message, that all people are equal, access to business must be based on vocational competence and not on position or family. On the document there is a further reference to the caliph Omar: 'One must exert oneself to attain recognition, and therefore he would not give his closest friend work for which the man in question was not competent' (op.cit.). The same quality was evoked by the Ottoman sultan Selim: 'I prefer not to reward kin, but rather efficiency and loyalty (*liyakat*)', he said. And in the running of the state he followed the principles of *liyakat* and competence' (op.cit.)

With Islam as the guiding thread it should be possible to resist the Western, non-Muslim dominance and develop a trans-national Islamic community:

> He has never entered into league with any non-Muslim state (kafir state) and he has always, and without fear of death on God's path, worked to recreate the Ottoman empire. This is Osman bey's outlook (op.cit.).

> We are not they who receive orders from the USA, Europe, Soviet, China, IMF, EU, Zionists, socialists, fascists and all the other 'ists' on how to run the state, and nor from any non-Muslim (*kafirden*) or slanderers. On the other hand we are pure hearted and courageous leaders who only wish to receive orders from God with a clean heart and an indefatigable and brave soul and the experience of our forefathers. That is our outlook (op.cit.).

> We have no wish to become a member of the EU, but to conduct a foreign policy in the Middle East along with the Islamic countries - in an expanded co-operative with improved trade, because this will serve us better. This is our outlook (op.cit.).

In these quotations we can also see hints at ideas about the establishment of a regional (Islamic) economy, which is not dictated by the leading world market forces. Finally it is firmly set down in the text that there is a reliance on industrialisation. Islam is a guarantee of progress and development and not an expression of traditionalism and stagnancy.

To cite the Islamic idea references are made in the document to selected *hadith*, to the tales of the rightly guided caliphs, in this case, more specifically, to the caliph Omar. One aspect specific to Turkish Islam is that references to the period of greatness during the Ottoman empire are given prominent place.

The text moves from an abstract definition of what the Islamic outlook comprises to, in the final points, comment on more concrete actual political questions but still at the broad abstract level: for example, the Palestinian conflict, EU, national self-determination and Islamic law.

If, meanwhile, we wish to gain some insight into the ideological thinking of the movement, as such, as regards the minority Muslim population in Western Europe, we are wasting our time looking at this document. Instead, starting with a speech held by Imam Hacir,[13] chairman of Mescid-i-Ömer, Berlin, along with excerpts from my interviews with leading Millî Görüş members in Berlin, Paris and Copenhagen, we can construct a realistic picture of the movement's basic manner of thinking.

I first encountered, in a shorter form, Imam Hacir's speech (in German translation) - in the Berlin Senate's Ausländerbeauftragte. The excerpt was shown to me as an example of the movement's hostility to the surrounding world and its opposition to segregation. Since the speech is reprinted in the Islamische Föderation's publication, there is good reason to assume that here it was not considered particularly extreme.

It might possibly seem odd to pick out a relatively random text in this context. I am, however, of the opinion that it is possible with this in mind to use the speech to offset a broader analysis later on. The text is relevant and unique to include here because it is explicit, while still remaining on the level of principles to give an Islamic perspective of the social position of Muslims in Western Europe. The text upholds the faith and the religious community, which it sees as being quite crucial to the survival of the Muslim population. The argumentation for this is thorough and is accompanied throughout by comprehensive references to holy sources, primarily the Koran, but also hadith.

3.B.4.1 Faith and the Need for Solidarity

Imam Hacir underlines two supporting elements for Muslim society, of which the first is unconditional belief in God. The imam supports his argumentation with a couple of verses from the Koran:

> 'And this is your only *ummah* and I am your God and have fear and hope (al-Mu'minun 52)'.

---

[13] The speech by Imam Hacir, which carries the title, 'Muslims of the world, unite..' (*Ey! Dünya Müslümanlari Birlesiniz...*) is published in the Islamische Föderation's periodical in June 1988 (a translation appears in Appendix F).

> 'This is your ummah, this is the only ummah. I am your God, pray only to me (al-Anbiya 92)' (Appendix F).

The imam goes on to stress that:

> If you have the intention of having a strong faith and of spreading joy among the Muslims and have made it your intention to help others, then you have *takva*. God says in the holy Koran: 'He who has followed *takva* shall have a high place on the day of judgement.' On that day neither sons nor material goods shall help. Only with *takva*, a pure heart and fear of God will you be content in Paradise (op.cit.).

The message of Islam is, of course, universal, a point taken up by other representatives of Millî Görüş:

> Millî Görüş has no purpose beyond Islam, Millî Görüş works for Islam, Millî Görüş is Islam. In that sense it does not differentiate itself from others. Millî Görüş is nothing special: all Muslims are brothers, all people come from Adam and Eve, therefore we are brothers with all people (....) (this work, p. 60).

> (...), we can open our hearts not only to the Turks, but also to the Danes, to the Pakistanis, to the Africans. Islam is for the whole world. Islam is not just for this world, but also about life after death (this work, p. 62).

> **MILLÎ GÖRÜŞ IS: 'Even were the Meccans to give me the sun in my right hand and the moon in my left, I would still preach the true faith of Islam', he said. Without being afraid of non-Muslims or the apostates our prophet preached the true faith Islam to all. That was his outlook (Appendix E).

> You are not a Mu'min if you would do something for yourself which you would not do for others! (Appendix I).

Faced with this decisive perspective, all the minor, more particular concerns stand aside so as to allow the good forces to rally around the Islamic project.

> There is a fundamental idea in Islam that every Muslim is a brother. Muslims are each other's brothers, this is how they should look upon themselves. God's messenger, Muhammed, once said that if a *Mu'min*, a believer, cannot feel his brother's pain on the other side of the world then he is not a true believer! (Mehmet, Appendix A,1).

This brings us onto imam Hacir's second bearing element for Muslim society, the importance of solidarity in the Muslim community. Furthermore the imam supports the Koranic authenticity of solidarity with references to various *ayat*:

> 'You are the best *ummah* of all people. You encourage the good and forbid the bad things and believe in God' (al-Imran 110).
> 'It is only those who are Muslims who are one another's friends' (al-Tevbe 71).
> 'Muslims are without doubt brothers. Reconcile between brothers and have fear of God, and God will be merciful to you' (al-Hucurat 10, Appendix F).

The imam's vision had as its immediate target group the Muslim immigrant society in Berlin. He points the way towards a re-Islamisation in his speech, - for Islam to be given a higher profile within Muslim immigrant groups. He points out the threat to the Muslim community in their country of origin as well as in exile:

> When one has established an Islamic society it is not permitted for anyone to follow non-Islamic principles, Jewish or Christian principles. This will lead to a division of Islamic unity, he who does so will distance himself from Islam (op.cit.).

> Our God says in the holy Koran: 'Oh yea faithful, if a group of you follow the other religions of the Book they will take you away from your faith and thereby make you non-believers (kafir)' (al-Imran 100) (op.cit.).

> He who does not follow the Islamic principles will without doubt become a part of those who have several gods. And they will come outside the Islamic community and they will not have any connection with the Islamic community, even if they say *shahada* many times (op.cit.).

The imam adds that the time of the Prophet and the four Rightly Guided Caliphs, the golden age of Islam, grew out of a strong Islamic community, while the times when it waned were caused by the faith and the community being repressed. Today the situation of Muslims is filled with so much pain that there is not enough will in the world to stop it. Islamic unity is the best weapon against the destructive forces. This unity is one that cuts across nationality, party, class, or any other kind of group allegiance. This is a unity based on faith and according to which the individual will be judged: And as noted, those who have followed Takva will come to sit at the high table on Judgement Day.

The source of this threat to the Islamic project comprises a destructive alliance consisting of capitalist greed and Judaeo-Christian-Communist conspiracy, which with almost diabolic logic leads the attack against the Islamic project. No help is expected from this quarter (this work, p.93f and 95f.).

As mentioned above, Millî Görüş followers also often see the Rushdie case in the light of a conspiracy theory. It is explained that *The Satanic Verses* is not the work of Salman Rushdie alone, but that the book is a part of a shrewdly thought out and slanderous campaign against the Muslims, arranged by the CIA and the British government.

Facing this destructive combination are its victims: *The Islamic community*. The antagonism appears to be absolute and it is often described with historical illustrations as well as contemporary examples of the persistent vitality of this constellation in that mankind are presented as the victims, alienated from God.

Islamic hopes for the future rest on Islamic forces, but there are also forces which work in conjunction with a societal tendency. As was seen in the evaluation of developments in Eastern Europe, there is a hope, which is almost founded on evolution, by which the possibilities and conditions for the realisation of the Islamic society are encapsulated.

3.B.4.2 Islam as the Guiding Thread

With the evocation of the threat of an all encompassing destruction of the Islamic community which builds on the individual's faith in God and which, in its broadest sense, depicts the hopes of mankind, there is also an appeal for goodwill, whose innermost spirit is an abstract (Islamic) reason which is removed from any kind of connection to the conflicts of interest of concrete social reality.

But the world as conjured up by Millî Görüş is not content with constructing this scenario for a divided Islamic community: The movement sets up at the same time an authoritative framework for the necessary change of course.

This framework is not, however, based on political priorities but, on the contrary, is founded on guidelines which extend from roots in the holy scripture of Islam. It is, on the basis of their formulations concerning the Islamic alternative, difficult to decide how to define these guidelines more accurately, in that they simply appear as a frame for the development of an Islamic society and are not more closely elaborated on. First and foremost, the prospect of the destructive forces has an influential effect on the individual as well as on humanity as a binding argument for the Islamic alternative. Taken further, society is to align itself with the laws of God and as such devote their life to his representative the khalifa. With this Millî Görüş has to distance itself from the Western European concept of democracy:

> An actual democracy, where people rule themselves, does not exist. 'Democracy' is an invented term and a term with no substantial content. In the capitalist society, 'die Demokratie-Ländern', chooses 'the people' in actual fact, not the government. On the contrary it is those who have the capital in their hands who choose their own people for government. They have founded various parties and the people only have the opportunity to choose between these parties (Appendix I).

Despite this, a draft of a form of rule, which in several crucial respects resembles the Western European, based on a parliament elected by the people, is put forward. Apparently, though, the view is that the candidates will be recruited from among vocational experts who presumably would be able to safeguard the common interest and on an enlightened foundation would be able to regulate eventual conflicts of interests (op.cit.).

It is difficult to decide what Millî Görüş's concept of God consists of other than conditions which support the Islamic utopian project. There are some indications in the interviews with organisation leaders in Denmark and Berlin. To get a clear message however we must resort to the pamphlet, 'What is Millî Görüş?' (Appendix E), Imam Hacir's speech 'Muslims of the world, unite!' (Appendix F) and the interview with the imam on 'The Islamic Alternative' (Appendix I).

The results of the interview can not unreservedly be regarded as definitive, authorised material, but bearing this reservation in mind, and along with the pamphlet and the imam's speech, I do believe that it is possible to illustrate certain tendencies which Millî Görüş and the Islamic movement as a whole *also* contain, and which perhaps represent immediate central underlying elements in the vague definition of the concept of God.

The Millî Görüş leaders proclaim frequently, and willingly, that the Islamic viewpoint, 'the new world view', pre-empts modern science:

> 'We must accept that we do not always completely understand what the holy texts are trying to tell us', the chairman explained. 'It was not possible in the day of the Prophet to know, for example, that television would one day be invented. Nevertheless this was anticipated in the Koran: The Prophet Muhammed told a story which today we can see contains a prediction about television. He foresaw, for example, that people would be able to move from one place to another faster than the eye can blink' (this work, p. 63).

> Es ist ja auch eines unserer Ziele, den Islam innerhalb der Wissenschaften wieder voranzubringen. Es gab ja lange eine Zeit wo der Islam die Führung innerhalb der Wissenschaften hatte, viele hundert Jahre her. Das möchten wir wieder haben, weil der Islam wirklich den Menschen mit ihren Wissenschaften dient (Appendix A, 2).

Even the Islamic system of government should - in the interpretation given by one Millî Görüş imam - be led by professional experts! (Appendix I). The reference to the scientific aspect of the Koran is utilised as a springboard in the creation of an Islamic cosmology which can integrate modern identity. It is clear that a worldview which can argue for its concordance with modern science is thereby seeking to create an important alliance partner.

In other words it is claimed that the demand to adhere to Islam's guidelines is in perfect agreement with modern conditions. The main principle is that Islam is a natural religion which has anticipated modern science. And as the precursor of modern science, Islam constitutes a gift to mankind, - a gift that can be used to reveal the depths of Islam.

But when all is said and done what matters is that Islamic solidarity reflects back to its positive origins, which supersede both race and nationality:

> We Muslims, living in Berlin, must accept the difficulties which are associated with living in another society and we must overcome the difficulties with an unshakeable faith and an unbreakable unity. We must understand and live in accordance with Islam. Islam is a world religion and it does not accept division and superiority. It measures each individual according to 'takva' ('the understanding and following of Islam'/LP). In this religion a Muslim Turk, Muslim Arab, Muslim Afghan and a Muslim German, are all brothers.
>
> The Prophet says, 'An Arab is not better than a non-Arab, and a non-Arab is not better than an Arab, and a white is not better than a black and nor is a black better than a white, but the measure of which one is the best, is the one who has 'takva'(Appendix F).

3.C Summary

AMGT has, over the last decade, undergone a transformation from being a Turkish Islamist movement in exile, whose interests lay primarily within the Turkish state-political landscape, to being a Turkish-European Islamic movement whose interests now lie to a great extent in the area of the organisation of Islamic identity among Turkish immigrant minorities in Europe.

The movement is divided internationally into regions, *bölgesi*, which are linked to a centre (in Köln), whose function is actually more that of implementing organisation rather than dictating policy - this allows for the exchange of experiences on a European-wide plan.

At the local level the movement's members constitute the main nucleus in a network of unions which receive public support under the national guidelines concerning this, whether it be in Aarhus, Berlin, or Paris. In this way it can be said that the movement's departments or sections, organise their members doubly: in part they are part of an international network centred around a common vision which, historically speaking, springs from a common national background. In part also they constitute the framework surrounding local activities with concrete social qualities which are important to the everyday life of the members of the centres and which run at their own tempo. The crucial service which the movement provides is the establishment of new opportunities for activities which are very varied in character and of relevance to the Turkish, Islam-motivated minority in Western Europe: sport, study groups, cultural activities, women's groups and of course mosques.

The extent of Millî Görüş's activities naturally rests on the fundament of its membership. The movement also does as much as it can, depending on local opportunities, to influence social processes in the country they are established in. This could be through seeking to establish Islamic private schools or by taking part in state advisory bodies.

- Millî Görüş's radical nature is therefore most vividly revealed in the more dogmatic texts and in the interviews with seek to illuminate the movement's worldview at a more general and abstract level, for example, in relation to the breakdown of the system in Eastern Europe.

-The high profile of Millî Görüş is also obvious in relation to their own analysis of the situation of Muslims in Western Europe, where a strong defence of the Islamic community is offered as the only possibility for survival.

-Matters such as their stance regarding the Rushdie case demonstrate Millî Görüş's ability to compromise in seeking to adjust to the democratic structures in Western Europe.

Millî Görüş seeks to link the religious and social practise through a global vision that is centred around an Islamic moral standpoint. One can say that the movement hereby contributes to the expansion of possibilities for the staging of the social and cultural interest among immigrant Turkish Muslims. In this manner the movement is explicitly challenging the Turkish state authority's assumed role as guardians of Turkish cultural heritage in Western Europe.

The movement criticises the lack of formal recognition of Islam in Europe, just as it criticises the Christian (Western) world for having aggressive intentions towards the Muslim world. But the movement's principle legalist and compromise-seeking orientation, and the movement's experience of functioning in surroundings hostile to Islam mean that the movement, generally speaking, is in a weak position as far as the European state public is concerned, and in regard to the ambition which it also has, of involvement in the political life on the country they are in, as a mediating stage between the minority Muslim population and the state authorities.

As mentioned I shall, in the concluding chapter (7), conduct a more comprehensive analysis of the universal aims of the movement as seen in the context of the social processes with which the members of the movement are involved in Western Europe.

In the following section I shall attempt a clarification which includes the way in which Islam is organised at the local level, and how the Islamic movements comprise a social opportunity which connects collectively to a religiously formulated identity among the individual members of the movement.

4 Islam in Daily Life

It was earlier ascertained that the new ethnic minorities, once referred to as 'fremmedarbejdere' (foreign workers), began to arrive in Denmark towards the end of the 1960s and the beginning of the 1970s (Pedersen 1991a). They worked for low wages in what were mostly dirty and difficult manual jobs which others were no longer prepared to do. Today, these immigrants are marginalised, both socially and economically. There is a high rate of unemployment and their future prospects on the labour market look bleak. They are, as the title of Günther Walraff's book so aptly puts it, 'Ganz unten', at the bottom. The story of the immigrants, the new ethnic minorities is, in this respect, a bleak one.

The discussion of the 'second generation problem' is important when seen in the perspective of the public institutions (ibid.). The institutions constitute an obvious arena in which to wage the battle over the 'second generation problem'. It is clear to those experts involved, counsellors as well as pedagogues and school teachers, that there are objective reasons for the problems between immigrants and the field of institutions. These affect general conditions in the structure of the institutions, and therefore also create problems for Danish children. The argument being that it is not only immigrant children who are affected by reductions in funding. When it comes to the immigrant children, however, it is implied that the problems are due first and foremost to 'subjective' causes which can be traced back to the particular, culture-specific backgrounds of the immigrants. These culture-specific aspects of the socialisation problematic are only ever given a cursory examination, and if so they are limited by specifying a particular aim of implementation. In Denmark, as in the rest of Europe, 'Islam' is not considered a 'natural/given' part of social life. On the contrary 'the Islamic' is rejected by society at large/the majority,- 'Muslims' are assigned a place among other sub-cultures.

We have seen that Muslim immigrants are 'culturally' disqualified and marginalised alongside their social and economic marginalisation. They are not only perceived as being culturally different, they are also seen as being different from 'us' by nature. They are fundamentally of another nature, and this compounds their disfavour. Their cultural values are looked down upon. 'Islam' is thereby forced to seek legitimacy where 'we' define the agenda. The assumption being that 'we' (non-Muslims) know what Islam is and are only content insofar as Muslims are prepared to confirm this knowledge.

The groups of immigrant Turks and Pakistanis often come from a rural background, from small towns and villages where Islam was an integral part of their daily life. While in itself this may be a banal fact, it is, nevertheless, an important point to recognise that the religious symbols and rites of Islam are not corroborated in and through the social environment which immigrants inhabit in Denmark.

The public circumstances under which these immigrants lived with 'Islam' are gone, which is why a new area of interpretation is developing for Muslims. This not only raises the question of how to live as a Turk/Pakistani and Muslim in a non-Muslim environment, but also, how to live as a Turk/Pakistani and Muslim in a non-Muslim, Western, industrialised society?

This question is central for the immigrant Muslims and these are questions which need to be answered not only in relation to the individual frame of reference, but must also be considered on a collective basis.

The most significant political currents and organisations among immigrants in Europe have always been linked to their countries of origin. That is to say that political conflicts and divisions, whether in Turkey, Pakistan, Morocco, or Algeria, have also been played out in Europe. There has, then, been a steady influx of political material and conflict into Europe. This can be applied equally to the left wing movements as to the nationalist right wing, and also to the Islamists.

Characteristically, immigrant groups do not find that existing European unions and political organisations cater sufficiently to their needs.[1] Conversely, a need develops to organise themselves into their own associations, be they of a political, social or cultural character.

The immigrants thus create institutional frameworks within which the religious life can be developed. Striving for organisation is not, however, restricted to this domain, but comprises other areas as well. There exists, therefore, a comprehensive and varied association life among immigrants in Europe which covers all aspects of life: religion, sport, education, music and folk dance, theatre. Usually it is the case that these organisations are structured along ethnic lines - association linked to 'home'. Looking only at organisations which are run by Muslim immigrant groups we find mosque associations, sports clubs, youth associations, and women's unions. There are associations which are linked at the

---

[1] See also Rex, Joly, & Wilpert (eds.) (1987) as well as Schoeneberg (1983).

international level, and there are nation-wide organisations. But the majority, by far, of all these organisations are those based on local activities, usually in connection with a particular housing area.

Most organisations have a purpose which extends beyond the narrowly defined activities mentioned above. Their aim is to create a cultural free zone which provides the skeletal structure for the development of a cultural identity through the organisation of activities for immigrants. Similarly, they see themselves as cultural administrators within a multicultural society. In this way, these organisations are not simply centres for the formulation of questions about immigrant policies, but are also centres for the re-interpretation of a new collective identity. These organisations mark the start of a new phase in the administration of cultural heritage. The existing associations offer a community for the immigrants on a basis of varied ideologies and cultural profiles.

On the basis of the collective framework which the Muslim immigrants have established in Aarhus we can identify three different discourses: 1) a secular, non-religious, and potentially anti-religious discourse, 2) a national cultural discourse and 3) an Islamist discourse. These discourses are central to the social life of the Aarhus immigrant organisations in their structure and perception of themselves (Pedersen 1991c):

Ad 1) The secular, non-religious or anti-religious unions.
This group, historically speaking, is the one which was the first to establish itself in Aarhus, as was the case throughout the rest of Denmark and the rest of Europe. It is they who, as Ralph Grillo (1985) demonstrates in the case of Lyon, France, are usually best placed to speak on the behalf of immigrants. It is this group which has the best means of dialogue with the counselling system. They are usually of a left wing orientation even though they stress their broad political appeal. They refuse to incorporate religious life into the activities of the unions because they say it is divisive. Taken on European-wide level, however, there are individual examples of left wing groups beginning to organise religious activities. The majority in the largest member groups in these unions clearly consists of younger, i.e. second generation immigrants - although first generation immigrants do also take part. In the case of the Turkish immigrants, we find the *Alevi* immigrants in this group. To a certain extent, Danes can also be found involved in their running.

The group is involved in 'immigrant politics' at a national level also, in the sense that most of these unions participate in the only existing nation-wide, inter-ethnic, immigrant association. At the local level they are organised on the grounds of national, ethnic affiliation.

Ad 2) The national-cultural unions
This group sees it as their task to formulate 'national values' which include stressing 'Islam' as the anchor point for a national-religious community. They regard the establishment of Koran courses as being crucial to the upbringing of their children in the Diaspora. They consist first and foremost of first generation immigrants. They are, broadly speaking, in agreement with the national political development in their country of origin. They criticise the Islamists for misusing Islam for political purposes and they criticise the secular unions for being atheists and Communists. They believe that these two groups undermine solidarity with the homeland and threaten national identity in the Diaspora.

Their local unions seek to establish mosques or smaller places of prayer in their areas of residence. If these mosques have many members and if they are Turkish, they will be manned by hocas dispatched and paid for by Turkey.

The unions which fall into this group are, according to the nature of things, organised on the basis of national ethnic affiliations. The Turkish unions have created their own national union at the nation-wide level which seeks to establish itself as an alternative to the above mentioned dominant associations. That is to say that they are increasingly involved in work with 'immigrant politics'. The Aarhus-based union participate in this nation-wide work.

Ad 3) The Islamist unions
This is the newest group of unions and was first established in the mid-1980s. Like the other unions, these also provide general social activities, such as sports. The central focus, however, is 'Islam'. Islam is regarded a the central axis in the definition of cultural roots and new identity - which does not mean that national background is ignored. Study groups on Islam is one of their fields of activity and they criticise the secular unions for denying Islam, jut as they also criticise them for placing too much emphasis on 'folklore' activities, which they regard as being irrelevant to modern life. They criticise the national cultural unions for using Islam politically, as an instrument for the national aims of their home country.

On the national level they are organised on the basis of their country of origin in that they are rooted in the Islamist movements of their homeland. At the local level this root is maintained although to a certain degree they also function on an inter-national and inter-ethnic basis.

The group is clearly dominated by younger forces who have recognised that their future lies in this country but who also have a need to underline a collective standpoint in Islam. The local leaders are often people who have grown up in Denmark.

There can be little doubt that by utilising 'Islam' immigrants can develop a space, culturally and consciously, in which the ruling norms of Danish society do not apply. This can form the basis for the development of a strength and pride within a world which looks down upon them arrogantly. The disorientation or confusion of norms which can occur in migration, can be softened or averted. Belonging to 'the Islamic' becomes a stabilising element for the faithful Muslim in the identity crisis which can be brought on by migration: How far this comprises a repression or short term solution to the problem will be looked at later, but this will obviously depend on what alternative possibilities the ethnic minorities can actually envisage for themselves.

To the German religious-sociologist, Niklas Luhmann, religion acts in the system of society by transforming the indeterminable into a definable complexity. His formulation goes as follows, 'Religion hat (...) für das gesellschaftssystem die Funktion, die Unbestimmbare (...) welt in eiene Bestimmbare zu Transformieren (...)' (Luhmann 1977, p. 26).

This does not, however, mean that he subscribes to the thesis about the integrating function of religion. On the contrary he criticises it. He advances the idea that history also testifies to religious movements that blow the system apart or disintegrate it. Religious experiences can support a given social order or they can bring them into question. They can lead an individual to a position of affirmation, or to one of denial. They can have a constructive or destructive effect, and they can also transform themselves from one to another (Luhmann 1977).

The Turkish or Pakistani youth relate, as we shall see later, to 'Islam'. For some, 'Islam' offers a viable alternative. There should, however, be no doubt about the fact that 'Islam' does not fulfil this function of identification for all Muslim immigrants - although all must somehow relate to it, for some it is a very problematic matter.

We cannot then, on the basis of this, assume that there is a merging of 'Islam' and identity, or of religion and the significant activities of Muslim immigrants. Islam can, on the other hand, as an ideological manifestation, be ascribed and expressed in a particular sphere in human subjectivity. As a medium of conscious action.

To estimate what practises Islamism, in concrete terms, actually gives rise to in Western Europe, it will be relevant to describe the social landscape which constitutes Islamism's local organisational space. In the following I shall outline this on the basis of using the example of Aarhus. It will become apparent that the development of this religious space has, to a large extent, become differentiated over the passing years, since the first mosque was established in 1979.

Since the young make up the most important players in the Islamic movements I shall attempt to describe Islamism's practices primarily through two activity profiles. This enables us to get an idea of the relevance of Islamism at the personal level, where both the subjective and the objective levels are integrated in daily life. Or, in other words, the participant's own (private) as well as collective experiences.

4.1 The Structure of Religious Life in Aarhus[2]

As noted earlier, the Turkish-Muslim immigrant society in Aarhus consists in part of a large group of *Sunni*-Muslims, the majority of whom come from a number of villages in the Sivas district, although a small minority also come from villages in the Konya district, and partly of a small group of *Alevi* Muslims, a sect which sees itself as a part of *Shia*-Islam. This group stems from villages in the +orum district. In Aarhus, most of the *Alevites* are ethnic Kurds, although there are a few individual Turkish-*Alevite* families.

It is characteristic that there are no large social exchanges between *Sunni*-Muslims and *Alevites* (also regardless of the intensity of the religious engagement). No Alevites live in *Sunni*-dominated areas and as was shown earlier, the differences are repeated in the structure of the unions.[3] This difference can be traced back to a theological difference, one which is ascribed importance partly because of the situation of the *Alevites* as a minority in Turkey, both in the past and at present. The *Alevites* have been, as was described earlier, discriminated against and persecuted in Turkey.

Here, I shall not go through the connection to the five pillars of Islam, or the important guiding threads of doctrine (See Selmer 1991 for this). I will settle simply for listing the most important visible manifestations which thereby comprise the distinguishable differences between the two religiously defined groups: 1) *Alevites* have no mosque, 2) *Alevites* do not perform the five daily prayers, 3) *Alevites* do not fast in Ramadan (but for 12-15 days in *Muharram*), 4) *Alevites* do not make the *hajj* to Mecca, 5) *Alevites* do not participate in Koran courses, and 6) Religious doctrine is not manifestly communicated in relation to the outside

---

[2] This section, which appeared previously in Pedersen & Selmer (1991) was founded on observations made in the period from 1986 to 1988.

[3] This observation, that religious differences are reflected in the organisational system, likewise shows itself to be the case in Norwegian and German research material, respectively, Næss (1986) and Wilpert (1986).

world.[4] Although the Alevites are not without their collective rituals, they do not assume a public character in the manner displayed by *Sunni*-Islam.

The religious life of *Sunni*-Muslims in Aarhus - mainly Turks, Pakistanis and Arabs, of which the largest single nationality are the Moroccans - has, since the middle of 1986, centred around two mosques, with their own hocas (imams): one in the centre of town and the other in the Gellerup area.

The mosque in Gellerup is run by the 'Tyrkisk Kulturforening i Braband' (Pedersen 1991b, p. 118) and manned by a hoca sent by the Diyanet (Diyanet Işleri Başkanligi), the Turkish ministry for religious affairs. The Islamisk Kulturcenter in Aarhus is linked via its leadership to the Islamisk Kulturcenter in Horsebakken, in Copenhagen.[5]

The Islamisk Kulturcenter is led at the local level by a committee of 8 men, chosen by the centre's community. "We talk over the matter of who it should be," says the chairman, who claims that in principle there is agreement that the committee should be as broadly representative as possible in terms of nationality, 2-3 Turks, 1-2 Pakistanis and 2-3 Arabs.

The Islamisk Kulturcenter does not receive public funding, - they 'don't want it.' Why not? 'Because it is not necessary, we could get it if we wanted, but we don't want it!' The chairman dismisses the idea that this is linked to a principle of not wanting to receive help from non-Muslims. To cover the smaller costs, such as minor repairs, a collection is made within the community. The cultural centre is, however, also financially linked to the Islamisk Kulturcenter, Horsebakken, Copenhagen, which, for its part, receives funds from Saudi Arabia and a lesser sum from Pakistan. The salaries of the imams have generally been covered by the countries that provide them; During the period up to the spring of 1986, for example, two Turkish imams were sent out by Turkey and Saudi Arabia, respectively. Their replacement is, likewise, a Turk. He is however being paid by the Islamisk Kulturcenter directly. The replacement of these two was explained

---

[4] This 'under-communication' of religious matters is in its own way religiously sanctioned by *Shiism's* principle of *takiya*, a pragmatic principle which, among other things, includes considerations about the necessity of caution in relation to social intercourse in potentially hostile surroundings.

[5] The Islamisk Kulturcenter, Horsebakken, is the oldest gathering place for Muslims in Copenhagen, according to a spokesman for the Islamisk Kulturcenter, Abdel Wahid Pedersen. The centre was set up in 1974 and moved to its current location, due to a shortage of space, in 1976. Since then, for a variety of reasons - linguistic, national, political, some divisions have formed. Today the place is used mostly by Pakistanis and Afghanis. The Turks have their own mosques. Abdel Wahid estimates that today there are 5-6 *jawami* (pl. *jami*, large mosques) and around 10 *masajid* (pl. *masjid*, smaller places of prayer) in Copenhagen.

to this ethnographer not as being due to religio-political considerations, as some in the Muslim community might believe, but with regard to the new imam's linguistic abilities. The former imams spoke only Turkish. The new one is a linguistic treasure for the community which is otherwise, in nationality terms, heterogeneous in that, apart from Turkish, he also spoke Urdu and Arabic. His theological education had been gained partly in Pakistan and partly from Al-Azhar in Egypt. Furthermore, he also spoke a little English!

These mosques, in the centre of town and in the Gellerup area, respectively, are known to those who frequent them by the name *jami*, which means that they are regarded as large gathering places for Friday prayers, among other things - in contrast to the smaller ordinary masjid. These jami are simply furnished and without undue ornamentation. The premises originally served other purposes and were not built with the idea in mind that they should serve as Muslim places of prayer. In this respect they are not oriented in the right direction, and the *qibla* is marked with the use of stripes, for example, on the floor.

Both mosques are used on a daily basis as well as for Friday prayers, just as they are also used for special occasions in connection with religious celebrations, such as *Ramadan, Id al-Fitr, Id al-Adha, Mawlid al-Nabi*, etc.[6] In connection with the celebration of these festivals guest hocas are often invited. The Turkish Diyanet sends several hocas to meet the great demand so that some can be invited to come from Germany, for example, both for the sake of Ramadan as well as for the Mawlid. The mosque is similarly used for prayer in connection with deaths.[7] There are,

---

[6] *Mawlid* (or *Veladet Kandili*) marks respect and love for the prophet in special ceremonies. Stories are told about the prophet's life and revelations. Special *dua* are said. There is agreement that the observation of *mawlid* is neither *farz* (mandatory) nor *sunna* (reccomended). Some claim that according to certain *hadith* it is forbidden in that it is associated with idolatry (c.f. also the Wahhabis and other later purifying movements). Since *Mawlid* is celebrated at night, it is usually celebrated here at the weekends.

[7] The funeral takes place normally in the homeland if the deceased is an adult, while children are usually buried here in Denmark. According to the funeral authority for the municipality of Aarhus, since 1973 there have been 'a maximum of 21 Muslims buried, of which 19 were children, in the municipality graveyard in Aarhus' (Letter from the funeral authority in Århus Kommune to the city's Muslim immigrant organisations). We know from other sources that the remaining two adults were refugees for whom burial at home was not an option. There are now Muslim burial sites linked to communal graveyards in other sites in Denmark. In Aarhus one such site was opened in the autumn of 1987 following efforts made by the Islamisk Kulturcenter, among others. The degree to which the mosque is used in connection with burials depends on where the burial is to take place. If it is to be in Denmark the

furthermore, Koran courses still being offered, both for children, and at times for adult men and women. Through the mosques the community are urged to pay *zakat*[8] and *fitr*,[9] even though none of them, according to the information given, is effectively responsible for the actual collections. Likewise, the mosques provide information about making the *hajj*.[10]

Which of the city's two mosques one chooses to frequent depends primarily upon where one is located. This, automatically, results in the mid-town mosque being a place where Muslims of all nationalities collect, while the mosque in the western part of Aarhus is by and large used by Turks who live there, although the Turkish Islamists actually gather at the mid-town mosque. Religious life is, meanwhile, a segregated practice in terms of the sexes. And it is the men who make daily use of the mosques. Mostly women conduct their practices at home, and in different forms on a daily basis.

Most Turkish *Sunni*-Muslims start and end Ramadan on the dates given by the Turkish authorities. These are marked in the national calendar which every Turkish home is equipped with. Over and above this the Diyanet sends out guidelines every year with dates for the beginning and end of the month of fasting, with the times given for when to start and break the fast each day.[11] The other *Sunni*-Muslims (Pakistanis, Arabs and

---

prayer, *Salat al-Janaza*, takes place in the mosque. After the body has been ritually washed from head to foot (*Ghusul abdesti*) in hospital, dressed in a body sheet, *kafan*, taken to the mosque where the prayers are to take place (this prayer does not include any *rakas*). In Denmark the dead are furthermore buried in a coffin.

If the burial is to take place in the homeland, the burial prayer will be conducted in the hospital, after which the body is transported home. In this case the mosque is not involved. Ordinarily the funeral prayer is done at the burial site, *janaza*.

[8] One hoca estimates that about half of the Turkish Muslims pay *zakat*, i.e. 2.5% of their total annual resources. Typically one would, he says, pay around half of this to one's own Turkish family and the other half to Turkish aid organisations, such as through the Diyanet.

[9] In contrast to *zakat* (c.f. note 8) according to one hoca everyone paid *fitr*, a fixed sum given to the poor at the end of *Ramadan*, just before *Bayram*. The sum of money is calculated by Diyanet and is set at 50Dkr and is equivalent to the cost of food for one person for one day. The money is usually sent to Danish aid organisations for people hit by famine, for example, he explained.

[10] Every Muslim who wishes to make the *hajj* has, in order to get a visa for Saudi Arabia, to document that he or she is a Muslim. In Denmark the Islamisk Kulturcenter or Rabita (Rabita al-'Alam al-Islamiya, i.e. Muslim World League) have to confirm this.

[11] The times are calculated for Copenhagen and corrected for a number of Danish cities: Aarhus, Odense, Holbæk, Køge, Slagelse and Roskilde.

Turkish Islamists) follow, as noted above, the guidelines distributed by the Islamisk Kulturcenter in Copenhagen.

Islamisk Kulturcenter 'follows' the moon as far as defining the beginning and end of *Ramadan* are concerned, effectively this means that they follow the practice in the Islamic world. In purely practical terms a message is received from the Islamisk Kulturcenter in Copenhagen. The imams from the mosques in Copenhagen gather the day before the expected start and finish of the month to attend short-wave radio or television broadcasts from Saudi Arabia and other Islamic countries. When sufficient information has been gathered, i.e. 6 or 7 countries have declared that the moon has appeared, agreement is declared. The month of fasting can begin. Islamisk Kulturcenter cannot accept Turkey's predetermined dates. Therefore the same celebration is only marked once in the centre. The chairman was of the opinion that Turkey was mixing politics with Islam, just as he meant that increasing numbers of people realised what correct Islam was.

This fact means that Ramadan does not always start and end in Denmark for all Muslims at the same time. Some follow the recommendations of the Islamisk Kulturcenter and others those of the Diyanet. Often it is the case of there being a day's difference between them. This also means that *Id al-Fitr* (*Ramazan Bayrami*) is started on two different days, as is the celebration on the 27th night of *Ramadan*, *Laylat al Qadr* (*Kadir Gecesi*) which fall on two successive days.[12]

Like the festival prayers, *Salat al-Id* (*Bayram Namazi*), which mark the start of Ramazan Bayrami just after sunrise, the festival prayer which begins the sacrifice of *Id al-Adha* is an event that nearly all Muslim men participate in. This does not imply that they all consider themselves to be religious, or in any way practising Muslims, but rather that this occasion affirms one as belonging to the community. Participation in the prayer at the start of *Id al-Adha* is also seen as a pre-condition for participation in the day's ritual slaughter of a sheep or cow, if for no other reason than 'for the sake of the family'. When, in some cases, this means that the existing mosque is not big enough, then other, larger premises have to be hired.

At these two events, *Bayram Namazi* in connection with *Ramazan Bayram*, and *Kurban Bayram*, the special Turkish greeting after the prayer, *bayramlasmak*, is made in its quite unique manner which distinguishes it from the daily after prayer greeting, *tokalasmak*. *Tokalasmak* is conducted out by the individual going around and greeting others with words which

---

[12] On the 27th night of *Ramadan*, *Laylat al-Qadr*, when the Prophet is said to have received his first revelation, the men gather for a common prayer and meal. For some, this ritual takes place every night throughout the month.

mean 'God has heard your prayer'. *Bayramlasmak,* is made to 'preserve love and respect for one another', and as such affirms the community, is made in a particular fashion. The community lines itself up according to age, after which, starting with the youngest, everyone moves along the line in turn until everyone has greeted everyone.[13] On these occasions it does, however, happen that some people do not wish to participate in this part of the ritual, but quite simply slip out of it. One of those who did exactly this explained that this part was not important to him, and that he did not wish to greet people whom he did not like. This shows, then, that daily conflicts can quite easily interfere the carrying out of the rite. He only participated in the prayer because later in the day he was to attend the slaughter of a cow on behalf of his family. The prayer which, on that occasion, he was to repeat with his hand on the cow's forehead, demanded ritual cleanliness.

At the *Id al-Adha/Kurban Bayram* a ritual slaughter takes place. In Denmark this usually takes place out in the country on a farm. For the farmers and merchants involved this provides them with a good day's income. That the traders prefer to avoid the limelight was vividly illustrated for me when I arranged with a Turkish family to attend the slaughter. After the ritual prayers, which took place in a community hall in Gellerup, and after the breakfast which followed with the family, we set off for the farm where the slaughter was to take place. The merchant expelled me from the proceedings immediately and I was told that I had no business being there. So as not to cause any offence to my Turkish 'hosts', I withdrew immediately. After the slaughter, the Turkish man whom I had arrived with was told by the Danish merchant that he would not deal with him again in future, something which he took quite calmly, saying that 'my family will help me' next time.

This slaughter, which for all immigrant Muslims is the symbolic re-enactment of God's intervention when Abraham was to sacrifice Ismail, and as such carries a great deal of significance, is, in the Danish context, actually criminalised. This was further illustrated when a newly opened *halal*-butcher, after having told a journalist that he knew of a great deal of such illegal butchering, was reported to the police for having knowledge of criminal actions.[14]

---

[13] Only the Turks have this special tradition for *bayramlasmak* after *Bayram Namaz*. *Salat al-Id* ends for the others with everyone greeting everyone with *taslim salam*. This greeting is used on other occasions too: Danish new year, Islamic new year, birthdays, etc., i.e. events that mark the beginning of a new cycle of a year.

[14] Outside the Copenhagen area it is difficult for Muslims to buy any *halal*-prepared meat other than chicken. Several slaughterhouses do produce *halal* meat, but this is with a view to the export market in the Middle East. The *halal* killing of chickens and cows can take place with the approval of the Islamisk Kulturcenter in

It should be noted that not all Muslims carry out this slaughter in Denmark. Instead they let the family back in the homeland carry out the sacrifice on their behalf. Some explain their not carrying out the slaughter in Denmark as being due to the lack of suitable conditions: the slaughtered creature should, in principle, be divided into three portions, one for the family, one for the neighbours and one third for the poor (*zakat*). But, they argue, the welfare state has done away with poverty in Denmark, which makes that particular third irrelevant and therefore the sacrifice should be dropped. Others would choose to give this 'poor' part to newly married couples who are trying to start a new life, and maybe even to a Danish neighbour, perhaps with the proviso that no alcohol be consumed with it!

As mentioned, taking part in the *hajj* is organised by both religious centres. As in the case of Ramadan, here too we find that there are differences. One mosque organises tours within the framework of the Turkish state, i.e. the pilgrims will make up part of the Turkish contingent. The other mosque organises *hajj* trips in connection with West German Islamic organisations.

4.1.1 Koran-i-kerim kürsü - Koranic Courses for Children[15]

Koran courses are now offered for children by both of the city's mosques in which both boys and girls participate. In principle, naturally, these Koran courses are open to all nationalities. In practice, in Aarhus, they are effectively only attended by Turkish children. The language barrier makes it complicated to mix nationalities. On the other hand however, the size of the non-Turkish Muslim community in the city is so small that independent continuous, 'publicly' administrated courses are impractical. These children are then left to the religious upbringing which can be provided within the family.

The extent of the teaching varies: two places offer teaching for two hours twice a week (Saturday and Sunday) and a third one offers 5 times, 3 hours a week (Sunday to Thursday). According to the figures provided, gathered through interviews, around half of the city's 6-14 year-old Turkish

---

Copenhagen. The Kulturcenter will assist abbatoirs in finding a qualified Muslim to attend the butchery. To get the necessary permission to butcher in the *halal* way in Denmark it is required that the creature be sedated before the air canal and the main artery are cut. There is a debate among Muslim scholars about whether or not the anaesthetizing of the animals is acceptable. Not all Muslims consider it necessary for the meat to be prepared in this way. The very fact that getting hold of *halal* meat is so difficult makes it not obligatory.

[15] This section previously appeared in Pedersen and Selmer (1991) was finished on the basis of observations during the period from 1986 to 1988.

Sunni-Muslims attended in the autumn of 1986. This is not to say that only half of the population attends organised Koran teaching. Participation in teaching varies individually, people do not sign up for a set course, as such. How long one attends depends on the level of insight and proficiency one wishes to attain. It is quite possible, although unlikely, that all Turkish *Sunni*-Muslim children will attend a Koran course at one time or another. Some will cease attending after reading and memorising the most important *ayat*, with regard to *namaz dua* (prayer), i.e. the last three verses of the Koran and the opening verse, *al-Fatiha*. Along with the learning of the Arabic alphabet, one hoca estimated that this would require perhaps 6 months with two hours twice a week. For others it is important that the entire Koran is read, and yet others wish to deepen their understanding through a form of recitation, such as *tecvidi* (Arab: *tajwid*) which involves reciting the Koran with the stress on the pronunciation and intonation, a deepening of the aesthetic dimensions of the reading in accordance with established rules. This is practised with the use of special *tecvidi*-booklets. According to one hoca there was no child in Aarhus who was *Hafez al-Koran* (Arab: *Hafiz al-Qur'an*), i.e. someone who has memorised the entire Koran. 'It would be an unreasonable demand to make on the child's time outside of school,' he says.

An average day's teaching would comprise the following: 1) The pupils would be heard reading a text from the Koran. Since the passage read is assigned individually, each pupil will have prepared their own piece. Depending on their competence this can vary, depending on the student, from a few lines to a whole page of text. The student sits and reads to the hoca, not to the class. The beginners, most typically the younger students, then practise the Arabic alphabet using special booklets. 2) The hoca then talks them through a few *ayat* about the founding of Islam, its outlook and particular rules regarding prayer, for example. 3) The pupils recite by rote, and according to age, chosen *ayat* at the hoca's request, often there is some talk about *namaz dua*. 4) *Namaz* (prayer) for those who read the Koran, and thus know the relevant *namaz dua*. The boys are all dressed in *tarkar* (small, often white, knitted caps), while the girls wear a headscarf.

The Koran courses are then an aspect of practising the Islamic faith including, among other things, the *ayat* required for prayer, in Arabic, and with accompanying explanation. In addition, the children's understanding of Islam is deepened, and this includes by means of the retelling of the prophet's Sunnah, and the stories of the Rightly Guided caliphs, and of the religious rites and duties.

The Koran courses are led by hocas, that is to say people with a special religious education. This education can take two forms, either a regular theological university education from a imam-hatip faculty, or else a period of learning at a Koran school in Turkey. In the last case this education would take place in parallel with the obligatory, secular school attendance, in some cases it more or less replaces ordinary school.

These last are often people who arrived in the country at the end of the 1960s or beginning of the 1970s as labour migrants. People who are not here primarily for the purpose of teaching Islam. They are on an equal footing, in that sense, with others who have to deal with the conditions in the job market. These are people, then, who have a good and thorough knowledge, not only of immigrants, but also of the history and conditions of immigration - which they have experienced themselves.

BEKIR is one such example. He is now unemployed after a work training scheme job with the commune. He arrived in Denmark in 1970. He found unskilled work, first in a tileworks and later in a machine factory. He spent the first eight years living in a single room without his family. In 1978 he managed to bring his wife and three children to Denmark.

From the start of his time in Denmark he has been engaged in trying to establish a place for Turkish immigrants to meet and pray. He helped to buy a property to be used as a mosque. He also helped to collect the money to bring a well educated hoca here from Istanbul for a couple of months. Since 1979, which is more or less when the mosque came into being, the place has been manned by a series of well educated hocas. In the last five or six years Bekir has, meanwhile, been teaching children in the remote district where he lives, just as he also contributes to the religious lives of the families living there.

Alongside the kind of religious education which Bekir represents there is another form, which is represented by those with high theological qualifications. They are usually in the country on two-year work permits. They fall into two categories: 1) Hocas dispatched by the Diyanet, the ministry for religious affairs, and 2) imams, employed and paid for by Islamic associations such as the Islamisk Kulturcenter which relies as much on the income from the 'community', as it does on what comes in from abroad. While with the first group, the hocas from the Diyanet are exponents of a Turkish-national Islamic orientation, the other group is not directly expounding the views of a particular state. At the moment this group has a modern, and thereby internationalist, Islamic orientation. These two categories of well educated Islamic theologians are, however, handicapped by the fact that they are only present on the basis of two-year stays, and in this way do not themselves gain the experience of being a part of the immigrants' lives.

4.1.2 The Growth in the Number of Mosques, 1979-1992

The first proper mosque appeared in Aarhus in 1979. The initiative for the mosque came from local Turkish immigrants who collected the money together to buy a suitable property. The mosque became known as the Islamisk Kulturcenter when it merged structurally with the Islamisk Kulturcenter in Horsebakken in the Copenhagen region in 1980. They thereby became one mosque and one community.

During the course of the 1980s the Diyanet involved itself to an increasing extent. Aarhus too received its own Turkish-state imams. In 1986, however, a division formed within the Turkish community, a break between the Turkish Diyanet supporters and the Turkish Islamists. As the Islamists enjoyed good support among the other nationalities, and since the Turkish Muslims on the west side of Aarhus wanted to have a local mosque, the Diyanet imam at the Islamisk Kulturcenter was transferred to a newly established mosque there (located in rather cramped basement premises more suited to storing bicycles). This automatically meant that the mid-town mosque drew Muslims of all nationalities while the mosque in Aarhus Vest was largely for the Turks who lived there, even though the Turkish Islamists still kept to the Kulturcenter in mid-town.

In 1989/90 the Diyanet decided they could no longer accept the Turkish Islamists' dominance of the Islamisk Kulturcenter and therefore used its authority within the honorary committee which backed the centre to force the Islamists' imam out in favour of their own candidate. When the Turkish Islamists found that they could not muster enough support among the other nationalities to oppose the pressure from the Diyanet, they chose to withdraw and establish themselves separately with their own mosque in 1990. At first this was in quite humble locations which belonged to a Turkish youth club. In 1991 the Sultan Eyyub Cami was inaugurated in a large villa in the centre of town. The villa also houses several Islamic associations.

The Diyanet community in Aarhus West has also improved its circumstances in that they were able to purchase a villa in 1990 which today is Diyanet Vakif. The site of the mosque does, however, give rise to some conflict with the municipality due to the insufficient parking facilities. The municipality has never approved of the villa functioning as a mosque. The Diyanet community in Aarhus South has also set itself up with its own mosque in rented premises.

This development in the organisation of immigrants and, by extension, of the young, so-called 'second generation', has given rise to the emergence on the one hand of a differentiation between the religious lives of the Turkish (but also other nationalities) *Sunni*-Muslim community, while on the other hand the individual is now faced with a choice, even when it comes to religious matters. The question of who 'I' am as a Muslim takes on an added dimension. Today, depending on the answer to that question, there are a number of organisations to which one can choose to align oneself.

It is characteristic of the current situation, in organisational terms, that the immigrants themselves decide who they want to have as a hoca/imam. If, for example, there is a hoca from Turkey whom they do not feel serves the interests of the community completely, or perhaps is too conservative, he will be boycotted and an alternative solution sought - possibly with somebody with exceptional religious insight from among the immigrant community standing in for a transitional period.

We can regard the above as an ongoing discussion, a continuing 'negotiation', and as an expression of an evolving, self-reflexive, independently minded extension of the awareness of God and man's place in the world. It has often been claimed that immigrants are under the sway of the religious leaders who have a great deal of authority, this, however, would not appear to be the case unconditionally. They have the leaders they choose to have!

4.2 Islamism as the Manager of Islamic Identity

Attempts to describe the relationship between religion and identity among Muslim immigrants can, as mentioned above, not simply be reduced to religion, in any meaningful way. Conversely, however, it does become apparent that Islam makes its presence felt, regardless of the degree of religious engagement. Islam enters the discussion, even if Islam far from fulfils the needs of identity, thus acquiring a function with regard to social identification for everyone.

For many of the so-called 'second generation' of immigrants the experience of being socially marginalised is very real, even in cases where they have enjoyed personal success in fields such as education. The result of this experience is manifest in the experience of finding companionship among other young people who come from similar backgrounds.

For many of these young people religion plays a marginal role. It is not a vital part of their everyday lives. Nevertheless they consider themselves to be a part of a cultural community in which they feel that they are obliged to defend Islam against what they see as incorrect interpretations of Islam, not least of all as demonstrated by the views of the average Dane. These young people would rather identify themselves with respect to an ethnic allegiance than to a religious one.

For other young people it is important to be able to consider their day to day life as being organised within two parallel realities. In one sense it is productive that they see themselves as people who can step in and out of two separate worlds. It can be regarded as a matter of greater opportunity rather than limitations. These possibilities, which one has to maintain, are given on the one hand by rules and cultural codes which might define the presentable young man with good manners, with respect and consideration to the family for example, while on the other a fashion-conscious engagement with Danish youth circles. This does not necessarily constitute an insurmountable identity problematic. One can see oneself as being a Muslim, but the actual engagement with Islam must, for the moment, give way to the life of a young person which has to be lived in the period until one gets married. There is, in effect, a time to be young and a time to be Muslim.

There are, then, young men and women who see a crucial difference between their own lives and those of their Danish peers. This difference can be explained in various ways. But regardless of what exactly it comprises, regardless of where one comes from, or what ethnic, or precise religious background, whether, for example, one is a *Sunni*-Muslim, or an *Alevite*-Muslim, or whether or not one keeps up with the latest musical hits and trends, regardless of what hopes one might have for one's future education or marriage, and regardless of whether one has spent all, or almost all of one's life in Denmark, there is still a quite distinct difference between this experience and that of Danes of a similar age.

In this connection we are, however, particularly interested in the young people for whom Islam lies at the centre of their social identification. This group see Islam as containing certain central authentic values which are binding and which demand the personal engagement of the individual. They know that not everything which pertains to be Islam is Islam and, conversely, that not everything which is ascertained to belong to a non-Islamic sense of consciousness, is necessarily non-Islamic.

For these young people it becomes possible - not despite, but because of Islam - to implement not just a critique of the family's inadequacy, in their quite individual biographical cases, but also a critique of a common socially agreed convention. One might say that this critique is partly a criticism of tradition and partly of the social stigma of immigration which they have been ascribed. Islam, in this sense, constitutes an opportunity for positive, individual identification.

In the following I shall expand on how engaged Islamists who are part of the Millî Görüş cemaat in Denmark administer Islamic identity. This centres around questions which concern Islam in daily life, Islam and work, the personal story, marriage and economy, the experience of being a Muslim in Danish society and the Islamic ideal.

The intention is to present material which can suggest an answer to 1) which experiences of life lie at the root of the impulse to join an Islamist community, 2) which interpretations of Islam seem to be relevant in daily life, and 3) what social role does the religious community play in relation to the development of social contacts (including marriage) and the conduct of financial investments (such as starting one's own business).

1. The young people who join the movement do not differ outwardly from other young immigrants. They live under the same conditions, i.e. socially, educationally, - unemployment is also high here. The generation of parents are often rooted in the peasant class. This fact does not apply only to the Islamists, but to the greater part of the old immigrant groups - Turks, Pakistanis, Yugoslavs and Moroccans. The parents have rarely acquired any significant amount of schooling, their fundamental knowledge of Islam comes from the village context. The young's knowledge of Islam is formulated by these parents in the migrant communities. It is, in this way, revealing that the relation of young people to Islam is enhanced in the migrant situation. Dayram and Ramazan are good examples of young people who have joined Millî Görüş cemaat. They both live with their wives and have, respectively, 3 and 2 children in their households and have their own independent incomes.

Bayram was born in 1962 in a village in the province of Sivas, in East Anatolia. At the age of ten he moved with his mother and siblings to Denmark where his father worked in a tileworks. Bayram now has an intermediate technical training education after having left school after the 10th grade. He has, in contrast to so many other young Turkish immigrants, been able to attain a good education - and to master, in the course of time, the Danish language.

Ramazan was born in 1964 in Konya. He arrived in Denmark in 1984 as a result of his marriage at the age of 20. His wife comes from the same village as he. Ramazan, in contrast to Bayram, spent all his childhood and early life in Turkey. He attended school for eight years (incl.junior secondary). When he was 15 years old he stopped going to school. His father saw no reason for him to continue with his schooling, and help was needed with the father's farming. In the winter, when there was not so much to do on the farm he went to the 'metropolitan cities', either Ankara or Konya where he worked in restaurants, hotels and at times in workshops. He is lucky to be working today. It was his father-in-law who got him the job; by actually giving his own job to Ramazan when he had to retire on invalidity pension. He spent the first couple of years in Denmark attending a variety of courses.

Since he arrived in Denmark he has lived on the Gellerup housing estate in Aarhus West. At first he and his wife lived with her parents. When they were to have their first child they moved into a three room flat in the neighbouring block. The stairwell is a mixed bag of nationalities; a couple of Danish families, Palestinians, Turks and a family from Vietnam.

Bayram lives in a large housing complex with many Turkish immigrants. The neighbours however, are all Danish. None of his family are there nor, for that matter, are any other Turks. He describes the relationship with the neighbours as a bad one. The flats are badly insulated as far as sound is concerned, he says, so they have to be careful not to make too much noise. His downstairs neighbours, for example, always complain that his children make too much noise running up and down in the flat. But, as he says, he cannot stop the children from playing. Ramazan on the other hand does not seem to have any problems with his neighbours, but he knows from others that Danes are not always pleased to have Turks or other foreigners for neighbours.

It is rare to encounter Turks who have regular contact with Danes on a private basis. Neither Bayram nor Ramazan, for example, has ever been invited to eat dinner in a Dane's house. Bayram has, however, eaten with Danes, on courses or similar occasions. They would not mind receiving such an invitation but they would, for example, make some demands regarding the food. They would not, for example, ever eat meat, but would eat fish or vegetables. Since, however, neither of them know any Danish neighbours privately - they only know Turks - the question is not particularly relevant. Neither of them take the trouble to attend resident association meetings, or other common arrangements with Danes. Bayram does sometimes go to the annual general meeting of his department.

Bayram's work experience is not particularly different from that of his peers despite his solid educational background. Unemployment and job offers for the long term unemployed have meant that he has worked in a couple of machine workshops. He has attended diverse courses for the long term unemployed and specially run initiative courses for immigrants. Ramazan's existence in Denmark was also characterised by various courses and job training schemes for immigrants until he got his present job in 1988. There is another Turk who works with him in the same place. The Danes do not like them talking Turkish between them.

Along with a couple of other people, Bayram has attempted to set himself up in business, dealing in foodstuffs, including halal beef. He also established an import-export business for a time along with several others, and he has also been active in organising courses for immigrants. These courses have since fallen through. He is full of initiative and dynamism and, according to him, will soon find another way forward.

All too many of their fellow countrymen are too lazy and cannot be bothered to make full use of what is available to them, according to both Bayram and Ramazan. Bayram in particular believes that too many of them are concerned with simply securing a place within the unemployment benefit system. People cannot be bothered to make an effort if it is not going to be rewarded. He believes that he actually thinks differently to those of his compatriots who first came to Denmark after they had completed their schooling. They turn inwards and cannot think in terms of what is beneficial to society as a whole (i.e. beneficial to others than themselves).

Bayram is of the view, like many in his Islamic group, that education and one's own initiative are the only way out of the stigma which affects the lives of immigrants. The prevailing Danish concept of success is also shared by Bayram and his comrades. They can see that it is difficult for Turks to find work, even for Turks who are well qualified: 'Danes would rather employ one of their own,' as Bayram says. Bayram shares the same experience as his Turkish peers of the job market in Denmark. On that point his life resembles theirs, which is why he perseveres and tries to create his own.

He is very well aware of whom he belongs with, whose fate he shares which is to say those who live under the same conditions as he - and those who have the same faith as he does. Bayram knows that his future is in Denmark, his upbringing was here and his education is Danish. He has put Turkey behind him. For Ramazan there is also no way of going back to Turkey, the opportunities are not better there. He does not want to go back to the village where he came from, which had electricity installed only a couple of years ago, and where oil lamps are still used. Turkish society is unfair, he says, one has to know someone who knows someone to get a decent job. Although the Danes might not believe it, there is much in Danish society which comes from Islam, the welfare society, for example.

Ramazan did not learn much about Islam in school, he says. He attended Koran reading for three months with the village hoca - but since he played truant a lot his father finally let him off - after giving him a sound hiding. But it was not very common for the children to attend Koran school. His father actually called himself a 'muhamadan' - which, as he explained, is what they had always been called, so he saw no reason to change it. Ramazan began to be interested in Islam before he arrived in Denmark, but it was when he arrived in Denmark that he began to take a stronger interest. At that time there was already a group of youngsters in Aarhus who were interested in discovering what Islam really was. It was his wife's brother who first introduced him. This was, in a manner of speaking, his introduction to Denmark.

He knows of other Turks who do not know Islam so well and who waste their lives away. Some become involved in a Turkish gambling-den where one can lose 2-3000 Dkr in an evening. The man who runs the place has now bought himself a villa. Several members of the Islamic community formerly used to visit the place, but it was a very bad way of spending one's time. 'Our Islam says that one must not play cards.'

'I never learnt anything about Islam in school,' says Bayram, 'or from my parents.' This does not mean that his father never talked to him about Islam. But that he regards as stories. What he had learned was in actual fact simply what was considered ordinary tradition in his home region. But his parents could not give him a reflected understanding of Islam. They were illiterates, he explains. He became a Muslim at 18, he says, after school. They were a group of 20-30 young people who studied together. This was not actual Koran courses, but rather had the character of self-tuition.

The beginning of Bayram's religious engagement coincided with the time when he and his family moved from one part of the country to another, one cannot say, therefore, as one might of others, that this development involved the changing of his circle of friends. On the other hand one can say that socialising within an active Islamic community defined his angle of approach to his new home. His new friends were from among a religiously engaged community. The timing was not accidental, he stresses, it was during these years that it became 'fashionable' among young Muslims to involve themselves more with Islam.

Bayram is currently seeking Danish citizenship and sees no reason to return to Turkey, since his entire upbringing and educational background encourage him to stay in Denmark. He would not dream of investing in Turkey, or of buying a house there. Bayram's father and his generation would not dream of seeking Danish citizenship, but the young people of Bayram's generation and their children in any case would not hesitate in changing nationality. Thoughts of returning to Turkey have been dropped, no one wants another split in the family. The future of the children is in Denmark.

Bayram also feels that his moral conscience/loyalty is aimed towards Denmark. It is Denmark which has given him the opportunities he has today: 'I will not turn my back on them, and this is also in accordance with Islam.' He is interested in Danish politics and exercises his right to vote in elections for the local municipality.

Although most of the young people who are the driving force behind this Islamic youth culture have completed most of their schooling in Europe they have not felt themselves drawn to other, i.e. Danish youth movements. For some of the newly arrived men the religious community has also been a means by which to tackle the formation of a social network in which they could circulate in a social sphere that was larger than that provided by the family.

2. The social marginalisation which characterises these immigrant groups is countered positively at the cultural level via the use of Islam. Islamism represents, in a manner of speaking, a trading position in relation to the surrounding society. This is an expression of the rejection of certain aspects of peasant society's traditions, but at the same time is an attempt to reformulate central moral values for use in modern society.

Individuals from among the older first generation of immigrants, who were the ones who initiated the community, can perhaps be characterised as worker intellectuals who see in this a vital alternative to a traditionalist way of life. The community can serve as a corrective to, and an extension of, inherited auto-didactic knowledge.

Although the Islamic movements often refer to a common heritage of great Muslim thinkers, including the Pakistani, Maududi, and the Egyptian, Sayed Qutb, there is a differentiation in their interpretation which does not cling to a fixed pre-existing pattern. One feature common to the formations of immigrant organisations in Europe is that they are constructed on national and ethnic qualifications. The same applies to the Islamists, although here the international link is more prominent and will continue to be increasingly so in the future. They tend towards assembling around their own mosques, or, where possible, to come together in mosques that do not have a definite allegiance, as opposed to mosques that come under the guidance of the Turkish state, for example.

This religious commitment constitutes a break with habitual and inveterate conceptions of Islam among Turks, according to Bayram and Ramazan. They see, primarily, that the Turkish state uses Islam to support Turkish nationalism, which is very remote from Islam. Bayram says, 'Turks are faithful to the state, and the *laik* state as well. It is a faith that is not good, since it hinders basic change.'

Bayram and Ramazan do not think that Islam, made subject to the Turkish national-state discourse, can provide an authentic claim for Islam's role in modern society. Religious motives are subject to political ones, Islam is abused by the Turkish state for its political aims. They believe that hocas who are sent by the Turkish state are, by and large, good Muslims; they are simply not able to speak openly and freely because they are bound to the state. Actually Turkey should not involve itself in religion. It is a Kemalist state, i.e. a secular state, so why should the state involve itself? This was an outcome of Mustafa Kemal's (Atatürk) revolution which was the start of the undermining of the religion, says Ramazan. This is why many Turks do not have a clear idea about Islam today, he thinks; there is still a lot of superstition. Amulets are still used, for example, but this is outside Islam, this is *hurafa* (superstition). One cannot protect oneself against *nazar* (the evil eye) with the use of *nazarlik* (eye-amulets). Those hocas who make *muska* (writing amulets) exploit people's ignorance. *Nazar* appears in the Koran and modern science also makes mention of it, says Ramzan, and explains that 'when one looks at others, the eye emits forces.' But, he continues, one cannot know when *nazar* is at work and what it means. Amulets are ridiculous and ineffectual and un-Islamic, there is only one thing which works against evil: prayer!

Millî Görüş is the best alternative to Diyanet Islam, according to Bayram and Ramazan. Millî Görüş is not a closed branch of Islam, like groups such as the Süleymani and Nurcu, and nor are they nationalist or nationally exclusive. Millî Görüş is internationally oriented, open to challenge and outward looking.

Neither Bayram nor Ramazan see any problem in adhering to Islamic rules in Denmark:

a) They only eat meat which has been prepared the *halal* way. The meat is now obtained from an Islamic butcher. The creature must not be sedated before it is butchered if it is to be considered proper *halal*.

Animals up to 70 kg. can, according to Danish veterinary legislation, be slaughtered without prior sedation, cattle on the other hand have to be sedated. It is possible to get cattle through private channels, he explains. But Danish merchants push their prices up to a level which Bayram cannot meet. Ramazan's family do not slaughter the animals, but buy them instead from others.

They obtain chickens delivered privately by friends and not from a factory so that they can be sure that they are slaughtered properly. One cannot be sure that this is the case in the factories. But he is, however, prepared to accept chickens from *halal* poultry factories, such as DANPO.

Why does no one ever make a fuss about the fact that Jewish animals are not sedated? Bayram asks. It was only with Muslims that it became a problematic issue.

b) Ramazan does not pay *zakat* as there is not much left over with only one income and after the rent has been paid, he explains. Bayram on the other hand does pay *zakat*. On the previous occasion he had paid the equivalent of 1000-1500 Dkr. *Zakat* is calculated as 2.5% of what one has over and above one's needs, and worked out on an annual basis. *Zakat* is actually calculated as that which is left over the value of 96 gr. of gold, he explains. The money is sent to poorer members of the family in Turkey. *Zakat* can be given to people who themselves cannot pay *zakat*, also, for example, to a cousin who is studying at university but has no funds, although this is something that Bayram would not approve of. In an Islamic state it is the state which collects the *zakat*. The collected funds have to be kept clearly separate from the rest of the state's finances. *Zakat* is to go to the poor. Turkey is not allowed to collect *zakat* and nor does it. Bayram finds this strange, as it could provide good political propaganda for the state. In Denmark, *zakat* payments must be private. No organisation can have the authority to collect, although one could envisage a number of people getting together to make a collection for a common cause.

In contrast to *zakat*, *fitre* is paid by the head, which is to say that children count too. Ordinarily, his family collects money together and sends it all together to poor family members in Turkey.

c) Fasting in Denmark is a private matter. In Turkey it is a public affair. Both Ramazan and Bayram naturally fast in *Ramadan* and even at other times during the year.

Ramazan and Bayram do not slaughter an animal in Denmark in connection with *Kurban Bayram*, the sacrifice festival. Instead Bayram sends money to his family in Turkey so that they can carry out the ritual there. Ramazan explains that the rules for the slaughter of *Kurban Bayram* state that one third should be given to the poor, a third to be shared with the family, and a third to oneself. This system is not practised in Denmark. Bayram and Ramazan think it makes no sense to make the sacrifice in Denmark because there is no one to give the poor third to. It should be given to people who are in need and cannot afford to buy meat. In Denmark the social system is so well supported that no one suffers actual want, everybody can have their requirements met. In principle the third that should be given to the poor could be given to Danes, but they would probably think it rather strange to be given meat. It would require a completely open relationship with a Dane and such relationships between Turk and Danes are rare.

d) All are free to make the pilgrimage to the *hajj*. Bayram would like to go on the *hajj*, but cannot afford it, and does not have the opportunity to save up for it. Ramazan also thinks that it will take many years before he will be able to go.

Islam is an easy religion, Bayram claims. He himself has been able to perform the five daily prayers and has done so since 1980. He has always been able to find places in which to pray at his place of work and during the times when he was studying, either in an empty room, or an empty corner. 'We can pray anywhere,' he claims. Not everyone, however, has had the same opportunities since the kind of places that Bayram has worked in, such as a number of projects for immigrants, have given him the chance to dictate his own conditions. If people do not adhere to their religious practices then it is not due to the lack of opportunity, but because they are too lax about it; some are afraid to ask their boss for permission, he says.

Many Turks are afraid of being fired. If one cannot pray then one can still do *salat-kaza*. Ramazan has also not experienced problems in being able to say his prayers. But not everyone has had the same experience. Many of those whom I have spoken to could not say their prayers at work, either because they could not find a suitable place to perform them, or because they felt that their employers did not want to have the bother of such problems. Instead they had to try and make up for it when they came off work.

The problem, according to Bayram, is not being a Muslim. The problem is that Muslims are excluded from their Danish surroundings, regarded as being different - and with suspicion. As a Muslim, one does not share the same manner of thinking, the same values, or views as the Danes do. One is different at every level, right down to the matter of language. Bayram would never use the same discourteous language that Danes use. In addition to this there are things such as the beer drinking culture, and even such things as the contents of one's lunch box which reveal the differences. In the relationship between Turks and Danes, it is apparently the external aspects of the Turks which count rather than anything else.

There are so many things associated with Islam which the Danes misunderstand, says Bayram, offering an example:

> Once my wife had to go to the dentist and so I accompanied her. The dentist, who was herself a woman, asked her whether it would not be easier for her if she learnt to speak better Danish. Then she could go to the dentist on her own, for example. Then I would not have to go with her, and then it would be easier for them to have a chat about everything, not just teeth.

> The dentist assumed, then, that my wife would go to the dentist *on her own* if she could speak better Danish. This is not the case, as she should not be going around town on her own, whether she speaks Danish or not.

> The dentist believes that she would tell her a different story if she was alone. She would not. It is not I who prevent her from saying anything other than what she does say.

Ramazan also believes that the Danes have misunderstood Islam, and think that Islam is fanatical and violent and that it is repressive of women. This is not true. Islam is, on the contrary, peace, he says and Islam sets men and women as equals, neither is more important than the other.

> Women are allowed to work. My wife would like to work. Islam says that the man should work and provide for his family. But when I work, it is not necessary for her to work too. Islam does not say that she must.

Many Danes think that it is repressive for women to have to wear the headscarf, but our Islam says that women should cover themselves. Those who do not cover themselves will burn in Hell.

The upbringing of children is a central issue for the Islamists: As a condition for adjusting properly to modern society it is important that the children are made familiar with Islamic principles. This inspires an awareness and consciousness around socialisation which was not present in peasant society. This method of bringing up children reflects precisely the loss of the social surroundings provided in the village. This is replaced by a radical and consistent self control which one is duty bound to pass on to the children.

Bayram has three children of, respectively, 2, 3 and 6 years of age: the two younger ones are looked after at home while the eldest now attends a kindergarten. He thinks it is nonsense to say that the children would not learn Danish if they did not go to kindergarten. His own eldest child learns new words all the time - swear words too. Children learn languages very quickly, he believes. Ramazan's children are 7 and 4 years old. His eldest boy has started school and is getting on well, but it is good that there are other Turkish children there. He does not spend much time with the Danish children.

Both fathers would prefer their children to be looked after at home by their mothers, so as to ensure they get a better upbringing. This is better than what the day care institutions can provide.

There is a widespread belief within the Millî Görüş cemaat that Muslim children are subject to Christianisation when they attend day-care centres and schools. Not so much because the personnel seek to influence them in that direction - perhaps the opposite even, says Bayram, but because life and culture, even in the kindergarten, for example, is founded on elements of Christianity. For example, they are encouraged to paint eggs around Easter time and to cut and glue paper for Christmas, also, birthdays are celebrated, which they are not in the Muslim tradition.

Naturally the Muslim children also enjoy doing these things, and they want to paint eggs and cut out paper shapes as Christmas approaches, and they would also like to get Christmas presents. They want to celebrate their birthdays and give sweets to the other kids in the kindergarten and invite them home. What happens is a kind of covert Christianisation of Muslim children in day care institutions and school.

Both Bayram and Ramazan believe, furthermore, that Turks - in contrast to the ideas which the municipality in Aarhus has - must retain the right to attend schools in their normal neighbourhood district. The school system and the individual teachers have to understand that Turks are

Muslims and that they also have the right to decide how to run their own lives. The problem with the school is that society fails to instil the child with good influences. The parents, both Turkish and Danish, have to understand that they have to teach children to treat one another well, Bayram says. Even six year-old Turkish children are not always accepted by Danish children. If his own child of six says that he has been playing with some 'kafirs', the child is reprimanded. It is not good for them to talk like that. In the same way Danish parents ought to step in when their children make some derogatory remark about immigrants.

Since Denmark no longer (since 1989) accepts double citizenship, Bayram's wife is not going to take Danish citizenship, as he will. She feels she does not want to do that, but is also thinking in terms of the children. He does not reject the idea that this is linked to keeping open the option of allowing their children to have their schooling in Turkey. Furthermore, the wife's Turkish citizenship prevents them from being shut out of Turkish legal processes.

Both Bayram and Ramazan realise that their lives are markedly different from those of Danes. The threat of marginalisation is countered at the cultural level by enhancing Islam as the representation of a set of positive values. Islam represents a generalised level of negotiation in the integration process in relation to the surrounding society which is founded on Christian values and traditions. They are no longer isolated social cases which are unable to cope in modern society. Bayram and Ramazan's position is derived from a collective identity which criticises fundamental values at the basis of Western civilisation. As a social critique, it is Islam which is confronted by an environment that is conditioned by Christianity.

3. The religiously based community is a crucial, but by no means singular, point of contact for the members of the Islamic movements: People also meet each other in the mosque outside of the times of prayer, often there are meeting places, and cafes associated with the mosque. People can meet on the premises of certain unions. On the other hand it is rare that people meet in public cafeterias.

The community is, though, not sharply cut off from the outside. An important indicator is that people prefer to go to relatives rather than to members of the community if, for example, help is needed with day to day matters, such as financial affairs, or in connection with marriage contracts.

The religious community that Bayram and Ramazan are members of plays a large part in their daily life, not as a substitute for family, but as an appendage.

When Bayram got married at the age of 21 the usual negotiation procedures involving relatives were set in motion. 'I grew up within a tradition,' Bayram says. Bayram's parents had, in the first instance, proposed a woman to him from his own family (FaBrDa). He turned down the proposal and found someone himself that he wanted. This was the daughter of his grandfather's daughter.

It was his own parents who, along with an uncle, acted as 'dünürler,' or 'marriage brokers'. In other words, it was they who presented the proposal of marriage and who agreed the brideprice and other conditions. The wedding was organised in great haste during a holiday in Turkey: One week after the engagement, Bayram was married.

For Ramazan it was also the case that he knew his wife before they were engaged and married. 'Everyone knows everyone in such a village'. In Ramazan's case, too, it was the parents who organised the marriage. They were engaged for a year prior to the wedding. The girl's parents, of course, travelled to Turkey. Prior to the wedding a party lasting several days was held. All the festivities were paid for by her father and they took place at their home. After the meal on the wedding day, the bride was collected in a car and she lived with them for a few days, until they could all travel back to Denmark.

Bayram does not know what the *başlik*, the amount paid by his parents to the girl's parents, was. Just as he cannot remember the value of the *altin* (gold jewellery, usually in the form of necklaces, armbands, earrings and rings) given to the girl - Bayram, on the other hand, does know that his wife did not have anything with her when she came into the marriage, none of the traditional *yatak*, *yastik* and *yorgan* (bed, pillows and eiderdown) or their more modern equivalents, such as a sewing machine: 'We were to live with my parents to begin with so we had no need of such things, and we could not bring them with us to Denmark anyway.'

In Ramazan's case it was her parents who were the ones who, in the first instance, had to provide everything that was needed. His parents did not pay *başlik* - 'We were in the same family' - he did though give an *altin* worth around 25,000 Dkr.

It was, then, not people from within the circle of their community of faith or conviction who were able to provide the right girl, but the family that took care of the matter. Bayram's own closest family knew the girl of course, who he had suggested himself. She was from the same village as he, but she was his own choice. Since she arrived in Denmark she has stayed at home and taken care of the children. Today she is one of the leaders of an Islamic women's group. Ramazan's wife has also stayed at home.

In Bayram's (failed) attempt to set up his own *halal* butcher business it was the Islamic community that was the starting point for the group of people who were to be co-owners. There were four owners - and all of them were members of the same Millî Görüş cemaat. The business was the initiative of these young people, but was made possible with family based finance, with internal loan conditions which made it possible for the young group to realise their ambition within a financial community that was also a religious community. It turned out to be a bad business venture that was not able to find the customers that were required: Muslims who wanted *halal* prepared meat and local Danish residents. As far as the Muslims were concerned there was actually no real market for them, since people by and large butchered their own livestock. In relation to potential Danes customers, what was offered was generally considered to be of insufficient variety.

Despite the fact that Bayram is unemployed and somewhat disappointed at the present time about his venture into the labour market, it was an advantage for him to start out from within a collective. The pooled energy has made projects possible and kept the initiatives going.

Even though the family is central, even to the Islamists, in the development of social contacts, such as in the arrangement of marriages and in conducting financial investments, Islam marks the centre of a community which also constitutes a new network as a supplement to the network provided by the family.

4.3 Changes

The majority of young Turkish immigrants are the children of labour migrants who originally come from rural areas. Migration brings with it socialisations associated with an agrarian society being confronted by a Western industrial society. In the agrarian context kinship played a strong role, and was applied in the allocation of work. New radical experiences are being made in Europe. These experiences are unique, not only articulated individually but also through social communities, communities of fate.

Perhaps what the old myth about Turkish immigrants is trying to tell us is, after all, correct; that the Turks lived together previously more or less as one individual minority group in Denmark - across and despite and the religious differences. People were simply Turkish.

From the end of the 1970s one can begin to detect, however, some differentiation within this minority group. Former political divisions between right and left were replaced by a differentiation on the basis of cultural revitalisation.

A variety of identity fora emerged. This change can be observed in relation to certain types of religious ritual functions, a change that was reflected throughout on the basis of ethnic, political and religious affiliations: here we find 1) a secular left wing oriented tendency, 2) a tendency by which Islam was cited within a national-cultural sense of awareness, and 3) an Islamist tendency.

Regardless of these various orientations, they shared the common experience of migration, and they were often manifest simultaneously within the context of the family. These combinations are often expressed along generation lines, where the second tendency will often comprise immigrants of the first generation, while the first tendency will often be a second generation phenomenon, as is the third tendency. In this the *Alevites* would constitute an exception: Here the first tendency would be present across the generations.

For 'second generation' immigrants as for 'first generation' immigrants unemployment is a collective experience. To some extent we can say that immigrant culture is also a culture of unemployment.

These changes are realised not only on the individual scale but also within organisational forms. These developments are mostly a phenomenon of the 1980s.

The conditions for forming a collective space is different for young women than for the men. While immigrant organisations generally make space available for the development of the men's social behaviour, their offer is more limited when it comes to women. The offers are organised on a weekly or fortnightly basis with specific aims in mind: folk dances or informative initiatives, or else they enter, as noted earlier, as 'mothers, wives or daughters'. Nevertheless the Kommune (municipality) and Amt (county) authorities have paid special attention to the situation of women, which is why women can find special opportunities in the area of education available in further schooling classes. These can take the form of purely immigrant classes (in such things as beadwork), or else in the form of specially designed educational offers geared to the job market. The informal gatherings must take place within a formal framework, but to a large degree also through the meeting of smaller groups of girlfriends, or in connection with family events and religious festivities.

The changes on the religious front seem to follow their own logic, and thereby have their own development dynamic among men and women, respectively. As was outlined earlier, religious life is not organised in the same way for women as for men. A number of the ritual areas are women's areas and are not institutionalised in the religious public institutions.[16] These forms, such as the use of *muska* and *nazarlik* and visiting holy graves

---

[16] This is not something which applies exclusively to the migration situtation, but also, for example, in Turkey where it can be argued that male religiosity is, due to its organisational structure, open to a greater degree to innovation (Tapper & Tapper 1987).

(*kutsal türbe*) have been criticised. These rites are seen as an expression of superstition (*hurafa*) not only in the general Danish understanding, but also in the mosques and to a marked degree among the Islamists. Religious life is subject to massive changes.

The Islamisation becomes a political-cultural medium for the cultural heritage and identity among *Sunni*-Muslims. This, then, marks a difference between them and the, mostly Kurdish, *Alevites*. These last have always, and do continue to under-communicate the religious and therefore also their relation to the *Sunni*-Muslims. A marked tendency among these, and especially among the young, is a Kurdishisation, as they frequently view themselves on the basis of their ethnic identity. To be Kurdish, is a part of the collective identity (cf. Pedersen & Selmer 1991).[17]

This difference manifests itself in the Danish context, but must, as was underlined above, also be seen in relation to the history of Islamisation within the framework of the development in the national-state Turkish discourse in recent years. In this process the *Alevites* are further marginalised and thereby not represented (op.cit.).

The experience of migration is one of learning, involving a broad spectrum of consciousness and activity forms, individually, as much as collectively. The background for this development among immigrants can be seen in a unity of several conditions, which will be further examined in Chapter 6, and which constitute the raw material for the concluding analysis of the potential of Islamism in Western Europe.

Before I turn my attention to the analysis of Islamism in Europe, seen in a more global perspective, I shall conduct a demarcation of yet another Islamic fundamentalist stance which also operates within Europe's Muslim migrant circles. This is the *Jama'at al-Tabligh*, who, successfully, manages to organise itself across a multi-ethnic foundation. This is, however, a form of Islamic activism that does not address itself to the question of power, and therefore, with regard to our introductory definitions, lies on the periphery of Islamism.

---

[17] This observation is also supported by Hjarnø (1988 & 1991).

5 On the Periphery of Islamism: Jama'at al-Tabligh[1]

Jama'at al-Tabligh, Tablighi Jama'at, Tabligh, Jama'at al-Da'wa, or to give it its correct name in full, Jama'at Tabligh wa Da'wa, The Community of Proclamation and Mission, lies on the periphery of Islamism.

Jama'at al-Tabligh is relevant to the context of this thesis as an example in relation to Millî Görüş. Jama'at al-Tabligh is an example of a fundamentalist, but non-Islamist movement. In itself, the intention of using this as an example is to enhance the profile of Islamism. Jama'at al-Tabligh is an example of an Islamic, non-intellectual activism which formulates its interests with respect to daily life, in the practical sense, and not in relation to the socio-political landscape.

The movement, Jama'at al-Tabligh, was founded in 1926 by the scholar, Mawlana Muhammed Ilyas (1885-1944) in India. Muhammed Ilyas attended the *Deobandi* school, where he studied the great *hadiths*, but he abandoned the order in 1918 after which Jama'at al-Tabligh took shape. The movement's two most important Indian centres are supposed to be in Lahore, in what is now Pakistan, and in Delhi (Kepel 1987, p.179; Ahmad 1991, p.512).

The international activities of the movement really began to take off in the mid-1960s. The movement has spread to Europe since then through migrants, Pakistanis and Indians, who have settled primarily in England, where the European centre is based, in Dewsbury. At the end of the 1960s Jama'at al-Tabligh made an appearance in France, where the first Tablighi were recruited from among workers from the Maghreb in North Africa.

Gilles Kepel (op.cit.) calls Jama'at al-Tabligh, as does Mumtaz Ahmad (op.cit.), the world's largest Islamic group. Hervé Terrel describes it as being the most cosmopolitan movement, seen from the point of view of its recruitment (Terrel 1986, p. 30) and one, furthermore, according to

---

[1] *Jama'at al-Tabligh* is also known as *Tahrik-i-Iman*, The Faithful Movement, and also as *Dini Dawat*, The Religious Mission (Robinson 1988, p.15).

Nadia Benjelloun-Ollivier (1986, p.52) which includes Muslims from all social classes, *Shi'ites* as much as *Sunnis*. The movement is, in this way, notable for - in contrast to other Islamic and secular organisations, being rooted in particular ethnic population groups - recruiting to a large degree internationally.

Ahmad (op.cit., p.457 ff.) gives one the impression of the movement's colossal appeal in comparison with the strongest Pakistani Islamist movement, *Jama'at-i-Islami*: In 1989 both movements held large public meetings over precisely the same days. In the case of Jama'at-i-Islami this was a large orchestrated event planned over several years and with many important guests; the leaders from all the large Islamist movements in the Muslim world - from Turkey, the Millî Görüş leader, Necmettin Erbakan was present. The meeting drew more than 100,000 participants and was covered by television. At the same time, 30 kilometres away, Jama'at al-Tabligh held their annual gathering with more than a million participants, although without, on the whole, the attendance of Islamic VIPs and without television coverage. The movement's annual meetings have also been described as the largest Muslim event in the world after the *hajj*.

The movement has an *amir* at the international level: Since 1965 the *amir* has been Sheikh In'am-ul-Hassan, who is the nephew of the founder of the movement, Muhammed Ilyas, who led the movement up until 1944. During the period from 1944 to 1965, Muhammed Ilyas' son Yusuf led the movement.

The movement is held together by regular MASHWARA, consultations: Every 3 months *tarib* (instructions) are given at Mashwara for the European Tablighi. The meeting is held in different countries with the participation of one or two representatives from each country.

Once a year there is a *Mashwara* in Dewsbury for the European Tablighi. Every 5th year *Mashwara* are held in the main centre in India with the participation of Tablighi-representatives from around the world. Every year after the *hajj* around 2 million Tablighis gather in Pakistan.

Despite its quite comprehensive level of activity the group rejects the idea that they have any kind of organisation, and stress that affiliation is without registered membership (Interview with representatives of Tabligh in Denmark, February 1992).[2] A condition which distinguishes them from Jama'at-i-Islami and AMGT.

The Tablighis whom I interviewed referred to the six principles which comprise the *leitmotif* of the movement, and as they were practised by the Prophet, to illustrate the central points for a Muslim: 1) *Kalima*, the

---

[2] This is confirmed by Ahmad (1991).

confession of faith, stressing that there is only one creator and one prophet: 'There is no other god than God and Muhammed is his messenger'. This acknowledgement ascribes a special responsibility to the individual Muslim which separates Muslim from non-Muslim, 2) *Salat*, the five prescribed prayers, which are a visible manifestation of God's greatness. These prayers are best performed in fellowship, in that such prayers are 27 times better that those made by individuals alone, 3) knowledge of God and *dhikr*, two sides of the same coin, partly knowledge of what God wishes of one here and now, partly to know how one can achieve knowledge of God and at the same time show that one recognises him through a repetition of his names, 4) respect for other Muslims, the sick, parents, the old and those who suffer want, by greeting them with *al-Saalamu Aleikum*, 'Peace be with you', 5) working earnestly for God's sake and not to achieve worldly gain. If the intention is worldly God will not approve of the work, for example, the prayer, and 6) to use one's time to strive to live like the Prophet. This selfless work will increase the individual's *iman*, faith.

The movement is characteristically missionary, and to this end makes great demands of its members: Each Tablighi must carry out at least 2.5 hours of *joula* (or *gasht*) a week in their local area. This *joula* is often conducted over two days, in part on the first day in the immediate vicinity of the local mosque and one day starting in a mosque nearby. In Denmark this would effectively mean in the Copenhagen area. After the prayer people leave the mosque in small groups, in the case of Copenhagen this would be the *Makki Masjid*. They contact people where they are, in their home, in the marketplaces, on the street, in the clubs, at certain restaurants.

Troll describes how this *joula* takes place:

> Each party going out for tabligh comprises about ten persons. One of them, with relatively better religious knowledge, is their mu'allim (instructor), and one with the capability of management of their group is amir (group leader). After gathering in the mosque for supererogatory prayers and prayers of supplication they move out with earnest looks and serious deportment (usually recognisable by their wearing of a beard, Muslim cap and kurta-pyjamas, and with each one carrying his blanket and travel bag) hymning the Glory and Sanctity of God and not indulging in anything which may be irrelevant to this sacred occasion. When they reach the locality where they are to deliver the 'call' they once again raise their hands in collective supplication (du'a) before God. They then go on their gasht (round) from door to door and collect the people at the mosque where they exhort them to observe their duty to Allah on the lines of the programme (set out above). Ladies may also be addressed on adherence to ritual prayer and on other points. They are also invited to take an active part in the movement. (Robinson 1988, from Troll, C. 'Five letters of Maulana Ilyas (1885-1944), the Founder of the Tablighi Jama'at,

Translated', Annotated and Introduced in Troll, C, (ed.), Islam in India: Studies and Commentaries. Delhi, 1985, p. 138-176).

In addition to this local mission every Tablighi must conduct *khuruj*[3] at least four times a year. Ideally speaking, one should devote one tenth of one's life to *khuruj* - equivalent to 3 days a month on average. The Copenhagen Tablighi can, for example, go on a 'small' *khuruj* to a nearby town for the weekend. The group would then use the local mosque as its base. They would ask to speak either just before or just after the sermon, depending on what traditional codes of hospitality towards religious people would permit. They would then go out on *joula* in the local area.

One can, meanwhile, use one's time in different ways. Some will, for example, go on 'big' *khuruj*. I was introduced this way to a seven man group of *Tablighi* from Pakistan, who were to spend a year in Europe. First three months in Denmark, after which they would move on to Sweden. There were no 'professional' religious people (such as imams) among them. They all had jobs to return home to: there were school teachers, farmers, and businessmen among them. The group had chosen an amir from among themselves who was in charge of the necessary paperwork for the trip.[4]

5.1 Denmark

Jama'at al-Tabligh in Denmark is just a small movement that is essentially rooted in the Pakistani immigrant community - not least of all in a large group of young people who have grown up in Denmark. At the same time the movement in Denmark also has an international fundament, according to the representatives whom I spoke to, and referred to some Danish converts, among others.[5] I have met Afghanis, Somalis, Pakistanis, and various Arab nationalities linked to the movement. The movement has very

---

[3] *In extenso*: Khuruj fi sabil-Allah, Exit onto God's Way.

[4] The group claimed that over a hundred *Tablighi-groups* left Pakistan every day on a large *khuruj*, around a thousand people. I, however, have difficulty accepting the accuracy of such a large figure.

[5] The term *converts* is mine. When I used this expression in referring to Danish Muslims in front of *Tablighis* they smiled and said that they were not sure that they were converts, as such. Yusuf, a Dane from Fredericia, had, on the other hand, explained to them that he had always been a Muslim but that he had only realized it when he had grown up!

few mosques, with *Makki Masjid*, the Mekkaner Mosque[6] in Copenhagen as their main centre. In Denmark the group is structured around an *amir* - who is of Pakistani origin.

The activities of the movement are based on respect for others, on giving without expecting to get anything in return, and on conducting a simple life (Interview with Danish Tablighi representatives, February 1992). The movement's Danish representatives explain that their simple message is to reinforce the fact that it is not sufficient to say that one is a Muslim, one has to act as a Muslim. Many people are Muslims, but they are not active. Tablighi Jamaat says that one should behave like a Muslim and it should be visible.

Muslims, on the other hand, are faced with quite a unique task, which sets them apart from other people. The *Tablighis* do not, for example, argue for worldly compromise in daily life. On the contrary, much emphasis is placed on the rhythm of Islamic life, and the outward symbols, such as, for example, wearing a full beard and jellabah, which to them is a means of bonding with the Islamic community at large.

The opportunity for *kadha* is quite restricted. God gave mankind five times for prayer, which shall be observed. Being unable to perform these every day is equivalent to arriving late for work every morning. *Kadha* is for exceptional cases, when there is 'no chance for salat'.

If one is not sure whether the meat one is buying is *halal*, one can easily come to an agreement with someone about buying chickens or livestock which one can butcher oneself. One must be certain and cannot assume that meat which claims to be *halal* was actually prepared that way. People who have worked in the chicken factories have been known to say that the chickens are not butchered properly. In addition, *ijtihad* has been given for both the half- and complete sedation of creatures.

Riba means to take advantage of another person while, on the other hand, it is allowed to invest and make a profit. It is almost impossible not to get *riba* in Danish society, but then one can use it for the 'general good', such as for the establishment of a drainage system, say. Those people I interviewed used a variety of financial institutions. They did, however, make it clear that they would not accept interest on their money, as this was *haram-money*. The Islamic Bank in Copenhagen was not a realistic alternative to, say, Den Danske Bank. The Islamic Bank was an integrated part of the Danish banking system - and not a privileged Islamic institution.

---

[6] The mosque's official Danish name is the *Islamisk Forsamlingshus*, or Islamic Meeting-house.

In other words it is not impossible to be a Muslim in a non-Muslim country, but the challenge is great, since one is actually confronted by material temptations. A life in moral ruin can easily be the outcome.

Tabligh has a particular task when it comes to giving Islam to the young, so that they are not simply Muslims by name, but also by deed. Every Saturday and Sunday they gather the young Pakistanis, not for Koran courses, but to tell them about Islam (one signs up for Koran courses oneself). The Danish school system is too free, the young lack respect for the teachers. Tabligh teaches the young that a Muslim behaves in a respectable manner and conducts his life in a simple manner.

It is this composite identity which characterises the movement's intervention - a condition that is also made clear in the organisation's founding rules of 1984, where, according to Bæk Simonson (1990, p. 100) the aims of the movement are as follows:

1) To look after the presence of Muslims in Denmark.

2) To create circumstances which make it easier for Muslims to exist under Danish conditions.

3) To help Muslim children to attend Danish schools without feeling different.

4) To maintain the original Muslim traditions without arousing contempt among the Danish population.

The word 'Islam' means 'to come in peace', which means to create a good atmosphere. Spiritual life is not dependent on nationality. It is a gift from God, to live in this world at peace with one's soul. This is a gift to all of mankind, who can thus enter Paradise. Tablighi Jamaat saves people all over the globe.

If we do not recognise this and believe in God we will all scatter in different directions. Problems will arise amongst us. A mental self-satisfaction will develop. With Islam we can live in an atmosphere of peace. With Islam we can overcome self-satisfaction and the darkness.

Achievement of this relationship to God demands a personal conversion. One begins with oneself, mankind are the first guilty ones - 'one must first sweep in front of one's own door!'

There is a need for more missionaries in Denmark to teach the community about their religion. The lack of legal recognition of Islam means, however, that it is very difficult to bring missionaries into Denmark.

Tablighi Jama'at is not founded on a 'state', to be Tablighi is not political. One cannot begin by building an Islamic state, what matters are the basic principles, which take the individual as their starting point. Every solid construction must start from the ground and build upwards - the same applies to the construction of an Islamic society. Islam is 'peace' - not 'force'.

If one has a strong faith and leads a simple life one will not end in Hell. The kingdom is the soul, it is not material (Interview with representatives for Tabligh in Denmark, February 1992).

5.2 France

The French section of Jama'at al-Tabligh was founded in Paris in September 1972 under the name *Foi et Pratique*, Faith and Practise.[7] Today the movement comprises around 40 affiliated organisations and has five mosques in Paris. The international appeal of the movement in France is clearly displayed by the majority of Algerians. Its administrative council has a very large Algerian majority, with a smaller number of Tunisians, a few Moroccans and Senegalese. The leader of Foi et Pratique, sheikh Mohammed Hammami is a Tunisian. Since 1977 the association has established itself with a primary school and a centre for Islamic studies on the outskirts of Paris, Château de Villemain in Seine-et-Marne.

The French section has not built up any large organisational apparatus. They do not, for example, organise pilgrimage journeys for the *hajj*: 'there are so many who do so privately,' on the other hand people go on the *hajj* in groups.

Sheikh Mohammed Hammami[8] explains that the association's only intention is to expound Islam to all the people on earth:

> To Muslims, to non-Muslims, to the West as much as to the East. We are all descendants of Adam and Eve, we are of the same origin.
>
> Foi et Pratique places a special emphasis on winning over those who are not believers, those who have been lost to Islam, or are on the wrong road. Therefore it is not sufficient, as some Muslims believe, to limit our efforts to the mosques. It is the duty of the believers to seek out people, there wherever they are so as to carry out tabligh.

People are actively sought out so as to get them to come to prayers. One conducts *joula*, as noted previously. *Joula* takes place most commonly at the weekends, it is explained. On Friday evening people leave the mosque in small groups after prayers. On the evening that I interviewed Sheikh Imam Hammami, a group of 6-7 left the mosque after the ceremony with him.

---

[7] According to Kepel the movement has been present in France since the end of the 1960s, but was registered as a union in 1972 with regard to the law of 1901.

[8] The interview with Sheikh Mohammed took place in May 1990 in the movement's most important mosque, Mosquée Omar, in the Belville section of Paris.

They approach people in public meeting places: in cafés, in market places, at cinemas and in mosques. 'we are careful and courteous to people when we meet them,' is the answer to my question about how they are received. It is the simple and harmonious aspects of the message which are always emphasised.

Sheikh Hammami stresses that Islam is not just *foi*, but also *pratique*. They believe that it is precisely this 'pratique' which distinguishes them with regard to, say, La Mosquée de la Paris, which in their eyes stands for ordinary Islam, passive Islam. Foi et Pratique is, on the contrary, a 'renovateur' which underlines the fact that Islam is the basis of all life.

The reason for the organisation being grounded in Muhammed Ilyas is explained as being due to his simple solutions and straightforward emphasis of 'pratique'. This should not, however, be construed as a rejection of other great Islamic reformers, such as Jamal ed-Din Afghani, or Muhammed Abdou, they are all on the same path, these ones though are just more theoretical than Ilyas.

Anyone wishing to be a Muslim one can become one. One must make up one's mind and there are no middle solutions, one cannot simply take up one aspect of Islam and leave others. Islam is a whole. A Muslim will always find time for Islam, there is not need to hang around in cafés. Music, dance, and gambling are incompatible with Islam. Sport, on the other hand, is good and the young who are linked to Foi et Pratique practise sport together. To understand Islam however, one must study the Koran and Sunnah so as to understand the importance of prayer, of alms, and of fasting, etc. My interpreter (who was Tablighi) explained as follows:

> I wasted many of my years when I was not a Muslim. I went to bars and I drank, I neglected my children. Ten years ago I met these people and, alhamdulilah, I am now a Muslim and have a good life. This does not mean that it does not matter that I threw so many years away. It is not unimportant, those years were wasted!

Society leads people to think in material terms, this however, is no excuse for not adhering to the laws of Islam. Prayer is a central part of this and the sheikh stresses that prayer shall also take place collectively - not just *juma*, but the five daily prayers. One should also allow oneself time to discuss the text so as to understand Islam.

Nor is there any reason not to maintain Islam's demands about prayer when one is working. One can always find a place to pray, those who say otherwise are simply seeking an excuse. If the employer does not give his permission to spend time praying, I ask, if people are afraid of creating problems with him by prayer, is there then no opportunity for *kadha*? Here the imam was clear and precise in his answer: 'Kadha does not exist in Islam. If God says that you should pray, then you must pray. There is no one greater than God, the boss is not greater than God.'

Foi et Pratique does not in any way wish to express, or be ascribed, any political standpoints. The debate about the veil, for example, has reached quite an unacceptable level, the Sheikh believes. Foi et Pratique does not wish to enter the debate, nor did they take part in demonstrations for the right to wear the veil:

> We are indifferent to politics. Our only intention is to explain Islam. For us politics is a superficial subject. We are concerned with Islam, not politics. To wear the veil is not a subject suited to politics, it is a religious command. There is nothing new about that!

Nor will they take a stance on the Rushdie affair. There was no taking part in demonstrations and Khomeini's *fatwa* was not recognised. One person in the group called Salman Rushdie a dog, but he was not the first to do so.

Sheikh Imam Mohammed Hammami was not invited to join the interior minister's new council on Islam and nor would he have any wish to do so even if he was asked: 'If the council makes decisions that serve Islam best, then it is only for the better, if they reach bad conclusions we are indifferent. We follow Islam anyway!'

5.2.1 An Interview and its Context - Meeting Sheikh Mohammed Hammami

My meeting with the leader of Foi et Pratique, Sheikh Mohammed Hammami, can provide some further insight to characterise the movement.

There was a marked difference between the interview situation which I had experienced with the Islamists of Millî Görüş and that which I encountered with the Sheikh of Tabligh in Paris. The leaders of Millî Görüş were people with organisational leadership skills while there was quite a different religious charisma about the Tablighi leader. This difference is reflected in their titles. The Tablighi leaders are typically *imams* and there is an *amir*, who is the ultimate leader. Millî Görüş is led by a *bölgebaşkan* respective to a *başkan* (i.e. regional chairmen, respective to a chairman).

The integrity of the Sheikh had to be protected with regard to the interview, several techniques were used with this in mind:

Although the roles are clearly defined in an interview situation, further distance was imposed by the circumstance of the Sheikh speaking in Arabic, despite the fact that he had just been speaking to me in good French: The Sheikh's answer had to be translated first into French, so I did not get the original reply. Revision of the interview was made impossible as I was refused the use of a tape recorder: 'that is not necessary,' it was explained to me. I could take notes and that would have to suffice, I was told. If my version of the interview was unsatisfactory, seen from the Sheikh's point of view then he could always insist that I had either misunderstood something or else that it had been wrongly translated.

There is, in addition, a reason to note that the Sheikh spoke not only in Arabic, but in *classical Arabic*. Thereby he spoke not only a language that I did not understand, but also a religious language, and one that was a practical demonstration of his position as far as his assistants were concerned. Furthermore the assistants would take over the task of answering my questions if they were deemed too polemic.

Since my command of the French language would have been sorely taxed if confronted with migrant-French, I wanted to ensure myself the use of an interpreter. However, my intention to use a female interpreter was immediately rejected by the Sheikh's assistants, who acted as go-betweens. A male interpreter was provided instead, who had great sympathy for my linguistic difficulties. In my meetings with various other Islamist representatives, and with the local representatives of state-religious representatives, I had never encountered this indication. It is, of course, pertinent to stress that it was the Imam's assistants who categorically refused me the presence of a female interpreter, it was not the Imam himself.

There was clearly no doubt about the fact that it was an honour for me to be allowed to interview the Sheikh. Up until the last moment there was some doubt about whether he would talk to me at all. I had no immediate person who could put me in touch with the sheikh. I chose therefore to go directly to the main mosque where I contacted a random group of believers who were about to leave the mosque. I explained that I wished to interview the sheikh.

A natural curiosity emerged about my intentions, and I then explained about my project. Two attitudes towards me immediately transpired - one group felt that it was very strange and suspicious that I had simply turned up from Denmark and had happened to approach them. The second group accepted my explanation, but said that I would have to return in three hours when the imam would be at the mosque.

The discussion continued, meanwhile, on the street outside the mosque where a great deal of energy was expended in explaining to me what Islam actually stood for. After a couple of hours in the company of these enthusiastic followers of Foi et Pratique, and after several Islamic books had been purchased for me,⁹ it was agreed that perhaps they might be able to help me. It turned out that the sheikh's youngest son, Hammadi, would be used as a messenger. Hammadi heard my story and promised to ask his father. Perhaps he would meet me the following day, Friday. If I could come along at around 4 p.m. then they would ask, although with no guarantee of the outcome. His father was actually quite tired of journalists and no longer wished to give interviews to them.

At 4 p.m. Hammadi came and explained that there was still no clear sign, and that his father was unfortunately very tired and had to take a rest. But if I could return at around 7 p.m. then perhaps there might be a chance. I recalled the innumerable other occasions on which I had made appointments which had simply come to nothing in the end. On the other hand I was received very obligingly by the son and others, which gave me hope. Only my persistence would show them that I was serious about what I wanted.

I arrived at 7 p.m. to find the sheikh busy sending out a group on *joula*, but he was willing to see me afterwards.

Right from the start of the interview the imam and his group were on the lookout for conflict-raising questions, and questions related to political life.

After an hour's time, a sign was made indicating that the interview was over, in that my attention was also drawn to the fact that it had been hoped that I would have shown a greater interest in Islam.

5.3 On the Periphery of Islamism

As it clearly emerges from my interview, it is a principle of the movement not to outline any political stance. Bearing this in mind, it is no coincidence that in its founding rules for the *Makki Masjid* in Copenhagen the movement includes among its aims, 'to maintain the original Muslim traditions without causing offence to the Danish population' (Bæk Simonsen 1990, p. 100). That they have no wish to associate themselves with any body of power is made clear from, among other things, the fact that they do not participate in the council of the French Interior Minister. This has been one of their characteristics throughout all their years in

---

⁹ I was given a book for children on fasting in Ramadan, and one with stories from the life of Muhammed. I have, in the course of my investigation, been given various small Islamic publications. The books I was given on this occasion, however, marked an interesting change from those that I had otherwise received. Previously, they have always been books of a scholarly Islamic nature, typically publications by Mawlana Maududi, or 'manuals' on Islam.

France. In this way Legrain asserts (1986, p. 14f.) that *Jama'at al-Tabligh* is the only significant movement which has not at any time wished to take part in gathering the Islamic organisations in France under a common umbrella - neither in *Rassemblement Islamique*, which was organised by *La Mosqué de Paris*, or in *la Fédération Nationale des Musulmans de France*.

Jama'at al-Tabligh distances itself clearly from the Islamists in not being oriented either politically or to a state. For the members of *Jama'at al-Tabligh*, what counts is being able to pass on Islam through simple explanations and through leading an upright life. Mumtaz Ahmad shows that the movement is fiercely 'anti-intellectual', deeply sceptical of the Islamic religious scholars (Ahmad 1991, p. 516f.). They are non-violent, they are courteous and present the message of Islam to de-Islamised Muslims - and to society in the widest possible sense.[10] They stress the importance of children learning Islam. And this leads us to an explanation of the apparent paradox of how a movement which *on the one hand*, according to Giles Kepel (1987, p. 179), can both be the largest Islamic group on the world stage, strongly missionary and, *on the other hand*, largely unknown in the West: it suffices to say that the movement is distinctively missionary, but the persistent anti-political grouping makes itself noticed by being highly activist in its orientation towards the daily life of immigrant Muslims.[11]

This activism is, meanwhile, met by a certain silence on the part of the official French and North African authorities, who would prefer greater discretion. On the other hand they perhaps see the movement as a buffer for the politically engaged Islamists (Legrain 1986, p. 14f; Diop 1989, p.8). This viewpoint seems also to be shared by the government of Pakistan in the 1960s. High ranking officials at the time have since said that direct

---

[10] The history of the movement is actually based on mission work among Muslims at a time when Hinduist revivalist movements were active among the formerly Hindu population who had converted to Islam. Jama'at al-Tabligh's mission was then, aimed at converts, who had not given up their Hinduist past in relation to the many rites which concerned the cycle of life (Ahmad 1991, p. 511 ff.).

[11] This anti-political line which is so characteristic of the movement has meant that they have remained indifferent to some of the most crucial socio-political themes in Pakistan. This has, conversely, led to the movement being criticized by Jama'at-i-Islami for thereby doing more to assist the anti-Islamic forces and secularism rather than Islam. The movement has, meanwhile, not managed to keep itself entirely clear of political controversy. In the 1950s, for example, a *fatwa* was issued against Jama'at al-Islami and their leader, Maududi. The movement was criticized for being only motivated by politics and for lacking interest in the spiritual dimensions. The movement has not, as such, taken a position on the Iranian revolution, while several of its leaders have criticized it for having nothing to do with Islam and for provoking divisions in the Islamic world (Ahmad 1991, p.518).

instructions were given at the government level to assist the movement so as to 'neutralise the influence of Jama'at-i-Islami and other politically activist ulama groups' (Ahmad 1991, p. 518).

Jama'at al-Tabligh can, however, also be taken as the first step towards political mobilisation: after having dug themselves into purely religious engagement, then crossing the line to Islamist activism.

This in any case is the view of the Tunisian Islamist movement's founder. Francois Burgat quotes a conversation from 1985 with Ahmida Enneifer:

> It was at that time (1970 was the year of the birth of the Tunisian movement), that a group, Jama'at al-Da'wa (yet another name for Jama'at al-Tabligh) came to us every year from Pakistan. In the beginning it consisted only of Pakistanis, but gradually they drew Tunisians to their school. Jama'at al-Dawa are people who travel in the Muslim world and preach a return to Islam, to religious praxis, etc. It is their simplicity which affected us, their way of life, which resembles the past in Tunisia. In this way one had two points of view. One way, which can be qualified as apolitical, was Jama'at al-Dawa, which proclaimed the good news to the people and their wish to see a return to the right path. There was however another tendency, much more intellectual, within the structure of l'Association pour la préservation du Coran, which wanted to hold conferences, organise meetings, create a small scientific research laboratory. But these two lines were quite different: one part was simple or popular, activist, etc., and the other part was striving towards the intellectual, and reached a much smaller number of people. It was so that this carried on until 1972 or 1973, those were the confused years. People did not really know what to do. One thing, however, was certain and that was that religious ideology could not be avoided. The religious aspect had become essential. The political aspect, however, still remained vague (Burgat 1988, p.25).

Francois Burgat, likewise, quotes a conversation from 1987 with Abd el-Salam Yassine, who for a number of years was a member of a *tariqa* until the sheikh passed away. Yassine is now one of the leading figures in the Moroccan Islamist movement. (Jamiyat al-Shebiba al-Islamiyya/Association de la jeunesse Islamique):

> In Morocco it happened in exactly the same way. It was they, the Tablighis, and not the Muslim Brothers who were the first. Before they came there were the occasional missionaries from the Muslim Brothers, but they did not produce any followers. The people from Jama'at al-Tabligh appealed to workers and doctors alike, in the same language without making any detours, without a political or economic dimension. These people, who are the voice of Islam's fundament, consult their hearts

before they consult their heads and their minds. They had, and still have, the healthiest influence on the Islamic movements. Their apoliticism is a plus for them since it allows them to travel freely, and much more easily. The West, which I also believe is spiritually dried up, finds in the Tablighis something which they are lacking.....With this simplicity, this pure religiousness, they have made conquests in Italy where people on the street ask them: 'Who are you?' and discover Islam for the first time in their lives. This also happens in Japan, in Canada, and in South Africa, even in South America. And their annual meetings today draw millions of people: I believe there were 4 million in Bangladesh last year...(Burgat 1988, p.26).

Jama'at al-Tabligh originates from a superficial, Islamised Muslim environment, whose praxis, according to the Islamist leaders was not inspired by the Koran, but by directives from Buckingham Palace, writes Gilles Kepel, and continues:

Sixty years later, despite the decolonisation and the independence of the Islamic countries, the cultural situation of the poor and poorly educated Muslim masses, immigrated into a very pregnant modernity where holy scripture has been ordered aside, has no structural comparison with that of the Mewatis in the time of Ilyas (Kepel 1987, p.179).

It could be said that the affiliation with *Jama'at al-Tabligh* is linked to the revitalisation of Islam generally, but the values, activities and institutions of the movement are completely different from those of the Islamists. However, the strength of the movement appears to be that it has set its sights on uncompromisingly bringing about the simple Islamic life here and now. This demands no special preconditions, everyone can join - Islam is belief and practise, not thick books. One should not wait for an Islamic state to bring about the optimal conditions. This taps directly into existing daily life at the personal level. This points also towards an ascetic movement among the marginalised, where faith becomes a dominant element in the structure of daily life. It is doubtful, however, in the long term, whether this will be sufficient to hold the attention of the young who need a vision in a global and modern context, something which the Islamists can provide to a much greater degree.

6 Migration, Marginalisation and Social Identity - Islam and 'Cultural Release'

In the preceding four chapters (Chapters 2-5) of this thesis I have analysed the development of Islamic organisations in Western Europe, primarily since the 1970s.

In *Chapter 2*, I illustrated that the wish of Islamic organisations to be able to function like European organisations has, to a large extent, been shaped and restricted by political and legal circumstances. I have shown that the institutionalisation of Islam in Western Europe is definitively influenced by the tendency within the European states to favour the initiatives advanced by the Muslim states on this matter - at the cost of autonomous organisations within the Muslim minorities of the European countries.

Furthermore, in *Chapter 3* I have outlined how one particular Islamist movement (Millî Görüş) has managed to establish itself among Muslim, Turkish-European minorities. I show that the movement offers a social platform which seeks to link religious and social practices with an Islamic moral stance fixed at its centre. As such the movement is an explicit challenge to the Turkish state's understanding of itself as the guardian of the Turkish cultural heritage among Turkish minorities in Western Europe.

In *Chapter 4* I went into how, at the local level, young Islamists who belong to the movement regard their Islamic consciousness at a personal level in relation to everyday questions. It has clearly been shown that the young people in the movement, often referred to as second generation immigrants, 1) do not differ markedly from other young Turkish-Danes with regard to their social profile, 2) they use Islam as a negotiating stance in relation to society as a whole, as the core of a positive form of social identification, as an alternative to the remote possibility of attaining positive social identification through the labour market, and 3) they are not socially limited by the religious community which they enter.

The community is not sharply cut off from the outside, - 'traditional' social strategies such as those of kinship also function.

Finally, in making an excursion into *Jama'at al-Tabligh* in *Chapter 5* I attempted to accentuate my profile of Islamism. I have demonstrated that this is a vivid illustration of the possibilities of developing a form of Islamic fundamentalist activism that restricts limits itself to the purely personal level within a moral perspective.

In *this chapter* the intention is to shift the perspective from the immediate level of the social players to the context of the society which defines the conditions under which the immigrants establish themselves as ethnic minorities. On the basis of this I shall, in the subsequent and concluding *Chapter 7*, turn back to Islamism's vision and strategy so as to discuss - and this time at a qualitative new level - the critical relevance of Islamism to its participants.

Bearing this in mind, the aim of the present chapter is to relate the development of the Islamic movement to a general theoretical frame of understanding. The question raised is as follows, how is it possible to conceive of Islamism within the structural conditions of social processes in Western European capitalist society in general? and the social processes that characterise the integration of the new ethnic minorities in particular.

6.1 Muslim Minorities, Labour Market Affiliation and Social Identity

Immigration to the European centres of growth, which, throughout the 1950s and 60s had a great demand for manpower, occurred simultaneously with the development of underdevelopment in so-called peripheral capitalist society.[1] There are quite specific conditions associated with the immigration of unskilled labour after the Second World War in each of the individual countries. France, Britain and Holland, for example, had

---

[1] These waves of migration are often seen as being a result of the so-called 'push and pull' factors. The migrants were 'pushed' out of their homelands or regions as a result of mechanisation, or because of low product prices which resulted in a surplus work force, and they were 'pulled' to Western Europe because of the shortage of manpower here. Considerations of the character and causes of migration stretch across micro- and macro analyses, as well as analyses of social networks, and psychological patterns of explanation. For a critical discussion of the dominant theories in the investigation of the nature of migration, see Christian Horst (1980). For a comprehensive analysis of labour migration's character as a function of the movement of international capital, and the ranking of countries in the international division of labour, see Saskia Sassen (1990).

previously experienced migration from their respective ex-colonies. West Germany, Belgium and Sweden first became involved at the end of the 1950s with the arrival of a work force from the Mediterranean countries. The labour migration into Denmark began in the 1960s and shared the same preconditions as the rest of Western Europe. It was only in the mid-1960s that Turks, Yugoslavs, and Moroccans began to make a noticeable appearance on the European labour markets.[2] Immigration occurred because of the demand for a work force which could no longer be provided by domestic resources. The picture varied, as mentioned, from one country to the next, however, generally it can be said that the work which the foreign workers were offered predominantly fell within the range of unskilled, low paid, labour intensive, often dangerous industrial production.

In Denmark these included the iron and steel industry (in particular iron foundries and rolling mills), and tileworks, - work force ghettos developed,[3] 'ethnic occupational ghettos' (Feuchtwang 1990 & Schierup 1993).[4] The foreign workers were, then, a replacement force for a Danish work force which at the time was being drawn in large numbers into the

---

[2] Regarding the labour migration in a selected number of European countries, see Stephen Castles (1984). In Danish, see also Christian Horst (1980).

[3] Of the Turkish workforce in 1981, 81% were unskilled, of the Pakistanis 76%, Morroccans 76%, and Yugoslavs 81%, compared to 25% of the Danish workforce (from; Henriksen 1985).

In 1972 61% of immigrants were employed within 'industrial production' against 27% of the Danish workforce. In 1974 the figures were 75.6% respectively, 26.2% (Klebak & Horst 1977, p.30), and in 1981 about 45% (between 29-52) against 26% (Henriksen 1985, p. 109). The figures for immigrants employed within the 'service sector' in 1972 were: 14.8%, in 1974: 10.1% and 1981:20-34 against 35% for Danes (ibid.).

A smaller survey carried out in the Glostrup area in 1971 shows a higher proportion of work injuries among foreign workers than among Danish workers in general. Thus around 7% of the male Danish workers in 1971 were injured, while 25% of the foreign workers in two selected businesses had suffered similar injuries (injuries that resulted in more than 3 days off work excluding the day of the injury itself). Although the survey does not include data that might tell us the extent to which the rate of injury among foreign workers was higher than that of Danes employed in the same jobs, we can conclude that foreign workers were engaged in branches that generally had a high frequency of injury (Mossing 1973). See also Klebak and Horst (1977, p. 31ff).

[4] I am using the term *work force-ghetto* here to refer to specific workplaces which are based on a narrow social recruiting foundation which runs along ethnic lines. Feuchtwang (1990) and Schierup (1993) employ the term *occupational ghetto* to cover the same condition, but which has a wider range as opposed to being related to a particular trade, as such.

rapidly expanding service sector. The foreign workers provided a temporary alternative to technological rationalisation in the labour intensive occupations they went into.

The 'crisis' came in the 1970s with the subsequent industrial structural changes following in its wake. It was in precisely those areas in which the foreign workers were employed that revealed themselves to be affected by the changes. As a result they suffered unemployment, at a considerably higher rate than that of Danes, and which continued to rise. By the mid-1980s unemployment was three to four times higher for foreign workers than for Danes.[5] In 1995 unemployment was three times as high for first generation immigrants than for the Danish population as a whole (Hummelgaard, et al 1995). Both Horst (1977) and Henriksen (op.cit.) as well as Hummelgaard et al. (op.cit.) note that once they have lost their jobs immigrants find it very hard to find work again, - unemployment tends to be permanent.[6] This can be caused by immigrants not being able to live up to the changes in conditions of qualification and in racist attitudes/ discrimination in the labour market.

The available statistical material shows that the level of unemployment among the immigrants can not be ascribed to education and language qualifications alone, in that higher unemployment is registered among immigrants that among Danes with similar professional qualifications. And although second generation immigrants generally manage better than their parents, they do not manage as well as the rest of the population.

This underlines the point that prejudice and discrimination figure as significant barriers to integration within the labour market. Several analyses, however, also show that the recruitment of new workers into industry occurs to a large extent via social networks (Madsen 1982, Feuchtwang 1990 and Csonka 1995), which usually do not cross ethnic boundaries.[7]

Csonka (op.cit.) shows that labour exchange offices are used less and less the greater unemployment is: the social networks in the companies take care of recruitment more easily. People who are already employed put

---

[5] This refers to the level of unemployment calculated according to full time unemployed in relation to those insured against unemployment (c.f. Statistik om Indvandrere, Danish Ministry of the Interior 1985).

[6] Ingrid Henriksen (1985) shows that the fact that many immigrants have moved away from 'production industries' is not a result of upward mobility, but of a further marginalisation of the labour market - in that the statistical move towards 'service functions', included projects for the long term unemployed organised by the municipalities.

[7] This is a condition that Schierup also addresses (1993, p.110.).

forward friends and acquaintances for vacant positions. The outcome of this recruitment strategy is, of course, that there is no way of gaining employment for those seeking work who are not already part of the social network of the company employees.[8] A self-supporting social and economic marginalisation process is thereby set in motion regarding the development of the labour market. This means an increase, among other things, in the development of an ethnically divided labour market and labour market relations along lines of ethnic affiliation. At the same time this produces a growth in the kind of jobs that take advantage of the marginal position of immigrants in the job market - the best known examples are continuous labour ghettos with bad working environments, minimum wages and very poor prospects for further employment.[9]

There are few who are *actively* interested in changing these conditions. The business community, of course, is not. They have a reserve work force in immigrants who are dependent on the employment. Nor are the immigrants themselves, who, in these work place ghettos see a conveyor system which allows them to continue receiving unemployment benefit, as a last chance to avoid ending up completely outside the labour market system, or who see it as an opportunity to gain access to the benefit system and also, despite everything else, to be able to contribute to their own livelihood. The trade unions have not developed a policy to deal with the matter and remain without any possibility of being able to suggest any realistic alternatives.

The social and economic vulnerability and marginalisation does not only apply to immigrant Muslim minorities in Denmark, a parallel situation is well documented in the rest of Europe (see, e.g. Castles 1984 and Cross

---

[8] The significance of the social network can also be seen reflected in relation to developments in the internal division of labour in a business (Schierup 1993 and Csonka 1995).

[9] Immediately after the publication of Günther Wallraff's book *Ganz unten*, Kiepenheuer & Witsch (1985) The Working Environment Service (Arbejdstilsynet) in Aarhus Amt carried out a survey which revealed quite unacceptable working conditions for immigrants and particularly for young women (Graversgaard 1986). This initiative was followed up by an extended hearing arranged with a Turkish immigrant union, the Anatolsk Kulturforening. The hearing also confirmed that problems of the above nature were widespread and were of quite a worrying nature in that the threat of being fired hung constantly over people's heads.

The director of the Arbejdstilsynet, Jørgen Rafnsøe, maintains that immigrants, especially Turks and Yugoslavs are not only employed in work places with a higher risk of injury than Danes, but that they are also persistently pushed into such jobs. That is to say that they are continually pushed into jobs that involve a relatively larger risk that their previous jobs. A continued marginalisation process is thus developing in this field too (Rafnsøe 1987).

1986). Globally speaking, the actual tendencies in terms of employment are linked, according to Sassen (1990) to the development of low paid jobs as a function of the rapidly expanding service sector. This is primarily service aimed at the specialised, export oriented service-sector and services aimed at high income groups within this sector (op.cit., p.22).

The economic and structural development in Europe after the Second World War was in fact based on the continued management of demand on the world market. The role of the state apparatus was to ensure that priorities were made to support this rationality - a role that demanded an extension of state competence with professionals in prominent positions. In other words, we can consider this as the development of a tendency towards 'technocratising', and thereby to a de-politicisation of state decision processes.

This also imposed a demand on the state apparatus to ensure social stability, such as through the development of public institutions, for example, to safeguard the socialising tasks which previously had primarily been confined to the home and the family. Today it is not just day care institutions that play a central role in this, but also schools and other social institutions.

In other words the economic development which gave rise to comprehensive social restructuring ascribed to the state apparatus the task of organising new fields. To use Habermas' terminology, which I shall return to further on, it could be said that social relations which were formerly organised in the *lifeworld*, that is to say the non-systemic organised social networks and communities, were instead now to be organised in the *systemworld*, in other words the fields of influence organised by the state and market (Habermas 1981).

As I indicated earlier it is characteristic of the new ethnic minorities that do not feel they are adequately represented by the traditional European unions and political organisations. The new ethnic minorities are primarily organised in their own organisations and movements. One of the reasons for this should perhaps be sought in the fact that the traditional European social organisations were an integrated part of the social development of Western Europe. This was a development which, as mentioned, delegated significant regions within the lifeworld to the care of the state. The role of the organisations has been subject to this process. Those ethnic minorities who arrived later have, therefore, as it was made clear above, developed a need for their own organisations that could articulate their social and cultural interests and which could function as intermediaries with regard to the outside world. The immediate demands made on the country of immigration are linked to work, accommodation, education and sports facilities. Looking inwards, however, it is the need to be able to develop networks which cross kinship and family bindings in the sense of organising cultural arrangements, tuition in the mother tongue, religious praxis, travel clubs, and funeral funds.

In the light of the terms *lifeworld* and *systemworld* which I shall incorporate (p. 160 below), the dynamics of the newer Islamic movements should be regarded as an articulation of social and cultural interests that are not represented. A need develops among the ethnic minorities for alternatives and supplements to existing interest organisations. This perspective should not immediately be taken as an approval of the explanation which argues that the Islamic movements have to be seen fundamentally as marking a 'value shift' among young people whose personal biographical experience has steered them into an orientation towards more spiritual values, as an alternative to falling back on a traditionalist type of world view.

I must admit that the strength of this explanation is, however, that it does address itself directly to some of factors which the movements' members cite individually as being the cause of their religious orientation. It is, however, also my belief that this 'value-shift' is not only related to conditions of life history, but also emerge from concrete social processes which, as I have touched upon, have had wide reaching social consequences.

When the ethnic minorities organise themselves independently in relation to the colonisation of the lifeworld, this does, therefore, relate, not least of all, to the fact that they are bound together in terms of identity to a process of migration and social development which is necessarily loaded with conflict:

-they enter Europe as a new social category, which is created through the development of socio-economic demands,

-they comprise a category that is still growing, but have at the same time radically lost their anchoring in a traditional lifeworld context. The idea of kinship as a basis for social organisation is actively threatened by, for example, the crucial element of the market based social system,

-their affiliation with the labour market is characterised by high unemployment, bad working conditions and strong tendencies towards a division of work along ethnic lines. This marginalised position makes them particularly reliant on the management of public institutions.

As a basis of identity this encourages ambivalence and a sensitivity towards conflict. The extreme pressure on living conditions gives rise to a development of unique cultural references based on a radical re-evaluation of cultural roots. Through this, virtually imposed, process 'Islam' enters into the discussion. Although basic insights into Islam might have been gained in the homeland, these are heightened by the process of migration to

Europe, and become a central reference in social identification (see also, Pedersen & Selmer 1991).

On this basis, then, I shall evaluate the growth of the Islamic movements as a consequence of structural developments in recent years concerning the economy and the expansion of the state. To talk of value changes alone in the light of this would be to reduce any understanding to the explanation of the participants themselves. The expansion of the *systemworld* continues to question the material-based systems of the *lifeworld*, the result being various types of conflict.

6.2 Reflections on 'Systemworld' and 'Lifeworld'

Let us in the following expand on the terms we have introduced, *systemworld* and *lifeworld*, with a view to a broader theoretical view of social processes in Western Europe. Following on from this we can try to link partial theories on migration processes with these analytical terms so as to set the development of the newer Islamic movements in a general theoretical perspective.

Habermas enables the distinction to be made, through the use of the above named terms, between the rules that decide the participants' course of action and the rules that stabilise subconscious actions (Habermas 1981). It is crucial to differentiate between the acting subject's participant perspective and the non-participating observational principle through a social system term. Society must be seen in the perspective of both lifeworld and systemworld at the same time. It is actually *lifeworld* which is the key term here.[10] Lifeworld should, in this way, be understood as the complex social relations that are reproduced by the processes of socialisation and the forms of community. The context of the lifeworld comprises in effect the continuity which links life experience, everyday life, and the religious orientation in association with the Islamic movements.

The *systemworld* on the other hand consists of the areas which capital (the market), and not least the state apparatus, organises. In principle the systemworld tends towards the domination of its surroundings and thereby to altering existing normative structures. The systemworld also has the character of *wanting* to 'colonise' the lifeworld by the logic of its rationality - which is to say that it almost adopts the form of a teleological

---

[10] Habermas' term *lifeworld* tendenciously coincides with the notion of *culture* as we find it in, e.g. Bauman (1973), or, more pertinently in Gramsci's term of *civil society* (1971), and Bourdieu's term *habitus* (1977).

principle. Historically speaking, this has been a notable characteristic of the spread of capitalism, i.e. in the form of urbanisation and migration. It can be said that because of the increasingly great differentiation of society and the destruction of traditional forms of solidarity, the state apparatus is forced to intervene increasingly in the life of the singular individual. It is, in fact, not given that the collapse of former structures in the lifeworld, ensures the emergence of new forms of solidarity (Habermas 1981, p.178). This also means that the systemworld is dependent on a well functioning lifeworld, on social networks and forms of fellowship, which do not, necessarily, have to be based on the family, but, as in modern society, can quite easily be conceived of on the basis of voluntary associations.

This provides, as such, the starting point for the idea that, as far as social practises are concerned, modern society is split into two fields which are in mutual conflict with one another. Habermas concerns himself with how the lifeworld is made subject to the rationality of the systemworld on a number of different levels.[11] Although the rationality of the *systemworld* is, as noted, guided by an overriding systematic principle of expansion, the changes do not occur in one smooth unchallenged course, on the contrary, they often occur non-contemporaneously, in between levels, and over a long period of time.

The different levels of rationality each have their own rate of development, which is why these processes in the cultural context have the character of being disproportionate, mixed, and having a lack of simultaneity: 'They are rather more insidious by nature, in that the changes can mostly only be felt from a distance, both in time and space'(Ziehe & Stubenrauch 1983, p. 29).[12] In this process certain former bonds are snapped, thus releasing potential energy. This 'release' from cultural

---

[11] According to Habermas, this 'colonising process' occurs on three levels of rationality:

(1) the level of the *objective world*, the world about which one can say something factual about and about which there is a consensus,

(2) the level of the *social world*, the world which regulates legitimacy in interpersonal relationships and thereby includes the collective symbols and comprehension of reality - to which Islamism relates itself directly,

(3) the level of the *subjective world*, the world which comprises mankind's subjective (inner) structure and thereby the experiences which are related to the individual's experience of life, and everyday life, and which it can account for.

[12] One of the examples given by Ziehe to illustrate the way changes at the cultural and biographical levels make their mark later on, is that in cultural terms the period after the war cannot be said to have been contemporaneous with the political and economic post war period, but only became apparent on a significant scale some 15 - 20 years later, during the 1960s (Ziehe and Stubenrauch 1983, p. 29).

traditions does not mean that the individual actually becomes more free, but is simply a release from previous objective preconceptions, such that an - albeit perhaps unattainable - expansion of expectations, transpires.

Ziehe describes the ambivalence of this cultural process of release. On the one hand it means in particular a release from the symbolic foundations of tradition, that the meaning of subjectivity can be re-evaluated. On the other hand this re-evaluation means that certain forms of load are increased. The gap between the longing and experience grows wider, the gap between reality and the resulting expectations is productive as far as the matter of change is concerned, but it can also give rise to paralysis (op.cit.,p.31).

It becomes meaningful to recognise that it is precisely in the discontinuity between systemworld and lifeworld that social and cultural conditions are disturbed, and that the cultural release thereby expressed becomes important to the newer Islamic movements. Or, to put it another way: the systemworld's reorganisation of social practices in the lifeworld does not automatically ensure social integration.

Habermas regards the tendencies towards disintegration as being a result of the systemworld's destruction of the conditions of communicative action in the lifeworld - i.e. as a 'reification-problematic'. One might say that with the system's expansion and intervention in the lifeworld there energies a need for legitimacy. This process, which is also characterised by *cultural release*, creates a need for resistance and social and cultural reorganisation - the alternative is anxiety or compensatory behaviour.

The social and cultural interests which the Islamic movements configure themselves around are, similarly, a result of the systemworld's dramatic colonisation of the lifeworld during migration. The Islamic movements in Europe can be viewed as a resistance to colonisation - as a symptom of social disintegration in the narrow sense, but more broadly as a pronounced attempt to express a social and cultural resistance to the dissolution of the lifeworld.

The matter of whether this social disintegration, and thereby also the Islamic movements, can be satisfactorily explained by reference to the crises in the systemworld's rationalisation of communicative action *alone*, is, however, open to debate. A model that was satisfied with this explanation would reduce the nature of the problem to an abstract, general, evolutionist analytic.

To read Habermas (op.cit.) that way would lead the analysis to side-step the specific, compound circumstances that are also linked to the social processes bound up in the conflict between systemworld and lifeworld, and in this case in relation to the conflict-filled processes of migration, of which the Islamic movements are a part.

This brings me to the end of my critical objections to the ontology of Habermas' project. Friedman (1994), for example, finds cause to regard Habermas ironically, as follows:

> Pure modernism as expressed in some of the work of Habermas would identify all social institutions as neurotic forms that hamper the development toward the context-free Utopia of communicative rationality (op.cit., p.221).

In contrast to Friedman, who hereby finds a reason to reject Habermas, I would, however, rather stress the historicity in this process in relation to the lifeworld.

As I touched on previously in this chapter, these processes must be seen in the context of the internationalisation of capital and the subsequent international process of integration which follows. Conditions which have given rise to comprehensive structural changes in the international division of labour and contributed to a continuing expansion of the state apparatus. These conditions are, as Friedman indicates (op.cit.), not in fact context-free. Processes of migration are social processes which occur under conditions that are not stable, but historical. This will become important in the following section in explaining the development and inertia of social processes.

6.3 Social and Cultural Interests among Muslim Minorities in Western Europe

Numerous social-anthropological works have examined the way in which the immigrants' struggle for existence is propagated along ethnic borders. Saifulla Khan (1978) stresses ethnic negotiation, the drawing of ethnic borders, as the rationale which defines the relationship between the ethnic minorities and the society of the majority. Others argue in accordance with this that the cultural baggage, motivations and orientations brought along play a crucial role in the situation of, say, Turkish and Pakistani immigrants (see, e.g. Dahya 1974; Hjarnø 1988, 1991). Conversely there is the argument that the ethnic borders are fluid and depend on social conditions in the group (Anwar 1979). Werbner develops and makes this standpoint relative in that she, in contrast to Saifullah Khan (op.cit.), prefers to see the cultural opposition as a result of inner power struggles within the ethnic groups:

..the community, as a discrete social entity, evolves relations of power, dominance and competing hegemonic tendencies within it; seen in interaction with the wider society, these processes of internal cultural consolidation and evolving power relations impact on its relationships with other segments of British society, creating both greater hostility towards it but also furthering the potential for personal and communal incorporation (Werbner 1990, p.341).

The economic and political context in which relationships between the ethnic minorities and the majority are thus played out underlines the significance of the distribution of resources and the character which the intervention of the state assumes in common concerns.

Against this background, the interplay between the new ethnic minority societies and the majority society cannot be taken as a smooth transition from traditionalist values to a modern value system, in which modernity is represented by the adjustment of the majority population to a general pattern of behaviour. The new ethnic minorities form networks which comprise every possible manner of reaction, created by the pressure from the systemworld.

This situation is also reflected by Schierup (1984) and Schierup and Ålund (1987), who, by introducing Bourdieu's term of the *social field*, provide an open and flexible understanding of the social forces that are active in the formulation of the social and cultural interests which comprise the reality of immigrants. The term refers to the fact that immigrant cultures, as such, relate themselves to both the outward as to the inward circumstances *and* to circumstances which characterise relations that look *backwards* to the region of origin (i.e., socially or in the form of kin, or in the form of property), along with relations which are aimed *forwards* to the country of immigration (i.e., new social networks and the labour market).

One important point is that those relationships which are aimed backwards are not diffuse and casual, but are founded on the fact that the act of immigration was based on chain-migration, and this social migration allows - at least to some degree - a reconstruction of family and/or village networks. This condition strengthens the migrant's interaction with the country of origin, for example, or with that part of the family which has not migrated. While these networks might be geographically remote, they can continue to be socially close to the migrated members.

The revaluation of the cultural heritage thus takes place in the local public, based on the social field which comprises a unit of complex forces which belong as much to the systemworld - as to the lifeworld. Seen in this perspective one can also then talk of the cultural resistance[13] assuming the form of *collective* fate, which finds expression in connection with the systemworld's demand for a reorganisation of the lifeworld of the new ethnic minorities.

The Muslim immigrants were, in point of fact, introduced during a time of socio-economic upheaval. The contribution of the state apparatus to the construction of national-state monocultures was, throughout the 1950s and 60s, strongly supported by the direction of movement of the economic undercurrent in the Western European centres of growth. This cultural *homogeny* (Friedman 1994) was broken in the 1970s and 80s in favour of a cultural heterogeneity. This *de-homogenisation*, which has caused some post-modern culture-analysts to talk of the tribalisation of youth, is explained by Friedman (op.cit.) as a phenomenon of the world system. The de-homogenisation springs from the development of a decentralised capital accumulation in the globalisation of production. This de-centred world economy has not only undermined the economic hegemony of the historical centre, but also the homogeneity of the centre itself, the cultural hegemony: '...the hegemonic structure of the world is no longer a reality; and with it, the homogeny which was its cultural form is also dissolving' (op.cit., p.141).

Stuart Hall, who talks of a 'shift in the subjective rhythm of life', and of the threat of a 'fragmentation of self-perception' (in Røgilds 1988), explains how young (white) unemployed refuse to spend their time hoping that they might find work. They constitute a new generation that, without illusions, invents alternative strategies of survival through, for example, motherhood or music: 'They are not completely lost. Their self-perception is not completely fragmented. They are definitely under great pressure, but their perception of themselves has not been completely fragmented' (Stuart Hall in Røgilds, p. 181).

The transformation of foreign workers into immigrants and their subsequent transformation into *Muslim minorities* (for example) coincides historically with the crucial structural changes in the social economy which were a prerequisite for this historical break.[14]

The new ethnic minorities are, so to speak, caught in a historic-economic trap. This implies that the lifeworld's conditions are distinctly different for these minorities than they are for the ethnic majorities, whose

---

[13] Ålund (1985) characterises this cultural resistance as *protective walls*. Ålund's application of this term includes the view that engagement with the surrounding world demands some safeguard to protect again the abuse of one's integrity.

[14] This is the same process that lies at the root of characterising society as 'post-industrial' or as an 'information society'.

social communities were transformed prior to this when crucial lifeworld processes were placed within the welfare state. The *local public*, as described by Schierup, does therefore look quite different.

The social communities and networks, which, for example, are related to kinship, ethnicity or Islamic identity become the answer to the threat of disintegration and break thereby from the systemworld's threats of fragmentation. Islamism's strategy becomes to produce symbols and institutions for this defence of cultural autonomy.

Gilroy imagines that the marginalisation of large minority groups produces the opportunity to form a common *black* youth culture which is a blend of various cultural sources. Gilroy cites a case where *hip-hop* music was capable of establishing a common cultural code which included both Afro-Caribbean and Asian youths:

> The explosion of interest in hip-hop culture which occurred in West London's Asian areas during 1985 is an important example of this creativity. For these young people, the language, symbols and artistic repertoires produced in the confluence of Afro-American, Hispanic and Caribbean cultures in the Bronx have yielded powerful sources of solidarity and pleasure as well as a means to organise themselves (Gilroy 1987, p. 217).

Examples can then be provided of the development of a cultural syncretism which redefines *Black Britain*. The question is, naturally, whether this syncretism is a marginal phenomenon with regard to Asian (Muslim) youth, or whether we can talk of a *tendency* which possesses the potential to create a new common identification, and one which also has the potential to include white youth?[15] Magnus Berg (1993) produces something of a parallel consideration, albeit in a different perspective, which can be briefly summed up as being that Turkish youth possess a 'secret identity', but an identity which finds nothing of interest within underground Swedish youth culture - on the contrary! Ground breaking youth culture is therefore forced to find its common roots in Afro-American culture (op.cit., p.49).

The decentralising of capital accumulation and the disarming of the economic and cultural hegemony of the historic, geographic centre results in the market, unlike in its previous interactions with the state, having to develop alternatives to the meaning of traditional social forms. The social and cultural interests are now firmly fixed in the lifeworld. The family and other traditional social networks can still show themselves to be central and crucial to the social processes in the lifeworld. Put another way, it is now

---

[15] Gilroy's project is to tackle conceptions of *ethnicity* and *ethnic absolutism*. He does not take up the matter as regards white youth.

left - insofar as this concerns the *systemworld* - to a large extent, up to the public institutions to contribute to the development of common cultural forms. This should not thus be taken as an argument for there being a special Muslim anthropology, special existential Muslim needs, which so to speak prevent such a process from within. The argument is, in contrast, of a historic character. Perhaps Pnina Werbner and Jørgen Nielsen are right when they claim to have observed that Muslim immigrants are less culturally vulnerable than, say, West Indians, who do not have the same well developed formal networks as the Pakistanis (interviews with, respectively, Pnina Werbner and Jørgen Nielsen, November 1988).[16]

The question can be approached from a slightly different angle as demonstrated by Courtois & Kepel (1988), Mouriaux and Wihtol de Wenden (1985, 1988), Subhi (1985) and Barou (1985), who show how Islam constitutes a new axis point in the organisation of the social life of workers in the workplace, and thereby also constitutes a third political force. The Muslim workers make new cultural demands of their places of work such as the presence of a prayer room, say, and the demand for the structuring of work schedules to allow Muslim festivals to be celebrated.

Against this background the workplace acquires a significance not only as a *place of production*, it is also the lifeworld, 'where the aspirations of the social actors concerned find expression which traverses a system of representation, traverses the imaginary' (Diop 1988, p.82).

This also constitutes a challenge to the discourse and practises of trade unions in formulating a collective negotiating tactic which also takes into account Muslim demands in the interaction between 'the private Islam of Muslim trade union members, the mobilising Islam of religious organisation leaders, and the peaceful Islam of the workers' (Mouriaux & Wihtol de Wenden 1988, p.49).

Courtois & Kepel (1988) propose an analogy between this process and that used by the French Communist Party (PCF) in the 1930s to stabilise, socialise and integrate the great southern European immigrant societies, mostly Italians, Spaniards and Portuguese - three million in 1931.

The trade unions and the PCF acted then as a kind of *integration machine*:

> If it is true that the PCF used its workforce to promote communist politics for 40 years as part of an international communist strategy, then it is even more true that a fraction of the French working class of rural and immigrant background have used the PCF as a similar kind of mediator

---

[16] *Pnina Werbner* is a social anthropologist employed at the Department of Sociology, University of Manchester. The Arabist, *Jørgen Nielsen*, was at the time director of the Islamic Centre at Selly Oak Colleges in Birmingham.

for four decades - to stabilise themselves during a difficult time and to quietly negotiate their integration into the French system (Courtois & Kepel 1988, p.36).

The trade unions and the French Communist Party do not play the same identification role in the case of the Muslim immigrants as they did in relation to the former Italian, Spanish and Portuguese immigrants. Courtois and Kepel's (ibid.) comparison between the immigrants from southern Europe and the integration of Muslim immigrants rests on the assumption that they represent a comparative point of departure: populations traumatised as a consequence of economic crises, social vulnerability, arbitrariness in life's circumstances and being subject to racism. The conjuncture of these forms the basis for a 'repli sur les valeurs propres'.[17]

Both phenomena - *Islam* and *Communism* - possess the same teleological and socially mobilising qualities:

> The communist phenomenon was a dual one, which certainly included an ideological-political dimension (teleological) that was subordinate to the imperatives of an organisation which belonged to the international communist system, and was a response to a global project (like Islam is), but which also included an anthropological dimension (societal), whereby it simply responded to the identity requirements of certain population groups (workers, peasants, etc.) (Courtois & Kepel 1988, p.35).

History has shown that the social dimension was stronger than the teleological as far as French Communism was concerned. In the case of Islam these two dimensions are not as yet decided.

The re-Islamisation of the Muslim immigrants represents a necessary step in the socialisation and eventual integration of these societies into the national community, but in the absence of the historic role of the trade unions and the PCF it is doubtful whether the same result could be carried through successfully (ibid).

There are two dominant and opposing viewpoints as regards the social function of the ethnic organisations. The *first* standpoint claims that the ethnic organisations maintain and encourage social segregation and cultural exclusion. The *second* view maintains that the ethnic organisations mediate between the minority and majority societies and thereby have an integrative effect on the individual as well as on the immigrant society as a whole. Schoeneberg points out a third standpoint:

---

[17] To the Communists *class* and *class party* represented a purity that was not to be *betrayed*, to the Muslim immigrants purity is represented by *Islam*.

...whether ethnic associations have a predominantly segregative or integrative effect will depend in large measure on basic orientations and activities they offer to their members and on the position they take to the rest of society (Schoeneberg 1985, p. 419).

Most of the organisations, the survey concludes, have a positive influence on social integration. Not surprisingly, however, it concludes that it is in fact the religiously oriented organisations which are characterised by encouraging social segregation in relation to the native European society.[18]

On the basis of this view the Muslim associations do not appear to have the ability to function as agents of integration; *partly* they do not have access to the area of political institutions,[19] and *partly* they encourage segregation and control of youth. Not even secular organisations such as SOS-Racisme and France Plus[20] can fulfil the role of social integration machines, according to Kepel, added to which they are too marginal in the social process (interview with Gilles Kepel).[21]

On the basis of what is outlined above we can allow ourselves to conclude that the difference between the two historical situations, as put forward by Kepel, cannot be reduced to a problem that only hinges on *Islam* or a Muslim anthropology. Islam does not rule out integration *per se*. The precondition, however, according to the interpretation of Courtois and Kepel, along with Schoeneberg, is that there are social players who can articulate the social and cultural interests that are historically in place within the Muslim immigrant community.[22]

It seems to me crucial, however, to stress that the *historic* context for North African migration is different to that of the Southern European case, and that this context makes a difference. The biggest wave of arrivals from Southern Europe is characterised by being contemporaneous with the industrial growth after the second world war in the European areas of

---

[18] This conclusion is also reached by Binswanger, K. and Sipahioglu (1988).

[19] The Islamic movements do not have access to political institutions because immigrants do not have the right to vote. Aside from a few exceptions the immigrants constitute a minority that will not be able to vote and therefore not attain political influence, according to Courtois and Kepel (1988).

[20] SOS-Racisme and France Plus are both 'beur' organisations supported by the Parti Socialiste.

[21] Bozarslan does not agree with this point of view. He, conversely, feels that these 'beur' organisations do actually constitute a politicisation based on the collective experience of demanding equal rights in French society. This introduces a perspective that transverses the horizons of previous ethnic organisations (Bozarslan 1989).

[22] In contrast, Binswanger and Sipahioglu (1988) believe that *Islam* obstructs the integration process.

growth. Campani et al. (1987) points to the mobility of the Italian workforce and that it is characterised by a higher proportion of skilled training than the later arrivals from North Africa - generally speaking.[23] Furthermore, Campani et al. (ibid.) stresses that there has always been a tendency in the debate to underline the fact that there was never an 'Italian problem', and that as far as the Italians are concerned they were *invisible* within French society and were accepted, - the same can be said to apply to the Portuguese (Hily & Poinard 1988).

On this point I would maintain that there are *qualitative* differences between the two examples given by Courtois & Kepel, which relate crucially to these being different socio-economic eras - where a factor such as visibility becomes central.

While Gilles Kepel explains that, historically speaking, it is a recent occurrence within the French context to speak of a *communauté musulman*, a Muslim community, as opposed to formerly referring to *travailleurs étrangers* and later of *travailleurs immigrés/algériens*...(Kepel 1987),[24] it does not appear to be due to the introduction of an *Islamic socialisation structure* alone, as he seems to suggest.

Dassetto stresses the need for a more cohesive understanding, one that considers the subjective experiences of immigration in a *cyclic migration perspective* - as he calls it: 1) the labour market constitutes the immigrants' first level of experience, which is why the social and economic aspect was at the forefront for the immigrants, 2) from the second half of the 1970s the family was to be the next new fundament of experience, in which upbringing and school life were the main concerns, and 3) sociability comes to the foreground: a series of civil, legal questions arise in connection with things such as marriage contacts, divorces and mixed marriages. A series of socio-political themes make their presence felt, including the unresolved *communication praxis*: How to tackle the multi-cultural/intercultural situation (Dassetto 1988). This, then, brings us to a problematic which, subjectively speaking, touches definitively on the matter of how the relationship between systemworld and lifeworld is articulated.

---

[23] Campani et al. (1987) does also mention that the Italian migration shows quite varied characteristics, which means that one has to qualify what one means with regard to *migratory entities*.

[24] This terminology for immigrants in France reflects a similar change in the rest of Europe. Research into *Islam* is surprisingly recent. In Michel Oriol's review of studies on Western European immigration history, from 1918-1979, studies of the religious life of the immigrants is absent. Up until 1979 the emphasis was on living conditions and on work, accomodation and education (Oriol 1980).

It was precisely this historically conditioned social situation which pushed the Muslim immigrants out onto the cultural periphery and left them without 'hegemonic power' (Stuart Hall in Røgilds 1988). This provides the lifeworld processes with a particular dynamic which gives the *Islamic socialisation structure* its significance in Western discourse. The newer Islamic movements represent, to my understanding, social and cultural interests that provide resistance to the systemworld's continued destruction of lifeworld structures.

The movements - Millî Görüş, in this particular case - constitute a network of regional and local self-help centres which, as was seen in chapters 2 & 3, organise social activities of very different characters: sport, information activities, courses and different forms of religious activities. These activities are aimed at both men and women, old and young. What separates the Islamic movements from other immigrant movements is that their religious and social practices point towards a moral centre which comprises a global Islamic vision. The reconquest of this social practise from the system is thus sought through the initiation of concrete social activities, and through an attempt to articulate the demands which spring from the process of social change.

What forms, then, does this resistance take in the lifeworld, and how do these forms relate to society as a whole: what potentials and perspectives do the Islamic movements comprise for dealing with the social conflicts of which they are a part?

The social and cultural needs expressed by the Islamic movements are a result of the systemworld's incursion into the lifeworld. By this definition certain demands are made on the movements to attempt to develop an ability to establish conventions and strategies which can construct a new social entity.

It is clear that a reorganisation of the social whole by way of an insistence on equal rights in the multi-cultural society, thereby securing a release from a humiliating power discourse, is a central notion of the Islamists - as it is for other immigrant groups.

In the concluding chapter, Chapter 7, I shall, on the basis of the material outlined here, conduct an investigation of Islamist expectations concerning this release and return to an evaluation of their development and the perspectives they contain, to gain an understanding of the current sociality. I would not claim that the Islamists' conceptualise a pluralist, multi-cultural society, on the basis of their specific invocation of equal rights, as such, since the consequence of their visions implies a necessary break with any social order that implicitly rests on a liberal democratic foundation. However, I would maintain that the term multicultural is broadly applicable with a spectrum of possible interpretations.

6.4 Public Institutions and Multicultural Society

The state administration of the life conditions of immigrants comprises a special field of conflict. To the immigrant movements this management represents the systemworld's colonisation of the lifeworld. The public administration is, seen this way, responsible for the guardianship and undervaluing of social and cultural needs and interests - the visions for change at this level require the recognition of these needs and the acknowledgement of autonomous institutionalised rights. Opposite this stands the public administration's political hinterland, which nowadays also expresses a need for decentralisation in its criticism of public management practices. In Denmark, early in the 1980s these concepts were addressed at such matters as the privatisation of public services - today they are concerned with the reduction of the scope of the state. One possible outcome of these notions of a smaller state might be that lifeworld expanding its scope.

In practice, however, in the beginning it was more a case of other parts of the systemworld taking over fields that were under state control through privatisation. Later it took on more of the character of a campaign of cutbacks aimed at the welfare state which are not met by the lifeworld's appropriation of the fallen bastions. Therefore, one could say that privatisation and cutbacks can go along perfectly well with the extension of administrative control. Schierup stated this clearly in relation to the situation in Sweden where *rebuilding self reliance* and *networking,*

> ...became synonymous with administratively controlling the clients' intimate lives and forcing them to take any job available rather than building up local autonomy and community responsibility (Schierup 1991, p.40).

As regards the new ethnic minorities one cannot speak of a limiting of administrative intervention. On the contrary, one can say that the 1980s and the beginning of the 1990s have actually meant an increasing desire by the public authorities, at both central and local state levels, to intervene to regulate the action opportunities and life conditions of the new ethnic minorities.

The reason given for this urge for monitoring, and regulatory intervention is that the ethnic minorities in particular are identified as by the state authorities as being a problem complex. (e.g. Grillo 1980, 1985; Werbner 1990; Pedersen 1991b; Schierup 1993 & Schierup & Ålund 1991).

It has become quite typical to regard the problem *vis-à-vis* immigrants as being ultimately a question of culture clash. According to this line of thinking these immigrants live 'in two cultures' or 'between two cultures', they live half in one and half in the other, or, even worse, in neither one nor the other. This implies that the tensions related to immigrants has to be understood as conflict and tension between two immutable value systems, between tradition and modernity and is not, therefore, due to a shortage of resources.

To a wide extent the cultural ballast of young people and of women is identified as being the real problem, rather than the strategy of the institutions towards immigrants. Talk of the *Muslim immigrant community* or *ethnic minorities* is, in itself, a sign of the development of a politicised relationship to the immigrants. Islam is seen as a *social problem*, Islam is politicised by the host community (Andezian 1986).

A survey of German studies on the situation of Turkish/Muslim immigrant women shows that they are considered in terms that stem from theories of underdevelopment, with *Islam* as the dominant factor of suppression. It might be claimed that the research perspective adopted towards these women represents a form of neo-colonialism - a perspective that would include the West German women's movement:

> Everywhere you find the theory that changed conditions of reproduction and changes in the distribution of work will only have a limited influence on the traditional status of women so long as their ideological orientation remains under the active influence of Islam (Lutz 1986, p17).

It is, then, a widely held view that *Islam* is the beast in the revelation, the devil's advocate and therefore as the cause of the problems, because *Islam*, it is said, is a way of life, a system of rituals, which also contains a fully developed and recorded set of laws governing daily life. This way of viewing the matter seems reasonable and in full accordance with widespread Muslim perceptions of themselves. It does, however, also appear to be a highly problematic standpoint, if we are to consider mankind, including Muslims, as part of the social world and not of the divine world. We would then have to turn away from the view of mankind and Muslims as being something created by God's hand, to see mankind and Muslims as being creative producers of culture, as acting human beings, who, among other things, look to their own god in seeking the secret principle of truth. This comprises the viewpoint that people relate to their god, their truth, their identity, but viewed in the light of experience in social life, and not the opposite. Man's relationship to God, the truth, or identity is thus taken as a social process.

The Turkish and Pakistani children and youth experience conflicts, but not between a particularly 'sacred' family and society. The immigrant families are in a double socialisation field which refers both back to a cultural normality that belongs to another world, and also to being alien to a cultural normality founded on another rationality. This social process influences the family's role and authority structure. This undermines the position of the father, not least of all (see also; Bøggild Mortensen 1989 and Hjarnø 1991). The fact that children are better at adjusting to conditions, the fact that they have a better grasp of the language, and the fact that their school education is better, all challenge the authority of the parents in general.

In Andezian and Streiff's (1982) interpretation, the position and importance of women to the group's identity is notably increased by migration. This is not related to the fact that they are the custodians of traditional order, but rather because their unbroken presence in the housing areas gives them the opportunity to establish a cohesive network which ensures social control in the immigrant community. Ålund, likewise, points out the increased importance of social networks centred around women in the immigrant communities of Stockholm suburbs (Ålund 1991, p.60).

The absence of elder women who would be in a position to represent the 'paternal power within the society of women' as in North African society results in the removal of the characteristics that traditionally would decide power status among groups of women:

> Social control based on status conferred by age and family hierarchy is replaced by joint control shared between the women of the same generation, in which the custodians of power must demonstrate that they can behave according to traditional roles as well as show a capacity for 'resourcefulness' in the host society (Andezian & Streiff 1982, p.309).

This situation is unique for younger women who are now forced to take a larger part of the responsibility for family life, inward as much as outward.

With the enormous unemployment that developed among men during the 1980s and 1990s Andezian & Streiff's analysis, based on field research in France in the 1970s, is not entirely adequate. The point of view has, of course, changed now since the social life of a large group of men has become narrowed and marginalised by their loss of work. The men, too, are now dependent on developing social networks in relation to the opportunities in the local area, such as through the local immigrant organisations, for example. To generalise, however, I would prefer to stress the importance of the quality of social competence in dealing with the institutions of the systemworld. Today, this social competence is in the hands of young people (male and female) of the second generation, thus replacing the hierarchy of age and family. And to take this as a basis for social control: in this sense, the young, second generation immigrants who are now adult quite simply represent the first generation which has its own experience of the European institutions and educational systems.

New answers are given to new questions. Modern society is in this respect characterised by social and cultural discontinuity, by breaks that continue to intervene in the lives of the individual. Just as Ralph Grillo has defined it in relation to France (Grillo 1985) we can also say that the 'immigrant problems' would seem to constitute a representation of the communicative relations between immigrants and the institutions of society. What is being discussed is the role of immigrants as users or customers of these institutions, such as the educational or health systems, etc., for example. The problems arise when the cultural or family patterns of the immigrants do not match the already structured consumer relations. The problems arise in the relationship between the institutions and the immigrants, but it is in the institutions' representation that the problems assume a political dimension.

This makes experience of the public administration a central pillar in the articulation of quite specific social and cultural interests.

One area that actually displays the experience immigrants have of institutional power is in the socialisation of children. The reaction of immigrants regarding education in the mother tongue in schools and the use of bilingual personnel in the day-care institutions shows (Pedersen 1991b) how 'the cultural field' is regarded with great seriousness. Immigrants consider this 'reception' as an invitation to debate cultural affairs, They do not feel that the question of who, for example, is to impart Turkish cultural norms to the children - in terms of teachers and other pedagogical personnel - is irrelevant. In a few cases there have been petitions organised to support a preferred candidate as an alternative to personnel chosen by those in charge of the language education and the day care institutions, without success, however. While the immigrants refer to cultural values as being the main criteria in these personnel, the institutions refer to a number of formal criteria as being pertinent to their choice of suitable personnel and argue that the criticism of the people employed is rooted in Turkish political discussions.

These formal criteria do not fulfil the expectation that mother tongue language teachers, and bilingual personnel in day-care institutions should function as conduits of Turkish cultural norms. There is, therefore, a conflict of interests in the definition of these instances. While to the organisers the teaching of the mother tongue is regarded as a chance for the children of immigrant groups to learn the Turkish language, the parents perceive it as an opportunity to assert a collective socialisation which exists as an extension of the socialisation of the family. We see, therefore, that the status of mother tongue education is taken up by the immigrants in order for it to gain the same systematic function for them as Danish public schools have for Danes.

In a number of day care institutions there has been an active attempt to adjust to the fact that immigrant children have begun to appear. Pedagogical research work has been started, but on a more general level it has been attempted to adjust the system by employing bilingual personnel. The municipality regards these bilingual personnel as some kind of 'cultural interpreters' who can assist the other personnel in their daily communication with the children, but also by representing the intentions of the institution towards the Turkish children and their parents. The parents 'misinterpret' this effort to oblige, and demand not only that these bilingual personnel act as interpreters, but that they should also be the representatives, guardians, and translators of Turkish culture in the institutions.

One conflict between Turkish families and Århus Kommune in connection with the employment of *Alevite* Kurds as bilingual staff in day-care institutions with children of *Sunni* Muslim Turks illustrates the two perspectives mentioned: A group of Turkish immigrant associations joined together in the autumn of 1988 to produce a petition in protest at the policy of the municipality towards Turkish immigrant groups. One of the points made was that they were unhappy with the engagement of Kurds as bilingual staff in institutions with Turkish children who were *Sunni* Muslims. The municipality dismissed the parents' objections as being irrelevant in that the qualifications required for the posts included a knowledge of Danish and not the applicants' cultural background.[25] And while there is little doubt that *Alevite* Kurds could fulfil the requirements of such institutions insofar as being qualified bilinguals, this does not necessarily imply that this measure would fully satisfy the demands of the ethnic Turkish immigrants that these personnel should also be their representatives.

School is one of the places where immigrant children encounter 'Danishness' on a massive scale. Here they have to acquire not only competence in the formal sense, but they must also build up the basis for their adult existence in the future. School is, then, the agent of socialisation and discipline.

School is, however, also the place where one expands one's life, broadens one's horizons, and this involves Danish peers and comrades. It is

---

[25] The conflict is reported in a number of articles in the daily newspaper *Århus Stiftidende*, i.e. the 28th November 1988, and was also well documented later in a special edition of the publication of the Anatolian cultural association, *MERHABA*, in January 1989.

quite characteristic that Turkish and Pakistani children and young people have a very poor - if any - personal development involving Danish children outside school hours. Even in the classes and in the schoolyard it is quite normal to split up according to nationality. Danes sit together with Danes, Turks with Turks, etc.. If, for example, there are sufficient numbers of Turkish pupils, then they play national matches in the schoolyard. As one teacher put it: 'Danish children are not bothered if their parents insist that they invite the whole class to their birthday parties because the Turkish classmates will not show up anyway.'

Let us turn now to how *Islam* figures as a pedagogically defined problem field in the county school system. What means of symbolisation and expression of religious affiliation are accepted in the publicly run primary school?

The laws and notices which define the organisation of teaching in the Folkeskole (county schools) presume that teaching is based on the circumstances pertaining to the individual pupil, in that values such as 'involvement' 'responsibility', 'freedom of spirit and thought', and 'democracy' are stressed at the same time. The interpretation of what this actually means can vary to a certain degree from school to school.[26]

The area of conflict in the schools with regard to Muslims who wish to emphasise Islamic principles is primarily noted in relation to the fields of sports, Christianity, sex education, as well as in relation to school camps, and days off on Muslim holidays and in relation to the use of the *hijab*.

Let me in the first instance define the basis of education in relation to the three subjects mentioned above:

Sports: This is an obligatory subject. The teaching comprises swimming, which is normally given in 3rd and 4th grade. One can be exempted for health reasons, but not for religious reasons. This fact was underlined in a ministerial circular on the participation of immigrant children in physical education. The ministry encourages schools to show respect and flexibility regarding the conditions for the obligatory bathing after the sessions are held. There are references to the possibility of using full suits, also for swimming, and they encourage practical solutions, such as the creation of separate shower units (Circulærskr 1986-01-13).

Sex Education: is an obligatory topic (not subject). It is mainly and normally given as an integrated part of the existing teaching curriculum,

---

[26] It should be remembered that responsibility for administrating the law governing the public schools (Folkeskoleloven) lies with the local authority, the kommune. The municipal councils can delegate certain competences to the school committees. Parent representatives constitute a majority in these school committees.

and not so often as an independently run course. Only in the vent of the last case is it possible to get special dispensation from participation (Bekendgørelse 172-06-15, nr 313).

Sex Education has given rise to criticism right from the start, from parents and others who regard it as obscene, and for intruding onto the space of parents. A writ was lodged at the European Council of Human Rights against the Danish state by three pairs of Danish (Christian) parents in 1972. The parents wanted their children to be exempted from the teaching. The Danish state was not found guilty, but the acquittal was based on a reference to the liberal Danish 'Free School Law' (Friskolelov) which gives parents the right to move their children to such a school (Eilschou Holm 1980). This case is still a leading one in the question of the right to exemption from certain topics in education in Denmark. It has also, among other things, prompted the fact that this teaching is given within the main teaching curriculum so as to ensure that the maximum number possible take part in it.[27]

Christian Teaching is centred on the Evangelical-Lutheran Christian teachings of the Danish national church (Folkekirke). Christian teaching occupies the centre of the Folkeskole's religious education, where it is also seen as the basis for understanding Danish culture, and understanding other religions (Bekendtgørelse 1991-06-20, nr.484).

Exemption from participation can be obtained, but this requires that the parents declare that they themselves will provide the teaching (Lovbekendtgørelse 1992-02-29, nr 669, pgf.59). The school authorities do not, however, have any legal grounds for controlling whether the parents actually live up to their promises.

Around 2% of the pupils in the Folkeskole are exempted from participating in Christian education, but there are wide local variations. There is no central registration of how many *Muslim* pupils do not

---

[27] It might be mentioned in connection with this that the number of private Islamic schools with public financial support is, relatively speaking, the highest in Europe. At the close of 1993 there were 12 such schools. Only Holland surpasses Denmark in actual numbers. In France there are none, in England there are none, in Germany there are none and in Belgium there was one. If we examine specific geographic regions then for a given nationality up to 30% of a particular grade attend a private Islamic school. Most schools are based on Arabic and Pakistani minorities. But during recent years the Turkish minority has also begun to establish private schools. The Islamic schools have been criticised from a number of sides for constituting a threat to integration on the basis of an abuse of the liberal Danish school system which is based on a Danish tradition of tolerance. The schools are allegedly being abused to further totalitarian aims. Officials from the Ministry of Education have also contributed to the debate using similar arguments.

participate in the teaching. An advisor at the ministry estimated that about 50% of Muslim pupils were exempted from taking part. My investigations show very large local variations. There are schools and classes in which nearly all the Muslim pupils participate, it very much depends on which way the subject is presented to the parents.

Different strategies are employed by the school leaders in approaching Muslim pupils and their parents when it comes to conflicts in relation to teaching. In my data I have identified the following three strategies:[28]

Strategy 1: The school qualifies not only as a Folkeskole, but as a *Danish* Folkeskole. When I began my interviews I somewhat naïvely interpreted the widespread use of the term *Danish* as a reference to a pedagogical norm that explicitly emphasised its positive method of approaching each child individually, in the way that the law is generally to be understood. This interpretation soon revealed itself to be mistaken when it came to *Muslim* pupils.

On the contrary, the stress on the term *Danish* should be taken as a means of constructing a pedagogical continuity that defines *Danishness* as the central cultural value of normality. This, thereby, banishes *Muslimness* into cultural marginality.[29] This discourse has its own patient, mildly repressive tolerant character. Practical solutions are sought to, among other things, nudity. People are free to hold Muslim holidays on the basis of mutual agreement being reached, and no questions are asked about the legitimacy of wearing the *hijab*, etc...If parents persist, and in the long run continue to question the need for their child to participate in certain aspects of the curriculum, then they are advised to move the child to a private Islamic school.

Strategy 2: The school also defines itself as a *Danish* folk school. *Islam* is considered a patriarchal form of repression. Islam defines a sustained pedagogical threat to the pupil and the social consequences of this have to be limited. The schools adopt a positive attitude to the pupil on the

---

[28] For a detailed account of my interviews with school leaders and imams concerning Islam and the folk schools, see Pedersen 1996.

[29] In her analysis of minorities and 'the idea of the national' in the Folkeskole, Jette Kofoed concludes that minority children are met on the one hand with a continued demand to behave in a Danish manner, while on the other hand, it is persistenly maintained that they will never really belong to the Danish world. This means that they are *not* offered an either/or choice with regard to a simultaneous possible identification with their parent's roots and an (imaginary) Danish background. They are not even offered an either/or choice with regard to the construction of social identity, but on the contrary, a neither/nor set of options (Kofoed 1994).

one hand and see themselves as their protectors. On the other hand the school adopts a tactical, in part menacing, and repressive strategy towards the parents. In particular the father is seen as a demonic organiser of the lifeworld. A take it-or-leave it strategy is adopted with no flexibility and without any effort being made to find solutions. To take the day off on religious holidays is considered unlawful absence. The use of the *hijab* is problematised partly as being repressive and partly as being destructive to efforts in developing the social life of the class. Parents are reminded of their option to enrol their children in a private Islamic schools if they are not prepared to accept the rules and systems of the school. Rather than regarding the establishment of Islamic private schools as one outcome of a failing in the Folkeskole, the law is used as a threat against the parents. At the same time Islamic free schools are considered an abuse of the tradition of liberal Danish schools.

Strategy 3: A small minority of school leaders define Islam as a positive starting point for the pupil. The Folkeskole law is seen as being on course for a head-on collision with freedom of religious belief as guaranteed by the constitution. One could say that these school leaders see themselves as being in a dilemma which requires a very elastic interpretation of the Folkeskole law. As one school leader puts it, 'I would have a serious problem if we had visiting school inspectors like they have in England here in Denmark checking on our teaching activities'.

We see then that the schools define the manner of the problems in different ways. But a grey area is established in the social life of the schools. The schools are involved in discussions that are complex and often quite contradictory in relation to Muslim pupils. The border line to an area formerly defined as a private sphere has been crossed.

It is important to realise that Danish Folkeskoles are based on an extended decentralised form of control which seeks to emphasise the necessity of a dialogue with the users, parents and pupils. This implies that religious interests are, to a large extent, received more positively in certain places than in others. The willingness can vary from one school to the next.

Despite the emphasis on dialogue, a central aspect of the Folkeskole's soul is a fairly unanimously critical view of the Islamic articulated values. The *symbolic violence* (Bourdieu 1977) is based on a blindness towards regarding this strategy as *cultural. Danish* values become, so to speak, considered as being universal, which leads to the idea that while the Folkeskole may actually be *Danish*, but is no longer a *folk* school as far as Muslim pupils are concerned. Islam continues to be treated as a foreign element which is not integrated or rooted in the social and cultural life of the schools. It can also be said that the conflict between school and Muslim pupil in the eyes of the school assumes, broadly speaking, the character of a conflict between *modernity* and *traditionalism*.

In the day-care institutions, the schools, etc. immigrants are simply objects. The institutions are, thus, important instruments in making socialisation a part of society. No matter which pedagogical strategy is used these institutions are directly involved in the administration that includes the cultural heritage of immigrant children. The emergence of the so-called 'bi-cultural/anti-racist' models expresses a critical awareness of this role. This does not provide an immediately applicable solution, but the establishment instead of a new point of departure which gives rise to new problems and therewith to new considerations, including the development of a critical awareness of culture as a technique of management.

Sivanandan (1983) views this multicultural education as a pedagogical method which is a response to expected revolt of the 'second-generation-immigrants', in other words an instrument for steering a crisis which is more likely to become a strategy of appeasement in a fundamentally racist society than a contribution towards change in the racist structure of the educational system. This multicultural strategy becomes a part of the development of a culturalism, not only in education, but also in the media and in the formation of policy.

This confronts the immigrants with a public debate which, as we also saw in Chapter 1, is essentially *culturalist*, i.e. it ascribes immigrants and cultural differences certain fixed and stylised qualities. This culturalism, *ethno-racism, ethnicism*, or *new racism*[30] (Schierup 1988) prevents them from furthering their own alternatives in the political centre (Schierup & Ålund 1987).

The power relationship towards the new ethnic minorities comes thereby to rest upon a superior knowledge of other cultures. Culture became a part of a larger control mechanism. *Cultural Management* has become the answer of the day to the limitations of social-technique.[31]

It also figures centrally in our comprehension in understanding the development of migrant culture as a culture of a particular minority - something which cannot be understood without taking into consideration the management of the cultural heritage of immigrants by a number of dominant social institutions. Migrant culture is seen as a dominated, and in

---

[30] These expressions shift the meaning of *race* from a biological definition to a cultural and ethnic definition of difference 'and subsequently qualified as pathological, problematic...and still subordinate..' (Essed in Schierup 1988, p.4.).

[31] Mary Searle-Chaterjee notes in a short article on anthropology in multi-cultural and anti-racist work that this multicultural education in England has been attacked by black activists as being a tool by which the whites can defuse black protest (Searle-Chatterjee 1987).

many regards an outwardly defined culture, which in its relations with the institutions will not allow itself to be swallowed up, but also offers further cultural resistance to the pressure to assimilate.

6.5 Cultural Release, Marginalisation and Social Identity

Schools experience that families are sceptical about the way in which the education they offer is structured. Much of what is allowed for boys is forbidden for the girls. This becomes particularly obvious when it comes to sexual matters where the girls adopt a set of norms, which, as far as Danish girls are concerned is regarded as a limitation of their world of experience, their personal development. From the onset of puberty in particular the family tightens its control over their personal contacts. This control manifests itself more strongly in Europe than in Turkey, Pakistan, respectively, and North Africa (Andezian & Streiff 1982; Bøggild Mortensen 1990 and Selmer 1991). The common normative reference falls away with migration, which is why Turkish and Pakistani parents feel forced to emphasise and take control completely. One could perhaps say that this control is imposed here in Denmark where the self-control of the individual can not be assumed to be internalised.

We see (cf. Chapter 4) that kinship continues to occupy a central role in socialisation patterns. We can witness the widespread adherence to tradition in wedding contracts. It is quite standard practice that young immigrants living here will, when they reach a suitable age, marry someone, often a distant relative, from the region their family originally comes from. The links to the home region are thus continuously maintained and renewed through marriage. The weddings, like other celebrations connected to the important milestones in life, such as the circumcision of boys (Turk.: sünnet)[32] or funerals, take place on the whole in the homeland.

---

[32] The age at which boys are normally circumcised can vary a lot from one nationality to another. Circumcision can take place a week after birth. In Turkey this circumcision (turk.: sünnet) usually takes place from around the age of five years. Migration, however, does introduce an element of disorder to this matter. The rule being that circumcision should take place in the homeland. In this way I witnessed a circumcision ceremony in Turkey in which three brothers, 1 year, 8 years and 10 years, respectively were circumcised on the same day. The ceremony involves a great deal of attention for the boys. The day before the circumcision, depending on interest and economic resources, they are dressed in a special outfit, an officer's uniform with a cap and a broad sash across the chest with the word 'Masallah'. Great show of this item is made during the migrants' summer holiday. The boys are taken for a treat, perhaps to a nearby picnic restaurant to eat. In the evening the whole family,

The change in the circumstances under which they live does not seem to impose any significant restraints on the business of marriages, these continue to reflect a persistent adherence to traditional cultural foundations. In all the interviews young people stressed the importance of the family and the large and positive significance of kinship, and they themselves see it as a contrast in their lives in relation to their Danish comrades and surroundings. Although the young are definitely founding new social networks and developing new social strategies in Western Europe, these are social networks that draw from chain migration a powerful counteractive force.

The young second generation immigrants investigated live an existence that is radically different from that of Danish young people. On the one hand they relate to the same institutional and social references as Danish youth, on the other to an immigrant community. The young reach this situation by different means.

This signifies that young immigrants not only represent a new situation in comparison with their parents who, as previously mentioned, do not have experience of European institutions and educational institutions, but also that they exist under markedly different circumstances than Danish youth, whose experience is not, for example, related to kinship.

The establishment of immigrants in society is a dynamic situation which continues to be influenced from a number of sides and in a number of ways. We can, though, schematise the elements we outlined above as the most important in the socialisation of the young immigrants: 'Hasan' and 'Fadima' are subject to four central *socialisation agents*. By socialisation agents we mean instances that formulate projects with 'Hasan' and 'Fadima', and as such set out intentions that are potentially outside their own life projects.

The two most noticeable socialisation agents for 'Hasan' and 'Fadima' might be said to be their own families and Danish institutions. If we talk of the family as the primary socialisation agent we must, in addition to the close family, the nuclear family, talk of the extended family which might include family in the country of origin.

It is of course the close relatives who, seen from 'Fadima' and 'Hasan's' point of view are the crucial ones, since it is they who represent direct intervention with demands and expectations.

---

neighbours and other associates are invited to a party. Food is served, perhaps raki for the adults, and music is played. The following morning the circumcision is carried out by a doctor while a prayer is read. The boys then remain in bed for three days while being waited on hand and foot.

The *Danish institutions* impose another set of demands on 'Hasan' and 'Fadima'. Out of this a project is formulated which promises them social mobility through education, but which at the same time characterises them as problems since they do not completely match the institution's set of values. The *collective associations* are agents in the close surroundings of the young people which not only attempt to supply content to leisure time, but also to provide content and a perspective on migrant life and life in general. Finally, the *state apparatus of the country of origin* can be seen as a part of those who formulate projects aimed at 'Hasan' and 'Fadima'. These states want something from their emigrants, and these expectations can have some legal character. It is, for example, only recently that Turkey has accepted double-citizenship, or that the Turkish state began sending hocas, etc.

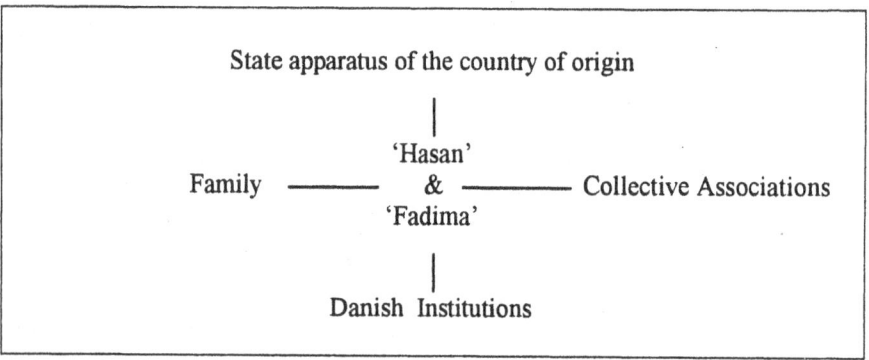

The two arrows in the figure above which point horizontally towards 'Hasan' and 'Fadima', can also be said to constitute an axis which represents crucial lifeworld relations, while the two arrows that point vertically can be said to constitute an axis that represents relations in the systemworld. It is the lifeworld relations which form the social foundations for 'Hasan' and 'Fadima' to formulate resistance to assimilationist strategies in the systemworld, such as are formulated by the state apparatus (the national as much as the local). The lifeworld relations are, in other words, a platform for the formulation of a meaningful life. Any attack on this platform is an attack on the chances of influencing the running of one's life. Therefore a great deal of the immigrant debate is 'life threatening'.

The marginalisation processes that characterise the development of society in general include, to quite a remarkable degree, large groups of immigrants. This definitively prevents them from differentiated personal development. This undermining of the ability of large groups of the population to have the opportunity to create a social identity for themselves through their associations with the labour market, or through a labour market that is characterised by ethnic work distribution leads to a crisis in social and cultural behaviour.

The marginalisation processes constitute, therefore, a large collective pressure that weighs heavily on the groups which it affects, not least of all the young.

It is of vital significance to the relevance of the immigrant organisations and the Islamic movements that they manage to channel this social force field into concrete manifestations of an alternative social context in which it is not the marginalised social processes which ascribe the significance of social identity. If this does not happen immigrant groups will be left to a diffuse form of social angst, criminal or other forms of socially destructive life.

A reorganisation of the social unit such as it is formulated by the Islamic movements also comprises a need for a cohesive conception of social and cultural interests of very different types. A public regulation which meets these needs will not arise spontaneously or all at once.

It can be said that the cultural release (cf. this work, p. 162) which is a generally ambivalent condition in Western European modernity should give rise to release from the former objective structure. This release has, though, at the same time deferred individuals in large numbers to marginalisation by a historical process. This can be confused with a collective destiny propelled along ethnic and religious lines. It is, therefore, both natural and relevant for the individual to construct his own truth about social identity in this context.

It is against the background of this composite understanding that I see the construction of a Muslim cultural identification that includes the creation of a specific Islamic identity manifested in the shape of Islamism in Western European modernity that arises from the asymmetric relationship between systemworld and lifeworld. *Identity* is, then, not inherited, but something that is told, remembered from the present and not from the past, such that it also, as in the case of Benedict Anderson (1991), applies to the biography of the nation: 'This fashioning, however, is marked by deaths, which, in the curious inversion of conventional genealogy, start from an originary present' (op.cit., p.205).

The question here is not, then, whether Muslims ought to behave this way or that. The crucial point is that it is possible for the individual to understand his life within a narrative unit as the grounding for his social identity.

One can say that if to be a Turk, Arab or Pakistani is defined as being a *Muslim*, which in turn is defined as rejecting an assimilation of European norms, then it follows that if one is a Muslim in a culturalist-based culture such as this, one must continuously deal with attacks on one's own sense of pride. It will not be sufficient to demand to be treated equally, *despite* being a Muslim, since this would imply complicity in the idea that - to a certain extent - being a Muslim is unworthy. The strategy, therefore, has to be to demand to be respected *as* a Muslim.

It is important how the social and economic marginalisation can be represented in the political language of the Muslim minority. Today the Islamic leadership in Denmark view this marginalisation to a wide extent as a confirmation of Islam's marginalisation (see Pedersen 1996).

7 Islamism in a Multicultural Western Europe

It will have become evident that the Islamic spectrum comprises a range of various forms of organisation and standpoints. In this concluding chapter I shall present a critical discussion of the relevance of Islamism, not least of all in the light of the social and economic marginalisation which characterises the immigrant Muslim minority's situation.

The analysis restricts itself in the first instance to shedding some light on Islamism by using material that concerns the Turkish Islamist movement, Millî Görüş. This is chosen firstly due to its clarity, partly because Millî Görüş constitutes the most significant Islamist movement among Turks and thereby is, so to speak, at the 'core' of the Islamic tendency in Northern Europe.

The material that is introduced comes, as it is made clear, from interviews with organisation leaders and with 'ordinary' members of the Turkish movement. The analysis is naturally, therefore, centred around this movement, although it can claim to a certain degree to apply more generally. Seen in relation to the various different positions within the Islamic spectrum however, the characterisation will necessarily be simplified - as in all cases of generalisation.

7.1 The Conspiracy and the Islamic Community

An abyss can be said to exist between the AMGT's vision of a future Islamic society in social harmony on the one hand, and the concrete initiatives associated with the movement on the other - and which are presented as an *Islamic outlook*. That the concrete initiatives displayed in the manifestation of an alternative strategy are not cohesive and at the same time lack a more detailed analysis of the societal interests and their internal relative strengths can be taken as being a central problem.

In the universe of Millî Görüş this problem does not, however, exist. This universe is ruled completely by an ideological figure who appears to span the gap between utopian vision and concrete initiatives in that it *shifts* the treatment of social conflicts to a level other than the traditionally political.

It is actually the relationship of the individual to God, here and in the hereafter, the vision of the apocalypse in other words, which is at stake. We saw how Imam Hacir stressed the importance to the Muslim minority community in Berlin that *unconditional belief in God*, was the first necessary bearing element, and that *solidarity within the Muslim community*, was the second. The golden age of Islam is proof, so to speak, that only by stressing the Islamic profile will Muslims be released from the forces of destruction.

The primary culprit at the root of the threat to the Islamic community is cited as being a destructive combination of capitalist greed and a Jewish-Christian-Communist conspiracy, which, by deed of its almost demonic logic, leads the attack against the Islamic project. These conspiring forces are visualised with reference to both historical as well as contemporary facts. Mankind is the real victim in his alienation from God. The believer and the Islamic community cannot, therefore, expect any assistance, but have only themselves to rely on.

The view of the world as far as the movement is concerned is singularly linked to a dualistic conflict between good and evil, victim and executioner, which in effect is a question about believing and not believing. The Islamic community threatened by this destructive conspiracy has no part in the threat: they figure as outside forces which humanity, as such, has a mutual interest in maintaining its struggle against.

This battle for the divine draws its starting point, naturally, from having absolute moral right on its side. What is needed to defeat the destructive system is the outspreading of the Islamic community which, on the basis of unconditional faith, will provide resolute resistance.

This dualistic universe also strikes a heroic pose on behalf of the Islamic forces that, not only in the interests of individual salvation, but also for humanity's sake take on the task of changing the direction of social development.

7.2 With Islam at the Helm

An appeal is made, invoking the threat of the complete destruction of the Islamic community, which is based on the faith of the individual in God and which, in the broadest sense, represents the aspirations of mankind. The core substance of this appeal is an abstract Islamic sense of reason, unhampered by any binding to the conflict of interests in actual social life.

To a non-Muslim of course the contents of such arguments would be debatable, if presented as a kind of absolute framework, let alone the idea that Islam's directives should as a matter of principle be indisputable. This, however, is not the crucial matter at hand here.

What is interesting in this context is that the development of society is, in the world of Millî Görüş, dictated by significant guidelines from God. These outlines, which are God given, as such, are fixed firmly in place and therefore not debatable in political discussion.

In the Millî Görüş view, God has the status of a subject whose *right* it is to dictate the conditions for human society. As far as Millî Görüş are concerned the precepts of Islam are in complete agreement with the projected aims of the movement. It is not possible, from the material at hand, to judge how flexible these projections are. Insofar as this tendency towards de-politicising the large social questions is taken to its extreme, it would be deeply alarming to other political positions and interests.

The above material sketches a picture of the movement's dual moral outlook on the world. The tendency to understand historical and social conditions through mythical figures (e.g. ummah, millât, kafir, müsrik, apocalypse, the caliphs, the Prophet) is taken to the point of pure mythology: the social conflicts disappear in favour of icons that represent good and evil.

This Islamic thinking, which claims that the social processes (and natural processes) are subject to divine laws, constitutes the core of the Islamic movements' holistic view.

The principles of Islamic politics and the radical social change derive from this holistic view: society must be brought into accordance with these fundamental laws. This argumentation, which places the Islamic movements at the centre of the necessary change, will not be examined here in detail.

What is striking, however, is that the principles and need for change derive from quantities that are said to govern actual social life, and that these quantities are rooted in the holistic oriented thinking.

Millî Görüş is not representative of the Islamic movements as a whole. However, it is reasonable to assume their basic form of argumentation as being characteristic of a large number of differently oriented Islamic trends, each of which takes the sacred texts as the point of departure for their social critique and demand for change. In this way they can refer to the positive nature of their beginnings which constitutes a diametric opposite to the marginalisation processes which undermine, so to speak, a form of socialisation which places *work* at the centre of identity formation.

The main outcome of founding the necessity of social change in references to God is, *firstly*, that it deprives the Islamic movement of the ability to differentiate between various types of contradictory processes in social development and thereby also inhibits the possibility of introducing nuance and differentiation into any conception of society. *Secondly*, this ideological subjection of politics to external, fixed parameters which are not open to debate, comprises totalitarian perspectives.

Several critics of the Islamic movements have previously pointed out the kinship of these movements with the fascist movements of former times in Europe. Manfred Halpern, for instance, has described The Muslim Brotherhood in Egypt as a Middle Eastern variety of Fascism. The stress on Islamic values that contain social indignation is reduced to a tactic whose actual motive is the suppression of any opposition, with a view to exercising power (Halpern 1963, p.135-146).[1]

The kinship to European fascist movements seems real enough as far as the kind of ideals and ideological figures are involved. The community's conceptions regarding conflicting social interests, the dual view of the world, with a clearly defined front between good and evil, the mythologising and naturalisation of the principles of social change have all helped to ground the self-perception of these movements.[2]

This does not, however, mean that one can stigmatise the Islamic movements as a budding new form of Fascism or any other form of totalitarianism, to the degree that, for example, is the case in the Berlin city council's strategy (cf. Section 3.A.3.1.1., p. 83ff.). On the contrary, the democratic conception which the group has of itself would seem to point in the opposite direction. As Hudson (1980, p.11) points out in relation to The Muslim Brotherhood, it is relevant in this context to note that the movement does not glorify 'nation' and 'race' in the same way as the European Fascists, just as their vision of a government system (Appendix I) does not call for a leader figure but builds on a parliamentary system. In their references to the holy texts, the *Koran* and *hadith*, they dismiss the notion that a mutual religiously sanctioned authority could be conceived of today (see e.g. this work, p.63) - the overriding traditions of *fiqh* are in other words rejected.[3] On the other hand, one should not be blind to the fact that the ideological figures which the movement thinks about and acts

---

[1] A similar analysis can be found in Lakhdar (1981), who comments on the new revitalisation of Islam, which led to the Islamic revolution in Iran in 1979.

[2] It also follows that they are also not to be distinguished from the Communist party tradition, or from large parts of the Western European left wing movement of the 1970s.

[3] This is also actually a trend in Islamic fundamentalism, which is historically constituted as Peters shows (1980).

according to, would, under different political circumstances be able, in principle, to assume a totalitarian character.

In the following I shall sketch out a possible contextual pattern underlying the rising tendency in Muslim immigrant circles towards the development of Islamist movements and tendencies and, taking this a little further, the resulting implications and perspectives will be discussed in relation to the processes of social release.

7.3 Muslim Immigrant Milieux and the Dialectic of Marginalisation Processes

In agreement with the central position ascribed to the destructive threats facing the Islamic community as it appears in the Millî Görüş universe, the subjective driving force which motivates both the individual and the movement as such, is resistance to the encroachment of the Islamic community; which represents humanity and its rightful relation to the divine, symbolised - among other things by the metaphor of apocalypse.

The question is whether this motivation, which subjectively speaking is undoubtedly very real, should be taken at face value. In other words, as the driving force in the rise that Islamism represents among Muslim immigrant groups, or whether we are dealing with a more complex background whose source should be sought elsewhere than in the threat of destruction to the Islamic community.

The mere fact that the threats in question are of an abstract and hypothetical nature might suggest the need to look for more deep seated, more concrete roots.

I have outlined how members of the Turkish Islamic movement live under the same conditions as the rest of the Turkish minority. Experiences of social marginalisation are combated in a positive manner via identification with Islam. The significant point in this identification is the break away from social stigma, tradition, thereby becoming a possible reservoir in reference to the composite elements. This identification with tradition does not, however, serve as a regression to a traditionalist position. On the contrary, it serves as a departure from traditionalism in favour of an insistence on being part of modern society (this work, p.129). The Turkish Islamists in Århus acknowledge modernism while at the same time finding themselves marginalised in relation to the job market. It makes good sense to them to be able to organise their lifeworld circumstances, which are, as such, threatened socially and economically, as a defence against Christian civilisation (this work, p.133).

My interviews show - not unexpectedly - that there is a perceived conflict between Islam and Judaeo-Christianity. My interviews also show that there is a lot of focus on the inferior position of Islam, that Islam does not enjoy positive significant recognition in Europe. The conflict thereby is directed at the social conditions, whereby the Muslim immigrants are subjected to being cast, defined outwardly, as being foreign, deprived of any kind of overview of their situation. Other analyses of the situation of immigrants support this interpretation.

The core in the motivation to take part in the Islamic community seems first of all to be an underlying resistance to being deprived of their autonomy with the accompanying loss of authority. Secondly, the motivation comprises a resistance to being deprived of control over one's own social relations.

Finally, a third motivation can be discerned from the Islamic literature and also films which are distributed and consumed to a considerable degree. On the one hand these are a fiction which tell of moral decay and destruction, on the other they are a fictional explanation of the harmony of a good Islamic life. This then, points towards the closely linked motivation which relates to the danger of social disintegration, lack of legal rights, and the brutalisation of inter-human relations. I would suggest that the source of this resistance to destruction, which occupies a central part of the movement's universe and which also has a structural influence on their conception of the world, and which draws substance from religious conflicts, lies in the life conditions of the Muslim immigrants. The question now is what conditions can more closely be said to have provoked this concept of conflict, as well why it has materialised in a resistance which is established in the conceptual world of the Islamic movements.

As it emerged in Chapter 6.2 the disintegration of social and cultural structures in the lifeworld due to the expansion of the systemworld is a fundamental and constituting fact. To the continued change in the terms of life, and the radical transformation of norms and traditions, as well as the attacks on the institution of the family, etc. there has, since the mid-1970s and at an increasing rate since then, been added another crucial problematisation of the central fundament of the circumstances of life for immigrants: their relationship to the job market.

The social marginalisation is added to an already dissolved part of the lifeworld, and tendentiously radicalises the dominant orientation of social functioning to diffuse passivity. The danger of losing a socially positive position, the danger of loss of identity appear very close.

This resistance can assume many different forms but there appear to be two general features to speak of:

-Firstly, positive images are produced to counter the conditions which give rise to opposition. These counter-images take the form of abstract negations of these social conditions, and since these manifest themselves diffusely the counter-images also take on the same character. At the same time the systemworld's colonisation of the social context and the undermining of the lifeworld's social relations linked to this ensure that the counter-images are not oriented towards sociality. In contrast, new orientations are sought which provide alternatives *outside of* that part of sociality which is occupied by the systemworld, whose experience does not span positive perspectives to which the counter-images can properly bind themselves. Since the sociality associated with the systemworld - which is subject to the strategies formulated by the state apparatuses - is characterised by conflicts, and appears insurmountable and lacking perspective, counter-images are articulated that express a need for harmony, clarity, simplicity and a context within life. Within this general tendency toward the negation of modern life conditions lies the fundament which the Islamic movements latch onto and organise.

-Secondly, the resistance appears to require a dual consciousness. Real existing Judaism and Christendom, having allied themselves with capitalism, represent the systemworld as a destructive demon to this way of thinking. The contrast between the individual and the system is experienced as a static relationship of opposites, as such. This experience of a dual contrast reflects true tendencies: the systemworld's encroaching dynamic, that not only undermines the lifeworld, but also poses the threat of social marginalisation to immigrants. Furthermore, the sociality that formerly managed the relation between the individual and society, also through kinship is, to a large extent, dissolved. This condition can be regarded as a clarification that the threats of division and destruction are real and thereby appear to encourage the establishment of dual consciousness.

This dualism channels resistance into a static and negotiable form, as the basis for the establishment of social action.

The resistance that springs from the systemworld's rationalisation of the social and cultural processes of the lifeworld already has, in this manner, features in common with the conception of the world of the Islamic movements.

Meanwhile, in relation to the general social and cultural problematic the emergence of the immigrant movements, including the Islamic movements, comprises a qualitative jump, depending on the realisation and aims of the resistance. They are associated with concrete social and cultural interests which provide new opportunities for orientation and action.

The international revitalisation of Islam, which has emerged in particular since the Islamic revolution in Iran in 1979, has also presented itself in Western Europe as a conceptualisation of social marginalisation as resistance to the logic of destruction of the conspiracy. Islamism in Western Europe is thus nurtured by some of the same systematic processes which are found at the global level. In the immigration countries too, the Islamic movements are the answer to comprehensive processes of social change, where the systemworld is regarded as the representative of a Western cultural, political and economic imperialism (cf. Johnsen 1981, Naïr 1984, Pedersen 1985 and Tibi 1985).

Furthermore, I should stress that the Islamic movements in Western Europe were not, of course, invented here, but that we are actually dealing with a global phenomenon. Nevertheless, I feel it is more important to underline the fact that the central point in the actuality and relevance of the Islamic movements in Western Europe appears to rest on local circumstances in response to local conditions. This is in the same way that Hannerz argues that the women's movements, environmental movements and peace movements, with all their global inclusiveness, arise out of local conditions (Hannerz 1992, p. 255). This, for example, is to say that the character of Islamism - on an axis with violent/terrorist strategies at one pole and legal negotiation strategies at the other - would certainly be defined at the local level.

The experience of the single individual of being surrendered to social marginalisation finds its counterpart in the threats against Islam. In the light of this the resistance to social marginalisation and the simultaneous undermining of the lifeworld structures could form the basis for a collective counter identity which delineates itself negatively with regard to the systemworld's economic, social and political content.

The dualism, and the thinking in terms of mythical figures that we find present in Millî Görüş complies with the need for stabilisation.

The myth of the pure and innocent Islamic community as the victim of a conspiracy has an influence on their concept world. The same applies to the condition that the reasons for the criticism and demands for change lie in the sacred texts. As a result of a crisis-laden sociality, a counter image is formed which suggests solutions which refer to a non-manmade common denominator which includes them and subjugates the enforced laws.

In an Islamic concept of the world then, the social processes are set in a perspective that refers to a law beyond the social which can explain social relations in a dualism, not spread and diffuse, but in an ideological system. In the following I shall discuss the consequences which the dynamics of this conceptual world can have for the movements, both as political and social factors, as well as in the broader sense of their perspective with regard to the founding of a positive cultural identity.

7.4 Multicultural Society and Equal Rights

Islamism's concept of the world directly constitutes a desire to set the social and cultural processes of the lifeworld in sharp opposition to the ruling rationality of the systemworld. Here, one is tempted to say that the integrity of Islamism seems, to a large degree, to be ensured.

Islamism's awareness of the problem is highly stylised. Trends in the development of society, which are not going to be rejected here, gain the status of irrefutable, total and one-dimensional facts. The threats preoccupy the entire Islamic outlook and as such prevent factors which might be aimed in an opposing direction, such as when Millî Görüş, for example, takes the conspiracy theory and the thesis of the Western world's complete cultural dissolution, seriously. As far as I am aware things are not that bad. In any case, such a viewpoint is open to debate.

Limitations as regards judgement and a sense of proportion seem, in other words, to be intrinsic to the universe of Islamism. The ability to localise contrasts and differences in the surrounding world is reduced. In the universe of Islamism the systemworld tends to simply embody the forces of destruction, which is why it is easy for criticism and demands to be aimed only at this as a whole - although they are not completely blind to those aspects of the systemworld which show Islamic characteristics, such as the social welfare system, for example. This, however, is not interpreted as evidence of the European social system's superiority, but rather as evidence that, on the strength of its character, *Islam* manages to realise itself as the natural religion of mankind.

It becomes then, impossible to distinguish between 'system-rationality' on the one hand, and complex social structures on the other. Social complexity easily becomes *identical* with the signs of crisis which characterise the negative aspects of modern society.

In the more specific critique of the *political* system, there is a tendency for Western democracy to be seen as heading for disaster - because it does not respect the universal laws. Democracy cannot find any common moral reference outside those which are manmade, which is fundamentally why democracy cannot, in itself, guarantee man's relationship with God. Such a system displays its arbitrariness both historically and in contemporary terms.

This is not, however, a rejection of the parliamentary system. On the contrary the Islamic system is put forward as fundamental for true democracy - which has to recognise God as the only absolute point of reference. This brings us back again to the parallel with Fascism made earlier. This comparison does not make Millî Görüş into Fascists wrapped in swaddling clothes, but it does highlight a critical element in the vision which the movement cannot simply dismiss.

This picture of society creates clarity in a chaotic world which forms the basis for the Islamic movement's collective identity. At the same time it makes it difficult to develop a dialogue between the social and cultural interests which Islamism organises and promotes on the one hand, and the existing social structures and other alternative social forces, on the other. This is difficult, not least of all when seen in the light of the discourse of abnormality that rules the Western image of Islam in the West (cf. Chapter 1.).

One prerequisite for a dialogue to be able to develop in the future is that the dual contrast be differentiated which, however, would appear to threaten the collective identity. This is certainly one place one might look for the reasons underlying the lack of compromise of smaller Islamic groups.

One could say that insofar as the Islamic movement's view of the world is ruled by a conspiracy rhetoric, this will also determine the processing of concrete social and cultural interests. Instead of reflecting these interests through dialogue with the surrounding society, the movement will tend to present its interpretation as being the only one valid. This understanding is further supported by references to holy scripture, which constitutes the real ally.

When interests are articulated in a static form this is due to the fact that social development, seen in a perspective of *systemworld* and *lifeworld*, block the immigrants' opportunities to realise former norms and traditional patterns, *at the same time* as the processes of marginalisation, to an increasing degree, appear threatening and bleak. In the lifeworld perspective, and thereby in a subjective perspective, this means that the development of society in general and in the immigrant environments in particular, does not seem to offer any positive possibilities.

As mentioned, this conception of the world comprises a reduced ability to enter into dialogue with the surrounding social structures. The hostile images and black/white views are a consequence of this situation. It is also primarily these aspects which characterise Millî Görüş's blueprint for change. The fundamental frame underlying the Islamic vision is the necessity for a *complete* break with the dominant social model, along with the accompanying orientation towards an Islamic society.

As it is made clear in certain parts of Chapter 3B (including p.102), and Appendix I, Millî Görüş's vision contains a number of elements which derive from the socialist tradition (including the responsibility of the state towards its citizens, and the limiting of private property rights). However, when brought into contact with the real world these aspects tend to fade into insignificance due to the fact that they are subordinate to a mythical universe. As has been shown, Millî Görüş does not found its vision of change on social concern, but instead on the ruinous decay of mankind which they seek to counter by appeals for Islamic reason to be applied via the establishment of an Islamic community. In relation to this the achievement of this conception involves fundamental conflicts of interest which Millî Görüş does not reflect.

The alternative considerations which the Islamic movement has for changes in international relations all circle within the dual universe in which there is a Jewish-Christian conspiracy that is on a firm footing with unbridled capitalism, and on the other hand a harmonious Islamic lifeworld, irreconcilably face to face. Europe and the European Community are depicted as an extreme complex which is placed within a lineage that can be traced unbroken back to the history characterised by the Crusades. Considerations regarding international economic pressure take a form in which regionalism is presented as an alternative to global economic integration.

Like other Islamic movements Millî Görüş considers *democracy* to be a Western construction. It is a construction that claims to make man his own master, raised above the laws of God. *Democracy* is, however, not only unwanted because it sets man apart from God, 'democracy' has no real substance, and is just a deceit.

1) Millî Görüş brings into question the democratic principle of majority rule with a reference to the absolute point of reference in the holy scripture, hereby making other positions illegitimate. 2) Millî Görüş postulates the possibility of a harmonious Islamic community. These are two tendencies that are potentially totalitarian and logically speaking constitute central elements in the movement's concept of the world.

In any case a blueprint is proposed for parliamentary rule, which closely resembles the European model, with an agenda whose concerns closely resemble those of a social democratic social state!

7.5 Islamism in Multicultural Society

The fundamental tendency in the Islamic concept of the world, to think in a *static* opposing structure between lifeworld and systemworld, to think in terms of *the Islamic community, ummah,* to seek a solution to the problems of mankind through radical references to the Koran and sunna, can be explained as a bid for their establishment as social players who wish to enter the life of society on an equal footing with others. In this sense it would be mistaken in this analysis of their world-conception to discount the movement's relevance in the social and cultural interests which are at stake among the new Muslim minorities.

Moreover, the changes that are at work within the Islamic movements could make it develop in a number of other different directions.

The analysis made above must however be said to be approaching a negative evaluation of Millî Görüş, and of the Islamic movement's immediate perspectives with regard to a social change. It seems sensible to modify this reasoning in the sense that there is not, necessarily, complete accordance between the conceived world, and social action at the local level. Precisely this lack of accordance makes this differentiation possible.

Let us, however, first recall which context the Islamic movement acts in. It is here that the movement has to find its legitimacy and relevance. In Chapter 6 I showed that the organisation of the *total social field* is bound to a conflict filled process which, at a general level, can be analysed as a transformation of the lifeworld. This is a transformation which has dramatic consequences for the organising of conditions in the lifeworld. This process creates a pressing need for resistance which can articulate the social and cultural interests.

Schiffauer (1988) draws attention to the fact that the structural entity which the immigrant Muslims inhabited prior to migration is broken by migration. Religious relations are not longer identical with the individual's other social, i.e. economic, political and social relations. They become explicit religious relations alongside other relations. The individuals no longer meet with other individuals in a religious society, under conditions of social exchange. The meeting will now have common viewpoints as its basis, and religion becomes a private matter. The individual leaves the society as a believer, to locate himself provisionally in the religious society. The religious society then becomes a contrast to the secular, as much as it is a place of refuge where one's dignity is recognised, away from discrimination and humiliation. In the migrant situation social relations make the specifically religious character become more pronounced and less implicit.

The basis of the mutual relations of village life are characterised by Schiffauer (ibid.) by a permanent oscillation between a secular and a holy order, a secular and a holy time. These orders are seen as being complementary and as preconditions for each other. The sacred order cannot, as such, make itself independent of the secular and assert itself at the cost of this - conflicts in secular reality are not removed by the sacred order. Conflicts in secular reality can, on the other hand, cross over and inhibit the performance of rituals. Although this does not bring into question the sacred order itself which in some cases would mean the disintegration of the society. In this context, which, as such, characterises village life, religious thinking takes the form of a collective consciousness (op.cit.).

Religious praxis, which was formerly an integrated part of society, changes its character with migration in that it is individualised, thereby changing its symbolic value. It now communicates the individual's limitations, in part with regard to the foreign environment, and in part with respect to other representatives of the minority group.

This fact makes possible the new departure that was discussed in Chapter 4.2., and which allows for a reorganisation of the community along new lines. The condition is not principally changed by the fact that we are dealing with collective social processes as discussed in Chapter 6. Migration implies that we are, structurally speaking, in a sociality which, while it is subordinate to the same general driving forces, also implements itself, for historical reasons, in quite a different manner.

On the basis of this it can be said that Millî Görüş, taken here as an organisation and movement, only influences social praxis in a *guiding* capacity. But there is not a necessary *coincidence* between ideological orientation and praxis - for example, in praxis the movement's local social activities exceed the norms delineated by the world-conception.

One might say that the various *cemaat* constitute a *community of interpretation* (Said 1981). Certain conceptions of *Islam* are set in circulation and form the basis for the individual as collective action, but the participants' engagement is flexible and varies in intensity. It is a virtue of Millî Görüş, in other words, to establish an alternative platform which can act to offset autonomous re-evaluations of the collective heritage.

In the same way as for Millî Selamet Partisi in Turkey (cf. Mardin (1984), the various Millî Görüş cemaat are not built around a religious order (tariqa). The various Islamic communities, Millî Görüş cemaat in this particular case, are organised in a formal union structure along local guide lines, both regional and national. One example, as we saw earlier, is the Millî Görüş cemaat in Århus, which organises initiatives of every type, social, cultural and educational. The intention is to give immigrants a collective initiative in local society.

In France one can say that access to French society is reflected in the formation of the TNUIF, the Tendence National Union Islamique en France, which actually has as an explicit aim to articulate a response to the immigrants' social and cultural interests in 'integration'. The leadership of the organisation is involved in the government's advisory body, Conseil consultatif de la communauté musulmane (c.f. this work, p.72), and hopes thereby to be able to contribute to ensuring the interests of Muslims in the future multicultural society. The French section also expresses a wish to participate in anti-racist initiatives (such as SOS- Racism).

The leader of Millî Görüş expresses himself with a keen awareness of the social questions and does not underplay the matter of reworking these into a dichotomy in which God's true representatives stand faced with their anti-thesis. There is a high degree of awareness surrounding social problems which also comprises an awareness that Millî Görüş and the Islamic organisers' success in the future depends on how they manage their role as intermediaries between the Muslim population and the French state apparatus (this work, p.73).

In the Berlin case there is a corresponding motivation to enter into dialogue with the authorities. Without much luck, as yet. On the one hand there is an insistence on one's own roots, and on the other a demand to be able to take up a social role as a player which extends beyond narrowly religious confines. Furthermore, one could say that social initiatives are set in motion that derive from the Islamic conception of the world. This could pave the way for new social processes which can develop much further then the actual horizon. The Islamic movements establish in this way social and cultural development possibilities that can demonstrate that it is possible to be socially active.

This, then, provides a local praxis that can release itself from the ideological intent, which means that the direction of Islamism cannot be decided in advance. The Islamic movement's running of social and cultural interests in the lifeworld in a religious concept of the world is specific. This administration does not carry an intrinsic necessity for all Muslim immigrant movements and is not the only possible organisational form.

The Islamic conception of the world comprises tendencies that are in no way unfamiliar to Turkish or other immigrant movements in Europe. One general tendency that can be identified is the tendency to ideologise associated with alternative package solutions, a condition that is documented, certainly in the case of the Turkish European movements (Özcan 1989).

The explanation for this condition is historical, in that the history of the Muslim world is marked by authoritarian forms of rule which, with the expansion of the systemworld, have prevented any alternative social and political reactions. As a consequence of this lack of democratic political culture the individual is in step with the dissolution of local collective communities, and is confronted by a state apparatus with no opportunity to ensure his own representation. This, in turn, leads to historic myth being offered a prominent place in the arrangement of the collective social identification (Gilsenan 1988, Harik 1972, Johnsen 1981, Naïr 1984, Pedersen 1985 and Tibi 1985).[4]

Millî Görüş and the Islamic movements as a whole are not, in this way, standing on barren ground but, on the contrary, within an historic tradition, which is why the movement has any kind of opportunity to gain broad appeal at all. This is, naturally, not *unequivocally* positive, since it is not necessarily linked to democratic forces.

Islamism creates a clear and concrete point of departure for the construction of resistance and positive social identification. The promotion of Islam and Islamic identity by Millî Görüş among the Turkish minorities therefore represents a breakthrough in social and cultural life in Europe. This also establishes a position, far from the centre of power, that insists on its own existence. There are references to the existence of de-central communities whose social and cultural common interests need representation. One could argue that this is where we see the tendency among Muslim immigrant communities to formulate a need to be regarded as fully valid citizens.

On this note the Islamist movements differentiate themselves in principle from *Jama'at al-Tabligh*, as I described in Chapter 5. Affiliation with *Jama'at al-Tabligh* should be seen as a response to the same social processes as an affiliation with Millî Görüş or any of the other Islamist movements. While *Jama'at al-Tabligh*'s activist fundamentalism refers to *faith* and *praxis* as a moral project within the framework of a narrow social and religious community, Millî Görüs's Islamism is more a symptom of a desire to enter the social dialogue. It is in this qualitative sense that it makes sense to call Millî Görüş in Western Europe *Islamist* rather than simply *fundamentalist*, that is to say, to consider it as a social *and* political movement. If, however, one is to judge the movement by the extent of its actual political participation in Western Europe it is perhaps actually more correct to consider it as a social, but politically embryonal movement.

As far as actual conditions are concerned, it has previously been noted, in relation to the chapter on Islamic organisations in Western Europe (Chapter 2), the closely linked assumption that the particular political and legal conditions in the institutionalisation of Islam in the individual countries has had a formative effect on the organisations. One could say that the increased tendency to handle relations with Islam at a state administrative level has placed the Islamic organisations in a perspective with identically positioned problems which has thereby also contributed to

---

[4] Benedict Anderson's analysis of nation-ness and nationalism shows us that we are dealing with a particular artefact, which is not restricted to the Middle East, but is global.

a generalisation of their outlook. However, it has, on the other hand, been of somewhat less importance as to whether this has assumed the form of interior or foreign policy.

The practical fusing of the Islamic movements, for example in national or international structures, is helped on its way by the state rejection of their legitimacy. The actual experience of the movements is negative throughout. These shared experiences of a rigid European state system constitute a continued affirmation of the mythical dual universe. What could, however, possibly reveal itself to be decisive in the future are those opportunities which the movement obtains for working with the fractures associated with Muslim minority environments.

As demonstrated, the Islamic vision of Millî Görüş is formulated in problematic forms, while the actual core of the matter is clearly obvious: it deals with marginalisation processes and the struggle for representation of the social and cultural interests in the lifeworld.

The new ethnic minorities' own organisations are perhaps the only ones which can articulate these interests, but their success will depend on the degree to which they can win a sympathetic hearing within the state apparatus system of treatment, at the local and central levels, as with established interest organisations, and not least of all with the trade union movement and established political parties. On this matter the Islamic organisations are on poorly placed - because they speak in a mysterious language which does not find positive resonance in Europe, nor with the pluralist-minded 'friends' of immigrants. The question is, then, how far, under these unhelpful conditions, can the Islamic movements induce the kind of development that will promote their interests. One cannot ignore the fact that to a great extent Western European societies would be able to integrate certain isolated demands and use them as stages in a necessary and positive renewal of the democratic foundations of multicultural society. This is not, however, any kind of miracle cure for social marginalisation.

7.6 The Concept of Minority Rights in Multicultural Society

Western European society is in the middle of a social process that comprises a complex and often conflict filled discussion regarding the integration of a growing Muslim-West European minority.

The integration of the new ethnic minorities has brought the question of equal rights onto the agenda. It is subjectivised by the minorities' own organisations and it is subjectivised even further by the state also, which, among other things, and to a certain degree, also drafts in representatives of these organisations into its decision making process. In

Denmark, for example, since 1989 there has been an immigrant council (the current Rådet for Etniske Minoriteter),[5] as advisory organ to the government on immigrant political questions. Later, in 1993, within the auspices of the state there was a wish to have the problem formulation given further attention through the setting up of a board for ethnic equality (Nævnet for Etniske Ligestilling).

The Western European political systems and public institutions are based on various traditions for the shaping of day to day relations between the public system and the citizens. We cannot, then, consider Western Europe as a monolithic entity at this level. At the same time we must also make clear that the individual public institutions have their own organisational peculiarities and characteristics, their own histories.

This has a number of consequences, including the fact that religiously motivated interests in the lifeworld are, as regards the systemworld, more easily met within certain institutional contexts than others. Despite the opposing currents and differences, we find in Western Europe an enhanced positively articulated identification with Christianity and a matching negative limitation towards Islamicly articulated interests. Although there is a certain institutional tolerance, *Islam* is met with scepticism and distaste. The conflicts are often politicised as a conflict between modernity and traditionalism. On the other hand it can be said that a blindness exists in the world of institutions towards the character of their own cultural traditions. Danish values, for example, are considered, so to speak, as being universal.

Islam is still considered to be a foreign religion that is not integrated into, nor rooted in, the social and cultural life of the state. But this is not an unequivocal situation. The relationship to Islam in Western Europe is persistently modelled, and the Islamic religious associations are admitted increasing social elbow room. This ambiguity in relations with Islam in Western Europe is at the same time played out with shifts in the relationship between systemworld and lifeworld.

For large groups in the Muslim minority the Islamic institutions constitute a defence of cultural autonomy, a counterpole to fragmentation.

---

[5] The council for ethnic minorities is the executive committee for the ethnic minorities' representative body (De Etniske Minoriteters Repræsentantskab). This body consists on the one hand of one representative from each of the immigrant associations who wish to participate and who, according to their regulations, ensure their members equal influence on choice of leadership. This is a creation of the state and not an umbrella organisation that emerged of its own accord, such as De Etniske Mindretals Sammenslutning i Danmark (formerly IND-sam) or, since their split in 1995, the new umbrella organisation POEM (*P*araplyorganisation for de *E*tniske *M*inoriteter i Danmark).

The Islamic movements constitute concrete attempts to meet the symbolic violence by pointing to the Islamic community as a possibility in social relations.

Against this background the organisation of an Islamic identity in Western European modernity can be taken as being created from an asymmetrical communicative relation which derives from social position. In accordance with our understanding of the systemworld/lifeworld relationship, the production of identity cannot be understood as youth entering a cultural continuity, but rather a cultural discontinuity. Identity, then, as Benedict Anderson (1991, p. 204-6) explains to us, is not something that is genetically inherited, but something that is remembered. It is not something that is remembered from the past, but something that is remembered from the present - it has a narrative character with a reversed genealogy.

This relationship to modernity has caused some of those engaged in immigrant research to discuss ethnicity as a form of role-play that relates only to a symbolic level. In the case of Necef (1992 & 1993), the concept of *symbolic ethnicity* is carried upon a concept of modernity as the total separation of symbolic forms from the social content, or even, perhaps, in that social ethnicity disappears. Modernity, according to this version, represents a tale of mobility, of the land of endless opportunity, of release from restrictive structures and social bonds in the family and in society. In Necef's dismantling of conceptions about ethnic essentialism and national romanticism, the social integration of immigrants is understood by means of a measuring stick where one end of the scale is comprised of tradition and the other of modernity.[6] Tradition in this process becomes, so to speak, represented by Turkishness, while modernity is represented by Danishness. The presumed cultural clash between the values of individual (Turkish) cultural migrants and the norms of European systems and structures are reduced to a uni-linear cultural universality, a new essentialism is installed.

The young people in those Islamic movements which I have studied reflect the choice of one survival strategy among several others. Young people reach inside to activate those elements in the sacred narrative which can be utilised to consider existence meaningful. In this manner these young people are also a part of modernity. At the same time it is worth dwelling on the fact that this process in the systemworld/lifeworld relationship is not just a continual process and history of the dissolution of the social.

---

[6] For a thorough criticism of Necef's all encompassing tradition/modernity modality, see Diken & Hamburger (1994).

Although socialisation in Western Europe is individualisation, the process is social and filled with contrasts. The social processes in the lifeworld derive still from personal networks and communities, territorial and non-territorial, traditional and post-traditional. Aleksandra Ålund stresses this point in relation to the development of so-called syncretic cultural forms, in an exemplary fashion:

> To conceive of the syncretic result of inter-cultural encounters in time and space simply as mixtures of style, would, in the above context, be too shallow an approach. The modern ethnic consciousness does not harvest its composite symbolic decor solely from the field of the modern cultural supermarket (Ålund 1991, p. 102).

The crucial factor is not, then, the degree to which Muslims ought to behave in one way and only one way. The crucial matter is whether it is possible for single individuals to understand their lives within a given consciousness and then use this as the basis for a collective, organised community. The Islamic community which derives from this rests as much on social relations as on territory.

In which capacity is it relevant to consider the question of social identity from a point of view of rights, and thereby as a public concern? Charles Taylor (1994) discusses the demand for recognition of cultural identities *vis-à-vis* public institutions. He argues that the institutions cannot refuse this recognition: the rights of the individual have to be protected, but the need of the individual to be a part of a special group must also be protected. Taylor sums up two central positions in his discussion of a policy of differentiation as follows:

A central argument *for* is that discrimination is, to a broad degree, based on a 'difference-blindness', and stresses that positive discrimination is necessary so that affected groups can achieve real social participation on equal terms. A consequence of this point of view is effectively that one has to positively recognise distinct cultural identities.

A central argument *against*, is that the question of recognition of cultural identities is a downward slide towards institutionalised culturalism. As such the criticism is not just aimed at discrimination on the basis of cultural differentiation, but also against positive discrimination, for example, in the job market. The sovereign right of the individual to their culture is an individual right, not a collective right. The public recognition of group affiliation will remove our individual rights from us.[7]

Regardless of which way we look at it problems arise when we examine the content of cultural forms and mixtures. One can, of course,

---

[7] Rockefeller (1994) argues this point.

also attempt to introduce a middle way, by highlighting the idea that culture is not static, but actually changes with time, but this would be more in the manner of talking around the problem formulation, in that culture may well change in the course of time, but not from one day to the next.[8]

If we attempt to view the problem formulation from a *systemworld/lifeworld* perspective in relation to the public institutions, we must make two things clear at the same time: 1) cultural release is inherent to modernity, culture is not essence, 2) the institutions may subscribe to the rationality of the systemworld, but the institutions are at the same time populated; in other words there is a lifeworld at work within this framework. In this way the concept of the institutions as being a neutral meeting place for people of all cultures is founded on an illusion.

The question remains though of how, given this situation, to tackle the recognition of new marginalised forms of cultural expression without compromising the basic principles that build on individuality and thereby, so to speak, betraying Europe's soul.

Jürgen Habermas, who remarks on Taylor's discussion, also formulates himself explicitly on this problem formulation:

> ...the coexistence of forms of life with equal means ensuring every citizen the opportunity to grow up within the world of a cultural heritage and to have his or her children grow up in it without suffering discrimination because of it (Habermas 1994, p. 131f).

Habermas' solution is that the social integration of immigrants must rest on an identity that is solely based on political socialisation and thereby does not require a more comprehensive internalisation of the local values of the country of immigration. He pleads in this way for an identity process that is based on 'constitutional patriotism', one that is 'founded on the

---

[8] For example, this question has been raised, and taken to extremes, in connection with the circumcision of female-children several times over the last few years: two viewpoints have demarcated the outer boundaries: The comprehensive Pharonic circumcision which has been testified to in the case of Somali refugee children, is the mutilation of minors, no less. In relation to a particular case, the social authorities in Århus, in accordance with this, decided that day-care institutions which learn of parents who have their girl children circumcised should contact the police without hesitation. The viewpoint opposing this is one that defines circumcision as a central part of cultural identity. Biologically women are simply not social women unless they are circumcised. To prevent these women from being circumcised is to exclude them off from their sex, their culture and thereby also from marriage. This point of view is formulated by the Ghanaian-Danish anthropologist, Christiana O. Knudsen (1994). The Somali-Danish psychiatrist, Fatuma Ali, recently produced a proposal to solve the conflict by a special law that includes a consideration of the identity perspective.

constitutional principles anchored in the political culture and not on the basic ethical orientations of the cultural form of life predominant in that country' (op.cit., p.139).

It is the *willingness* to enter into the *political culture* of the new homeland that is the crucial requirement the individual must be faced with in multicultural society. This is not just a problem formulation that is raised as a consequence of the comprehensive migration movements, but also as a consequence of the regional identities which have grown out of the European states in recent years.

This *willingness* to participate in political culture excludes the fundamentalist migrant cultures, Habermas makes explicit. Why this addendum is necessary, he does not explain. A term like 'fundamentalist' does not increase our insight. The Islamic movements grow out of a social need, their character varies and cannot be predicted, but must be examined in their concrete manifestations. By excluding 'fundamentalists' or 'Islamists' from the arena of political socialisation in advance, we simply fence out and level over quite different positions, which have quite different aims, to create a meaningless common denominator.

My analysis indicates that 'fundamentalists' can also be integrated at this level, in that this is not dependent on the perceptions, 'cultural background', or character of the individual. 'Fundamentalists' have also become part of the institutional and organisational structures in Western Europe and participate, as we have seen, in various activities. It depends more upon the institutional forms of the systems and thereby on which models are utilised at the level of cultural negotiation in deciding what is possible.

Postscript

In this thesis I have attempted to describe and evaluate the development of what is, culturally speaking, a new situation, as represented by Islamism within the Muslim minorities in Western Europe. This analysis of Islamism's European dimension is conducted by drawing on experiences, primarily with a starting point in empirical material from three countries, namely, Denmark, West Germany (West Berlin), and France. In this postscript I shall attempt to supplement, expand and variegate with regard to a number of problem formulations in the thesis.

The analysis begins with a critique of the essentialist and instrumental politicising categories which are present within the media (1986-87). The analysis is placed in juxtaposition to the existing social science discourse on Islamism (1947-85) (Chap. 1). In what follows I shall discuss the continued validity of this representation, along with its significance in the development of a multicultural society. This includes a more precise definition of my understanding of the importance of cultural heritage with respect to the conceptual world of Islamism, which relates to the political history of Islam. Moreover, I shall discuss the development of the social scientific discourse of Islam and Islamism and I will fix the present thesis with regard to this.

Finally, I shall define my use of the term 'second generation immigrant'.

Islam in the Media

As it has emerged in this thesis, the Islamic movement views itself as being in a defensive position, being placed in a hostile world. On the basis of my analysis of the representation of Islam in the newspaper *Information* (a publication generally considered sympathetic with regard to immigrants) in the period 1986-87, this view would not appear to be unfounded. The image Islam presented constitutes a unilaterally hostile scenario.

I have, furthermore, concluded that the development of Islamism in the multicultural society will be conditioned by the way, in which the dialogue is conducted. Therefore, naturally, the way Islam is represented in the media is not irrelevant. The question remains as to the degree to which the media's representation of Islam, such as I concluded in my analysis of the years 1986-87, is still valid.

That the Islamist's viewpoint of the media appears unchanged is confirmed by a number of sources. During the period of 1993-94, I interviewed a number of Islamic leaders (imams and leaders of Islamic organisations) in Denmark about Islam in Western Europe. From this it emerged that all of them, the Millî Görüş imams as much as the others, considered the coverage of Islam as being too heavily (negatively) weighted. In September 1996, during a public debate on, 'Muslims, New Danes or New Enemies?'[1] the speaker for the Union of Muslim Students expressed the fact that she felt that the media demonised Islam. From the angle of participants in the Islamic movements there is still no doubt that the image of Islam in the media is a negative one. If we turn our attention to the electronic media *flow,* here too, there is also little doubt that Muslims, on the whole, find themselves represented in negative terms. The positive reports on Islam are swamped, so to speak, by the flood of information that, as far as Islam is concerned, is related to international conflicts and terrorism. Evidence of this can be found, for example, in the media analysis of Islam in media representation, conducted by researchers linked to religious science at Tübingen University (Medienprojekt Tübingen Religionswissenschaft 1994).

As noted in this thesis (p.2) the use of religious language was utilised in association with the Gulf Conflict of 1991-92 by both the Iraqi regime and the USA's Middle Eastern allies. The fight for Islam became one part of the conflict's themes. Could the outcome of the Gulf War not perhaps be taken as an invitation to the West, and to the Western media, to differentiate their view of Islam? If the conclusion drawn from the image of Islam in *Information* was that *Muslims* had to choose between *Islam* and *modernity*, then it would now seem that, apparently, there are two types of Muslims in existence - the good and the bad; where the good Muslims are pious ones who want only to live out a personal relationship of faith in moral integrity, while the bad Muslims are the fundamentalists.

Jurgensmeyer (1995) shows in his 'reading' of the media's representation of 'fundamentalism' in the early 1990s, that the term is

---

[1] The public arrangement was organised by SOS-Racisme in cooperation with the Prehistoric museum, Moesgård, Århus. The speakers comprised a representative of the Foreningen af Studerende Muslimer, FASM (The Union of Muslim Students), along with experts on Islamic and European history.

heavily loaded with negative connotations, *and* that the authorities use 'the fundamentalist threat' to justify it's infringement of human rights. *Fundaphobia* he calls this irrational fear of fundamentalism. Countless examples testify to the fact that is a serious matter to be accused of 'fundamentalism'. As such, 'fundamentalism' was utilised by the state apparatus in Algeria to legitimise it's termination of a democratic process. In the West this action was by and large met by tacit, if not by unconditional approval. While on the one hand it went against all principles there was general relief that an Islamist government had been prevented from becoming an actuality (op.cit. 345).

Conversely, Jurgensmeyer believes (ibid.) that it is characteristic that *fundamentalism* is seen in the academic discourse as being a cross-cultural, anti-modernist religious activist phenomenon. Thus an acceptable way of avoiding the term 'fundamentalism' is sought on the presumption that it should not lead up to a value loaded evaluation of it.

One consideration does, however, appear to be relevant in that in the written as much as in the electronic media today emphasis is placed on Islam being represented by *Muslims*. In my study of the representation of 'Islam' and 'Muslims' in the newspaper *Information*, the journalists most commonly referred to academic experts on Islam when in need of someone to provide the correct facts. This, by the way, applied not only to *Information*, but also to all the mass media. Today these professional experts are often either replaced or matched with non-academic experts from among the Muslim minorities themselves. Whereas previously it was the expert who spoke on behalf of Islam, today it can be the faithful Muslim who acts as witness and lends authenticity to the journalistic account. It does of course have more media impact if a Muslim spokesman speaks on the role of Islam than if a non-Muslim Islamic expert does. This, however, only gives an impression of greater authenticity. The possibility of consolidating unequivocal images of Islam still remains unchanged. It is, as such, still a representation that is prepared and edited journalistically.

While it is true that representations in the media which provide a positive image of Islam are more common today than they were perhaps ten years ago, the Islamic players have had a hard job registering this as anything other than a peripheral phenomenon in an endless media bombardment.

In other words, what is actually new about the media representation is perhaps not so much what is being said about Islam, but relates rather to the fact that the objects being discussed are themselves now also players in the debate, much more than they were before. In the field of the media there are thus openings so that 'Muslims' can find themselves represented as participants in society, which is important!

The Media, Multicultural Society, and the Significance of Cultural Heritage

Probably it could be said that the media's representation[2] of Islam is important in the establishment of a multicultural society, insofar as Muslims here can rediscover themselves as citizens with equal rights. On this basis it would not suffice to insist that the media attend on courses in political correctness. The universe of Islamism is confirmed by the media's representation, but it is also the lack of social equality, broadly speaking, that makes Islamism relevant to its participants. While this concerns social inequality, it also, equally, involves the way religious interests are channelled at the societal level. On this last level the same rules of access do not apply to the Muslim minority as they do to the, religiously speaking, well-established Western European majority population (Pedersen 1996; Shadid & Van Koningsveld (eds.) 1996).

Following on from this it can also be said that the form of Western European Islamism is determined by social developments in Western Europe including, in particular, the degree to which Muslims can identify themselves with this. Roughly speaking, one can question the degree to which Muslims can claim that they are unemployed, for example, because they are Muslims, or whether we will witness a social mobilisation and differentiation that will drain such a claim of any content.

The European Islamism with which I am concerned manifests itself on the basis of an ambivalence about identity which is linked to the history of immigration and which manifests the need to reconsider the cultural heritage (c.f. p.159 above). A central thesis in this work is that the opportunities and relevance of Islamism derive from the marginalisation of Muslim minorities (and Islam) in European societies and especially in relation to affiliation with the job market.

The cultural heritage has to be administrated and as I have shown, Islam constitutes an indispensable aspect of the social identification of Muslims in Western Europe. Islamism is a form of administration which

---

[2] By 'representation' in this context I mean the content of meaning in the message, as much as who the messenger is.

consciously reflects on the cultural heritage and places Islam and its political history at its centre. Islamism grows, then, out of a need for social identification and thus constitutes an offer of cultural reorganisation which configures the cultural heritage in the context of Islam's long history.

One can say that establishing the new ethnic minorities in Western Europe is not primarily characterised by cultural continuity passing from parent to child. The transmission of culture is, on the contrary, rather characterised by discontinuity - or even worse: the transmission of culture is characterised by the continuity of discontinuity.

Islamism is not, thus, explained by references to the cultural heritage. The cultural heritage can be said to constitute the reservoir of symbols to which Islamism refers. Like other immigrant movement culture administrators, Islamism is selective as regards its culture and history and frames it, so to speak, in a narrative form which is meaningful in a contemporary context. Islamism is just one medium among several in the management of the cultural heritage - cultural heritage is always administered and re-evaluated, and transformed from one social (herewith geographical) context to another.

Islamism is an expression for a particular selection of elements in the world of religious concepts which are not restricted to the local minor cultural context and tradition. Islamism lays claim to a universal legitimacy whose universe of symbols is drawn from holy scripture and the political history of the Muslim world, and primarily from the age of the Prophet and the Rightly Guided caliphs.

The strength of Islamism lies, as I have sought to show in this thesis, in having its centre on the periphery of society where it can link itself to the cultural heritage or, as Burgat puts it, with 'the passed down and intuitive culture' making 'the symbolic lineage' more possible:

> It then allows for a fundamental reconciliation: insofar as it reintroduces the use of the 'local' referents whose 'expropriation' from the public sphere had progressively limited it to those of the private one (family law), it would first of all permit Homo Politicus Orientalis to reconnect with his inherited and intuitive culture. In this way, it would reconcile him with the culture of an ancestor (real or mythological, this is not what matters), thus making symbolic lineage again possible. And doubtless herein probably lies the secret of the Islamist formula: by reinserting the language and referents of their forefathers into the representational system, it restores historical continuity in the collective imagination which the intrusion of Western categories has interrupted. In doing so it

contributes - at the symbolic level - (....) to close the colonial parenthesis (Burgat 1995, p.4, n.1).

Islamism in Western Europe occupies, one might say, the collective need for repositioning and positive social identification with regards to the hegemonic discourse about Muslims and Islam here.

Islamism becomes the expression of a counter-position whose articulated centre is placed on the cultural periphery of European society. On the one hand this allows us to claim that Islamism can be explained in ways other than with reference to the cultural heritage. At the same time it can, conversely, be asserted that the universe of symbols which inhabit the discourse of Islamism can quite well be located within, and relate to, the political history of the Muslim world.

Islam in Social Science Discourse

Social science discourse, such as it is to be found represented in the selected contributions to analyses of Islamism in the Middle East, has founded the basis for the positioning of my analysis of Islamism in Western Europe. I refer here to two positions that were relevant to my analysis: the 1st position views Islam and modernisation as being incompatible, and the 2nd position points to Islamism as the result of blocked possibilities of opportunity. My interest in these positions lies in their attempt to understand *Islamism* within the parameters of the direction of the capitalist system's development. These are works that seek to think of Islamism within a modernising theoretical frame of understanding. My conclusion, however, was that *Islam* was considered as a cultural system that should stand up against 'change' and which thereby provided an inadequate answer to 'modernising' (see this work, p.11).

I have tried to focus attention on the social actors of Islamism and thereby focus on the local, social and specific economic factors, and from this point to understand the development of the movement in Western Europe as a (partial) answer to its social positioning: Seen in this way Islamism becomes an enduring means of expressing the values of a particular minority population in praxis.

I have criticised the fact that in the social science debate it is *Islam* that is placed at the centre of analysis. The question of Islamism's characteristics, possibilities and directions are more likely decided by the social reality than by Islam and Islamism as an abstraction, where Islamism is understood in terms of the intellectual or political history of Islam, or on the basis of the categories of Islamic theology.

I am not alone in making this criticism. In connection with his analysis of the Egyptian Islamic movement, *al-Jama'a al-Islamiyya*, Fandy (1994) criticises the widespread tendency to favour the study of Islamism's intellectual history so as to characterise the social-revolutionary movements. Instead of focusing on the local and social conditions, one allows oneself to be side-tracked into falling into 'the trap of the Islamists': 'journeying back with the Islamists to their idealised vision of the prophet Muhammed's state in Medina' (op.cit., p.608). Fandy's criticism indicates that studies of Islamism still privilege this point of view. [3]

Fandy demonstrates how the movement in southern Egypt developed its own character in response to the particular regional factors. Thus the movement developed an agenda different to that of the radical Islamic movements in the north of Egypt. Fandy's conclusion constitutes a new and important perspective on why the movement is so strong in Southern Egypt and how it challenges the legitimacy of the state. His attention to precise detail concerning local conditions contributes to Fandy being able, in contrast to others who fell into 'the trap of the Islamists', to pick out the group's regional character.

A crucial point in my analysis is that *Islam* and *Islamism* cannot be taken as a homogeneous reaction against development, which can already be described as being anti-modern. On the contrary, the argument is made that Islam should be regarded as a language and therewith as a possibility for legitimisation. This view is also one which, as it will appear, has gained recognition in the social science discourse on Islam in the Middle East during the 1990s.

Eickelman & Piscatori (1996) also show in their tour de force on 'Muslim politics', that Islam adopts a position as a symbolic language in social and political praxis, and that the way in which the language is set up is intimately related to the degree to which common identities are constructed, and how the players further and defend their intentions. Krämer (1993) also shows this in her analysis of the Islamists' flexible use of classical Islamic terms on state leadership in Muslim society. Among other things, Krämer concludes that;

---

[3] Here Fandy is referring to a number of social science analyses which deal with Islamism in Egypt in the 1980s.

> It is not possible to talk about Islam and democracy in general, but only about Muslims living and theorising under specific historical circumstances. This may sound evident enough, and yet it is all too often ignored (Krämer 1993, p.4).

It is then the connection between the strategy of the Islamists and the process of social development which constitutes the analytical field of this thesis. It is clear that social science literature on Islamism in recent decades has pointed in several direction: On the one hand the first significant new tendency relevant to my project centres on 'post-modernism' and the crisis of values associated with this. The second new, significant tendency centres on the introduction of the terms concerning 'civil society' and democratic processes in the Middle East.

One might say that my access to Islamism in Western Europe is compatible with - although not identical to - the newer tendency to analyse Islamism and 'fundamentalism' in relation to 'post-modernism' - which includes viewing Islamism as an identity project. However, my analysis differs from these, not only by relating itself to theories about modernity in general, but also in localising this in the historical conditions of modernity. The motives of the participants are, thus, not simply analysed in the perspective of the participants themselves, but - and this is crucial - also in a distanced perspective of observation which seeks to find its focus in theoretical positions which follow the social, local, process of change and perspective, - structured as it exists in the global economy.

In both Ahmed (1992) and Ahmed & Donnan (1994) Islam is tied to post-modernism in a thesis that describes Islamic fundamentalism on a par with the flourishing of other contemporaneous 'ethno-religious movements';

> Fundamentalism is the attempt to resolve how to live in the world of radical doubt (...) In fact an argument can be made, that ethno-religious revivalism is both cause and effect of post-modernism (1992, p.13).

Akbar S. Ahmed criticises fundamentalism in that he believes that it betrays the essence of Islam which by nature represents *'the religion of equilibrium and tolerance'* (op.cit., p.48).

This point of view, that *Islamism* is an answer to a post-modern age is similarly to be found in the American 'fundamentalism project', in which the emergence of fundamentalist movements is compared on a global scale.

The intention of the analyses in this mega-project[4] is to put forward data with a view towards a global comparison of different 'fundamentalisms': Protestant in North and South America, Catholic in the USA, Jewish in Israel, Islamic (Sunni as much as Shi'a) in most of the Muslim world, Hindu, Sikh, Confucian...

The analyses generalise and even out on a number of themes which show that the discourse and strategies of the fundamentalists *can* be broken down into themes such as worldview, education and media, politics, social economy and activism, and that fundamentalists are characterised by the fact that they *fight*, they have a case: they 1) hit back in response, are reactive, 2) fight for a worldview, 3) fight with a means (i.e. such as an imagined ideal), 4) fight against others (a world that is generally bad, or specified others), and 5) fight in the name of God or another transcendent reference (Marty & Scott Appleby 1991:ix-x). In other words the marks and characteristics which could in theory be applied to a similar degree to other non-religious political movements, whether they be social and political movements, sexual politics or environmental movements. In this way the same formula applies to the Jewish settlement movement, Gush Emunin, on the West Bank, the Islamic social movement, al-Jama'a al-Islamiyya, in Egypt, the Turkish Naqshibendi-Tarika, and the Protestant missionary movement in South America, along with many other movements.

In 'The Fundamentalism Project' it is 'fundamentalism' which is the central analytical category, and not the social positioning of the players, which, to me, is the crucial problem.

In Kepel's (1992) view also the Christian, Jewish, and Muslim movements are seeking revenge in God's name on the basis of the global crisis of values which has arisen as a result of the breakdown of the great utopias of modernity, both moral and analytical. To Kepel, the religious movements herald a new era of world history. It could be said that the main contribution made by Kepel and 'The Fundamentalism Project' is that they contribute to increasing our understanding of Islamism as being neither the protest of tradition bound circles, and nor concerned with modernising Islam, but is, on the contrary, about Islamising modernity.

Kepel feels, however, duty bound to stress that:

---

[4] The results of this project, which is financed by The American Academy of Arts and Science, are published in 5 volumes and add up to over 3,500 pages, in the period from 1991-1995.

At the end of the day the re-Islamisation, re-Judaeoisation and re-Christianisation do not have the same effect and profile in their respective societies - other than their coincidental development since the middle of the seventies (op.cit., p. 219 f.).

Kepel does not offer much hope to the re-Chrisitanising movements, in that he considers Western democracies as a guard against this.

In one of the concluding chapters from 'The Fundamentalism Project', Almond, Sivan and Scott Appleby (1995) speak in favour of a similar way of thinking about the term 'civil society' in that,

It makes a great deal of difference if a society has strong and independent trade unions, civic associations, communications media, and political parties, capable of draining off anxiety and resentment in response to social and economic crises, and converting them into secular politics and public policy. We would fail to understand Islamic movements, for example, if we did not take into account the fact that civil society in Islamic countries has been reduced over the last century by the interventionist state (op.cit., p. 434).

The writers mentioned operate with the thesis that the Islamic movements are strong, where civil society has been reduced by the interventionist state. The Islamic movements are not, then, a part of 'civil society' but stand, on the contrary, in opposition to it.

To Gellner (1992) this absence of 'civil society' is a result of the fact that Muslim society is, and always has been, built into a special power relationship. A church-state dualism has never developed, and society does not, therefore, have a need to defend itself against a state. Right from the start, society was the state, so to speak, in that the principles of religious and political legitimacy rest upon the sacred message, consensus, and sacred leadership.

To Gellner the current revitalisation of Islam is an expression of the fact that the great pendulum is now swinging in favour of high-Islam in a reform of low-Islam - and now, on the strength of modernity, perhaps for ever.[5] That the thesis of secularisation does not apply in the case of Islam is not due to a historically established coincidence but is a consequence of a quality of Islam. Islam has its own in-built alternative. Islam is immune to the secularism that is implicit in modernity in any society other than one

---

[5] Gellner's theory about the pendulum swing is found in his book 'Muslim Society', Ch.1, 1981.

which is Muslim. Gellner's thesis that Islam constitutes a social whole whose essence is immune to the influence of history is, according to Sadowsky (1993), central to the American 'new-orientalists' approach to an understanding of developments in the Middle East. This thereby provides a basis for linking essentialism and the rejection of the relevance of Western colonialism and imperialism in social science analyses - and in politics.

The debate about 'civil society' as the central category in the question of the development of democracy, as it emerges in the contributions in Norton (ed., 1995) becomes central to Middle East research and is relevant also to the analysis of the Islamic movement in the Middle East. The actual term 'civil society' provides an opportunity to shift the central analytical focus away from 'Islam' and 'fundamentalism', transforming it into a category which belongs to the social level of the actors, and thereby also ensuring that we do not remain trapped by the cultural essence.

To Norton (1995, p.7f.) and Ibrahim (1995, p.27f) 'civil society' refers to a positively defined, empirical social category which constitutes a buffer between state and citizen, which is to say diverse voluntary organisations and vocational associations. At the same time, 'civil society' is defined as being a part of modernity, and is defined in opposition to the so-called traditional social circles. This is, then, a (very) restricted application of a term which leaves (very) open the question of whether the Islamists are at all part of 'civil society'. 'Civil society' in the contributions mentioned is not in actual fact categorised simply as consisting of voluntary associations, but also presumes a 'civility', a particular normativity, - which sees attitudes such as tolerance, understanding, pluralism, and social behaviour as being implicit in qualifying as a 'civil society'. This presupposes the implicit understanding of the fact that one is participating in a peaceful, common cause - within a democratic process. This understanding of the term 'civil society' introduces a normativity that to a large degree is influenced by empirical coincidence.

Burgat (1995) offers an understanding of 'civil society' which reflects the historical origins of the term to a larger extent, as an instance that deals with society's ability to resist the state. Burgat points out that the term 'civil society' plays a rhetorical role in the struggle for power in the Middle East. 'Civil society' is staged in the political game as a term which deals with society's ability to resist a specific political power, namely the Islamists - and not the state. This thus makes it the (repressive) Middle Eastern state powers which have, so to speak, secured representation of the term and which can thereby be regarded as constituting the subject in an assumed process of democratic development. This successful hegemony in the representation of the term of 'civil society' is symptomatic of the Middle Eastern regimes' - including Algeria's - communication with Western political circles. To the extent that the authoritarian regimes manage to convince the West, the West participates in a political struggle on the side of these regimes and thereby enters effectively into an alliance against society, including the actual 'civil society', Burgat writes.

To Burgat 'civil society' constitutes a collectivity of all social practise that does not directly derive from state and market. In other words it is not, as Norton (op.cit.) and Ibrahim (op. cit.) would have it, the characteristics that could be defined as positive which ascribe the term, 'civil society' with its noted lack of internal contrasts. - 'Civil society' in the case of Burgat, is rather characterised by its treatment of those relations which the state and market do not organise and this includes also the so-called traditional milieus. 'Civil society' is in this way not an established and clearly organised institution with a unique content. It is better characterised as being a category that refers to a potential of contrasts and conflicts which can be channelled in a number of directions. The interests of 'civil society' thereby express social processes which are capable of expanding the democratic fundament, but can also - depending on the context - lead in other directions, such as towards violence and oppression, for example. This interpretation of the term 'civil society' can thereby be said to be in accordance with the understanding which I presented earlier on the basis of the terms *lifeworld* and *systemworld*, which demarcate a general frame around a reservoir of complex social experiences and interests and which are then anything but free of internal contrasts.

The frame is set out in such a way that Burgat views Islam's opportunities as deriving from the marginalisation of Islam as a political language through the European imperialist phase. Islamism thus fulfils the same collective need for repositioning with regard to those in power as the nationalist movements formerly were (c.f. quote on p.212 above, from Burgat 1995, p.4, n.1).

Insofar as the relationship between 're-Islamisation' and social or political 'modernisation' is concerned, Burgat stresses that these cannot be represented academically as being in conflict or mutually exclusive of each other:

> ..the reislamisation process gives room to a complex, ambivalent and contradictory process of re-expression of the hard core of Western

political modernity using the terminology of the endogenous Islamic culture (op. cit.).

It can be said that alongside the heavily value laden and negative discourse on Islam and Islamism, there is now a discourse which takes a more positive, realistic, expectant view and which allows open analyses.

The So-called Second Generation

In analysing Islamism I have (primarily) directed my attention towards the development of what is, culturally speaking, a new development among young Muslims, - among the so-called second generation. This group is, as I have described it, characterised by being the first generation which has its own experience of the European institutions and educational systems (see above, p. 174f.).

My attaching of the prefix 'so-called' when using the term 'second generation' is due to the fact that this term applies to a social reality that is filled with contradictions and cannot unequivocally be summed up by the term 'generation'. Although the process of immigration itself does not run an unhindered course, but describes, on the contrary, a complex lack of simultaneity. In fact, one might say that most of the participants in the Islamic movements whom I interviewed were not born in Denmark and could, from a certain point of view, be taken as being 'first generation'. The generation term can be criticised for covering over this social complexity.

Sayad (1994) asks what is actually meant by 'generation', which implies that the chronology of immigration in some way describes the course of immigration meaningfully. It is in fact unclear in which sense generation is actually used: do we mean a chronology of successive waves of immigration which imminently refers to national origins in the country of immigration, a time before immigration, or does the term refer to a meaning in the familial context - where the 'second generation' are simply the descendants of their immigrant parents but born after the immigration, having grown up and socialised within the immigrant situation (op.cit., p. 7).[6]

---

[6] Paradoxically, writes Sayad, it was only with the introduction of the term 'second generation' that their parents became the 'first generation' - so it is the children who make the parents citizens in the actual sense of the term, granting

The generation term introduces, meanwhile, another new quality, - a generation which is different from previous ones. This is striking in its own way, according to Sayad, but at the same time one does not understand the generation if it is to be understood only in the sense of being in conflict with the parents - there is also a third party, - namely the immigrant society. (op.cit., p. 9). It lies within the power of the immigrant society to objectify and categorise. When the subjects of power have got their objects - in this case the so-called second generation - to recognise themselves as such, the project will have succeeded; the group then constitutes a social category. The distance which the term thereby introduces in the relationship between parents and children thereby becomes the guarantee of power in the socialisation process. The power can now speak on behalf of the 'real concerns' of the object which, by necessity, has to fit badly in one place so as to fit comfortably somewhere else. Considered in this way the generation term exists both unequivocally and as a term that can be instrumentalised politically (op. cit., p.18).

There is, meanwhile, a reason to hold on to the term 'second generation'. The term appears to me useful - for the present time in any case[7] - if the above-mentioned consciousness of its contrast filled and manifold content is to be preserved intact. When there is no reason to get rid of the term it is because the generation term, qualified as 'second generation' actually denotes a quality which is significant in that it demarcates the transition to a new reality in the socialisation in relation to the parents generation. It is this experience which needs representation, simultaneously with a critical awareness of the power structures of social construction which turn the so-called 'second generation' into a political social problem category that can be subjected to cultural management.

---

them, therewith, their complete social and political identity. It is the children who make the parents exist, feeding them to public life (Sayad 1994, p.4).

[7] For the moment, because the relevance of the term will abate in time with the emergence of new 'generations' (sic!).

Bibliography

Ahmad, M. (1991), 'Islamic Fundamentalism in South Asia: The Jamaat-i-Islami and the Tablighi Jamaat', in M. Marty and R. Scott Appleby (eds.), *Fundamentalisms Observed*. Chicago and London: University of Chicago Press.

Ahmed, A.S. (1992), *Postmodernism and Islam. Predicament and Promise*, Routledge, London, New York.

Ahmed, A.S. & H. Donnan, (1994), 'Islam in the Age of Postmodernity', in A.S. Ahmed and H. Donnan (eds.), *Islam, Globalization and Postmodernity*, Routledge, London, New York.

Algar, H. (1976), 'The Naqshbandi Order: A Preliminary Survey of its History and Significance', *Studia Islamica*, No. 44. Paris.

Algar, H. (1985), 'Der Naksibendi-Orden in der republikanischen Türkei', in J. Blaschke and M. Bruinessen (Hg.), *Islam und Politik in der Türkei*. Jahrbuch zur Geschichte und Gesellschaft des Vorderen und Mittleren Orients 1984. Berlin: Express Edition.

Ally, M. M. (1979), 'The Growth and Organization of the Muslim Community in Britain', Research Papers 1. Centre for the Study of Islam and Christian Muslim Relations. Selly Oak Colleges. Birmingham.

Almond, G. A, H. Sivan, and R. Scott Appelby, (1995), 'Explaining Fundamentalisms', in Marty, M.E. and Scott Appleby, R. (eds.), *Fundamentalisms Comprehended*. The Fundamentalism Project, vol. 5., The University of Chicago Press, Chicago, London.

Anderson, B. (1991), *Imagined Communities*, Verso, London & New York.

Andezian, S. (1986), 'L'Islam dans la France d'aujourd'hui', *Revue Autres Temps. Les Cahier du Christianisme Social*.

Andezian, S. & J. Streiff (1982), 'Transpositions and Reinterpretations of the Traditional Female Role on an Immigration Situation', in *Living in two Cultures. - The Socio-Cultural Situation of Migrant Workers and their Families*, England, The Unesco Press.

Anwar, M. (1979), *The Myth of Return: Pakistanis in Britain*, Heinemann, London.

Arjomand, S.A. (1984), *From Nationalism to Revolutionary Islam*, Oxford, Macmillan.

Asad, A. (1987), 'De to-kulturelle klasser styrker ikke modersmålet', *Samspil 1/1987*.

Barou, J. (1985), 'L'Islam. Facteur de Régulation Sociale', *Esprit. Change la Culture et la Politique*, No. 6. Paris.

Barth, F. (1969), 'Introduction', in Barth, F., *Ethnic Groups and Boundaries: The SocialOrganization of Culture Difference*. Boston.
Bastenier, A. (1988), 'Islam in Belgium: Contradictions and Perspectives', in Gerholm T. and Y.G. Lithman (eds.), *The New Islamic Presence in Western Europe*, Mansell Publications, London.
Bauman, Z. (1973), *Culture as Praxis*, Routledge & Kegan Paul, London & Boston.
Bekendtgørelse (1972), *Bekendtgørelse om seksualoplysning*. Bekendgørelse 1972-06-15, nr. 313.
Bekendtgørelse (1991-06-20), *Om formålet med undervisningen i folkeskolens fag*. Bekendtgørelse1991-06-20, nr. 482.
Benjelloun-Ollivier, N. (1986), Les Immigrés Maghrébins et l'Islam en France. Identité et intégration, *Hommes et Migrations*, No. 1097.
Berger, M. (1970), 'Economic and Social Change', in Holt, P.M. et al (eds.), *The Cambridge History of Islam*, Vol. 1., University Press, Cambridge.
Berg M. (1993), 'Double normality· Reflections on Style and Turkish Second Generation Immigrants',*YOUNG*, Nordic Journal of Youth Research, nr.1.
Berlin Islâm Federasyonu, Haziran 1988, (Islamisk Føderation Berlin. Juni 1988). Berlin.
Binswanger, K. & Sipahioglu, F. (1988), 'Türkisch-islamische Vereine als Faktor deutsch-türkischer Koexistenz', Benediktbeuren: RießDruck und Verlag.
Bjørklund, U. (1986), 'World-Systems, the Welfare State and Ethnicity', *ETHNOS*, 1986: 3-4.
Blaschke, J. (1985), 'Islam und Politik unter Türkischen Arbeitsmigranten', in J. Blaschke and M. Bruinessen (eds.), *Islam und Politik in der Türkei*. Jahrbuch zur Geschichte und Gesellschaft des Vorderen und Mittleren Orients 1984, Berlin: Express Edition.
Bourdieu, P. (1977), *Outline of a Theory of Practice*, Cambridge.
Bozarslan, H. (1989), *Strategies Beurs de Conquete de l'Espace Politique: les Cas de Memoire Fertile et de France Plus*. Upubl. paper.
Burgat, F. (1988), *L'Islamisme au Maghreb*, La voix du Sud. Karthala, Paris.
Burgat, F. (1995), 'Islamists versus "civil society"', paper presented at seminar, *State, Individual and Civil Society in the Middle East*, Magleås Kursuscenter, 13-14th November 1995, The Middle East Network, Denmark.
Bæk Simonsen, J. (1990), *Islam i Danmark*, Aarhus Universitetsforlag, Aarhus.
Bøggild Mortensen, L. (1989), *'At være eller ikke være' - Om tyrkisk ungdom i København og Ankara*, Akademisk Forlag, Copenhagen.
Campani, G., Catani, M. & Palidda, S. (1987), 'Italian Immigrant Associations in France', in J. D. Rex and C. Wilpert (eds.), *Immigrant Associations in Europe*, Gower, Great Britain.

Castles, S. (1984), *Here for Good. Western Europe's New Ethnic Minorities*, Pluto Press, London.
Cibedo-dokumentation (9/1980), *Beiträge zum Gespräch zwischen Christen und Muslimen*. Frankfurt.
Cirkulæreskr (1986-01-13.), *Cirkulæreskrivelse vedrørende indvandrerbørns deltagelse i idræts undervisning*. Direktoratet for folkeskolen og seminarier m.v. 1986.
Courtois, S. & Kepel, G. (1988), 'Musulmans et prolétaires', in R. Leveau and G. Kepel (eds.), *Les Musulmans dans la Société Française*, Presse de la Fondation Nationale des Sciences Politiques, Paris.
Cross, M. (1986), 'Migrant Workers in European Cities. Forms of Inequality and Strategies for Policy', in *Proceedings from An International Seminar on Migration Research*. The Migration Initiative of the Danish Social Science Research Council.
Csonka, A. (1995), *Når virksomheder rekrutterer*, Socialforskningsinstituttet, Copenhagen.
Curtis, M. (1981), 'Introduction', in M. Curtis (ed.), *Religion and Politics in the Middle East*, Westview Press/Boulder, Colorado.
Dahya, B. (1974), 'The Nature of Pakistani Ethnicity in Industrial Cities in Britain', in A. Cohen (ed), *Urban Ethnicity*. ASA Monographs.
Dam, N. van (1983), 'Minorities and Political Elites in Iraq and Syria', in Asad, T. & R. Owen (eds.), *Sociology of 'Developing Societies'. The Middle East*. Monthly Review Press, New York.
Dassetto, F. & Bastenier, A. (1984), *L'Islam Transplanté*, Editions EPO, Belgium.
Dassetto, F. (1988), *Musulmans de Belgique: Processus d'implantation et de visibilisation*, Unpublished paper, Département de Sociologie, Université Catholique de Louvain, Belgium.
Diken, B. & Hamburger, C. (1994), 'Tyrkeren og ghettoen på modernitetens limbo', *GRUS*, nr. 42. Ålborg.
Dindler, S. & A. Olesen (red.) (1988), *Islam og muslimer i de danske medier*. Århus Universitetsforlag, Aarhus.
Durand, J.-M. et al. (1990), *La Course a la Representation de l'Islam. La Creation du Conseil consultatif. Enjeux et Debats*, unpublished paper, Institut d'Etudes Politiques de Paris, Paris.
Eickelman, D.F. (1981), *The Middle East. An Anthropological Approach*. New Jersey.
Eickelman, D. F & Piscatori, J. (1996), *Muslim Politics*, Princeton University Press, Princeton.
Eilschou Holm, N. (1980), *En sag for Menneskerettighedsdomstolen*, København: Juristforbundets Forlag, Copenhagen.
Encyclopaedia of Islam (1983), London.
Etienne, B. (1987), *L'islamisme radical*, Hachette, Paris.
Fandy, M. (1994), 'Egypt's Islamic group: Regional revenge?', in *Middle East Journal*, vol. 48, no.4. Washington DC.
Friedman, J. (1994), *Cultural Identity & Global Process*, Sage Publications, London.

Gellner, E. (1981), *Muslim Society*. Cambridge Studies in Social Anthropology.
Gellner, E. (1992), *Postmodernism, Reason and Religion*, Routledge, London, New York.
Gerholm T. and Lithman, Y.G (eds.) (1988), *The New Islamic Presence in Western Europe*, Mansell Publications, London.
Gibb, H.A.R. (1947), *Modern Trends in Islam*. The University of Chicago Press, Chicago.
Gillette A. and Sayad, A. (1984), *L'mmigration Algérienne en France*, Éditions Entente, Paris.
Gilroy, P. (1987), *'There Ain't No Black in the Union Jack'*, Unwin Hyman, London.
Gilsenan, M. (1988), 'Popular Islam and the State in Contemporary Egypt', in F. Halliday and H. Alavi (eds.), *Ideology in the Middle East and Pakistan*. Macmillan Education, London.
Gramsci, A. (1971), *Selections from Prison Notebooks*, Lawrence and Wishart, London.
Graversgård, J. (1986), *Indvandrerne særligt truet*. Arbejdstilsynet. Århus.
Grillo, R.D. (1980), 'Social Workers and Immigrants in Lyon, France', in R.D Grillo (de.) *'Nation' and 'State' in Europe. Anthropological Perspectives*. Academic Press, London.
Grillo, R. (1985), *Ideologies and Institutions in Urban France. The Representation of Immigrants*. Cambridge.
Guenena, N. (1986), 'The 'Jihad'. An 'Islamic Alternative' in Egypt', in Cairo Papers in Social Science, vol. 9:2. Cairo.
Habermas, J. (1981), *Theorie des Kommunikative Handelns*. Frankfurt am Main.
Habermas, J.(1994), 'Struggles for Recognition in the Democratic Constitutional State', in A. Gutmann (ed.): *Multiculturalism. Examining the Politics of Recognition*, Princeton University Press, Princeton.
Hacir, A. (1988), 'Ey! Dünya Müslümanlari Birlesiniz...', in *Berlin Islâm Federasyonu*. Haziran 1988.
Halpern, M. (1963), *The Politics of Social Change in the Middle East and North Africa*. Princeton.
Hammer, O. (1984), 'Ryd forsiden, indvandrerne er her ... også!' in *Dokumentation om INDVANDRERE*, Nr. 3. MS.
Hannerz, U. (1992), *Cultural Complexity. Studies in the Social Organization of Meaning*. New York: Columbia University Press.
Harik, I. E. (1972), 'The Ethnic Revolution and Political Integration in the Middle East', in *The International Journal of Middle East Studies*, No. 3.
Hedman, L. (1985), *Indvandrare i Tystnadsspiralen. En rapport från Diskriminerings-utredningen*. Stockholm, Arbetmarknadsdepartementet.
Henriksen, I. (1985), *Indvandrernes levevilkår i Danmark*. Socialforskningsinstituttet, Publikation 142. København.

HFR (1987), Undersøgelse af Hotel- og Restaurationspersonalets Forbunds langtidslediges situation. Hotel- og Restaurationspersonalets Forbund.
Hily, M.-A. and Poinard, M. (1987), 'Portuguese Associations in France', in J.D. Rex, D. Joly and C. Wilpert (eds.), *Immigrant Associations in Europe*, Gower, Great Britain.
Hjarnø, J. (1988), *Indvandrere fra Tyrkiet i Stockholm og København*. Esbjerg: Sydjysk Universitetsforlag.
Hjarnø, J. (1991), *Kurdiske Indvandrere*. Esbjerg: Sydjysk Universitetsforlag.
Horst, Chr. (1980), *Arbejdskraft: Vare eller Menneske? Migration og vesteuropæisk kapitalisme*. Kultursociologiske Skrifter, No. 10. Akademisk Forlag.
Hummelgaard H. et. al. (1995), *Etniske Minoriteter, integration og mobilitet*. København: AKF Forlaget.
Ibrahim, S.,E. (1982), 'Islamic Militancy as a Social Movement: The Case of Two Groups in Egypt', in A. H. Dessouki (ed.), *Islamic Resurgence in the Arab World*, Praeger Publishers, New York.
Ibrahim, S.E. (1995) 'Civil Society and Prospects for Democratization in the Arab World', in Norton, A.R.(ed.), *Civil society in the Middle East*, Brill, Leiden, New York, Köln.
Israeli, R. (1979), 'The New Wave of Islam', *International Journal*, Vol. 34, No. 3. Toronto.
Johansen, B. (1981), 'Islam und Staat im Imperialismus', *Das Argument*, Nre.129 og 130, Berlin.
Joly, D. (1988), 'Making a Place for Islam in British Society: Muslims in Birmingham', in Gerholm T. & Y.G. Lithman (eds.), *The New Islamic Presence in Western Europe*, Mansell Publications, London.
Joly, D. and Nielsen, J. (1985), *Muslims in Britain: an Annotated Bibliography 1960-1984*. Bibliographies in Ethnic Relations No. 6. Centre for Research in Ethnic Relations, University of Warwick, Coventry.
Juergensmeyer, M. (1995), 'Antifundamentalism', in Marty, M.E. and Scott Appleby, R. (eds.), *Fundamentalisms Comprehended*. The Fundamentalism Project, vol. 5., The University of Chicago Press, Chicago, London.
Kepel, G. (1987), *Les Banlieues de l'Islam. Naissance d'une religion en France*, Éditions du Seuil, Paris.
Kepel. G. (1992), *Gud tager revanche*. København: Gyldendal.
Klebak, S. and Horst, Chr. (1977), *Fremmedarbejderes viden om social- og sundhedsvæsenet*. Publikation 7. Institut for Social Medicin. KU.
Knudsen, C. O. (1994), *The Falling Dawadawa Tree. Female Circumcision in Developing Ghana*. Intervention Press, Århus.
Kofoed, J. (1994), *Midt i Normalen*. Københavnerstudier i tosprogethed, bd. 24. København: DLH.
Körmendi, E. (1986), *Os og de andre. Danskernes holdninger til indvandrere og flygtninge*, Socialforskningsinstituttet, København.
Krämer, G. (1993), 'Islamist Notions of Democracy', *Middle East Report*, no. 183. USA.

Lakhdar, L. (1981), 'Why the Reversion to Islamic Archaism?' *Khamsin*, No.8, London.
Legrain, J.-F. (1986), 'Aspects de la présence musulmane en France', *Dossiers de SRI*, No. 2, (Secrétariat de l'Episcopat par les Relations avec Islam).
Leveau, R. (1988), 'The Islamic Presence in France', in T. Gerholm T. and Y.G. Lithman Y.G. (eds.), *The New Islamic Presence in Western Europe*, Mansell Publications, London.
Lings, M. (1961), *A Muslim Saint of the Twentieth Century*. London.
Lovbekendtgørelse (1992-02-29), *Lov om Folkeskolen*. Lovbekendtgørelse 1992-02-29, nr. 669.
Lutz, H. (1986), Migrantinnen aus der Türkei. - Eine Kritik des gegenwärtigen Forschungsstandes. *Migration & Ethnizität 0/86*. Berlin.
Mardin, S. (1984), 'A Note on the Transformation of Religious Symbols in Turkey', *TURCICA. Revue d'Etudes Turques*, No. 16. Éditions Peeters, Paris.
Marty, M.E. and Scott Appleby, R. (1991), 'Introduction. The Fundamentalism Project: A User's Guide', in M.E. Marty and R. Scott Appleby (eds.), *Fundamentalisms Observed*. The Fundamentalism Project, vol. 1. The University of Chicago Press, Chicago, London.
Medienprojekt Tübinger Religionswissenschaft, (1994), *Der Islam in den Medien. Studien zum Verstehen fremder Religionen*, Gütersloher Verlagshaus, Germany.
MID (1995), *Muslim i Danmark*. Årg. 2, nr. 7. København.
Mossing, N. (1973), Arbejdsskader hos gæstearbejdere. *Ugeskrift for læger*, 139, 9.
Mouriaux, R. and Wihtol de Wenden, C. (1988), 'Syndicalisme français et islam', in R. Leveau and G. Kepel (eds.), *Les Musulmans dans la Société Française*, Presse de la Fondation Nationale des Sciences Politiques, Paris.
Moustapha Diop, A. (1988), 'Stéréotypes et stratégies', in R. Leveau and G. Kepel (ed.), *Les Musulmans dans la Société Française*, Presse de la Fondation Nationale des Sciences Politiques, Paris.
Naïr, S. (1984), 'Social Formations, Power Structures and Ideology in the Arab-Muslim World', *Praxis International*, vol. 4, No. 2. Great Britain: Basil Blackwell Publisher Ltd.
Necef, M. Ü. (1992), *Etnisk kitsch - og andre (post)moderne fortællinger om 'de andre'*, Institut for Kultursociologi, Copenhagen.
Necef, M.Ü. (1993), Tyrkeren og ghettoen. *GRUS* nr. 41. Ålborg.
Nielsen, J. (1981), *Muslims in Europe. An Overview*. Muslims in Europe 12, Centre for the Study of Islam and Christian-Muslim Relations, Selly Oak Colleges, Birmingham.

Nielsen, J. (1987), *Islamic Law and its Significance for the Situation of Muslim Minorities in Europe*. Muslims in Europe 35. Centre for the Study of Islam and Christian-Muslim Relations, Selly Oak Colleges, Birmingham.

Norton, A.R (1995), Introduction. In: Norton, A.R. (ed.), *Civil society in the Middle East*, Brill, Leiden, New York, Köln.

Norton, A.R. (de.) (1995), *Civil society in the Middle East*, Brill, Leiden, New York, Köln.

Næss, R. (1988), 'Being an Alevi Muslim in South-Western Anatolia and in Norway', in T. Gerholm and Y.G. Lithman (eds.), *The New Islamic Presence in Western Europe*, Mansell, London.

Olsen, G.R. (1988), 'Islam: What is its Political Significance? The Case of Egypt and Saudi Arabia', in K. Ferdinand and M. Mozaffari (eds.), *Islam: State and Society*, Curzon, UK.

Oriol, M. (1980), *Bilan des Etudes sur les Aspects Culturels et Humains des Migrations Internationales en Europe Occidentale, 1918-1979*, Fondation Europeenne de la Science. Strasbourg.

Pedersen, L. (1984), *'Det islamiske alternativ' blandt (mandlige) studenter i Cairo*, unpublished fieldreport, Dept of Ethnography, Aarhus University, Aarhus.

Pedersen, L. (1985), 'Islamisk opposition i Ægypten: Mellem tradition og modernisering?', unpublished conference thesis, Etnografisk Afd., Aarhus Universitet, Aarhus.

Pedersen, L. (1988), 'Islam, muslimer og indvandrere i *Dagbladet Information*', in S. Dindler and A. Olesen (eds.), *Islam og muslimer i de danske medier*. Aarhus Universitetsforlag, Aarhus.

Pedersen, L. (1991a), 'Fra fremmedarbejder til indvandrer', in L. Pedersen and B. Selmer, *Muslimsk indvandrerungdom. Kulturel identitet og migration*, Aarhus Universitetsforlag, Aarhus.

Pedersen, L. (1991b), 'Magten og indvandrerne', in L. Pedersen and B. Selmer *Muslimsk indvandrerungdom. Kulturel identitet og migration*. Aarhus Universitetsforlag, Aarhus.

Pedersen, L. (1991c), 'Tyrkiske og pakistanske indvandrerorganisationer i Århus', in L. Pedersen and B. Selmer, *Muslimsk indvandrerungdom. Kulturel identitet og migration*, Aarhus Universitetsforlag, Aarhus.

Pedersen, L. (1996a), 'Islam og stat i Vesteuropa (EU). De muslimske minoriteter, religionsfrihedens grænser og demokratiet', Forskningsrapport, SHF.

Pedersen, L. (1996b). 'Islam in the Discourse of Public Authorities and Institutions in Denmark', in W. A. R Shadid and P.S. van Koningsveld (eds.), *Muslims in the Margin. Political Responses to the Presence of Islam in Western Europe*, Kok Pharos, The Netherlands.

Pedersen, L. (1998), 'Islam and Socialization Among Turkish Minorities in Denmark: Between Culturalism and Cultural Complexity', in S. Vertovec and A. Rogers (eds.), *Muslim European Youth. Reproducing ethnicity, religion, culture*, Ashgate Publishing Ltd, UK.

Pedersen, L. and B. Selmer (1991), *Muslimsk indvandrerungdom. Kulturel identitet og migration*. Aarhus Universitetsforlag, Aarhus.
Peters, R. (1980), 'Idjtihad and Taqlid in the 18th and 19th Century Islam', *Die Welt des Islams XX:3-4*.
Pontoppidan, L. (1985), *Litteratur om indvandrere. Supplement 1983-1985. En annoteret bibliografi*. MS-Indvandrerdokumentation, Denmark.
Raffnsøe, J. (1987), *Arbejdsulykker og arbejdsbetingede lidelser blandt indvandrere, 1983-1985*, Arbejdstilsynet, DK.
Rahman, F. (1970), 'Revival and Reform in Islam', in P.M. Holt et al (eds.), *The Cambridge History of Islam*, Vol. 1. Cambridge of the University Press.
Rex, J., Joly, D. and Wilpert, C. (1987), *Immigrant Associations in Europe*. Aldershot, GB.
Robinson, F. (1988), *Varieties of South Asian Islam*. Research Papers in Ethnic Relations no. 8. Centre for Research in Ethnic Relations, University of Warwick, Coventry.
Rockefeller, S.C. (1994), 'Comment', in Gutmann, A. (ed.), *Multiculturalism. Examining the Politics of Recognition*, Princeton University Press, Princeton.
Roy, O. (1985), *L'Afghanistan, Islam et modernité politique*, Le Seuil, Paris.
Røgilds, F. (1988), *Rytme, racisme & nye rødder. - En bro mellem sorte og hvide?* Politisk Revy, Copenhagen.
Sadowsky, Y. (1993), 'The New Orientalism and Democracy Debate', *Middle East Report*, no. 183. USA.
Said, E. (1978), *Orientalism*. London: RKP.
Said, E. (1981), *Covering Islam*. London: RKP.
Saifullah Khan, V. (1978), The Pakistanis: Mirpuri Villagers at Home and in Bradford', in Watson, J. (ed.), *Between two Cultures*, Basil Blackwell, Oxford.
Saribay, A.Y. (1985), Die Nationale Heilspartei, in J. Blaschke and M. Bruinessen (Hg.), *Islam und Politik in der Türkei*. Jahrbuch zur Geschichte und Gesellschaft des Vorderen und Mittleren Orients 1984, Express Edition, Berlin.
Sassen, S. (1990), *The Mobility of Labor and Capital. A Study in International Investment and Labor Flow*, Cambridge University Press, Cambridge.
Sayad, A. (1994), Le mode de génération des générations immigrées. *Migrants-Formation*, No. 98.
Schierup, C.-U. (1991), '"The duty to work": the theory and practice of Swedish refugee policy', in Schierup, C.-U. & A. Ålund (eds.), *Paradoxes of Multiculturalism, Essays on Swedish Society*, Avebury, Aldershot.
Schierup, C.-U. (1993), *På kulturens Slagmark. Mindretal og større tal taler om Danmark*, Sydjysk Universitetsforlag.

Schierup, C.-U. and Ålund, A. (1987), *Will They Still be Dancing? Integration and Ethnic Transformation among Yugoslav Immigrants in Scandinavia*. Göteborg.

Schierup, C.-U.and Ålund, A. (1991), *Paradoxes of Multiculturalism. Essays on Swedish Society*, Avebury, Aldershot.

Schiffauer, W. (1988), 'Migration and Religiousness', in T. Gerholm and Y.G. Lithman (eds.), *The New Islamic Presence in Western Europe*, Mansell Publications, London.

Schoeneberg, U. (1985), 'Participation in Ethnic Associations: The Case of Immigrants in West Germany', *International Migration Review*, vol. 19.

Searle-Chatterjee, M. (1987), 'The Anthropologist Exposed. Anthropologist in Multicultural and Anti-racist Work', *Anthropology Today*, Vol. 3, No. 4.

Selmer, B. (1991), 'Indvandrerkvinder. Religiøse og kulturelle traditioner', in L. Pedersen and B. Selmer, *Muslimsk indvandrerungdom. Kulturel identitet og migration*, Aarhus Universitetsforlag, Aarhus.

Shadid, W.A.R and van Koningsveld, P.S. (eds.) (1996) *Muslims in the Margin. Political Responses to the Presence of Islam in Western Europe*. Kampen: Kok Pharo.

Sivan, E. (1985), *Radical Islam. Medieval Theology and Modern Politics*, Yale University Press, New Haven.

Sivananda, A. (1983), 'Challenging Racism: Strategies for the 80s', *Race and Class*, Vol. 25, No. 2.

Slomp, J. (1988), *Muslim Minorities in the Netherlands*. Muslims in Europe 37. Centre for the Study of Islam and Christian-Muslim Relations, Selby Oak Colleges, Birmingham.

Slomp, J. (1985), *Statistik om indvandrere*, Indenrigsministeriet, DK.

Slomp, J. (1991), 'Statistik om indvandrere og flygtninge', *Dokumentation om INDVANDRERE*, Nr. 2. Mellemfolkeligt Samvirke.

Stenbæk, J. (1987), 'Om ægteskabsindgåelse, anerkendelse af trossamfund og religionsfrihed i Danmark', in Kristensen and Riis (eds.), *Religiøse minoriteter*, Aarhus Universitetsforlag, Aarhus.

Subhi, T. (1985), Musulmans dans l'Entreprise. *ESPRIT. Change la Culture et la Politique*, No. 6. Paris.

Tapper, N. and Tapper, R. (1987), 'The Birth of the Prophet: Ritual and Gender in Turkish Islam', *Man*, No 1, Vol. 22.

Taylor, C. (1994), 'The Politics of Recognition', in A. Gutmann (ed.), *Multiculturalism,Examining the Politics of Recognition*, Princeton University Press, Princeton.

Terrel, H. (1986), 'L'Islam Arabe en France', *Les Cahiers de L'ORIENT*, No.3.

Tesli, A. (1979), *Turkish Labour Migrants in Århus*. Workingpaper.

Tibi, B. (1981), *Die Krise des Modernen Islams. Eine Vorindustrielle Kultur im Wissenschaftlich-Technischen Zeitalter*. C.H.Beck.

Tibi, B. (1985), *Der Islam und das Problem der kulturellen Bewältigung sozialen Wandels*, Suhrkamp, Frankfurt am Main.

Turner, B.S. (1974), *Weber and Islam: A Critical Study*, RKP. London.

Voisard, J. and Ducastelle, C. (1988), *La Question Immigrée dans la France d'Aujourd'hui*, Calmann-Lévy, Paris.
Wallraf, G. (1985), *Ganz Unten*, Kiepenheuer & Witsch.
Werbner, P. (1990), *The Migration Process: Capital, Gifts and Offerings among British Pakistanis*, Explorations in Anthropology, Berg, New York, Oxford, Munich.
Wilpert, C. (1988), 'Religion and Ethnicity: Orientations, Perceptions and Strategies among Turkish Alevi and Sunni Migrants in Berlin', in T. Gerholm and Y.G. Lithman (eds.), *The New Islamic Presence in Western Europe*, Mansell Publications, London.
Ziehe, T. and Stubenrauch, H. (1983), *Ny ungdom og usædvanlige læreprocesser*. Politisk Revy.
Ægteskabsloven (1984), Kommenteret. Jurist- og Økonomforbundets Forlag, 2. udg, DK.
Özcan, E. (1989), *Türkische Immigrantenorganisationen in der Bundesrepublik Deutschland*. Berlin (West): Hitit Verlag.
Ålund, A. (1985), *Skyddsmurar. Etnicitet och Klass i Invandrarsammanhang*. Stockholm.
Ålund, A. (1991), 'The power of definitions: immigrant women and problem ideologies', in C.-U. Schierup and A. Ålund (eds.), *Paradoxes of Multiculturalism. Essays on Swedish Society*, Avebury, Aldershot.

Appendix A

Interview with Mehmet, Spokesman for AMGT-Berlin Bölgesi, March 1990
(Transcript of original recording in German)

(1) On the Community
Es gibt im Islam den Grundsatz, das jeder Moslem der Bruder ist. Die Moslems sind unter anderen Brüdern, sie müssen sich so kennen. Der Gesandte Gotten, Muhammed, hat einmal gesagt, wenn ein mu'min, das is ein Glaübiger, den Schmerz seines Bruders auf der anderen Seite der Erde nicht fühlen kann, dann ist er kein richtiger Glaübiger! Wir müssen so zusammenhalten - und zu diesem Zweck machen wir solche Treffen, Ausflüge.

(2) On Knowledge
Es is ja auch eines unserer Ziele, den Islam innerhalb der Wissenschaften, wieder voranzubringen. Es gab ja lange eine Zeit wo der Islam die Führung innerhalb der Wissenschaften hatte, viele hundert Jahre her. Das möchten wir wieder haben, weil der Islam wirklich den Menschen mit ihren Wissenschaften dient.
    Für die Bildung interessieren wir uns sehr, den Mitlgliedern den richtigen Islam lehren, nicht den Islam den DITIB lehrt. DITIB lehrt z.B. fünfmal täglich beten, dann Fasten, *Zêkat* und Pilgerfahrt nach Mekka, und das ist alles. Aber im Islam ist das nicht alles, wir versuchen dann darüber hinaus noch den gesamten Islam zu lehren.

(3) On the Accusation that Islamische Föderation is a Cover Organisation for Millî Görüş
Das ist Unsinn! Das ist ganz einfach: In der Islamischen Föderation sind doch auch andere Vereinen, es sind zum Beispiel auch Vereinigungen, die mit Millî Görüş nicht sympatisiert, nicht mögen. Wenn es in Wirklichkeit so wäre, daß die Islamische Föderation gelenkt wird, dann müßen diese Vereinen austreten - oder Barbara John sagt 'diese Vereinen sind dumm, die sehen das nicht, aber ich sehe das!'. Das ist Unsinn, es ist richtig, daß die Mehrzahl der Mitgliedern gleichzeitig Millî Görüş angehören, aber das hat nichts darüber zu sagen, daß Millî Görüş jetz übergebe Einfluß. Die Islamische Föderation hat ihre eigene Satzung, die Arbeitsbereiche der

Föderation ist ganz anders, die Föderation arbeitet in Berlin, in der berliner Gesellschaft. Millî Görüş arbeitet....nur mit den Türken zusammen, sehen Sie, die Arbeitsbereiche ist ganz anders. Die mischen sich auch gar nicht ein und zu. Die Islamische Föderation macht dann alles so offiziel, mit Schriften und so weiter. Millî Görüş machen dann mit Hilfe, wenn hier renoviert werden, dann kommen wir schnell, und helfen, nicht offiziel und so weiter. Das ist der Untershied. es gibt sehr viele Sachen, was die Barbara John falsch sagt. Die Barbara John, die glaubt, wir sind eine straffe Organisation, militärisch, alles was Köln sagt und praktiziert, es wäre schön. Wir Muslims wollen, das was Barbara John sagt richtig ist, aber es ist nicht so. Es ist unser Wunsch und wir waren glücklich so eine cemaat zu sein, und alles funktioniert. Mieinandern zusammenarbeiten ohne Konflikte, was der einen sagte ist der andere einverstanden und so weiter, das wollen wir, aber das schaffen wir nicht, und Barbara John sagt das überall die Millî Görüş ist, so wir müßten uns davor achten und so weiter.

Die Schule ist genau so wie die Fernsehen (Türkish-Deutsche Fernsehen), genau sowie die Frauenvereinigungen. Die Schule hat mit Millî Görüş... nichts zu tun wäre falsch, das ist richtig...nichts zu tun wäre falsch, weil wir sind Muslims, und das sind auch Muslims, wenn die helfen brauchen, helfen wir mit, zum Beispiel bei der Renovierung haben wir mitgeholfen. Wir haben gemalt, wir haben mitgeholfen, das ist ganz klar. Aber Millî Görüş kann keinen Answeisungen geben und die können uns keine Answeisungen geben. Wir sind so unabhängig, plus wenn die umfangende Hilfe Brauchen, stehen wir zur Verfügung. (....) Das ist so, und die Schule ist hier untergebracht, das auch der Grund, weil Barbara John sagt, das der Schule hängt von Millî Görüş ab. Dieses Gebäude gehört der *vakif*, ist eine Stiftung, und alle Räume werden von Muslime umsonst vermietet. Diese Mosche bezahlt zum Beispiel keine Miete, andere Moscheen müßen Miete zahlen. Und die Schule zahlt auch keine Miete, weshalb, aus diesen Grund ist die hier. Wir würden zu beispiel gerne in einen viel größeres Gebäude kaufen, damit vielleicht viel größeres Schule errichtet werden können,...aber im Moment ist das hier das billigste.

(4) On Interest on Payments for Attending the Hajj
Das bleibt irgendwo in die Tasche von Hoca oder so, und es kann auch sein, das es auf die Bank kommt, aber dann nur ein Girokonto - ohne Zinsen. Weil wir sind hier von Millî Görüş, von Islam gegen Zinsen.

(5) On DITIB's Hajj
Und wenn die Pilger jetz nach Mekka gehen, dann gehen die dorthin, sitzen zur Hause, und gehen zur den Gebetszeiten in die Moscheen, kommen

wieder zurück, und kommen wieder hierher. Die sehen nichts, die hören nichts, die erleben das nicht.

(6) On When Ramadan Should be Held
Deshalb haben wir letzes Jahr ganz anderes gemacht. Wir haben gesehen das die früheren Jahre, wenn wir zum Beispiel ein paar Tage vorher den Ramadan verkünden, dann gab es einige, die haben gesagt warum macht ihr das, warum seid ihr gegen den Türkischen Staat, die machen doch auch, die rechnen das. Unser Prophet hat uns gesagt, wir sollten mit den Fasten anfangen wenn ihr den Mond sehen, und ihr solltet aufhören, wenn ihr den Mond seht. Also die einzige Bedingung ist, den Mond sehen. Er hat nicht gesagt 'rechnet', aber das wissen die meistens nicht. Aus diesen Grunde haben wir letztes Jahr die Verkündung des *Ramadans* nicht öffentlich gemacht, sondern wir haben gesagt, öffentlich machen wir genau so wie Diyanet, aber, jeder der es wissen will, kann uns anrufen und wir geben Antwort. Und jeder, der es wissen wollte, hat uns angerufen und wir haben gesagt, ja der Mond wurde gesehen, ihr können anfangen. Dann wird es öffentlich nicht verkündet.

Dann schlagen wir unser Mitgliedern ganz einfach vor, das die Söhnen genau so wie der Vater tut, weil in Islam soll man den Vater auch nicht kränken, und deshalb sagen wir unsern Freunde mal, macht so wie dein Vater und hoffe, daß Allah dir vergibt. Früher haben wir richtige Auseinsetzungen gemacht, ja. Ein Tag vorher, nein nein ein Tag danach! Das machen wir jetzt nicht mehr, weil das bringt nichts. Es ist jedes Jahr immer derselbe, immer derselbe, dadurch verlieren wir Zeit, und nicht anderes. Deshalb machen wir jetzt, jeder soll machen wie er will. Die Islamische Föderation sieht, beobachtet und mann sagt wir haben den Mond gesehen, jeder der uns glaubt soll anfangen mit dem Fasten. Und jenigen, die das nicht glauben sollen, bitte schön, nicht Fasten, daß ist für uns egal.

(7) On Accusations of Being Anti-Jewish
Sie sagen das wir judenfeinlich sind das stimmt nicht, wir sind Feinde der Zionisten. Zionisten sind jüdische Faschisten, die also davon überzeugt sind, daß das jüdisches Volk hier das Herrenvolk auf der Erde ist, und alle andere Völker unterdrücken muß, und gegen dieser Volk sind wir. Und Israel ist zionistisch, was dort mit der Palästinensern gemacht wird... haben Sie vielleicht ins Fernsehen gesehen, die schnappen sich die Kindern, und schlagen ihn die Arme kaputt, weil es in ihren Buch so steht. In ihren Buch steht: 'Wenn ihr andere Menschen findet, dann schlagt sie die Arme kaput, dann schneidet ihre Ohren ab, und schneidet die Nasen ab'. (......) Es steht darhin in diesen Buch, ins Torah!.....Und genau das praktisieren sie auch, im

Gefängnissen schneiden sie die Näse und Ohren ab, und gegen dieses Volk sind wir. Und in die Millî Gazette zum beispiel, es ist eine Zeitung die mit Millî Görüş sympatisiert, in dieser Zeitung erscheinen oft Artikeln, die dann sagen 'barbarischer Juden'. Weil wenn die Juden sagt, meint sie immer Israelis, aber das versteht John[1] nicht. John denkt auch das wir hier gegen die Juden sind.

Also anti jüdisch ist korrent, wenn man mit Jude wirklich die Juden in Israel meint. Aber die Juden hier leben nich nach ihrem Buch, die leben ja hier nach der Verfassung. Die haben ihren eigene Religion etwas umgeändert, etwas gemildert, und die leben hier nach der berliner Verfassung, genai so wie wir. Die sind Bürgern, die uns niemal etwas getan und wir haben die nie etwas getan, das ist ganz klar. Aber die Juden dort... jeder seht, was die machen gegen die Palästinensern. Palästinensern sind Muslems und unser Brüder, wenn man dort ein Palästinenser tötet, hat man mein Brüder getötet, dann muß ich einfach judenfeindlich sein.

Man schreibt auch 'Israelis' und 'Zionistern', aber die Millî Gazette erscheint in der Türkei, und die schreibt das jetz in den türkischen Millieu. Also wenn man in der Türkei 'Jude' sagt, versteht man sofort 'Israel'. Weil es gibt kein andere Juden, aber wenn man *hier* Jude sagt, dann versteht man in erster Linie die Juden hier in Deutschland. Aber wenn man in der Türkei 'Jude' sagt, versteht man *die* Juden, deshalb!.

Wir haben in die Millî Gazette mehrfach gesagt, die sollen ein bißchen aufpassen, daß die nicht 'Jude' sagen sondern 'Zionisten'. Wenn die 'Juden' sagen, meinen die 'Zionisten', aber wenn sie 'Jude' schreiben wird es hier falsch verstanden, und dann haben wir dann Probleme bei der Schule zum 'helft uns!', sagen die 'nein, ihr sind judenfeindlich!'. Das ist die Schuld von Millî Gazette in der Türkei, aber wir haben keine Weisungsbefugnisse, wissen Sie, wir können nicht sagen, 'jetz müßt ihr das so machen', wir können nur bitten (Interview, op. cit.).

(8) On Right/Left and Accusations of Terrorism
Jeder spricht aus eigen Kopf, und es gibt sehr viele Meinungen über Millî Görüş. Es gibt Menschen, ich kann Ihn Menschen zeigen, das sehr nationalistisch geprägt sind, es gibt solche Menschen, so gibt es ja über alle. Auch in Millî Görüş gibt es Flügel, rechter Flügel und linker Flügel. Wenn man von ganz recht jemanden nimmt, und sagt was ist Millî Görüş, dann sagt er, daß Millî Görüş ist das, das, das und das. Und das veröffentlicht man. Das ist natürlich nicht richtig, man muß jemanden aus dem Mitte nehmen, nicht wahr? Die Zuständigen im Senat werden dann

---

[1] Barbara John is the leader of the Senate's 'Ausländerbeauftragte'.

verwirrt - das ist ganz normal - und glauben die Millî Görüş ist eine terroristische Vereinigung. Die haben sogar Verbindungen zwischen uns und Iran hergestellt, wobei ich sagen muß, das wir uns mit dem Iran nicht verstehen mit dem Iran. Das ist der Kaplan, er hat sich abgespaltet, bei dem stimmt es das er mit Iran zusammenarbeitet, aber bei uns nicht, wir arbeiten mit Iran nicht zusammen, wir verstehen uns auch nicht mit Iran.

(9) On the War in Afghanistan, Being a War for All Muslims
Der Krieg in Afghanistan war ja ein Krieg zwischen den Sowjetunion und den gesamten Muslims auf der Erde. Jede Muslim hat Afghanistan unterstütz finanziell, einige Freunde sind dorthin gegangen, 2-3 Monate, hat dort Krieg mitgemacht, und sind wieder zurückgekommen. Solche Freunde haben wir auch. Und alle Muslime auf die Welt hat diesen Krieg gewonnen, oder sagen wir fast gewonnen - zwischen die Muslims gibt es auch Meinungsverschiedenheiten. Solche Sachen diskutieren wir natürlich in Versammlungen so diskutieren.

(10) On the Fall of Communism and Islam's Opportunity
Wir sind fast alle der Meinung, daß das der erste Schritt ist, Kommunismus ist kaputt gegangen. Der zweiter Schritt wird sein, daß der Kapitalismus kaputt geht, das dritter Schritt wird dann Islam kommen, und die gesamte Welt dann wird den Islam akzeptieren. Davon sind wir überzeugt, weil Islam ist etwas von Allah.... für den Menschen und für die menschliche Gesellschaft. Und diesen ganzen Gesetze, freien Markwirtschaft oder Kommunismus, wenn mann die jetzmal analysiert, wird man feststellen, daß die freie Markwirtschaft ein Teil von Islam genommen hat, und ein Teil selbst, also von die Kopf, Kommunismus auch, ein teil von islam und ein Teil von Kopf. Es ist nicht zu Ende gegangen: Die Kommunismus ist kaputt gegangen, die freien Markwirtschaft wird ein bischen schlauer, die hat es gesehen, das es so nicht weiter geht, und hat sich verändert, und verändert sich immer weiter. Der Kommunismus hat sich nicht verändert, der Starke ist sehr schnell kaputt gegangen. Der freien Markwirtschaft verändert sich, aber die verändert sich immer in Richtung Islam, also das stellen wir fest. Und wir hoffen das es irgendwann mal im Islam endet.

Appendix B

Interview with Yahya Schülzke, vice chairman of Islamische Föderation, Berlin, November 1989, and March 1990.
(Transcript of original recording in German)

(1) On the Evangelical Church's Opposition to Islamic Religious Teaching in Public Schools
...die Evangelische Kirche hat sich gegen diesen islamischen Religionsunterricht ausgesprochen. Und da die Evangelische Kirche in Berlin den grössten Bevölkerungsanteil darstellt, war das für die Politiker natürlich auch eine wichtige Entscheidung. Sie werden nicht gegen ihrer Wähler, die sie also wählen, entscheiden. .....die Evangelische Kirche hat in Berlin vorher 1.250.000 Angehöriger gehabt und nach die lezter Zählung hat sie noch 970,000. Aber bei 2 millionen Menschen ist das immer noch die Hälfte, die also jetzt die Evangelische Kirche angehört, und deshalb ist es auch eine wichtige Frage für die.

(2) On the Relationship between the Evangelical and the Catholic Churches
Jetz im Augenblick - hat man mir gesagt - ist das Stand so, daß die Evangelische Kirche nicht mehr gegen die islamische religionsunterricht ist, sondern nur noch gegen die Islamische Föderation als Träger. Aber das ändert eben dem Empfehl nichts. Die Sache darüber müssten wir noch diskutieren. Es ist natürlich das Problem, das viele Christen, evangelische Christen, die also in die leitende Stellungen sind, auch fürchten, wenn jetzt der Staat, mit dem Muslimen einen neuen Vertrag macht, das auch ihrer alten Verträge dadurch beinflusst werden. Das ist eine logische Sache.

Die Katolische Kirche hat sich bis jetzt zurückgehalten. Wir haben also mit der Katolischen Kirche erst jetzt vor kurzen einen Dialog angefangen, wobei sich herausgestellt hat, daß unsere Dialogführung mit den Katolischen wesentlich einfacher ist als mit den evangelischen Christen. Komischerweise zum Beispiel, wir.....diskutieren im Augenblick jetzt - in diesem Jahr - die Frage sehr stark: Gibt es einen einzigen Gott oder gibt es also mehrere Götter? Für die Katolische Kirche und für die Muslime gibt es keine Schwierigkeit: Es gibt nur einen Gott für beide.

Die Evangelische Kirche hat eine grosse starke Gruppe von Evangelikalen, die also behaupten, daß das also nicht so ist. Der Gottvater des Evangelikalen wäre nicht gleich zu setzen mit dem Gott der Muslime. Ich habe bis heute nicht genau verstanden, warum es bei dem evangelische Christen so unheimlich schwierig ist. Ich habe nur Unterlag, ich kann Ihnen also zeigen, wir diskutieren das also. Das ist hochgekommen dadurch, daß der Bischof Kruse, der ja gleichzeitig Bischof der Evangelische Kirche Deutschland ist. Der Bischof hat uns ins frohen Jahr gesagt 'ein Gott aber welcher?', das war die Diskussion, die wir geführt haben schon,....am Horizonte Festival war das.

Das Bischof hat uns in den vergangen Jahren dieses Grusswort gesendet (well wishing in connection with the end of the fast/LP), die Linien war dieses hier, ...ich will es nurmal zitieren: 'Wir stehen mit Ihnen in der gemeinsamen Verantwortung uns dafür einzustezen, daß Gottes Name geehrt werde'. Er hat also von der Gemeinsamkeit gesprochen und also auch von einen Gott gesprochen, nicht. Diese Zeitung der Evangelikalen, haben ihm fürchtelich angegrriffen. Haben also geschreiben hier 'synkritismus'....Und besonderes schlimm war es natürlich für die Missionäre, die also Muslime missionieren in Afrika,....sie haben ihn sehr angegriffen. Und daraufhin hat er in diesem Jahr geschrieben,...(das ist diesen Satz hier)....: 'Sie haben in der vergangen Wochen um Ihres Glaubens willen viele Enthaltungen und Anstrengung auf sich genommen und feiern nun ein Fest zur Ehren Ihres Gottes', Ihres Gottes - Ihre!...Das ist die Reaktion auf diese Angriffe die er bekommen hat. Er hat also versucht, so ein Lösung zu finden. Aber wie auch der Pfarrer Jan Slomp (responsible for the Dutch Reformed Church's relation to Islam/LP) eigenlich meinte, ist es ein Rückschritt im Dialog,....Das ist ein Rückshritt, weil wenn wir also wirklich ein Dialog mit einandern führen wollen, dann wäre es unheimlich wichtig, daß wir uns daraufhin verständigen können, das es nur eine einzig Gott gibt, für alle Religionen. Das ist die Basis für Dialog. Dadurch wird natürlich Missionsarbeit fragwürdig, wenn wir alle derselbe Ziel haben, und nur die Wege dahin verschieden sind, dann warum sollte der Eine nicht seinen Weg gehen und der Andere nicht den anderen Weg gehen. Aber ich glaube, das ist auch das Problem dieser evangelikalen Leute, das sie sagen, 'nur ein Weg und nur ein Ziel und wir haben nicht deselbe Ziel'! Das ist also eine Frage über die evangelische Missionswirksamkeit.

Die Katolischen haben auf grund des 2. Vatikanischen Konzils eine Aussage gemacht, wie die Muslime zu sehen wollen, und sie haben darin gesagt, so haben wir das verstanden, wir sind Gläubige. Die Evangelische Kirche hat das bis heute nicht gesagt. Und sie haben mir erklärt, daß ist für uns so schwierig, weil wir so vielen Gruppen haben, ja. (.....). Aber wir haben immer noch nicht gehört: Sind wir für sie Gläubige oder Ketzer oder was sind wir also für sie? Das ist noch nicht gesagt. Das ist natürlich so, wenn den solche Sache passieren wie mit dem Grusswort, und jetz wird von Ihren Gott gesprochen, dann gehen wir also wieder zurück, dann fangen wir wieder von vorne an. Dann wissen wir gar nicht mehr, was sind wir jetz für sie.

(3) On Islam and the Constitution
Daß es im Islam die Möglichkeit gibt, Verträge auch mit anderen zu schließen, und daß diese Verträge gültig sind. Wenn wir hier leben, haben wir diesen Vertrag Grundgesetz anerkannt, und wir sind bereit danach zu leben. Deshalb werden wir den Koran nich wegwerfen, wir werden immer noch sagen, das ist unser Idealbild, aber wir haben jetzt dieser Vertrag mit diesen Gesetz. So habe ich es versucht, zu erklären. Die haben es erst akzeptiert nachdem Steppart (German expert on Islam/LP) gesprochen hatte.

Die halten nicht nur Milli Görüş für Terroristen, sondern alle Muslime! Wir sind alle Terroristen, sehen sie das! deshalb wollen die uns politisch hier keine Rechte einräumen.

(4) On the Lack of Recognition of Islamische Föderation as a 'Körperschaften...'
...es ist die Politik etwas zu finden! Etwas zu finden - und sagen wir wollen das nicht zulaßen. Wir Muslime müßen jetzt leider versuchen einen Punkt nach den anderen auszuräumen. Nun haben wir das Problem, das unsere Leute von Millî Görüş so eine Selbstdarstellung nicht gemacht haben.

Das Hauptproblem scheint mir eigenlich zu sein, und da bin ich jetzt erst von einen christlichen Pfarrer darauf gebracht worden. Er hat mir gesagt, das kommt an welche Ausländerpolitik man macht. Wenn man eine Ausländerpolitik macht, die auf Rückführung ausgerichtet ist, dann wird man es nicht zulaßen wollen, daß wir hier Institutionen bilden, islamischen Institutionen. Sondern man will nur Institutionen hier zulaßen, die an das Heimatland gebunden sind, das ist der politsche Gedanke, der da hinter steht. Deshalb benutzt man also jetzt die Türkisch generalkonsulat um alle religiöse Sachen (....) zu machen, weil das bedeutet Rückführung. Denn diese Leute werden nicht ausgebildet hier in dieser Gesellschaft zu leben, sondern ausgebildet zu Hause. Wird alles auf Türkisch gemacht, wird der Islam so erklärt, wie der in der Türkei erklärt wird.... Ich habe hier (In his above mentioned defense statement to the administrative courts/LP) (...) gesagt, daß wir Muslime anstreben, eine Loslösung von den traditionellen nationalistischen Staatsislam, wie in der Türkei, in Syrien, überall getriebt worden. Wir streben an ein freien europäischen Islam, der von den anderen Einflußen frei ist. Das können wir naturlich nicht mit den Institutionen erreichen wie DITIB ist, staatliche Organisationen gibt es überhaupt nicht. Deshalb wenn die Leute hier unseren Versuch, diesen Gesellschaft mit Islam zu verbinden, eine Verbindung hier zu stellen, nicht akzeptieren, dann wird Islam in eine Ghetto gehen müßen.

(5) On Islam and Religious Freedom
Ich meine, daß der islamische Staat eigentlich seine Berechtigung daraus herleitet, daß er Religionsfreiheit, daß er also Gleichheit der Menschen, das was z.B. die französische Revolution in Europa gebracht hat. Das hatte eigentlich Prophet Muhammed seit tausend und vierhundert Jahren gebracht! Die französische Revolution war also im Essenz eine Islamische Revolution war? So sehe ich es! Ich meine das eigentlich ein Staat gewünscht wird, der alle diesen Freiheiten garantiert, das wäre also ein islamische Staat. Islamischer kann der gar nicht sein, und es wird also nicht dadurch garantiert, daß die es unbedingt die Muslime die Macht haben. Sondern die Muslime können diesen Staat mitarbeiten, sie müßten nur darfür sorgen, daß diese Freiheiten für die Muslime auch gelten. Das ist der Hauptpunkt.

Appendix C

Yahya Schülzke's Defense Statement Presented at a Parliamentary Hearing of the School Committe of the Berlin Senate, 14th Febuary 1990.

Mir ist (...) vorgeworfen worden, daß ich 1985 gesagt habe, daß ich es als eine Ungeheuerlichkeit ansehe, daß man den Koran, ein 1400 Jahre altes göttliches Gesetz, mit unserem Grundgesetz vergleichen will. Dazu stehe ich auch noch heute. Ich habe nie davon gehört, daß man die Vereinbarkeit des Alten und des Neuen Testamentes der Bibel mit unserem Grundgesetz habe überprüfen wollen.

Ich halte solche Überprufungen auch für unzulässig, ohne meine Verfassungstreue zum Grundgesetz, das ich für ein gutes menschliches Gesetz halte, deshalb in Frage stellen zu wollen.

Die von uns gegründete Islamische Grundschule, Islam Kolleg, war am Anfang ein Projekt der muslimischen Frauen.

Die muslimischen Frauen in Berlin gründeten vor Jahren, den Islamischen Frauenverein, Cemiyet- Nisa e.V., den Islamischen Frauen Sportverein e.V., die Kindertagestätte und den Kinderhort, die sie in alleiniger Zuständigkeit leiten. Nach ihren Erfolgen mit diesen Frauenprojekten, die auch von Politikern als integrationsfördernd angesehen und deshalb zum Teil auch vom Senat unterstützt werden, haben sie den Mut Gefaßt für ihre Kinder auch eine eigene Grundschule zu schaffen, die ihnen die Kindererziehung erleichtert und die Ausbilbung für die Kinder verbessert.

Gerade auch im Hinblick auf die zur Zeit gravierend zunehmende Ausländerfeindlichkeit, die innerhalb kurzer Zeit, für uns Muslime durch die mehrfache Schändung des Türkischen Friedhof am Columbiadamm dokumentiert worden ist.

Die Frauen haben uns Männer davon überzeugt, daß die Errichtung dieser Grundschule notwendig ist. So ist diese Schule enstanden, das erste gemeinsame Projekt von muslimischen Männern und Frauen. Diese gemeinsame Zusammenarbeit von muslimischen Männern und Frauen ist für uns Muslime genau so neu, wie es diese Schule für die Politiker ist. Sie werden hier in Berlin nichts Vergleichbares finden.

Diese Zusammenarbeit von Männern und Frauen auf der Grundlage des Koran und der Sunna des Propheten Muhammed ist möglich geworden, weil es im Islam in Berlin, in Deutschland, ja in Europa, den Beginn einer Entwicklung gibt, die immer weiter von der frauenfeindlichen Tradition des nationalistischen Staatsislam wegführt zu einer neuen Form des religiösen islamischen Zusammenlebens von Mann und Frau in einer multikulturellen Gesellschaft, wie wir sie in der zukunft in Europa haben werden.

Diese Entwicklung steht natürlich erst am Anfang und die Lösung von den unislamischen Tradition nationalistischer, staatlicher Prägung wird auch für die Muslime schwierig sein und einen längeren Zeitraum benötigen.

Sie muß auch deshalb als besonders integrationsfördernd angesehen werden, weil mit ihr zum ersten Mal versucht wird, demokratische Strukturen in islamische Vereingungen einzuführen, und damit zu arbeiten. Diese demokratischen Strukturen werden Sie im traditionellen und nationalistischen Staatsislam vergeblich suchen.

Es ist für mich, als jemand der für diese Entwicklung entscheidende Verantwortung trägt, unverständlich, daß diese Bemühungen der Muslime, die im Hinblick auf eine große und selbständige europäische islamische Gemeinschaft eingeleitet worden sind, so wenig von den zuständigen Politikern geachtet und verstanden werden, besonders deshalb, weil diese Entwicklung auch den ernsthaften Versuch einer wirklichen Integration des Islam in unsere heutige europäische Gesellschaft darstellt.

Sie wird besonders von den Muslimen angestrebt, ir für immer hier leben werden und sich deshalb von Einflüssen des traditionellen, nationalistischen Staatsislam lösen wollen.

Ich denke in diesem Zusammenhang auch die Bemühungen dieser Muslimer, einen ständigen Dialog mit den anderen Religionen und gesellschaftlichen Gruppen in unserer Stadt zu führen, mit dem Ziel, zu einer gegenseitigen Achtung und Anerkennung zu kommen, die für unsere multikulturelle Gesellschaft der Zukunft unbedingt notwendig ist, wenn wir auch künftig friedlich miteinander leben wollen.

Während unserer gemeinsam gestalteten Veranstaltungen der Christlich-Islamischen Begegnung im Rahmen des Evangelischen Kirchentages in Berlin, an denen auch ich beteiligt war, haben über 2000 Kirchentagsbesucher Moscheen der Islamischen Föderation und auch der staatlich islamischen Organisationen besucht, und Hunderte von Muslimen waren in den christlichen Kirchen. Dabei haben stundenlange Diskussionen zwischen Christen und Muslime über alle uns betreffenden Probleme stattgefunden. Und Christen und Muslime waren sich später darüber einig, daß es eine gute gemeinsame Veranstaltung gewesen ist.

Zur Stellung der Frau im Islam, die ja hier auch bei der letzen Sitzung schon eine besondere Rolle gespielt hat, möchte ich folgendes sagen. Bei den bisher stattgefunden Diskussionen unter Muslimen hat sich herausgestellt, daß die Muslima eine Abkehr von dem der Tradition verbunden nationalistischen Staatsislam fordern, weil durch ihn die Rechte der Frauen in der Vergangenheit stark eingeschränkt worden sind, und er sich dabei nicht mehr auf islamische Grundsätze stützten kann.

Wir haben bei diesen Diskussion auch die verblüffende Feststellung machen müssen, daß die heute immer wieder erhobene Forderung nach der Gleichstellung der Frau für die Muslima bedeuten würde, wenn wir Grundsätze des islam und nicht die Tradition zugrundelegen, daß die muslimischen Frauen bei dieser Gleichstellung auf die besondern Frauenrechte, die ihnen der Islam gewährt, verzichten müßten. Das bedeutet, die völlige Gleichstellung von Mann und Frau, würde die muslimischen Frauen benachteiligen und sie müßten Rechte, die sie behalten wollen, aufgeben, um dafür andere Rechte zu bekommen, die sie selbst gar nicht wollen. Die Stellung der Frau im Islam ist besser als die des Mannes. Und er bedarf noch sehr eingehender und gemeinsamer Diskussionen, um die vielen Vorurteilen und falschen Darstellungen zu beseitigen, die z.Z. darüber im Umlauf sind. Wir sind aber gern bereit, im Hinblick auf unsere gemeinsame Zukunft, mit allen Interessierten offen darüber zu diskutieren.

(.......)

Ich bin fest davon überzeugt, daß die Entwicklung des Islam in Berlin, in Deutschland und in Europa zu einer freien und selbständigen Gemeinschaft der hier lebenden und auch hier bleibenden Muslime auf die Dauer nicht verhindert werden kann.

Wir befinden uns im Augenblick in einer Phase der Entwicklung, in der viele Dinge zwischen dem Islam und dieser Gesellschaft durch starke Vorurteile belastet werden, die zum Teil auf Unkenntnis des wirklichen Islam beruhen.

So könnten in gemeinsamen Verhandlungen vertraglichen Regelungen und Absprachen getroffen werden, weil der Islam solche vertraglichen Regelungen mit allen Beteiligten zuläßt und von den Muslimen die strikte Einhaltung der geschlossen Verträge fordert. Wir halten dies für den besserern Weg, als den, die Muslime dazu zu zwingen, sich ihr Recht nur über die zuständigen Gerichte holen zu müssen.

Sie werden jetzt darüber zu befinden haben, ob der Islam und die Muslime endlich gleichberechtigte Teile dieser Gesellschaft werden können und sich innerhalb dieser Gesellschaft und mit ihr zusammen weiter entwicklen dürfen, oder ob Sie auch die Muslime zwingen werden, in einem Ghetto zu leben, wie es in der europäischen Vergangenheit mit anderen Religionsgemeinschaften geschehen ist.

Appendix D

AMGT Hac.
Advertisement for AMGT's Pilgrim Excursions to Mecca in 1990
(Translation of document shown on following page):

* Would you like to make your journey to the *hajj* by aeroplane with all services and expenses included?
* Would you like to visit your close family in Turkey before and after the *hajj*, by air, and with all services and expenses included?
* Would you like to have all your questions regarding the *hajj* answered?
* If you are looking for a *hajj* organisation in Europe, or an organisation that has won public awards (the Saudi *hajj* authorities/LP), then you should choose AMGT's *hajj* organisation.

The price for a one month return direct flight is given as 3350DM. The price for 5 weeks direct by bus is given as 2300DM.

246 *Newer Islamic Movements in Western Europe*

Appendix D
Advertisement for AMGT Hajj Organisation

Appendix E

What is Millî Görüş?
(Translation of original Turkish document which follows)

To remind people what Millî Görüş is we hereby reproduce a publication that was written a long time ago in Turkey.[1] We do not wish for those who say that they are religious and faithful to the traditions to smudge Millî Görüş and thereby come to stand side by side with Zionists,[2] communists, socialists and non-Muslims.

***Milli Görüş:* 'Even if the Meccans were to offer me the sun in my right hand and the moon in my left hand, I should still preach the rightful faith of Islam,' he said.[3] Without fearing non-Muslims, nor the infidels, our Prophet preached of the rightful faith Islam to all people. That is his outlook.

** *Millî Görüş:* 'If a wolf eats a sheep by the Dicle then God shall hold Omar responsible', said Omar.[4] He also wrote to his wali (governor/LP) in Damascus, 'I have heard that you are building a palace. If it is out of your own pocket then it is extravagance, but if it is from the state coffers it is betrayal', said he who himself carried a sack of flour on his back for the wife and children of a martyr. He said, 'One must exert oneself to achieve

---

[1] It is not clear from the pamphlet when it was originally written. A qualified guess by a Millî Görüş member dates it as being later than 1973, partly because of the reference to Cyprus, which can be taken as a topical comment on the conflict with Greece. The pamphlet was reprinted, signed by Avrupa Millî Görüş Teşkilâti, i.e. Organisation Millî Görüş in Europe and by Avrupa Islâmci Gençlik Teşkilâti, i.e. The Islamic Youth Organisation in Europe. The explanations which are included in this text as notes do not appear in the original Turkish text but are given by a Danish member of the movement.
[2] In the Turkish text the word *mansonlars* is used which is literally translated as *freemasons*. The usual understanding in Millî Görüş is that the lodges of the freemasons (including the Rotary and Lions clubs) in Turkey represent foreign zionist interests.
[3] The Prophet Muhammed is speaking here to Abu Talib.
[4] The Dicle is a river in Turkey and Iraq which in the time of the second caliph Omar marked the outer border of the caliphate.

recognition' and therefore he would not give his closest friend work for which the person in question was not competent. That was Omar's outlook.

** *Millî Görüş*: After cuma (Friday) prayers he removed his royal cape and put on some white clothes and said, 'If I die, these clothes shall be upon my corpse. Then you must follow my son Kiliç Arslana and swear biyat (allegiance/LP) to him'. After this he went out against the Byzantine army of 300,000 men who were led by Diyojen whose army was six times as large as his. He was victorious and took the leader and many soldiers prisoner and said to him, 'I release you. You can go and gather a new army and meet me again', said the conqueror of Malazgirt, Alparslan.[5] That was his outlook.

** *Millî Görüş*: In a place that he came to as a guest he saw that the holy Koran was hanging on the wall as decoration. Therefore he could not sleep, but remained standing in honour of it. He has never entered into any alliance with a non-Muslim (kafir) state and he has always and without fear of death on God's road worked to recreate the Ottoman empire. That was Osman Bey's outlook.

** *Millî Görüş*: In the Kosova encounter, 'our parents did not take elephants to protect them against the enemy's attack, but turned to face the arrows on the field of battle. It was in this way that they were victorious and conquered many fortifications', as Yildirim Bayazit said. That was his outlook.

** *Millî Görüş*: When he was only 14 years old he said 'father if you become padishah (sultan/LP) then you must come and lead your army - your enemies plan to attack. If on the other hand it is I who is padishah, then I order you to lead your army'. When he was 22 years old he would accept no hindrances and in his wisdom he invented a canon. 'Either the Byzans will conquer me or I shall conquer the Byzans', said he, the one who moved ships across land and horses across water. 'That which my teacher accepts, I too accept', he said, he who was the person whom the Prophet had praised,[6] namely the conqueror, Mehmet Han. That was his outlook.

---

[5] Alparslan (Brave Lion) crushed the Byzantine emperor's army in 1071 and thereafter controlled all of Little Asia.

[6] In one *hadith* the Prophet says: 'The commander who conquers Istanbul is a good commander (and a strong Muslim) and the soldiers are also good soldiers (and strong Muslims)'. Istanbul was the centre of the Byzantine empire and therefore was a goal of great symbolic importance.

** *Millî Görüş*: I do not care for distinction in kin, but on the contrary, for competence and loyalty (liyakat/LP)', he said. And in state affairs he followed his principles of *liyakat* and competence. 'This world is too small for two leaders', he said. 'The mud which flies up from the horse of my teachers is my medal of honour. When I die you shall bury me with this cape on, just as I have written it in my will',[7] he said. In the very last part of his life his orderly, Hassan Can, said to him, 'Great scholar, now you shall meet God'. To this the sultan replied, 'naughty child, did you believe that up until now I was outside of God?' This was said by Yavis Sultan Selim, who met God, that is his outlook.

** *Millî Görüş*: You have burned our ships and that is the same as if you had shaved off our beards. When one shaves a beard it grows back even thicker, but we have conquered Cyprus from you and that is the same as if we had cut off you arms - and an arm which has been cut off cannot grow out again. This Sokullu Mehmet Pasha said to the courier of the (kafir) enemy. That is his outlook.

** *Millî Görüş*: Palestine is not my property, and nor is it the property of the people who live there. It is the martyrs who lie buried there. One cannot buy land for money, only with one's blood can one buy land, he said to Theodor Herzl and sent him away.[8] He has never listened to the infidels and the slanderers and he has remained faithful to God's word. In 36 years he has kept the Ottoman Empire alive in a cold war against Jews, Armenians, Romans, Jonturks,[9] and against all who slandered and tried to

---

[7] Sultan Selim Hans' personal teacher was also his *mufti*, just as he was also *Sheikh ul-Islam* for the entire Islamic world. The story goes that once sultan Selim Han and *Shiekh ul-Islam* were riding along with others, the Sheikh's horse stumbled and mud from the horse soiled the sultan. Some consequently believe that this made the sultan look foolish. The sultan repeats these words so as to rehabilitate the sheikh and to show his own deep respect for him.

[8] Theodor Herzl came to the sultan to buy land in Palestine for the early Zionist settlers.

[9] The JonTurks are said to be a part of the early Turkish tribes. Instead of wandering from the Mongolian plains to what is now Turkey the Jonturks followed a northerly course which brought them to the Balkans. While the first groups became Muslims, the others became Christian. One feature common to both is that they were known as possessing courage and strength, qualitites that were good in

destroy the Ottoman empire, this sultan Abdulhamit Han the 2nd said...And that is his outlook.

** *Millî Görüş*: To set aside the non-Muslim (küfür) laws which were imported from Europe and introduce a constitution as our forefathers had, God's laws, is our outlook.

** *Millî Görüş*: We are not those who say religion is one thing and the state another, and thereby keep religion under the control of the state. We are the state leaders who will give religion freedom and wish to rule by the laws of the creator of the universe, the laws of God. This is our outlook.

** *Millî Görüş*:: We are not those who for the control of the state take orders from USA, Europe, the Soviet Union, China, IMF, EEC, Zionists, Socialists, Fascists and all the other 'ists, and nor from the non-Muslims (*kafirs*) and slanderers. We are, on the contrary, pure of heart and courageous leaders who wish only to take orders from God with a pure heart and a tireless and courageous soul and the experience of our forefathers. This is our outlook.

** *Millî Görüş*: We do not wish to become members of the EEC but to conduct a foreign policy in the Middle East along with the Islamic countries - in a greater co-operation and with increased exchange because this will serve us better. This is our outlook.

** *Millî Görüş*: Finally we will work wholeheartedly and fearlessly to improve in all areas and with a view to industiralising the Muslims. This is our outlook.

---

war. Therefore Christian JonTurks were used as an attacking army by the Christian world against the Muslims.

Appendix E
What is Millî Görüş? - Original Text in Turkish

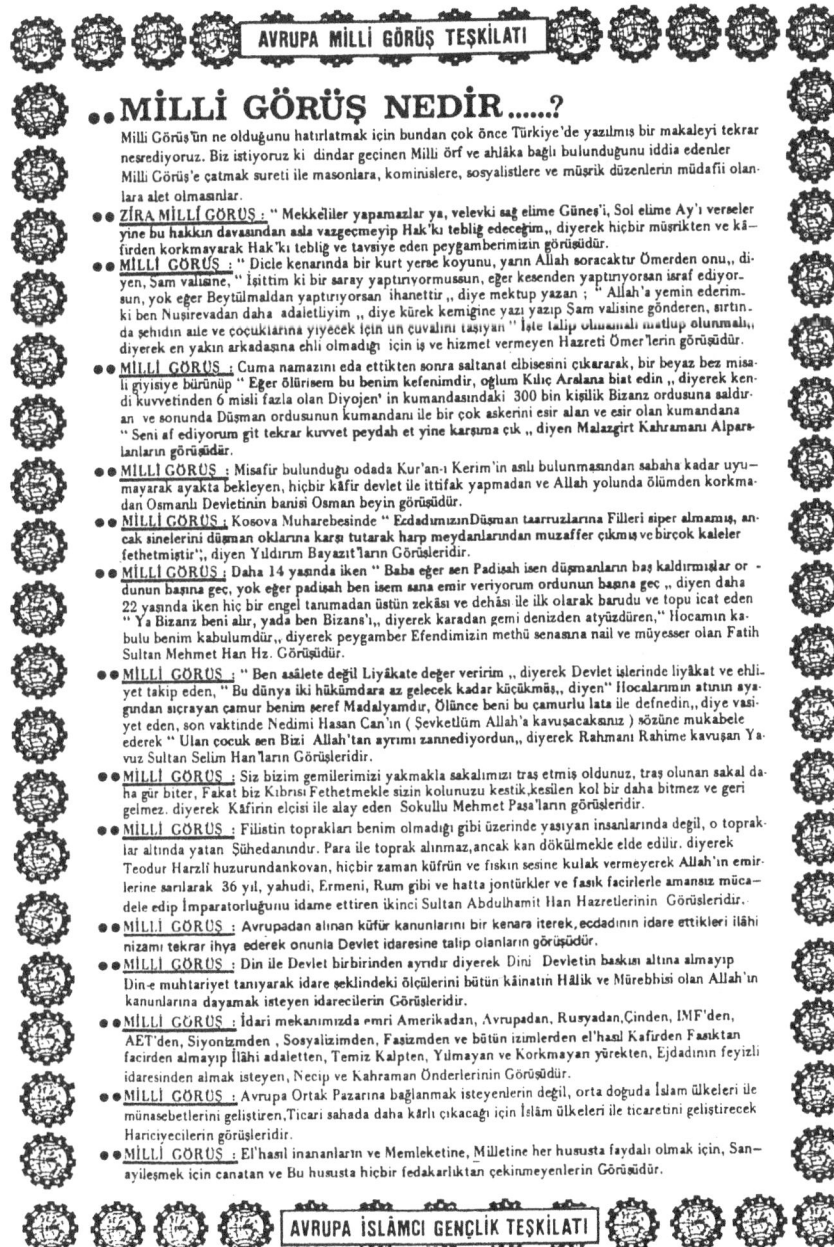

AVRUPA MİLLİ GÖRÜŞ TEŞKİLATI

..MİLLİ GÖRÜŞ NEDİR......?

Milli Görüş'ün ne olduğunu hatırlatmak için bundan çok önce Türkiye'de yazılmış bir makaleyi tekrar neşrediyoruz. Biz istiyoruz ki dindar geçinen Milli örf ve ahlâka bağlı bulunduğunu iddia edenler Milli Görüş'e çatmak sureti ile masonlara, kominislere, sosyalistlere ve müşrik düzenlerin müdafii olanlara alet olmasınlar.

● ● ZİRA MİLLİ GÖRÜŞ : " Mekkeliler yapamazlar ya, velevki sağ elime Güneş'i, Sol elime Ay'ı verseler yine bu hakkın davasından asla vazgeçmeyip Hak'kı tebliğ edeceğim,, diyerek hiçbir müşrikten ve kâfirden korkmayarak Hak'kı tebliğ ve tavsiye eden peygamberimizin görüşüdür.

● ● MİLLİ GÖRÜŞ : " Dicle kenarında bir kurt yerse koyunu, yarın Allah soracaktır Ömerden onu,, diyen, Şam valisine," İşittim ki bir saray yaptırıyormussun, eğer kesenden yaptırıyorsan israf ediyorsun, yok eğer Beytülmaldan yaptırıyorsan ihanettir ,, diye mektup yazan ; " Allah'a yemin ederim. ki ben Nuşirevadan daha adaletliyim ,, diye kürek kemiğine yazı yazıp Şam valisine gönderen, sırtında şehidin aile ve çocuklarına yiyecek için un çuvalını taşıyan " İşte talip olunmalı matlup olunmalı,, diyerek en yakın arkadaşına ehli olmadığı için iş ve hizmet vermeyen Hazreti Ömer'lerin görüşüdür.

● ● MİLLİ GÖRÜŞ : Cuma namazını eda ettikten sonra saltanat elbisesini çıkararak, bir beyaz bez misali giyisiye bürünüp " Eğer ölürsem bu benim kefenimdir, oğlum Kılıç Arslana biat edin ,, diyerek kendi kuvvetinden 6 misli fazla olan Diyojen' in kumandasındaki 300 bin kişilik Bizans ordusuna saldıran ve sonunda Düşman ordusunun kumandanı ile bir çok askerini esir alan ve esir olan kumandana " Seni af ediyorum git tekrar kuvvet peydah et yine karşıma çık ,, diyen Malazgirt Kahramanı Alparslanların görüşüdür.

● ● MİLLİ GÖRÜŞ : Misafir bulunduğu odada Kur'an-ı Kerim'in asılı bulunmasından sabaha kadar uyumayarak ayakta bekleyen, hiçbir kâfir devlet ile ittifak yapmadan ve Allah yolunda ölümden korkmadan Osmanlı Devletinin banisi Osman beyin görüşüdür.

● ● MİLLİ GÖRÜŞ ; Kosova Muharebesinde " EcdadımızınDüşman taarruzlarına Filleri siper almamış, ancak sinelerini düşman oklarına karşı tutarak harp meydanlarından muzaffer çıkmış ve birçok kaleler fethetmiştir'', diyen Yıldırım Bayazıt'ların Görüşleridir.

● ● MİLLİ GÖRÜŞ ; Daha 14 yaşında iken " Baba eğer sen Padişah isen düşmanların baş kaldırmışlar or - dunun başına geç, yok eğer padişah ben isem sana emir veriyorum ordunun başına geç ,, diyen daha 22 yaşında iken hiç bir engel tanımadan üstün zekâsı ve dehâsı ile ilk olarak barudu ve topu icat eden " Ya Bizansı beni alır, yada ben Bizans'ı,, diyerek karadan gemi denizden atyüzdüren," Hocamın kabulu benim kabulumdur,, diyerek peygamber Efendimizin methü senasına nail ve müyesser olan Fatih Sultan Mehmet Han Hz. Görüşüdür.

● ● MİLLİ GÖRÜŞ : " Ben asâlete değil Liyâkate değer veririm ,, diyerek Devlet işlerinde liyâkat ve ehliyet takip eden," Bu dünya iki hükümdara az gelecek kadar küçükmüş,, diyen" Hocalarımın atının ayağından sıçrayan çamur benim şeref Madalyamdır, Ölünce beni bu çamurlu lata ile defnedin,, diye vasiyet eden, son vaktinde Nedimi Hasan Can'ın (Şevketlüm Allah'a kavuşacaksınız) sözüne mukabele ederek " Ulan çocuk sen Bizi Allah'tan ayrımı zannediyordun,, diyerek Rahmanı Rahime kavuşan Yavuz Sultan Selim Han'ların Görüşleridir.

● ● MİLLİ GÖRÜŞ ; Siz bizim gemilerimizi yakmakla sakalımızı traş etmiş oldunuz, traş olunan sakal daha gür biter, Fakat biz Kıbrısı Fethetmekle sizin kolunuzu kestik,kesilen kol bir daha bitmez ve geri gelmez. diyerek Kâfirin elcisi ile alay eden Sokullu Mehmet Paşa'ların görüşleridir.

● ● MİLLİ GÖRÜŞ ; Filistin toprakları benim olmadığı gibi üzerinde yaşıyan insanlarında değil, o topraklar altında yatan Şühedanındır. Para ile toprak alınmaz,ancak kan dökülmekle elde edilir. diyerek Teodur Harzlî huzurundankovan, hiçbir zaman küfrün ve fıskın sesine kulak vermeyerek Allah'ın emirlerine sarılarak 36 yıl, yahudi, Ermeni, Rum gibi ve hatta jontürkler ve tekfirlerle amansız mücadele edip İmparatorluğunu idame ettiren ikinci Sultan Abdulhamit Han Hazretlerinin Görüşleridir.

● ● MİLLİ GÖRÜŞ : Avrupadan alınan küfür kanunlarını bir kenara iterek, ecdadının idare ettikleri İlâhi nizamı tekrar ihya ederek onunla Devlet idaresine talip olanların görüşüdür.

● ● MİLLİ GÖRÜŞ ; Din ile Devlet birbirinden ayrıdır diyenleri, Din Devletin baskısı altına almayıp Din-e muhtariyet tanıyarak idare şeklindeki ölçülerini bütün kâinatın Hâlik ve Mürebbisi olan Allah'ın kanunlarına dayanmak isteyen idarecilerin Görüşleridir.

● ● MİLLİ GÖRÜŞ ; İdari mekanımızda emri Amerikadan, Avrupadan, Rusyadan,Çinden, IMF'den, AET'den, Siyonizmden , Sosyalizimden, Fasizmden ve bütün izimlerden el'hasıl Kafirden Fasıktan facirden almayıp İlâhi adaletten, Temiz Kalpten, Yılmayan ve Korkmayan yürekten, Ejdadının feyizli idaresinden alrmak isteyen, Necip ve Kahraman Önderlerinin Görüşleridir.

● ● MİLLİ GÖRÜŞ ; Avrupa Ortak Pazarına bağlanmak isteyenlerin değil, orta doğuda İslâm ülkeleri ile münasebetlerini geliştiren,Ticari sahada daha kârlı çıkacağı için İslâm ülkeleri ile ticaretini geliştirecek Hariciyecilerin görüşleridir.

● ● MİLLİ GÖRÜŞ ; El'hasıl inananların ve Memleketine, Milletine her hususta faydalı olmak için, Sanayileşmek için canatan ve Bu hususta hiçbir fedakarlıktan çekinmeyenlerin Görüşüdür.

AVRUPA İSLÂMCI GENÇLİK TEŞKİLATI

Appendix F

'Muslims of all the World, Unite'
(Translated from the Turkish document; 'Ey! Dünya Müsülmanlari Birlesiniz.....' written by Imam Hacir)

For centuries the Islamic world has existed on the basis of two strong points. It could not have existed without either one of them. Only when the two points were united could they exist, in the same way that two things are needed to make water, hydrogen and oxygen. The desired outcome can only be attained by remaining firm on both points and this can only happen if God wishes it to be so. Each basic element (*esas*) has a value according to its placing, if it is not in its place then it is of no value. Just as gold, when buried in the earth along with other materials has no value, only when it is prepared by the goldsmith does it gain its value. The two elements which form the basis of Muslim society are these:

1) One must believe unconditionally and unrestrainedly in God.
2) One must remain true to the basic rule which is called the Muslim community.

These two points are confirmed by many Koranic verses, by the sunnah of the Prophet, and by the history of Islam.
When Muslim civilisation was at its height, these two points were very prominent.
When one examines the history of the time when Muslim civilisation fell, one can see that either one or both of these points had been neglected. When God speaks of *ummah* in the holy Koran, he always says that one must remain true to God, unconditional faith and *takva* (conducting one's life according to Islam/LP) that one should pray to God.
Again our God says in the holy Koran: 'And this is your God and have fear and hope (*korkun = fear of god*/LP)' (Mu'minun 52).
In another *aya* it is written: 'This is your ummah (*tevhid* and Islam's *millat*/LP), this is the only ummah. I am your God, pray only to me' (Enbiya 92).

In another *aya* Canabi Hak (i.e. God) praises those cemaat who carry out their duties correctly: 'You are the best umma among all mankind. You encourage the good things and forbid the bad things and believe in God' (Al-Imran 110).

God says that Muslim groups are each other's friends and that they are brothers in Islam: 'It is only those who are Muslims who are each other's friends' (Tevbe 71).

In another *aya* God says: 'Muslims are brothers without doubt. Reconcile between brothers and have fear of God, then God will show you compassion' (Hucurat 10).

When first an Islamic society is established it is not permitted for anyone to follow non-Islamic principles, Jewish or Christian principles. This will lead to the division of Islamic unity, and he who does so will distance himself from Islam.

Our God says in the holy Koran: 'Oh, you faithful, if a group of you follows the other religions of the book you will distance yourselves from your faith and thereby make yourselves unbelievers (*kafir*/LP)' (Al-Imran 100).

He who does not follow the principles of Islam will undoubtedly become one of those who have several gods. And they will come outside the Islamic community and they will not have any connection to the Islamic community, even if they say the *shahada* (profession of Islamic faith/LP) many times.

Our Prophet says:
'One must never kill anyone. This is only permitted in the following three cases:
1. Spouses who have been unfaithful.
2. Someone who has killed someone else for no reason.
3. One who leaves Islam to go to another' (Bukhari and Muslim).

The aim of the Islamic society is the Islamic community (*ummah*).
Our Prophet says:
'You shall not be those who step outside the community and thereby begin to kill one another'.

These *ayat* and *hadith* forbid all conflict within the Islamic society and show that one should be conscious of this and forbid any form of racism and hostility within the Muslim society.

An Islamic community (cemaat) which has a strong faith and a strong solidarity will feel liberation in this world and in life after death.

Our forefathers, since the time of the Prophet and since the time of the four Rightly Guided caliphs, have had a good and dignified influence on history, and history is filled with many conquests. This they could do because they had endless belief in their creator, God, and it was an Islamic community with a very strong sense of solidarity.

The Muslims are today in a situation where they have lost a lot. And it is a great shame that they are enemies of one another. All these things have happened because the two fundamental points are lacking.

God, may He always show mercy to sultan Abdülhamid, said these historic words which today we have need of more than ever before.

'O, Islamic world, unite, unite!..'

Honour be sultan Abdülhamid Han. He was capable in his day of defending the faith, solidarity and land of the Muslims.[1]

He responded to the divisions with *iman* (*faith*/LP) and the principles of Islamic fellowship. What we have ascertained is this: that the situation of Muslims in the Islamic countries is filled with suffering today, grief, greed and suffering and nothing but this. One could go on, with even more complaints, from east to west, but there is not sufficient paper or strength to do so.

We Muslims who live in Berlin must accept the difficulties which are associated with living in another society and we must overcome these difficulties on the basis of an unshakeable and unbreakable solidarity. We must understand and live up to Islam. Islam is a world religion and it does not accept division and superiority. It measures each individual according to *takva* (understanding and living in accordance with Islam/LP). In this religion a Turkish-Muslim, an Arab-Muslim, an Afghani-Muslim, and a German-Muslim, are all brothers.

The Prophet says: 'An Arab is not better than a non-Arab, and a non-Arab is not better than an Arab, and a white is not better than a black and nor is a black better than a white, but the measuring stick for the best is the one who has *takva*'.

One can only live in accordance with this hadith if one knows what *takva* is. Takva means that one is godfearing, both when one is

---

[1] *Land* here refers to Palestine.

alone and together with others. One must accept the fate which God has chosen for one.

If you have succeeded in having a strong faith and spreading joy among the Muslims and have made it your aim to help others, then you are one who has *takva*. God says in the holy Koran: 'He who has adhered to *takva* will have a high place on Judgement Day'. On that day neither material goods nor sons will help. Only with *takva*, a pure heart and godsfear will one be content in Paradise.

With the fear of God go in the way of Islam. It is this way that the Koran has shown and the Prophet has taught and for centuries the people and the leaders have gone this way together. This way is a strong faith and a strong Islamic community. To become a valuable Islamic society again you must heed the words of Abdülhamid:

'Oh, Islamic world; unite, unite!'

The chairman of the Bilal-Habesi mosque and Islamische Zentrum in Aachen, our older brother (term signifying honour/LP), Isam Attar says this: 'The Muslims are those people who, with their faith and their observances, are as God would have them. It is not simply a matter of etiquette, Muslims are Muslims through their faith, not because they belong to this or that group'.

Finally our God has put it very beautifully: 'Only those who are believers are brothers' (Hucurat 10).

Appendix G

Islamische Föderation Statement on the Rushdie Case
(Translated from German original).

In the name of the one and only God, the Merciful and Compassionate.

The position of The Islamic Federation, Berlin.

We Muslims are against murder and against the offer of a reward for this purpose, because both things are totally incompatible with Islam!

In that Satanic book it is written: 'Where there is no faith, nor can there be any blasphemy!'

Any person who believes in God is challenged by this sentence.

We Muslims testify that we believe in the one and only God, and that Muhammed is God's messenger. And we believe in Jesus, in Moses and in all the other prophets, which the one and only God has sent to mankind and we do not distinguish between them.

The protectors of free speech who oppose the protesting Muslims have so far killed 15 Muslims. We demand that in future a limit is set on the spokesmen and business people who support such insults. One person's freedom must end where the next person's freedom begins.

How then should we explain to our children that religion is an important and sacred part of our lives if we allow it to be dragged through the mud in this fashion.

We call on all people who believe in God to stringently object to human values, which include faith, ever being accosted in the future!

In contrast to some disappointed Muslims, we are still of the opinion that this problem should *not* be solved by violence, but with reason and insight. We Muslims also wish to live in peace in the future with all groups within modern day society. However, the current freedom of speech must have a limit which respects the values which people who believe in God have, and protect them from infringement.

Appendix H

Islamische Kulturzentren Statement on the Conflict in Azerbaijan, 1989 (Document)

ASERBAIDSHAN
Um die Völkertötung in Aserbaidshan zu verstehen, muß man tiefer in die Geschichte Aserbaidshands eingehen.

Lage und Geschichte Aserbaidshans:
Sie ist eine historische Landschaft, westlich Kapischen Meeres mit 8 Mio. Einwohnern im nördl. Teil Aserbaidshan, wo die Rote Armee Gorbatschows tausende Menschen umbrachte und immer noch umbringt. Im 8. un 11. Jh. setzte sich in ganz Aserbaidshan - ausgehend von Schirwan - der Islam durch. Der größte Teil Aserbaidshans verlor eine Unabhängigkeit erst 1221 durch den Feldzug der nach Westen verstoßenden Mongolen: 1236 wurde Schirwan Teil mong. Reichs. 1453-1607 war Schirwan von den Osmanen besetzt. In der zweiten Hälfte des 16, Jh. setzten die Versuche Moskaus ein, Azerbaidshan unter seine Kontrolle zu bringen; ein Verstoß nach Baku schlug 1722 fehl.

Zu beginn dieses Jh. fing eine aserbaidshanische Nationalbewegung an, die durch dir rußische Revolution 1918 blockiert wurde. Die Briten besetzen Baku in der letzen Phase des ersten Wetlkrieges im August 1918, wurde aber von den Osmanen und Deutschen vertreiben. Die Rote Armee nahm mit brutale Gevalt Baku ein und proklamierte am 28.4.1920 die Aserbaidshanische SSR.

Die neue Bewegung, die vor rd. einem Jahr anfing, richtet sich in Richtung FREIHEIT und GERECHTIGKEIT, d.h. Glasnost und Perestroika.
Am 23.9.1989 stellte die aserbaidshan. Bevölkerung folgende Forderungen für ihr Land:
1. Vollständige Kontrolle die aserbaidshan.SSR über die natürliche Rohstoffe in Aserbaidshan
2. Vetorecht gegen alle die Republik betreffenden Allunionsgesetze
3. Aser als Nationalsprache und russisch unter-etnische (dem Verkehr mit den anderen Sowjet-Völker dienende) Sprache

4. Uneingeschränktes Recht der Republik zum Verlassen der UdSSR
5. Garantie der Intergrität des Territoriums, also auch Verbleib von Nachitschewan und Berg-Karabach bei Aserbaidshan

Es is nicht zu verstehen, warum Gorbatschow seine Rote Armee wie seine Vorgänger ganz brutal gegen waffenlose und wehrlose Bürger, die friedlich demonstrierten, einsetzte, wobei tausende Aserbaidshaner erschossen wurden und werden.

War es nicht Gorbatschow höchst persönlich, der von Glasnost un Perestroika gesprochen hat?

War es nicht, der Honecker zur Reformierung in der DDR aufrief?

Warum sieht Gorbatschow zu, wie täglich Hunderte von Aserbaidshaner durch die Rote Armee niedergeschossen werden?

Warum sieht sich Herr Gorbatschow nicht die blutbefleckten Straßen in Baku an, auf denen die Leichen der Aserbaidshaner liegen?

Und was mit den Menschenrechtsorganisationen?
Obwohl die Aserbaidshaner unter Hungershot und Obdachlosigkeit leiden, keine medizinische Hilfe erhalten, können sie von niemanden eine Hilfe erwarten.

Es ist für uns unbegreiflich, warum alle internationalen Organisationen (z.B. die Vereinigten Nationen, EG Menschenrechtsorganisation) zu dieser Massentötung in der EdSSR schweigen.

Schweigen ist das gleiche wie die Beteiligung an diesem Massenmord selbst.

Türkische Förderung in Europa.

-Vereinigung der neuer Weltsicht in Europa (Berlin)
-Deutsch-Türkischer Akademikerbund
-Türkisch-Islamische Anstalt für Religion
-Freiheitlich Türkisch-Deutscher Freundschaftsverein
-Rat der islamischenm Einheit.

ISLAMISCHE KULTURZENTREN

Appendix I

'The Islamic Alternative', - A Millî Görüş imam explains
(Document prepared from the transcript of an interview with an imam who is a press spokesman and who appears as a hoca on the television channel, Türkischen Fernsehen Deutschland, TFD. The interview was conducted in November 1989 and March 1990. Direct quotations from the transcript appear in the original German).

In the so-called 'Islamic' states the politicians seek only to exploit those Islamic rules which suit their purposes and other rules, which do not match their political direction, they ignore, states a Millî Görüş imam. Islam, then, is utilised to a variety of aims. The Iranians have theirs, the Iraqis theirs, the Saudis theirs. The Syrians have something different again, just as the Turks have their own. Therefore, the many faithful Muslims, like us, feel that there is no real Islamic state in existence. There are simply states in which Muslims live. One cannot simply pick out the bits of Islam that suit a particular point of view. Islam has specific instructions and rules.
Islam is a complete understanding, which can define basic alternatives, such as, for example, in relation to 1) economy, 2) systems of government, 3) the rights of workers, 4) human rights, 5) women's' rights, and 6) the protection of nature. The foundation in achieving the desire for these alternatives lies in a *hadith*, explains the Millî Görüş imam: 'Du bist kein Mu'min wenn du was willst, und für die Andere nicht willst!' ('You are not a Muslim if you do not wish for others what you wish for yourself.')

The Islamic Economy
'Jemand sieht das sein Nachbar hungrig ist und gut schlafen ist kein Muslim!' (*hadith*). In other words, he who sees that his neighbour is poor, and does not help, is not a Muslim. It is a duty to give *zakat*, *fitre* and *sadakât*, but one should also help if there is further need: He who does not help will not go to paradise! It is a sin (the imam's use of the term *haram* is translated into German by the interpreter as 'Sünde' or 'sin') to hoard one's wealth. One should invest, not for the sake of one's own gain, but to benefit the people. The state has a responsibility to see that production in the final instance meets the needs of its people.

The imam continues: I actually believe that the Islamic state should only interfere in the economy to a very small degree, but that it should nevertheless ensure the freedom of the population. For example, the population in the DDR are afraid of 'freie Marktwirtschaft' ('free market forces') and would rather talk of a 'soziale freie Marktwirtschaft'. Under an Islamic state it is from religion and not from the state that intervention comes. In other words, a moral element is introduced which dictates, 'what you should do and what you should not do'; 'help the poor', etc..

The state does not dictate production at all. All means of production should be decided by the producers. Any means of production can then be conducted, so long as it is not damaging, or of no benefit: If the production is damaging, or of no benefit, then the state should possibly intervene and say, 'No, that should not be produced!'. The production of alcohol, for example, would be such a case, where the state perhaps should intervene with a ban. One can also, however, discuss whether problems are at all solved by this kind of intervention. The ban on alcohol in America proved not to be a solution at all!

Islam's approach to the ownership of land is also a terribly important aspect which is not currently respected in the Muslim world. Islam land rights are based on the principle that all land possessions belong to God and that man only borrows it. This means that someone who wishes to occupy a piece of land must work that land if he is not to lose it. The Prophet Muhammed has provided a very clear example of this:

> Der Profet Muhammed hat Bilal, den Sklaven der Adhan gemacht hat als erster, ein Stück Land geschenkt, und Bilal hat es also nicht bearbeitet. Der Kalif Omar hat zu Bilal gesagt, wenn du es nicht bearbeitest werden ich es dir wegnehmen! Und Bilal fragt, wie kanst du mir etwas wegnehmen, was der Profet mir gegeben hat. Und Omar hat gesagt, er hat es dir unter diesen Bedingungen gegeben, wenn du es nicht erfühlst verliehre du es.

One does not, then, have the right to 'own' a property, but the right to 'use' it, and this can be lost. The role of the Islamic state is to see that this right is not abused. After three years of disuse, the right to work a piece of land should pass to someone else. However, there are still large groups of people who have nothing to eat, which would be impossible according to Islamic law.

The Islamic economy rests on conditions of a free economy in business life, but these are not the same as capitalism. For example, profit is taxed in the capitalist state, while it is not in the Islamic state. On the other hand property is taxed (capital and private wealth).

The Islamic economic system and herewith business enterprises cannot work on the basis of making interest. Therefore it is not right that certain banks call themselves 'Islamic' today, when they still operate with the use - one way or another - of 'interest rates'.

The Islamic System of Government
How should an Islamic system of government be defined, what does Millî Görüş regard this as being? The imam starts by commenting on the term 'democracy' when I ask him about 'Islamic democracy'. Real democracy, where the people rule themselves, does not exist. 'Democracy' is an invented term with no real substance. In capitalist society 'the democratic countries' choose 'the people' in actual fact, not the government. On the contrary it is they who have capital in their hand who choose their own people for government. They have founded various different parties and the people only have a choice of choosing between these parties.

In Islam the system functions differently. In Islam it is the *ulama*, who make up the parliament and choose the government, *shura*. The ulama should not be taken in its strictly religious sense. *Ulama* should be understood as 'scholars, or 'learned men' who cover all aspects of knowledge. It is important for the imam to stress that talk of an Islamic system of government requires an Islamic population, and that this system is not being practised today. There is a faithful population led by a faithful government of which all are *ulama* in the religious sense: 'Denn jede, auch der kleinste Mann auf der Straß, muß - so wie so - vieles, über die Religion wißen und so wie so *Ulamas* sein'. But this parliament of *ulama* does not only represent the religious, but as mentioned, all aspects of knowledge. The parliament's ulama can deal with all areas, also areas which lie beyond the expertise of the individual.

It is the people who elect the *ulama* to parliament, and this *ulama* chooses a *shura* from amongst its members and this *shura* conducts the laws, The people will know who these ulama are. They will know their lives and know that they are orderly people. This will guarantee that people without morals will not enter into the leadership of the state.

This Islamic system of governing is guided by skilled experts. A peasant or a labourer can not be elected to parliament since they could not be defined as ulama: 'Nicht so eiene einfache Mensch, der z.B ein Traktor fährt!', but an agronomist, for example, could.

The Islamic system also ensures religious minorities rights and influence. They fall within the guarantee of the Islamic state. The state gives them the freedom to establish their own schools and churches, in the same way as they have the right to conduct business just like anyone else. They also have almost the same duties as other people, including paying taxes. They must, however, acknowledge certain conditions: They must acknowledge the Islamic system and not form opposition to or disturbances against Islam. Nor may they transgress the moral guidance line which Islam sets, they may not, for example, produce porno-films.

The religious minority is represented in parliament, but cannot enter the *shura*. If we refer to the Christians, they are not necessarily represented by a priest, but by any *alim*.

In the Islamic state the minority have their own laws, in particular their own penal codes. They can punish their own people with their own laws, it is not up to the Islamic state to carry out this punishment. A representative of the *shura* participates as an observer in the court, which otherwise consists of (e.g.) Christians. The Christians create their own laws according to Christianity, and the Jews according to Judaism. It is not the Islamic state authority which makes their laws.

The Christians have their own legal state, so to speak, which though is under the control of parliament. They have their own penal code such that Christians are treated in a Christian legal system. If two people from two different faiths are involved in a case against one another then it takes place either in an Islamic or a Christian court, but in an 'unbiased court'. An example of a conflict between Sultan Fatih Mehmet and a Jew is an exemplary case of how a 'free court' is conducted.

Workers' Rights in Islam
In the capitalist countries the state authority is more or less in the hands of the capitalists who have poor regard for the rights of workers which is why we have trade unions, said the imam. The intention of the trade unions is to protect the rights of workers. There is no need for this in an Islamic state, he continues, because the state will guarantee the workers' rights.

In one *hadith*, Muhammed says: 'Bevor der Schweiß von Stirn trocken wird, muß der Arbeiter schon ihr Geld bekommen haben'. This means, said the imam, that the employer should pay wages due as soon as the working day is over and should not wait until the next day, this applies regardless of whether he is satisfied with the work or not. The imam added that the wage is automatically regulated according to prices.

In an Islamic state the guarantee of rights is quite different, also with regard to labour market conditions:

> In die islamische Staat ist jede berechtigt ohne jemanden in zwischen zu kommen in oberste Gericht oder Parlament zu gehen. Die Türen sind also offen für jeden, jede einfache Mensch.

If the individual feels that he has been treated badly, the person concerned has the immediate right to stand before the highest legal authority, or the parliament even without waiting for a convenient opportunity to occur.

In Islam, Muslims are encouraged to speak the truth and to always point out injustices, even if it is the president who has committed them. The imam refers to testimony from the first two caliphs:

> Die erste Khalif Abu Bakr hatte die Leute gesagt: 'Wenn ich irgenwas falsch mache, - das ist in Türkisch 'Krumm mache' - dann sollte ihn mich mit einen Schwert gerade machen', der präsident Abu Bakr hat das gesagt! Zweiter Khalif ist Omar. In Moschee hat jemand sogar ihn nach seine Meinung Unrecht gefunden, und meinte das er etwas nicht richtig macht. Also der dem Präsident auch offen sagen das er Unrecht tat, ist eine guten Muslim.

The trade unions, which are regarded as being necessary organisations in fighting to protect the interests of workers in the capitalist system, become irrelevant in Islamic society. Instead of trade unions, *ahilik* are organised 'brotherhoods', which is to say unions for each vocation which negotiate on their behalf regarding demands, wishes and product prices. These *ahilik* are standard institutions, whose approval in each and every case is a prerequisite for products to be put onto the market.

Islam's Human Rights

There are numerous hadith which illustrate that the founding principle in Islam is that right belongs to those who are right, and not to those who have power, the imam explained. He stressed the five different characteristics of Islam which Muslims must regard as being fundamental human rights:

> '1) Die garantie das leben und leben (T: can) lassen, 2) glauben (T: din) lassen, 3) eigentum (T: mal) haben lassen, 4) würde (T: namus) haben lassen, stoltz, moral und 5) vermehren und leben lassen.'

Womens' Rights in Islam

The imam underlines that womens' rights in Islam are very comprehensive, but that they can all be boiled down to:

> Kurz gesagt die Frauen brauchen nichts zu tun, nicht mal waschen, kochen u.s.w. für ihre eigene Kinder und Mann. Sie braucht nichts zu tun, ausser eins, damit die Moral oder Befriedigung den Mann nicht zu den Fremden geht, soll die Fraue zu hause dem Mann ihre Geschlechtswünsche befriedigen.

The only duties of a woman are therefore, to make herself available sexually to her husband and to bear his children.

The imam rejects any notion of Islam advocating that a woman's place is in the home, to prepare food and also to take care of the house, in the same way that responsibility for the children is not hers alone:

> Das also im Volk solche Pflichte dem Frau gegeben ist, nicht weil sie Muslime sind, aber weil sie nicht Muslime sind. Die wissen nicht wie ein Muslim seien soll, deswegen hat man die Frau viele Arbeit gegeben. Also das ist traditionel, und in jeden anderen Volk ist das anderes. Aber das hängt mit dem Islam nicht ab.

The inferior position of women in Islam was herewith dismissed by the imam. It is not Islam which dictates that a woman's place is in the home with the children, it is a consequence of 'tradition'!

The duties of women do not differ from those of men. The most important duties for both men and women is to learn still more: 'Wissenschaft ist für jeden mann oder frau *farz* (translates as 'duty'), das ist ein wort von Gott - ein *aya*'.

The imam outlines a view of the social position of women which is radical in relation to the usual Islamic interpretation. Woman can be scientists, they can run businesses, they can bear arms, yes, even become generals or lead of armies, just as they can also become heads of state. Women who earn money also have the privilege of not having to put so much as one 'pfennig' of their money towards the housekeeping, it is all for her own use! In one area women are, however, excluded; women cannot become judges:

> Weil die vielleicht mehr gefühlvoll ist, also von Natur her, und falshce Urteile geben kann,....von natur ist die Frau gefühlvoller als der Mann, und deswegen kan vieles verzeihen und nicht bestrafen kann.

But this surely could be a problem if there was to be a woman general or president?

> Wichtiger ist es wenn vor Gericht. Ein 'Unrechter', also ein der Unrecht hat, kann durch ihren Weinen, und alles was er machen kann eine Frau weiss machen, aber es ist nicht so wichtig wenn ein General ein fehler macht!

The tendency of women to allow themselves to be ruled by their emotions is also precisely the imam's argument for why Islam demands two female witnesses for every one male in legal wrangles. Although women are guided by emotions rather than by logic, it would be unlikely that two female witnesses would have exactly the same feelings at the same time. The imam, however, was also eager to explain on this point that not just any *man* could step forward as a witness:

> Nicht jeder Mann kann Zeuge sein, z.B. wer Alkohol trinken, mit fremden Frauen geht, wer lügt u.s.w., der kann überhaupt kein Zeuge sein. (....) Wenn er zum Hause z.B. seine Kinder schlägt oder Frau schlägt, das er unrechte macht, der kann auch kein Zeuge sein. Um Zeuge zu sein verstehen wir, erstmal Muslim zu sein, aufrichtig.

Protection of the Environment in Islam
Regarding the environment, Islam is also up to date, according to the imam, who continued: The first question which any person, that is to say, any Muslim is faced with regards the state of the world's health. Because health is valuable to man, one must show regard to the environment, so that it does not suffer damage. This concerns everything that has anything to do with the environment: Animals, plants, stones. One must not just discard rubbish wherever one please, nor should one spit in the street!. Any enterprise which fouls the environment will soon lose its license to produce and will in addition also be severely punished.

There is a *hadith* which states that one should treat the environment with care: 'Wenn man auch gerade beim sterben liegt, irgendwo, muß man in der Hand ein Grünes haben!'. This means that one must give a lot of consideration to plants in Islam, the imam explains, and goes on:

> Im Türkischen gibt es ein Sprichwort: 'yash kesme, bash kesme', das bedeutet 'wer einer lebendige Baum oder pflanze schlagtet, schlagtet schon ein Kopf.

Companies which make too much noise, or create a lot of dust, or in some other way are harmful to human health should not be conducted in towns where people live. Islam dictates even that they should lie around 100 km. from the towns.

Finally, the imam added, with a glint in his eye:

> Wenn wir den Grünen hier den Islam so um diese Umwelt erklären könnte, wäre fast alle Grünen Muslime, weil sie so mit den Umwelt sich so befaßen!

Appendix J
Letter from Senator für Schulwesen, Jugend und Sport, Berlin

Der Senator für Schulwesen, Jugend und Sport

BERLIN

Senator für Schulwesen, Jugend und Sport
Postfach, D-1000 Berlin 19 (nur Postanschrift)

Dienstgebäude: Bredtschneiderstraße 5
Berlin-Charlottenburg

Rechtsanwälte
Dr. Lehmann-Brauns
Dr. Mahlo
Kurfürstendamm 37

1000 Berlin 15

Eingegangen
1 4. JULI 1982

RA Dr. Lehmann-Brauns
RA Dr. Mahlo

☎ (030) 3033-1 (Vermittlung)
3032 (Durchwahl)
(987) (Intern)

GeschZ. (bei Antwort bitte angeben)	Bearbeiter	Zimmer	Datum
II - C A 7/I b C 1		250/696	12.7.1982

Sehr geehrte Herren Rechtsanwälte,

ich beziehe mich auf die bisherige Korrespondenz mit der Föderation Islamischer Vereinigungen und Gemeinden in Berlin und auf Ihre Schreiben vom 2.6. und 30.6.1982, die Sie mir als Bevollmächtigte der Föderation übersandt haben.

Dem Anliegen der Föderation, in der Berliner Schule islamischen Religionsunterricht durchzuführen, vermag ich aus den nachstehend genannten Gründen gegenwärtig nicht zu entsprechen:

Wie Sie wissen, besteht in Berlin - abweichend von der Rechtslage in den anderen Bundesländern - nach § 23 Abs. 1 des Schulgesetzes für Berlin (SchulG) für Religionsgemeinschaften die Möglichkeit, in eigener Verantwortung Religionsunterricht in den Schulen zu erteilen, ohne daß dieses Recht jeder religiös orientierten oder interessierten Vereinigung eingeräumt wird. Maßgeblich für ein solches Privileg ist das Selbstbestimmungsrecht der Religionsgemeinschaften nach Art. 137 Abs. 3 Satz 1 WRV in Verbindung mit Art. 140 GG. Wesentliche Voraussetzung für die Durchführung von Religionsunterricht ist somit zunächst das Vorhandensein einer Religionsgemeinschaft.

Nach eingehender Prüfung bin ich zu dem Ergebnis gelangt, daß die von Ihnen vertretene Föderation diese Voraussetzung nicht erfüllt. Der Begriff der Religionsgemeinschaft (gleichbedeutend mit Religionsgesellschaft) hat im deutschen Verfassungsrecht einen bestimmten Inhalt, der auch für § 23 SchulG maßgebend ist. Danach ist Religionsgemeinschaft der Zusammenschluß von Personen aufgrund übereinstimmender Auffassungen in religiöser Hinsicht, der den vorhandenen Konsens in umfassender Weise bezeugt. Demzufolge muß es sich um einen Zusammenschluß von natürlichen Personen handeln. Diese Voraussetzung erfüllt die Föderation jedoch nicht, da nach § 4 Abs. 1 ihrer Satzung nur juristische Personen die Mitgliedschaft in dem Verein erwerben können. Die Mitglieder der einzelnen

- 2 -

Appendix J
Letter from Senator für Schulwesen, Jugend und Sport, Berlin

Vereinigungen als natürliche Personen sind nicht zugleich auch Mitglieder der Föderation. Als Dachverband juristischer Personen könnte die Föderation dann als Religionsgemeinschaft angesehen werden, wenn die einzelnen Mitgliedsvereinigungen selbst Religionsgemeinschaften wären und der Zusammenschluß nicht nur partiell religiöse Belange bezweckte, sondern eine hinreichend umfassende religiöse Zielsetzung hätte. Für einige in der Föderation zusammengeschlossene Vereinigungen, wie z. B. den Türkischen Kultur- und Solidaritätsverein e. V., muß bereits die Erfüllung der Voraussetzungen einer Religionsgemeinschaft in Zweifel gezogen werden. Außerdem ist nicht ersichtlich, daß die Angehörigen einzelner Vereinigungen der Föderation sich zur Erfüllung aller Aufgaben, die zur Verwirklichung einer Religionsgemeinschaft gehören, zusammengeschlossen haben und ein gemeinsames Glaubensbekenntnis praktizieren. Nach meinem Eindruck bestehen erst recht innerhalb der Föderation keine einheitlichen, übereinstimmenden Auffassungen in religiöser Hinsicht. Ferner deutet die Satzung der Föderation in § 3 darauf hin, daß die Föderation für die religiösen Belange der Moslems lediglich gleichrangig mit sozialen, rechtlichen und kulturellen Interessen Sorge tragen will. Als Hauptzweck wird dort die Vertretung der Interessen der Föderation gegenüber den Behörden herausgestellt und die Anerkennung als Religionsgemeinschaft als ein wesentliches Ziel genannt. Aus der Beschreibung der Ziele in der Satzung und der Aufgaben der Föderation kann gefolgert werden, daß die Föderation nicht - bzw. noch nicht - die Tatbestandsvoraussetzungen einer Religionsgemeinschaft erfüllt, weil sie keine hinreichend umfassende religiöse Zielsetzung hat. Dies wird nicht zuletzt durch die Passage in der Satzung bestätigt, wonach die Föderation selbst erst die Anerkennung als Religionsgemeinschaft anstrebt. Auch die Aufgabenbeschreibung, nach der die Föderation vor allem als Interessenvertretung der in ihr zusammengeschlossenen islamischen Gemeinschaften verstanden wird (§ 3 Nr. 1 der Satzung), legt den Schluß nahe , daß die Föderation keine Religionsgemeinschaft, sondern lediglich einen religiös orientierten Verein darstellt, da die Universalität des Wirkungskreises, die einer Religionsgemeinschaft eigen ist, fehlt und sie somit nur einzelne religiöse Zwecke verfolgt.

Im übrigen ist noch auf ein weiteres Bedenken hinzuweisen,. Es bestehen rechtliche Zweifel, ob § 23 Abs. 1 SchulG in seiner jetzigen Fassung auch islamischen Religionsgemeinschaften das Recht einräumt, Religionsunterricht in der Berliner Schule zu erteilen. Sie ergeben sich aus der Entstehungsgeschichte dieser schulgesetzlichen Regelung. Das Spektrum des möglichen Religions- oder Weltanschauungsunterrichts, das der Gesetzgeber im Jahre 1948 im Auge hatte, bezog sich auf die damals in unserer Gesellschaft vorhandenen Erscheinungsformen, offen sicherlich für gewisse Veränderungen innerhalb dieses Spektrums. Ich meine, daß der Islam, so wie er sich heute in Berlin religiös und politisch darstellt, für die Erteilung von Religionsunterricht ganz neue Fragen aufwirft - bis hin zur Fragestellung, inwieweit die Aufgaben der öffentlichen Schulen und der von Religionsgemeinschaften zu verantwortende Religionsunterricht kollidieren dürfen.

Der von Ihnen erwähnte Aufsatz (Eiselt, Islamischer Religionsunterricht in den Ländern der Bundesrepublik Deutschland, DÖV 1981 S. 205 ff) ist mir bekannt. Darin wird, soweit er die Rechtslage in Berlin betrifft, zur Vermeidung von Widersprüchen zwischen staatlicher und religiöser Erziehung im Schulbereich

Appendix J
Letter from Senator für Schulwesen, Jugend und Sport, Berlin

```
                           - 3 -

eine gesetzliche Regelung für nötig gehalten (S. 210 a.a.O.).
Auch der Senat erwägt zur Zeit die Frage einer gesetzlichen
Lösung des Problems. Sofern diese Überlegungen - mit wahr-
scheinlich legislatorischen Konsequenzen - abgeschlossen sind,
werde ich Sie hierüber informieren.

Ich bitte um Verständnis, daß Ihnen augenblicklich keine andere
Antwort gegeben werden kann.

Hochachtungsvoll
In Vertretung

Koch
```

Appendix K

Flyer for the Alternative (Islamic) Theatre in Berlin
The text in translation reads as follows:
   THE APES LEAP INTO THE PRESENT.
(In other words; Darwin's apes, the Kemalists, pursue their aim by hanging Islam on the gallows).

Appendix L

Interview with Mustafa Doğan, chairman of Millî Görüş in France
This interview took place in the movement's French centre, Paris Fatîh Camisi, in May 1990 (transcript of tape recording).

'There are not as many Turks here in France as in Germany. There are between 200,000 and 300,000 here, most of whom live in Alsace, the Paris region and in Lyon.

Not all have access to a mosque, but Muslims are ordered by God, Allah, to pray five times a day. To practise our faith we can use mosques, prayer rooms, congregation halls, small conference rooms, etc...But at the present time we do not have enough imams for our sections. We have around sixteen or seventeen imams. We need qualified people and we do not have them.

We also lack well-educated women. We only realised this problem when it was much too late. We need women who are not imams, but who know a lot about religion, who know of the problems Muslim women have in France and in the West.

Our personnel, and in particular, those who run the religious services all have university certificates of graduation and have practical experience in Turkey and in Europe. They are all qualified for the service they provide. Aside from these imams we need personnel who can provide social counselling and help. We lack, for example, personnel who speak good French, who speak other languages and who can receive the public, who can inform them of our activities. For example, you found me here today by chance, if you were to come looking for me here tomorrow, you would not have found me. You were lucky!

We are an 'association but non-lucratif' (ASBL) according to the French 1901 law, i.e. it has no commercial aims, it is an association which serves the needs of ordinary people in every manner; financial support, education, social, sports. It is aimed at children and at people who have arrived here and who have need for moral and economic support.

Apart from the imams, we have university students who are carrying out postgraduate work here in France and who help children and the young who attend French schools. Their task is to answer the questions which arise in the course of their schooling and for which they might need extra help or knowledge. Aside from teaching the Koran and prayer, the young are also educated in Oriental culture - we are, of course, of Turkish origin. They inform the children about the history, geography, language and traditions of Turkey.

We are not, as such, a religious association in the narrow sense of the term. We are an association which encompasses everything: the daily life of people, life in the streets, the humanitarian, the spiritual life, the cultural, the social, the educational, financial, athletic and so on.

Put another way: Thirteen years ago immigrants believed that they would return to the country they came from, to Turkey or Morocco. More than anything else, we have, since 1985, come to understand that the Muslims will remain here in France and in Europe. They will not be going back - unfortunately, in my opinion - to their countries of origin. Therefore, we have to realise that this Muslim population has to be integrated into the countries where they are living. Ideas have to be produced, information has to be distributed to people: Western society must understand that Islam is not a religion which rejects everything.

We have begun to take part in the work of those organisations which seek to calm the spirit of the spectres which racism contains, among those who are not realistic, one might say.

TNUIF is working, above all, to make French society understand that Islam can exist alongside other religions, other traditions, and that Islam can be integrated. We are ready to be integrated into French society, that is why we have added *Tendance National* to *Union Islamique en France*.

TNUIF gathers the individual UIF-unions around the integration of its members in France. That is to say that the ambition of TNUIF is to be integrated into French society. When we created the UIF these integration problems did not exist because the population had not yet begun to create problems. People first began thinking about staying in France or Europe from the middle of the 1980s on. Only then did we think about the fact that we should live here, that we had to be integrated and accepted and not remain marginalised, foreign and hidden in the West. Of course we can live in France and Europe and remain Muslims, become Western and at the same time practise our religion.

We are working towards Islam being integrated into French society. There are about 4 million people who are not recognised by the state authority, who have no representative organisation, and there are many problems, more than in Germany, for example. The problems of Muslims remain to be solved. Above all the youth problems, their criminalisation and marginalisation in society. For example, Le Pen has emerged as a consequence of the poor education of these young people, therefore we have to be motivated and we must co-operate with the state authorities to solve our problems. The government has also decided - and this is good, that a solution has to be found to the problems of young people.

The insecurity surrounding certain rights relating to Islam is indisputable, also with regard to youth, who need to have a goal.

The girls' veil is a religious duty a duty given by God. But the mass media have interpreted this in their own fashion - and the racists have reacted quickly. The media have ignited a fire. The question of the Islamic veil has existed for a long time. But journalists will always create sensation. The problem is formulated incorrectly. It is a religious duty, it is God's order, sent down via the Koran. If you are Muslim you must practise the faith completely.

We are against the marginalisation of the Muslim people in French society and in the West as a whole. We want young people, young girls women and men to be instructed and to practise their Muslim religion. They should live in French society and represent Islam as it really is.

Islam is not a religion that, as certain journalists say in the mass media, is an 'integrist religion', 'fanatical', and 'terrorist'. The journalists have a quite mistaken understanding of Muslims. We do not have the same aims as the Iranians, or what can be seen happening in the Middle East. Islam ought to be pacifist. Muslims ought to bear peace to mankind, peace to themselves, peace to their enemies as well as to their friends.

We believe that French society or the West in general must understand that the Muslim religion is not a religion that rejects.....even though historically it has been in conflict with Western culture....but the Muslims demand that they are accepted like other religions in a spirit of brotherhood. We demand that 'Freedom, Equality and Brotherhood' should apply to everyone!

I think that secular people in a tolerant atmosphere will be able to understand that we are not seeking to create an anti-social climate in French society. Above all when we say that when young girls want to wear the veil it is not to create problems in society but because it is a religious duty. If one respects our ideas - and we are asked to respect the ideas of others, other forms of belief! - one can ask why we wear this veil and the answer would be that it is because it is a duty. (...) The mass media have created this problem.

It is apparently not possible to introduce Islamic teaching in French schools, but in my opinion one could introduce 'des course civique' (....), which would correspond to religion. Alongside the secular schools we ought to set up Muslim schools which conform to the reality of French society. Just as there are Catholic schools and Jewish schools. We plan to be able to open such an independent school in year's time. Since we are specialised in Turkish immigrants we will make them for Turks.

In France there is no organisation which is recognised by the state authorities (le pouvoir public), to issue a *halâl* certificate. We strongly need a solution to this problem. We are, if you like, a minority in relation to the collected Muslim population in France. We are around 4 million Muslims, above all Arabs, we are only a few in relation to them. We are specialised in the Turkish population groups, where we are well represented, but we are not represented in the other groups.

We not have the same rights as the Jewish community. The Jews are well organised. The Muslims in France are not organised.

They (Muslim organisations/LP) have not shown themselves to be responsible, they have not yet shown an engagement *vis-à-vis* the Muslim population, *vis-à-vis* the young people. In my opinion we should unite at the initiative of the government, we support that solution. The government has been waiting, the government is now helping the Muslims to form this council.

The minister's decision (to form a consultative council/LP) has oriented us towards representing Islam in France, this is a subtle point. It is now up to us to be accepted by the Muslim population. We are a link between the public authorities and the immigrant Muslims. (...) We are, in my opinion, duty bound to find concrete solutions for the public authorities, solutions which will be accepted by the Muslim community, which will be approved from below and if we find solutions that are satisfactory to the public authorities.

The most immediate problems for Islam in France are those associated with the establishment of Muslim burial grounds, *halâl* butchers, the marginalisation of the young and their education. These are very thorny problems, but ones that should be solved as soon as possible.

We get along with Diyanet without a great deal of difficulty. Unfortunately, they had greater resources at their disposal than we do. The Turkish government has an advantage in terms of the imams and organisations which work with Diyanet, above all on the personal level. But they do not provide the right solutions for society, for the young generation. They have the advantage of resources, but you could say that they are not sufficiently engaged. We have the advantage of having motivated members, more motivated that the unions which are supported by Diyanet. We are much more motivated than they are, unfortunately we do not have the same resources. But we are neither for nor against them.

We find a consensus at the national level in France, with the other Muslim communities in France: with the North Africans, with the Pakistanis, with the French converts, with the blacks. That is to say that this year is the first time that we have had a consensus, and that has made a great impression. We follow the first Muslim country which observes the moon. We exchange viewpoints on the matter with AMGT, but we do not take precisely the same line.

The organisation organises the collection of *zekât* to help the poor and students who need bursaries. To help people who have need and who otherwise fall outside the system. But first and foremost it is with regard to helping the young gain an education, says the chairman.

Appendix M

Letter from the Danish Directorate for Aliens
Direktoratet for Udlændinge

Lars Pedersen,
Etnografisk afd.
Århus Universitetet, Moesgaard
8270 Højbjerg

Dato **20 SEP. 1990**   Sagsbehandler IMH/gn   Udl.nr./journalnr. 1990 HJ 453-12
Bedes anført i svarskrivelser

Under henvisning til Deres skrivelse af 13.8.1990 skal direktoratet for Udlændinge oplyse, at man i 1989, efter samråd med Justitsministeriet og Kirkeministeriet, indførte den nugældende praksis vedrørende tyrkiske imamer, der er udsendt og aflønnet af den tyrkiske stat.

Praksis vedrørende disse imamer er herefter, at de meddeles opholdstilladelse med henblik på midlertidigt ophold og at tilladelsen ikke forlænges ud over et samlet ophold i Danmark på 4 år.

Som nævnt i direktoratets skrivelse af 20.02.1990, kan der efter udlændingelovens § 9, stk. 2, nr. 4 efter nærmere konkret skøn meddeles opholdstilladelse til udlændinge med henblik på virke inden for et trossamfund i Danmark.

Vedrørende de forhold der indgår i skønsudøvelsen skal direktoratet bemærke, at hver enkelt ansøgning bliver afgjort på baggrund af en individuel bedømmelse af samtlige fremkomne oplysninger.

Direktoratet stiller dog som generelle krav, at ansøgeren har en uddannelse, der kvalificierer vedkommende til at virke som imam, samt at vedkommende har praktisk erfaring indenfor faget. Endvidere stilles der normalt krav om, at ansøgeren skal afløse en imam, der tidligere har haft opholdstilladelse i Danmark.

Appendix M
Letter from the Danish Directorate for Aliens

Direktoratet for Udlændinge

- 2 -

Såfremt ansøgeren ikke skal afløse en imam i Danmark, vil direktoratet, eventuelt efter samråd med Kirkeministeriet, vurdere, hvorvidt den pågældende ansøger kan få meddelt opholdstilladelse.

I vurderingen heraf indgår blandt andet, om der må antages at være behov for en ansættelse af en udenlandsk imam og om et eventuelt behov ikke kan dækkes ved ansættelse af herboende udlændinge/danskere.

Direktoratet skal afslutningsvis bemærke, at det er en forudsætning for meddelelse af opholdstilladelse til udenlandske imamer, at pågældende er økonomisk sikret under et eventuelt ophold i Danmark.

E.B.

Marianne Birger Møller

Ingrid Munch Hansen

Appendix N

Letter from the Danish Directorate for Aliens
Direktoratet for Udlændinge

Lars Pedersen
Etnografisk Afd.
Århus Universitet
Moesgaard
8270 Højbjerg

Dato 2 0 FEB. 1990   Sagsbehandler IBT/tm   Udl.nr./journalnr. 1990HJ453-12
Bedes anført i svarskrivelser

Under henvisning til Deres skrivelse af 12.01.1990 vedrørende udenlandske imamer kan direktoratet oplyse, at der efter udlændingelovens § 9 stk. 2 nr. 4 efter nærmere konkret skøn kan meddeles opholdstilladelse til udlændinge med henblik på virke inden for et trossamfund i Danmark.

Efter direktoratets praksis meddeles en sådan opholdstilladelse med henblik på midlertidigt ophold og som hovedregel for et samlet ophold af 2 år, idet man dog for så vidt angår de anerkendte trossamfund ikke har nogen tidsbegrænsning, men løbende vil forlænge opholdstilladelse sålænge den pågældende er beskæftiget inden for trossamfundet.

Til udlændinge, der virker inden for et trossamfund, hvis præster af Kirkeministeriet kan bemyndiges til at foretage kirkelig vielse med borgerlig gyldighed, kan der, såfremt den pågældende har opnået kirkeministeriets bemyndigelse til at foretage vielse, meddeles opholdstilladelse i op til et samlet ophold af ialt 4 år.

Der vedlægges en fortegnelse over de nævnte trossamfund.

Efter direktoratets praksis meddeles der herudover opholdstilladelse i op til 4 års samlet ophold til tyrkiske imamer, der er direkte udsendt og aflønnet af den tyrkiske stat. Det drejer sig om ca. 9-10 imamer, der på denne måde er udstationeret i Danmark.

Summary
Newer Islamic Movements in Western Europe

The intention of this thesis is to describe and evaluate the development of the cultural shift represented by the newer Islamic movements among Muslim immigrants in Western Europe.

Beginning with a presentation of the way Islam is organised in Western Europe, and via an investigation of the most significant Islamic tendency among Turkish immigrants in Western Europe, it emerges that Islamism provides a clear and concrete starting point for creating a positive identification within Muslim immigrant environments.

Islamism represents a consciousness which markedly insists on an alternative to the dominant cultural and social marginalisation. There is an insistence on the validity of certain social and cultural interests in the struggle between *lifeworld* and *systemworld*. The investigation suggests the existence of decentralised communities whose common social and cultural interests are in need of representation. Islamism reveals a tendency among Muslim minorities to formulate the demand to be considered as fully valid citizens.

The above noted investigation of Islamism among the Muslim minorities is presented in the thesis from a number of different strategies and levels of analysis. I then attempt to integrate these into a progressive presentation of the case.

In the introduction, I criticise (Chapter 1) the representation of *Islam* and *Islamism* in Western discourse. Western discourse on *Islam* and *Islamism* constitutes a problematic mental landscape for multicultural society. My criticism is built upon an analysis of representations in the media. Similarly, I criticise the representation by Western social sciences of the Islamic movement which in recent years has become highly noticeable in the Middle East. I follow this with a closer definition of the term *Islamism*, which my analysis relates to:

While *Islamism* can, among other things, be said to be formulated upon the basis of a criticism of *traditionalism*, *fundamentalism* can be said to be the basis of *Islamism*. *Islamism* distinguishes itself from *fundamentalism* by its stress on the socio-political dimension in the religious context. *Fundamentalism*'s project meanwhile can be said to be more concerned with underlining the authenticity of the holy scripture. In this way *Islamists* can be said to be *fundamentalists*, while the reverse does not necessarily have to follow.

In *Chapter 2*, I present an account of the institutionalisation of Islam in Western Europe. The aim is to uncover the foundations of the growth of the Islamic organisations. I show that the Islamic organisations' wish to function like European organisations is limited to a large degree by political and legal circumstances. Even at the state-political or administrative levels the development of autonomous Islamic organisations is opposed.

On the basis of the development of the Islamic scene in Europe it can be seen that it is the political and judicial conditions for the establishment of Islam which decide which sociological players emerge: either 1) the Muslim state apparatuses, or 2) the Muslim immigrants themselves.

Although we could say that the management of Islam is in the hands of these two main groups of participants, it could also be said that there is a general trend for the European countries to favour the initiatives of the Muslim states on the Islamic scene. The social scene for Islam in Europe must be considered to constitute a democratic problem.

Avrupa Görüş Teşkilâtleri (AMGT), or as it is usually known, Millî Görüş, which is the most important Turkish Islamic movement in Western Europe, is introduced in Chapter 3. The aim is to clarify the perspectives which a chosen Islamist group offers to the (primarily Turkish) Muslims minorities in the European context. Which type of community the members are offered. Which organisational framework is linked to participation in the movement. I sketch an outline of the organisation in Denmark, Berlin and France and present background material for the subsequent analysis of the movement's positions. The chapter is built on material which I have gathered through interviews with representatives of three of the movement's regions: Denmark, France, and Berlin.

The movement has, during recent decades, undergone a transformation, from being a Turkish Islamic movement in exile to being a Turkish-European Islamist movement, whose primary interests lie in the organisation of an Islamic identity among the Turkish immigrant minorities in Europe. The movement is organised into regions (bölgesi) which are linked to a centre (in Cologne), which however, acts more in the organisational capacity than in dictating opinion - this enables an exchange of experience on the European level.

Millî Görüş seeks to link religious and social praxis through a global vision which is centred around an Islamic moral standpoint. One could say that the movement contributes thereby to an expansion of the possibilities in the construction of social and cultural interests among the immigrant Turkish Muslims. As such, the movement explicitly challenges the Turkish state authority's own view of itself as the administrator of Turkish cultural heritage in Europe.

In the subsequent chapter, *Chapter 4*, I expand on how Islam is organised at the local level so as to approach a clarification of this which can be linked to a formulated religious identity among the participants in the Turkish Islamist movement. The Turkish Islamism scene in Aarhus is used as a concrete example of Islamism as a social possibility, both collectively and individually. It emerges that the development of religious space has differentiated itself to a large degree over the years since the first mosque was established in 1979.

I expand on how the engaged Islamists who are part of a Millî Görüş cemaat (community) in Denmark interpret their Islamic identity. This expansion, which focuses on two activist profiles, centres around questions which concern Islam in daily life, Islam and work, personal background stories, marriage and economy, the experience of being Muslim in the Danish community, and the Islamic ideal. With this it is possible to gain an impression of the relevance on Islamism at the personal level which integrates, as such, the subjective and the objective levels in Daily live. Or, in other words, the participant's own (private) as well as collective experiences.

1. The young, who are part of the movement, do not distinguish themselves outwardly from other young immigrants. They share the same conditions, i.e. socially, educationally, and in relation to the job market - unemployment is also high here. The parents' generation are often rooted in peasant society. This condition applies not only to the Islamists, but also to a large part of the old immigrant groups. The parents rarely have any extended schooling in their background, their basic knowledge of Islam comes from a village context- The younger people's knowledge of Islam is provided by these parents in the migrant environments. It is, as such, characteristic for the young peoples relation to Islam to be sharpened in the migrant situation.

2. The societal marginalisation, which characterises these immigrant groups, is received positively at the cultural level through the increased stress on Islam. Islamism represents so to speak a negotiating position in relation to the surrounding society. It is an expression of a rejection of certain aspects of peasant traditions, while at the same time an attempt to reformulate central moral values for use in modern society. The

raising of children assumes a quite crucial importance for the Islamists in this sense.

3. The religiously based community is crucial but is in no way the only point of social contact for the participants in the Islamic movements. The community is not sharply delineated outwardly. One important indicator is that people prefer to approach relatives rather than members of the community if they have need for help in the day to day context, e.g. on financial matters, or in connection with entering into marriage.

Before I turn my attention to a more global analysis of Islamism in Western Europe I attempt, in *Chapter 5*, to delineate another Islamic fundamental position active within the circles of Europe's Muslim minority. This is *Jama'at al-Tabligh*, which has successfully managed to organise itself on an inter-ethnic foundation.

Jama'at al-Tabligh differs markedly from the Islamists in being neither state, nor politically oriented. Members of *Jama'at al-Tabligh* are concerned with the transfer of Islam through simple explanation and through a conducting an honourable life. The consistent anti-political grouping makes itself noticed in being markedly activist in its orientation towards the daily life of immigrant Muslims. This is, however, a form of Islamic activism which does not associate itself to the question of power and which therefore with reference to my opening definition is situated on the fringes of Islamism. The chapter is built on interviews with participants in the Danish section of the movement and with the leader of the French section.

I wish to show that although Islamism is exclusive, it is not an answer to particular anomalies and stories of individual lives. On the other hand it can be said that Islamism is a collective answer to a marginalised position in Western society. The perspective of the analysis shifts then in *Chapter 6* from the immediate level of the social players to the societal context which defines the actual historic and social for the establishment of immigrant environments in Western Europe. This chapter constitutes an attempt to compare the structural conditions for societal processes in West European capitalist society in general, and those processes which characterise the integration of immigrant societies in particular.

This leads us through a discussion which centres around the terms *system* and *lifeworld* (Habermas 1981) as a general theoretical frame for the understanding of the Islamic movement's articulation of social and cultural interests.

The social and cultural interests which the Islamic movements organise themselves around are analysed as being a result of the *systemworld*'s dramatic colonisation of the *lifeworld* in migration. The

Islamic movements in Europe are considered then as a resistance to colonisation - as a symptom of social disintegration.

The social communities and networks which are related, for example, to kinship, ethnicity or Islamic identity become the response to the threat of disintegration and break thereby with the systemworld's threats of fragmentation. The strategy of Islamism then becomes one of producing symbols and institutions for this defence of cultural autonomy.

The immigrant ethnic minorities are, so to speak, trapped in a historical economic trap. It is precisely this historically conditioned societal situation which has sent Muslim immigrants out to the cultural periphery and left them without 'hegemonic power' (Stuart Hall in Røgilds 1988) gives the lifeworld processes a particular dynamic which gives the Islamic socialisation structure its significance in Western discourse. The newer Islamic movements characterise then, to my understanding, social and cultural interests which exercise resistance to the systemworld's continued destruction of lifeworld structures. The re-conquest of a social praxis from the system is thus attempted through the implementation of concrete activities and via the articulation of the demand for changes.

Against this background I turn back in the concluding chapter, *Chapter 7*, to the vision and strategy of Islamism so as to discuss the critical relevance of Islamism at a qualitative new level - in the light of the social and economic marginalisation which characterises the situation of the immigrant Muslim minority.

The Islamic spectrum contains a varied range of organisation forms and positions of a very different nature. The analysis limits itself to viewing Islamism through the material which concerns the Turkish Islamist movement, Millî Görüş. The analysis is therefore, naturally aimed primarily at this movement. It does, however, seem reasonable to assume that their basic pattern of argument is characteristic of a long list of differently oriented Islamic currents, each of which take the holy texts as the basic point of departure in their social criticism and call for change. In this way they can refer to a common source of origin, which forms a counterpoint to the undermining by marginalisation processes of a socialisation in which identity is centred around work.

One could say that there exists a gulf between, on the one hand, a vision of a future Islamic society in social harmony and on the other, the concrete initiatives which are linked to the movement - and which are advanced as an Islamic outlook. That the concrete initiatives to envisage an alternative strategy do not make sense when taken together and also lack a closer analysis of the societal interests, as well as of their strengths relative to one another, should be viewed as a major problem.

In the universe of Millî Görüş this problem does not, however, exist. This universe is ruled completely by an ideological figure, which seeks to close the gap between utopia and concrete initiatives. This is achieved by deferring the matter of dealing with social conflicts to a level other than the traditionally political. What is actually at stake is *the individual's relationship to God, here and in the hereafter*, or in other words, *the vision of the Day of Judgement*. There are two structural supports upon which the Muslim society rests, the *first* of which is *unconditional belief in God*, and the *second* is *solidarity within the Muslim community*.

The source of the threat to the Islamic project consists of a destructive combination consisting of capitalist greed and a Jewish-Christian-Communist conspiracy which, by deed of an almost demonic logic, conducts the attack against the Islamic project.

The movement's view of the world is also unambiguously linked to a dualistic conflict between good and evil, belief and non-belief, sacrifice and executioner. The tendency to understand historical and social conditions through mystical figures (i.e., ummah, millat, kafir, müsrik, Day of Judgement, the caliphs, the Prophet) are developed into a pure mythology: the social conflicts disappear in favour of icons which represent good and evil.

But Millî Görüş's vision of the world does not end with the construction of the complete scenario for a threatened and divided Islamic community: At the same time the movement projects authoritatively compelling frames for the necessary change of direction.

These frames are founded on arguments rooted in the holy texts of Islam. First and foremost, the conception of the destructive forces as having an impact on the individual as much as on mankind as a whole acts as a compelling argument for the Islamic alternative. In broad terms society must subject itself to the laws of God and as such devote their lives to his representative, the Khalifa.

The Islamic movements are capable of criticising the social marginalisation processes which characterise the establishment of the immigrant environment in Western Europe. The worldview which dominates the Turkish Islamist movement is formulated in problematic terms, but its strength lies in being able to place Islam at the centre of social identity as an alternative to the lack of opportunity to establish a positive identity via affiliation with the labour market. I show that it makes good sense for the Islamists to organise their lifeworld conditions which are, as such, threatened socially and economically, as a defence against Christian civilisation.

The key to the motivation to participate in the Islamic movement appears first of all to be an underlying reluctance to losing one's autonomy, with the subsequent loss of authority which follows. Secondly the motivation comprises a resistance to having control over one's immediate social relations being taken away.

I also maintain that the source of this resistance lies in the living conditions of the Muslim immigrants. The question of which conditions are more specifically responsible for provoking this conception of conflict, along with why this grows into a resistance that is established in the world as conceived by the *Islamic* movements is also discussed.

In the first instance the analysis probably leads to a negative evaluation of Millî Görüş and the Islamic movement's immediate perspectives with regard to societal change. This reasoning is, however, modified later in that there is not necessarily complete agreement between the concept of the world and locality or individual social action which transgresses the community. It is precisely this lack of agreement which enables the differentiation.

One can say that the different cemaat, religious communities comprise a *community of interpretation* (Said, E, 1981). Specific conceptions of Islam are set in motion and form the fundament for individual and collective action while the engagement of the participants is flexible and of varying intensity. Millî Görüş' significance is, in other words, to establish an alternative platform which can serve as a depository for autonomous re-evaluations of the collective heritage and identity.

On this basis social and cultural development opportunities are established which demonstrate that it is possible to be socially active. Thus the Islamist movement establishes a position, removed from the centre of power, which insists on its own existence. Thereby asserting that de-centralised communities exist, whose social and cultural common interests have need of representation. One could ascertain as such that from this position too, we witness among the Muslim immigrant minority the tendency to formulate the demand to be considered as complete citizens. This is why I bring the discussion about minority rights onto the agenda in the concluding section.

As shown, the Islamic vision is formulated in problematic forms, but the actual core is very clear: it deals with marginalisation processes and the struggle for the representation of social and cultural interests in the lifeworld. The movement's future character will depend on which opportunities it gets for working with those contact surfaces which relate to Muslim minority milieux.

In the *Postscript* I augment, expand on and make more explicit a number of the problem formulations relevant to my analysis of Islamism in Western Europe.

I discuss the continued validity of the analysis made in this thesis of the media's negative representation of Islam in the period 1986-87. Although today there seems to be a greater degree of willingness to present more positive representations, it would appear that the substantial and decisive new factor in the media representation is that Muslims are now themselves participants or players in the media debate on Islam and Muslims. This factor is important in the development of the multicultural society. Furthermore, it encourages the introduction of nuance into the formulation of Islam and the cultural heritage, and the particular contribution of Islamism in this, - leading on from this I describe the level of Islamism's relationship to the cultural heritage.

I then locate this with regard to the most significant trends in the social science discourse on Islamism in recent decades, which essentially centres around the terms 'post-modernism' and 'civil society'.

Finally, I discuss the problematic term 'second generation immigrant', which I define as covering a social reality which is both contradictory and complex. This, therefore, invalidates the term to a certain degree, while however indicating an independent quality with regard to the 'first generation', and which therefore requires representation.